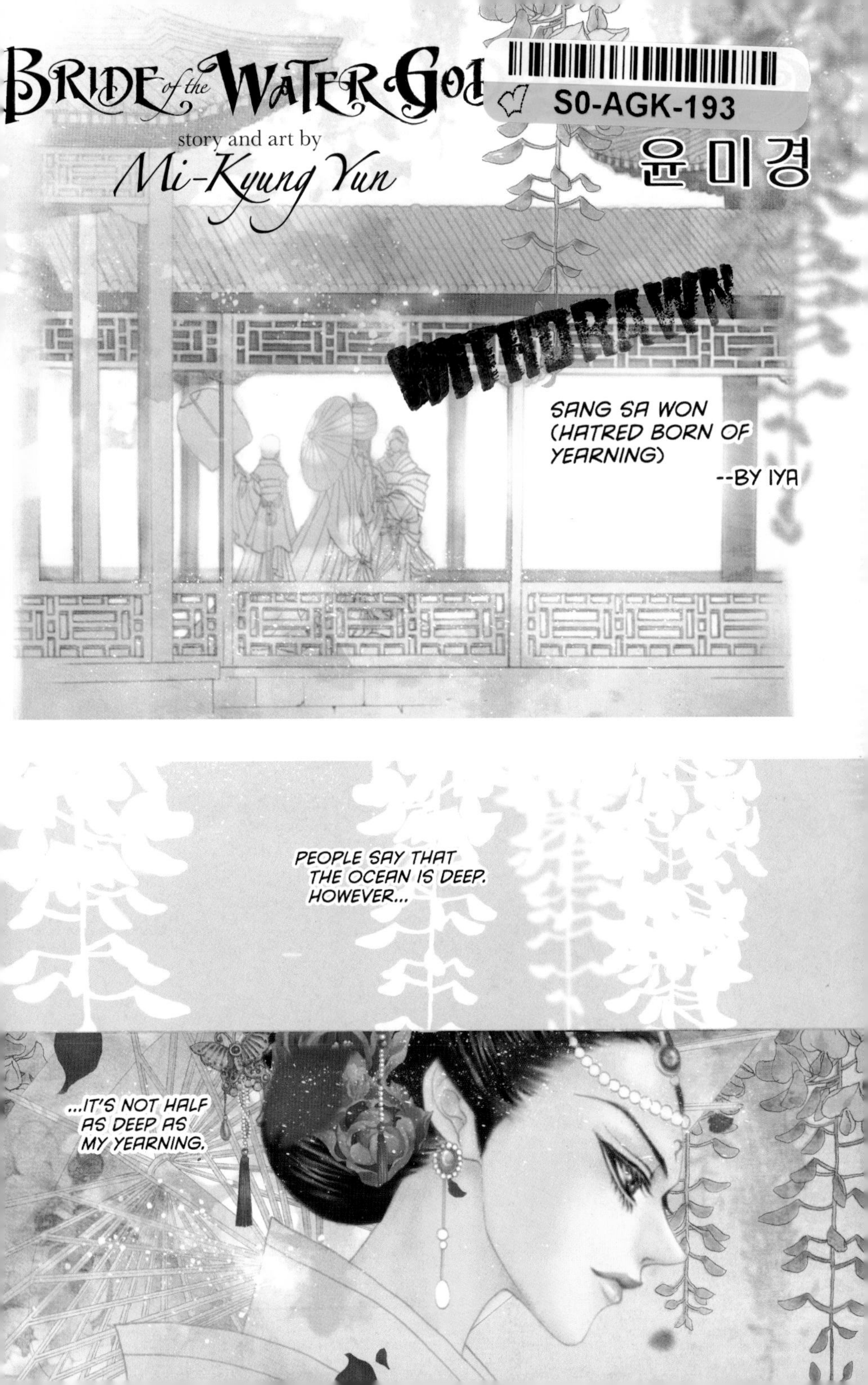
BRIDE of the WATER GOD
story and art by
Mi-Kyung Yun
윤미경
SANG SA WON (HATRED BORN OF YEARNING) --BY IYA
PEOPLE SAY THAT THE OCEAN IS DEEP. HOWEVER...
...IT'S NOT HALF AS DEEP AS MY YEARNING.

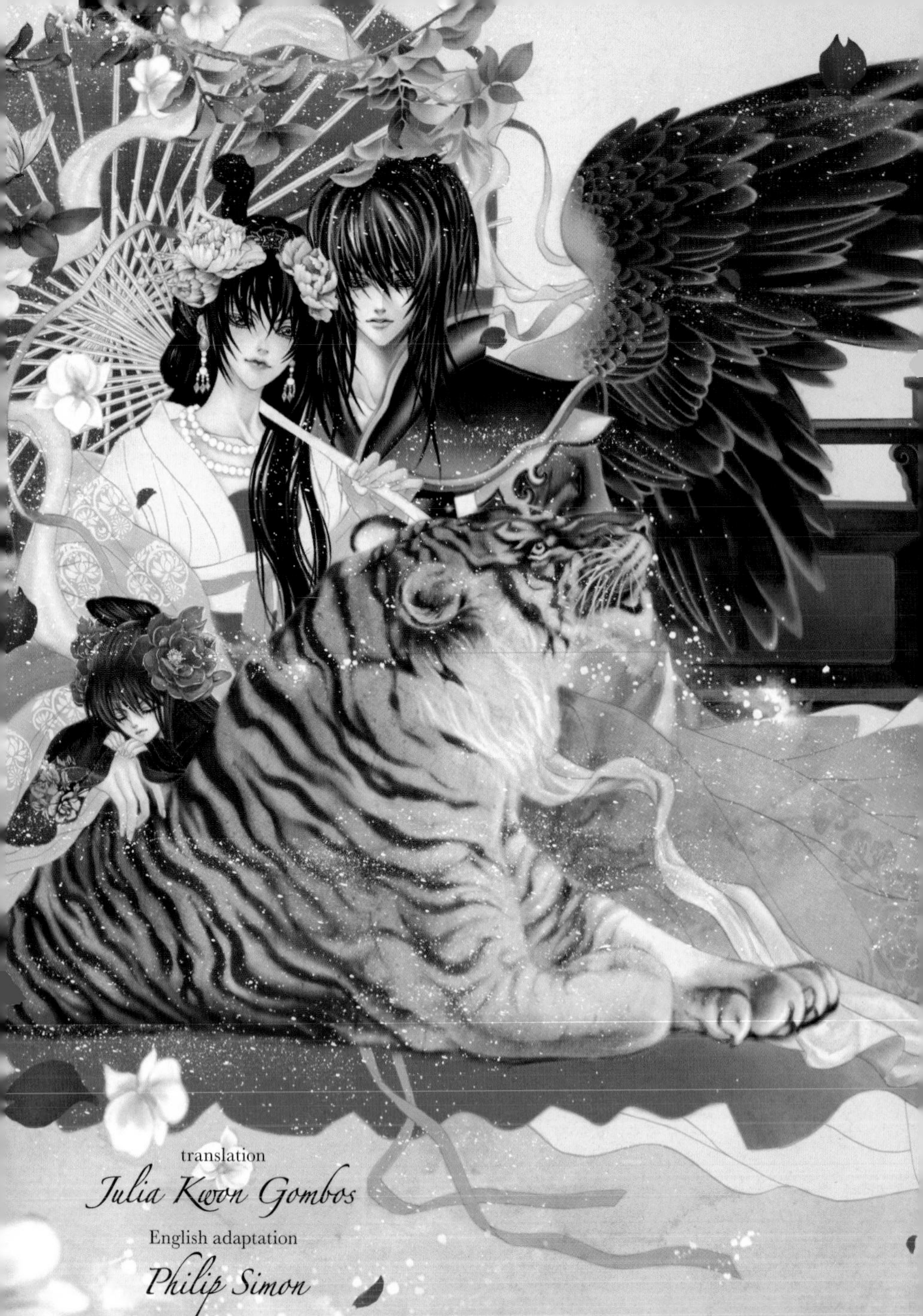

translation
Julia Kwon Gombos
English adaptation
Philip Simon
lettering
Andy Grossberg &
Studio Cutie

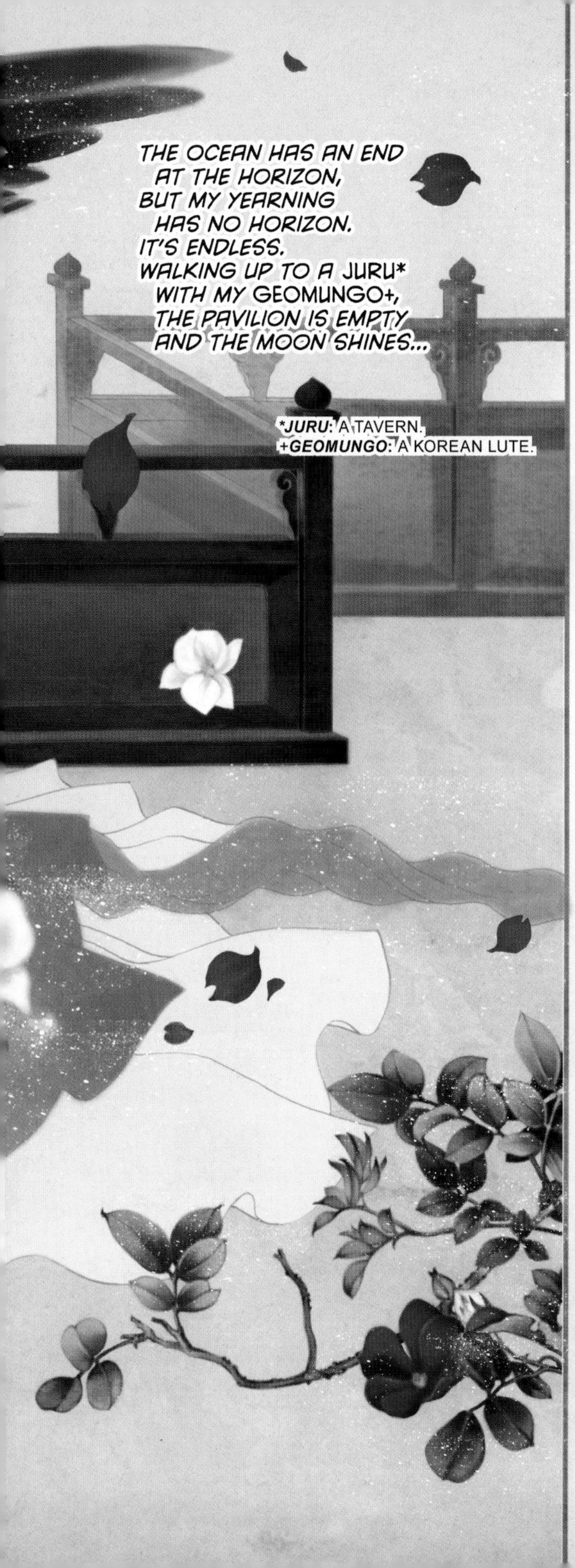
THE OCEAN HAS AN END AT THE HORIZON, BUT MY YEARNING HAS NO HORIZON. IT'S ENDLESS. WALKING UP TO A JURU* WITH MY GEOMUNGO+, THE PAVILION IS EMPTY AND THE MOON SHINES...
*JURU: A TAVERN.
+GEOMUNGO: A KOREAN LUTE.
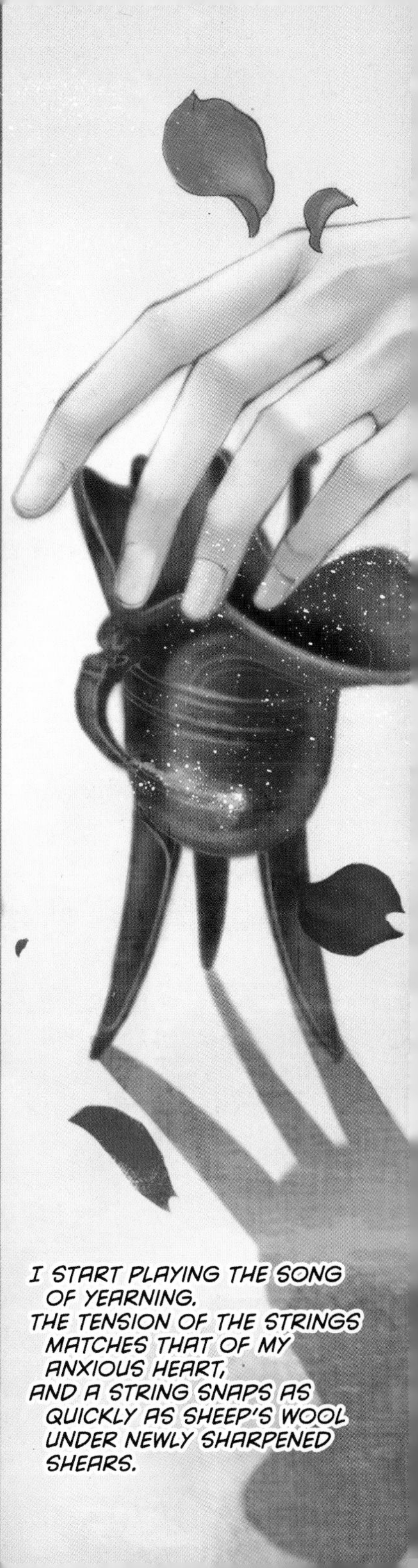
I START PLAYING THE SONG OF YEARNING. THE TENSION OF THE STRINGS MATCHES THAT OF MY ANXIOUS HEART, AND A STRING SNAPS AS QUICKLY AS SHEEP'S WOOL UNDER NEWLY SHARPENED SHEARS.

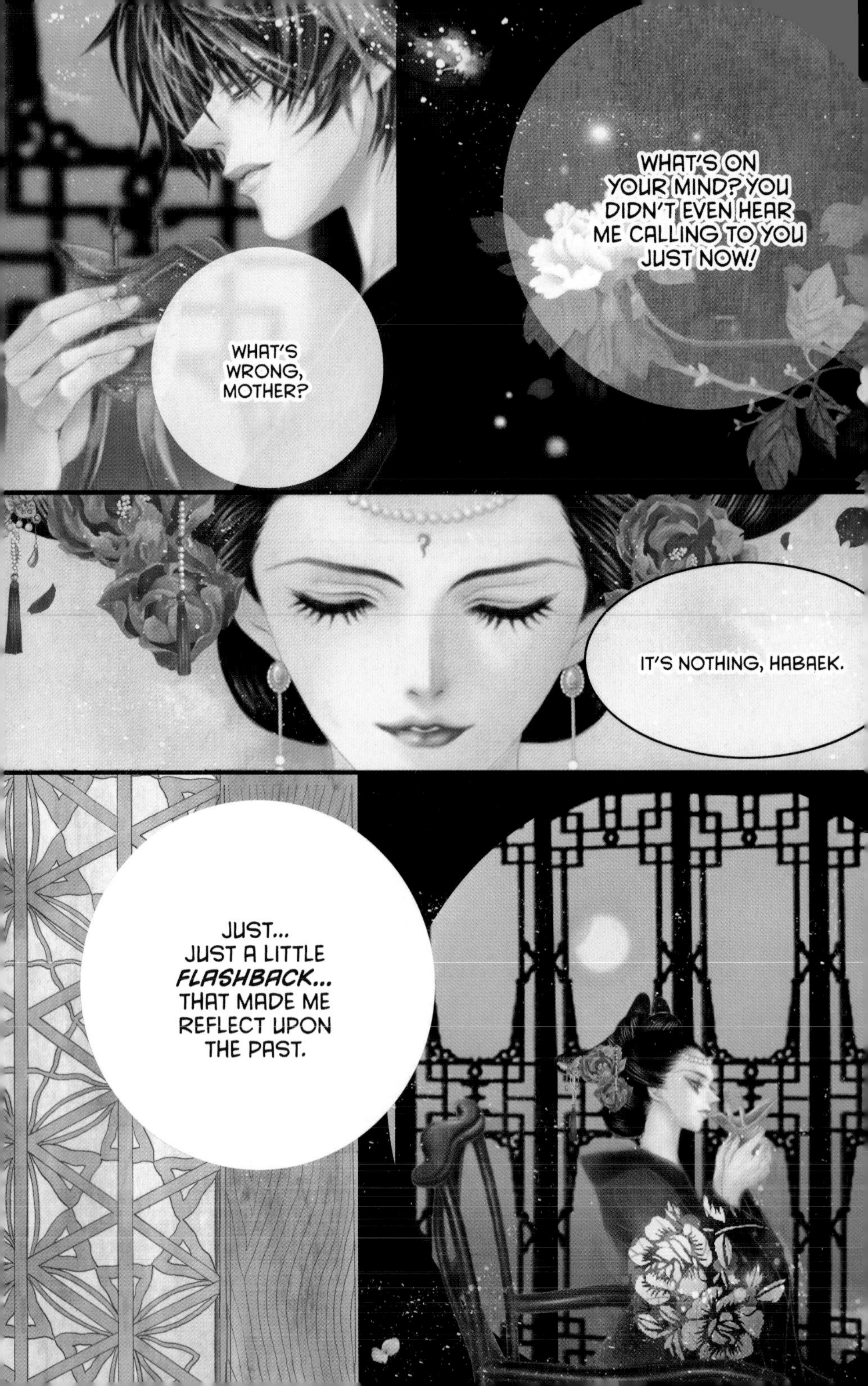
WHAT'S WRONG, MOTHER?
WHAT'S ON YOUR MIND? YOU DIDN'T EVEN HEAR ME CALLING TO YOU JUST NOW!
IT'S NOTHING, HABAEK.
JUST... JUST A LITTLE *FLASHBACK...* THAT MADE ME REFLECT UPON THE PAST.

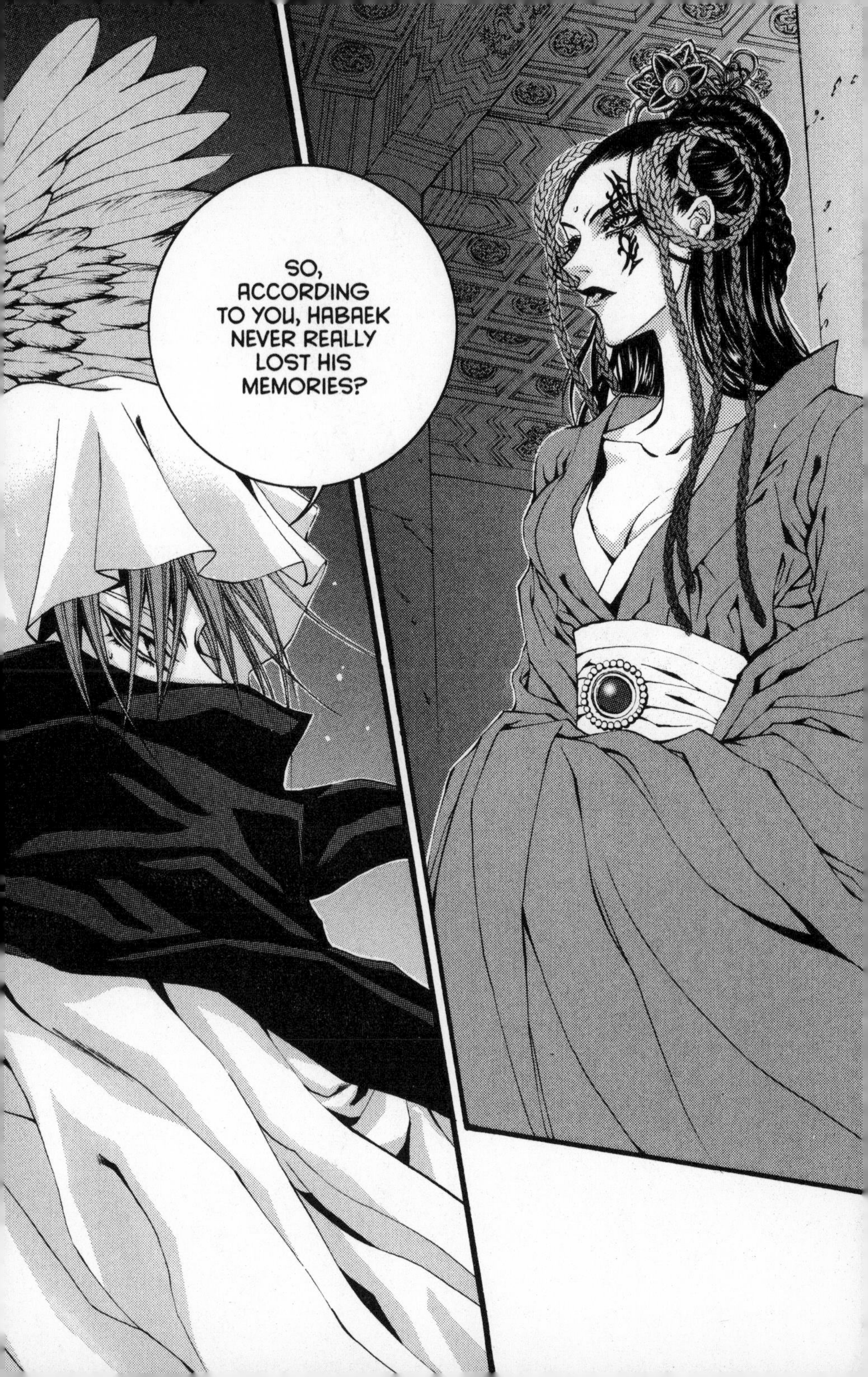
SO, ACCORDING TO YOU, HABAEK NEVER REALLY LOST HIS MEMORIES?

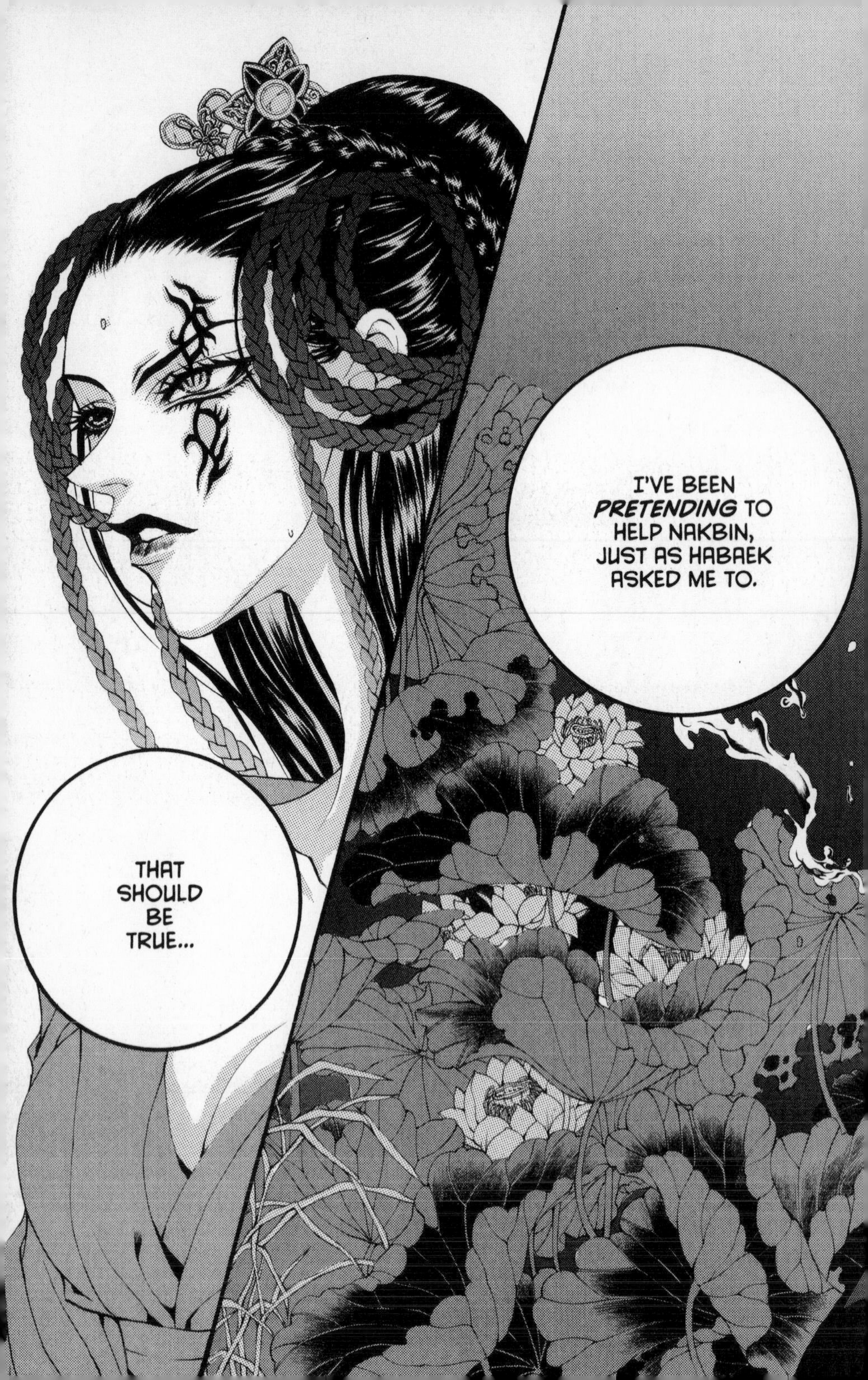
I'VE BEEN *PRETENDING* TO HELP NAKBIN, JUST AS HABAEK ASKED ME TO.
THAT SHOULD BE TRUE...

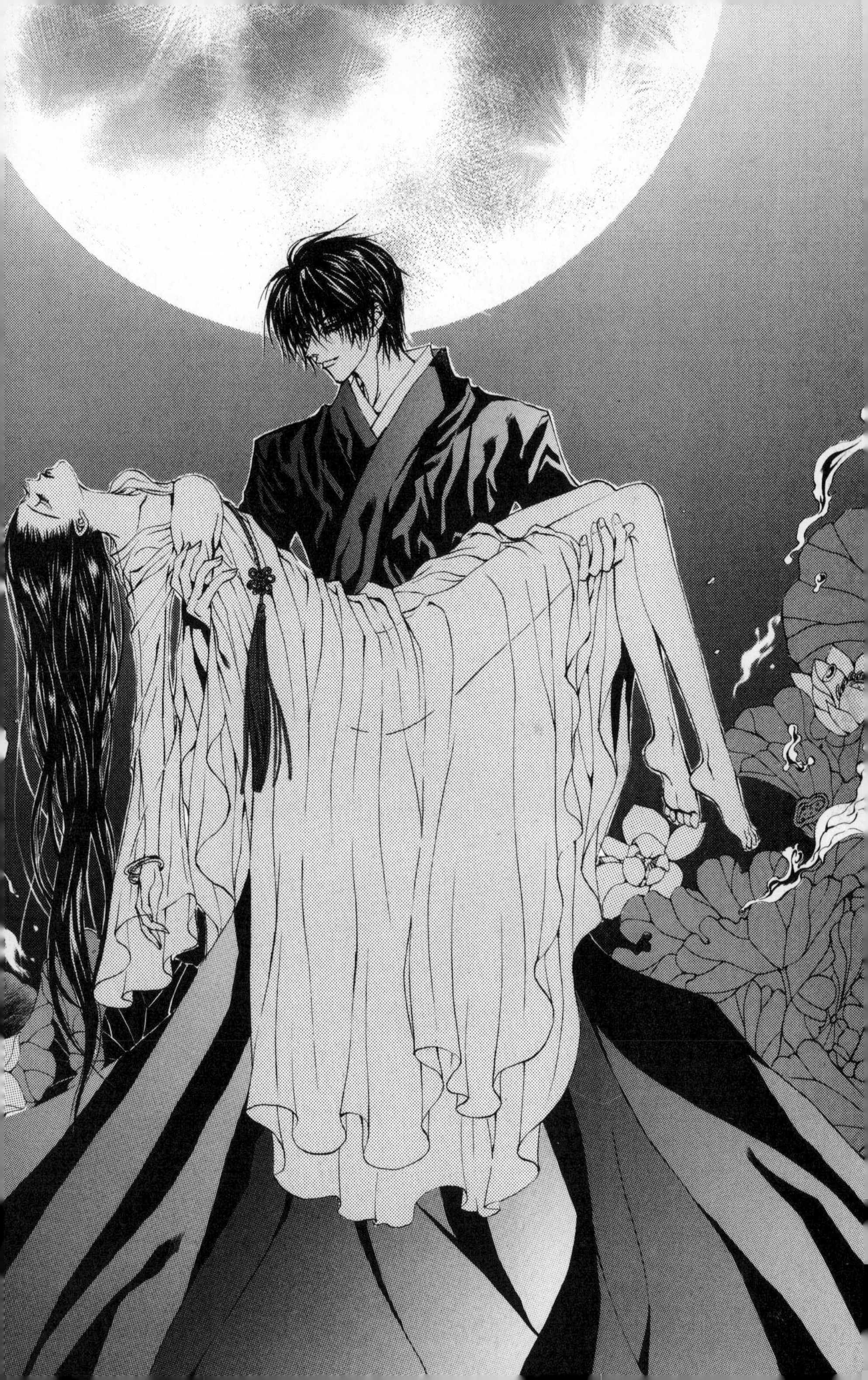

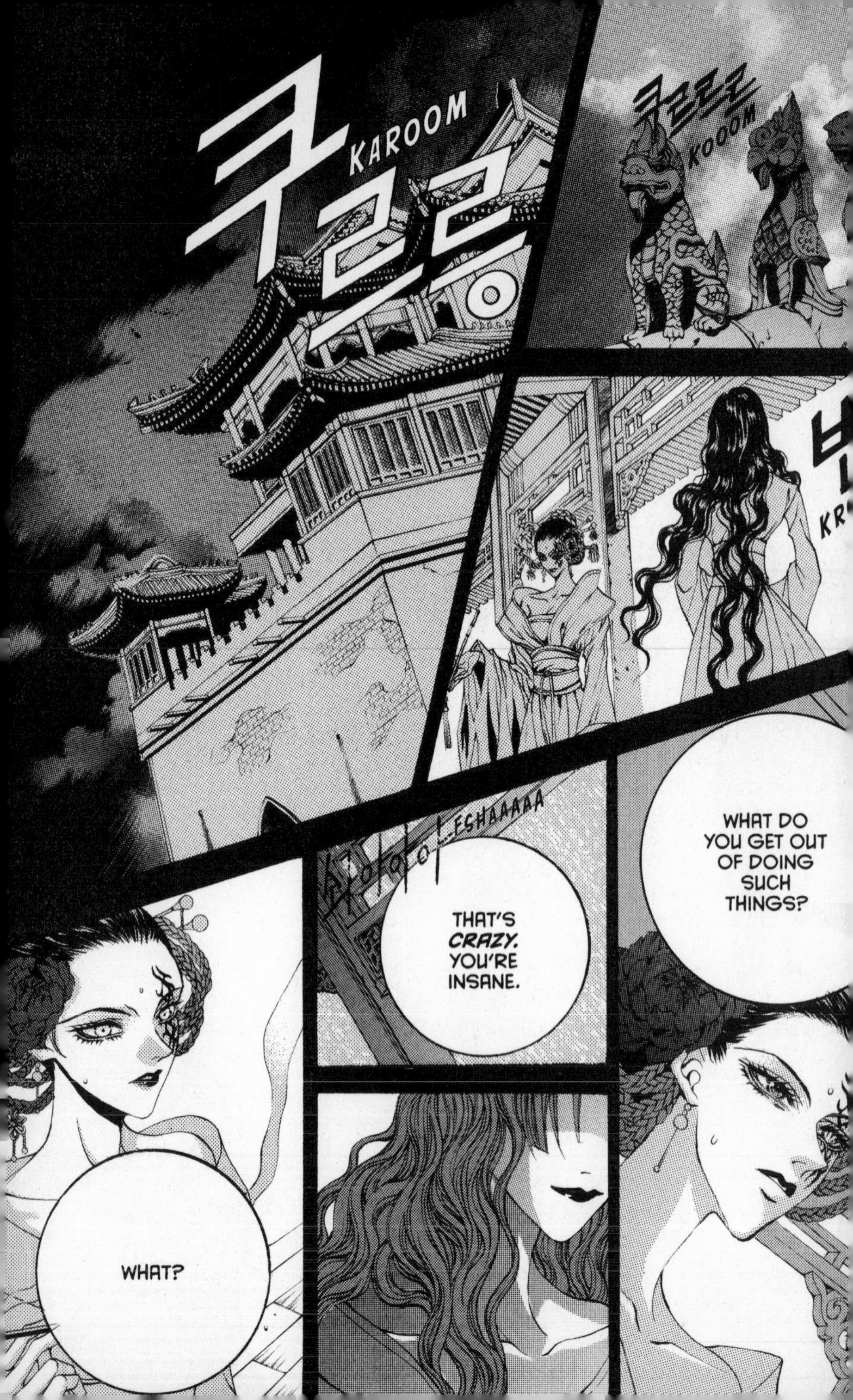

쿠르릉
KAROOM
KOOOM
FSHAAAAA
WHAT?
THAT'S *CRAZY.* YOU'RE INSANE.
WHAT DO YOU GET OUT OF DOING SUCH THINGS?

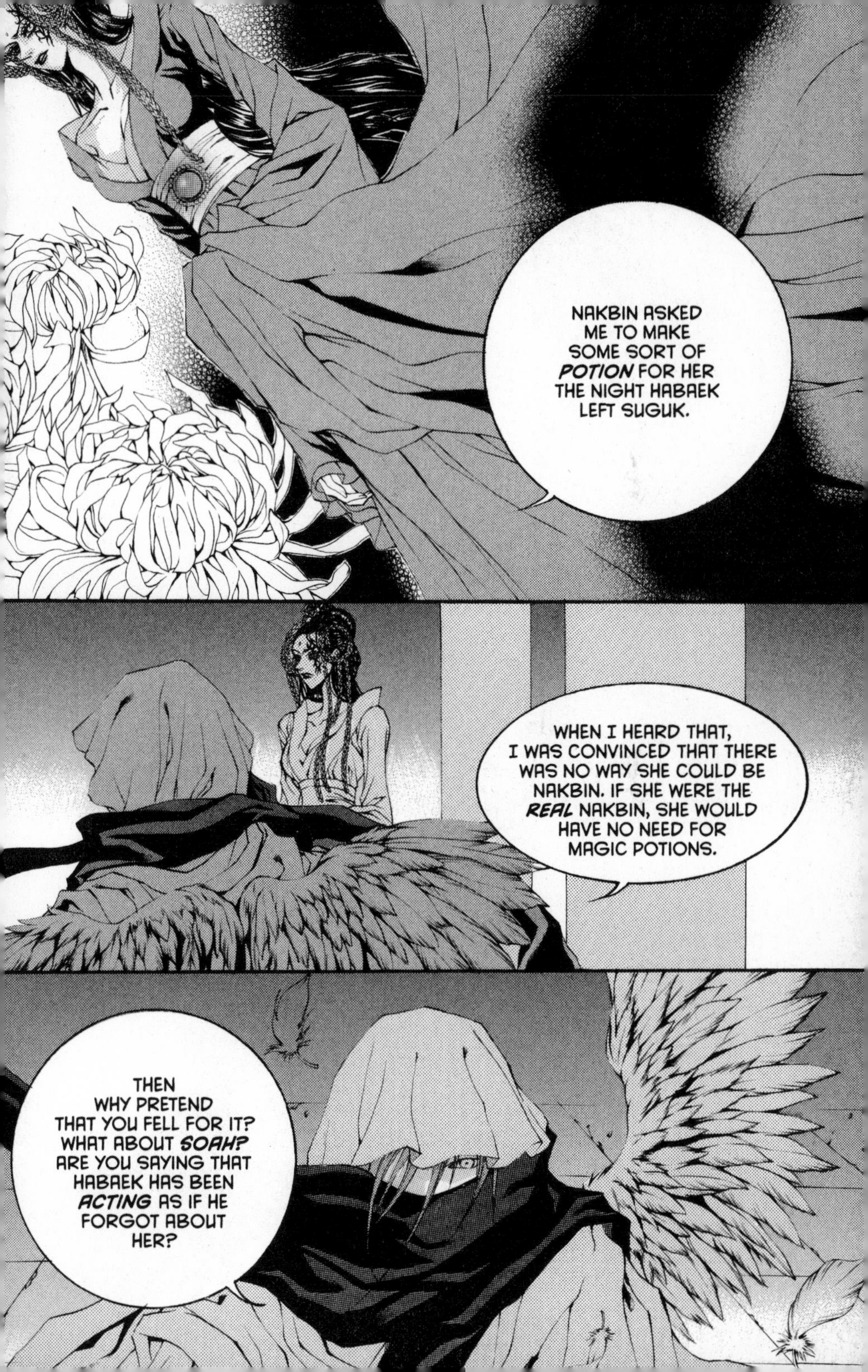
NAKBIN ASKED ME TO MAKE SOME SORT OF *POTION* FOR HER THE NIGHT HABAEK LEFT SUGUK.
WHEN I HEARD THAT, I WAS CONVINCED THAT THERE WAS NO WAY SHE COULD BE NAKBIN. IF SHE WERE THE *REAL* NAKBIN, SHE WOULD HAVE NO NEED FOR MAGIC POTIONS.
THEN WHY PRETEND THAT YOU FELL FOR IT? WHAT ABOUT *SOAH?* ARE YOU SAYING THAT HABAEK HAS BEEN *ACTING* AS IF HE FORGOT ABOUT HER?

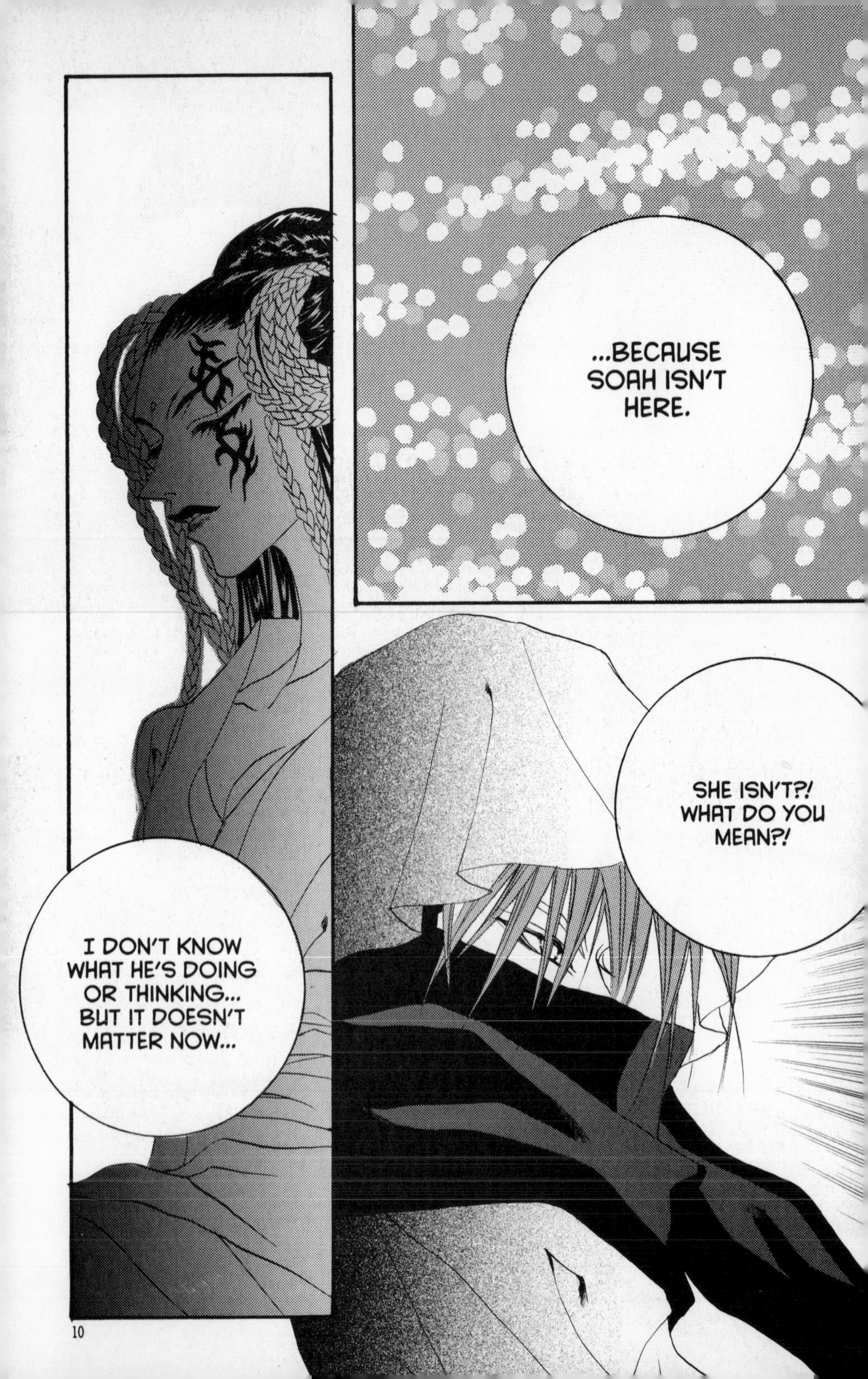
...BECAUSE SOAH ISN'T HERE.
SHE ISN'T?! WHAT DO YOU MEAN?!
I DON'T KNOW WHAT HE'S DOING OR THINKING... BUT IT DOESN'T MATTER NOW...

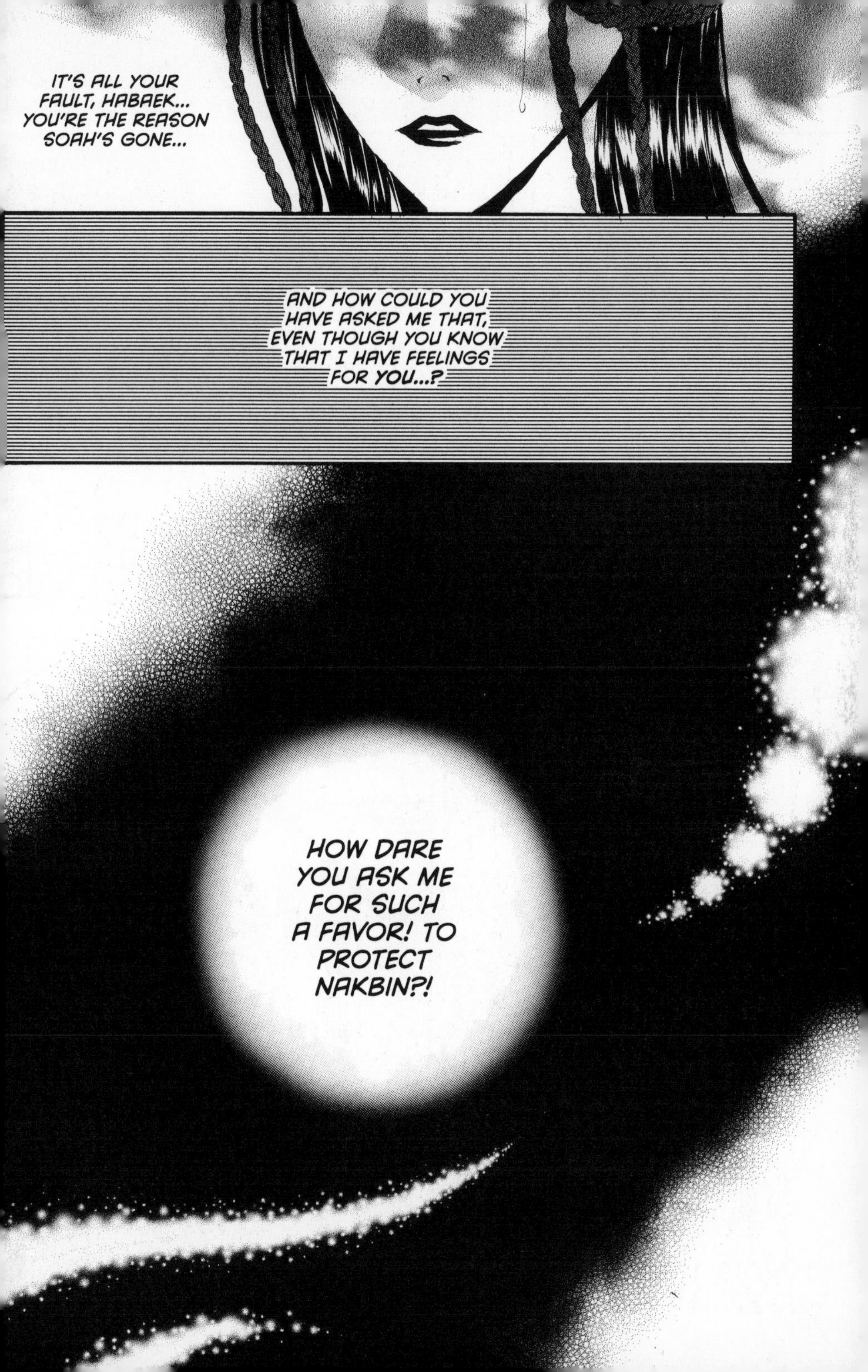
IT'S ALL YOUR FAULT, HABAEK... YOU'RE THE REASON SOAH'S GONE...
AND HOW COULD YOU HAVE ASKED ME THAT, EVEN THOUGH YOU KNOW THAT I HAVE FEELINGS FOR YOU...?
HOW DARE YOU ASK ME FOR SUCH A FAVOR! TO PROTECT NAKBIN?!

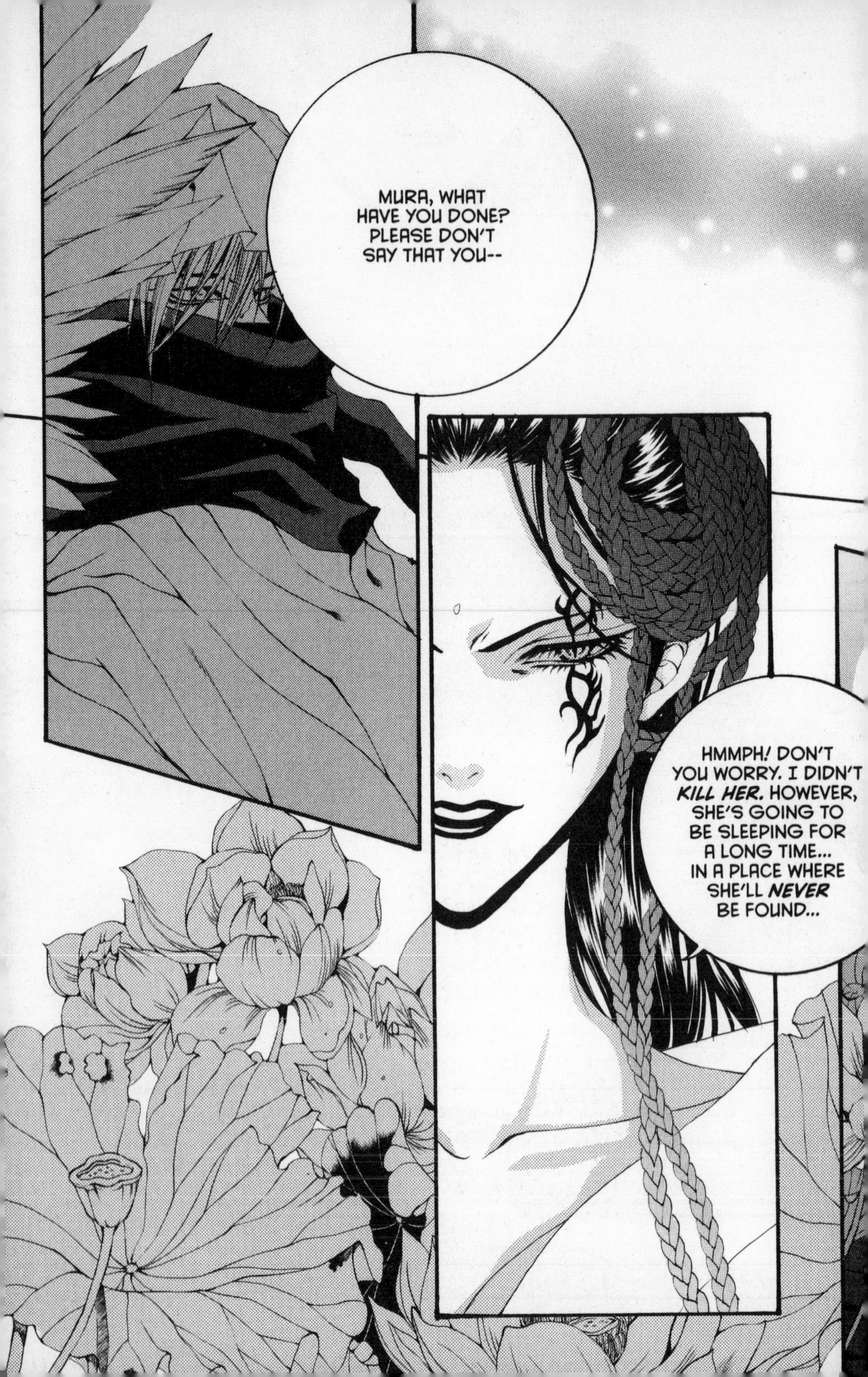
MURA, WHAT HAVE YOU DONE? PLEASE DON'T SAY THAT YOU--
HMMPH! DON'T YOU WORRY. I DIDN'T *KILL HER.* HOWEVER, SHE'S GOING TO BE SLEEPING FOR A LONG TIME... IN A PLACE WHERE SHE'LL *NEVER* BE FOUND...

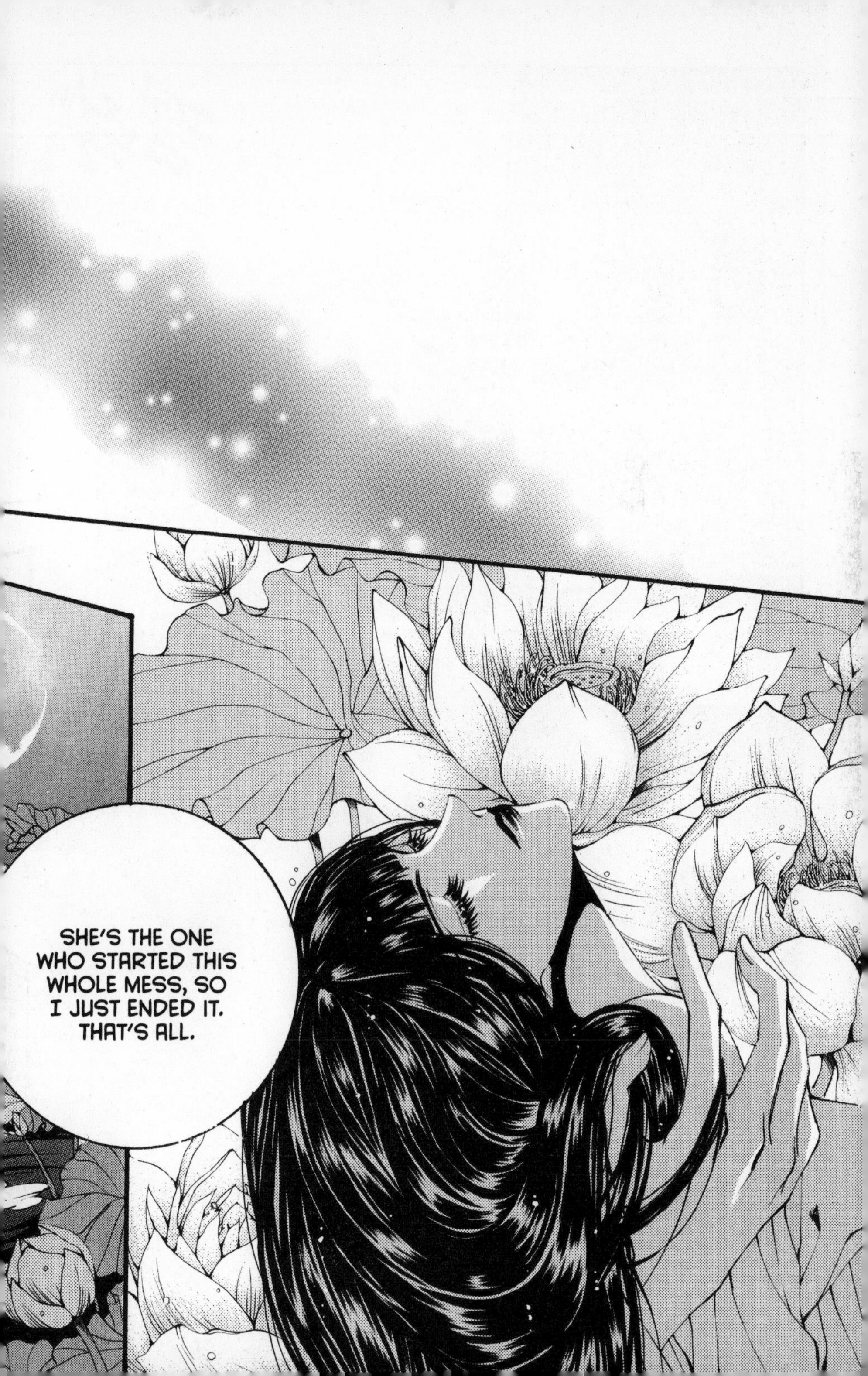
SHE'S THE ONE WHO STARTED THIS WHOLE MESS, SO I JUST ENDED IT. THAT'S ALL.

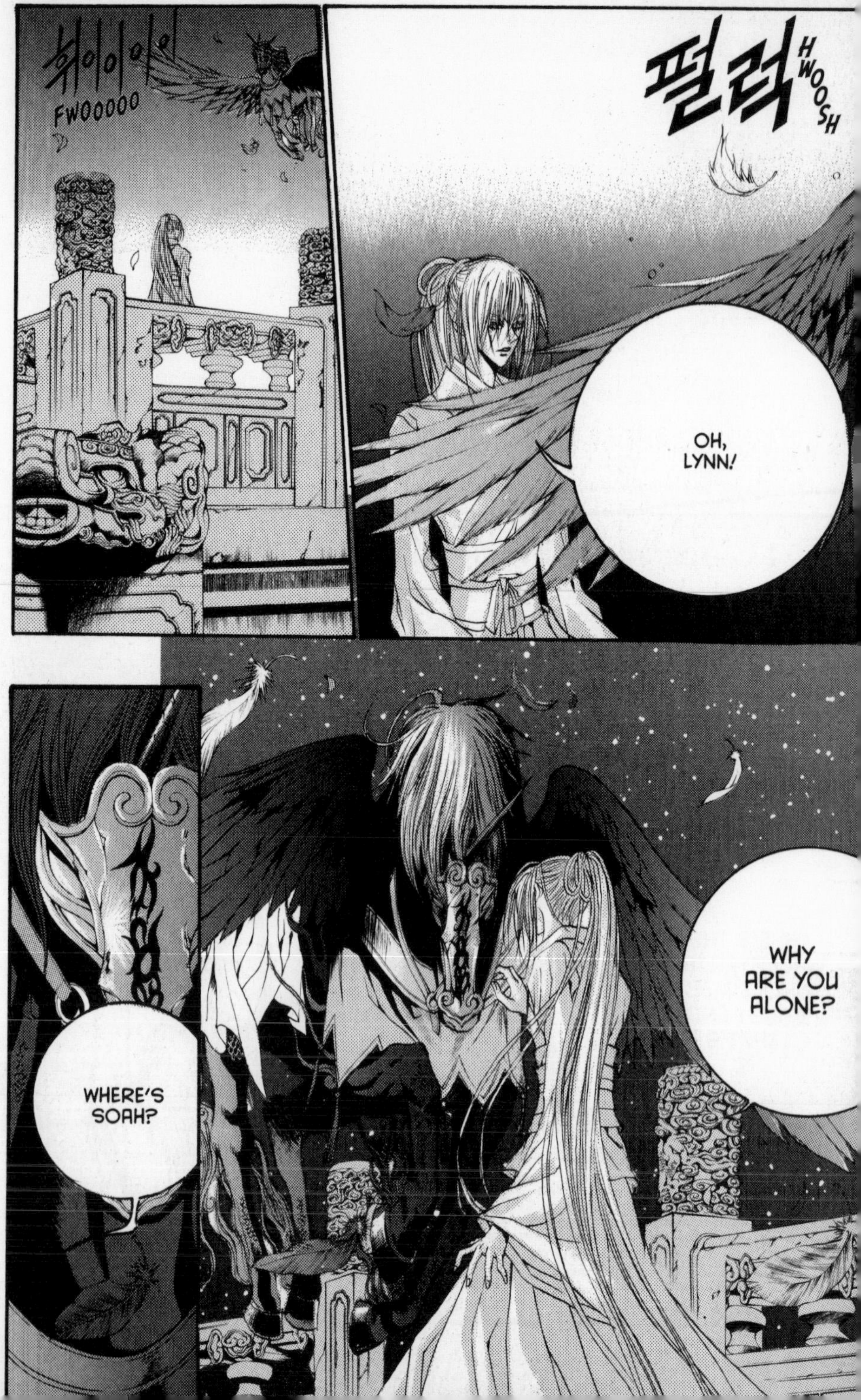
휘이이이이
FWOOOOO
펄럭
HWOOSH
OH, LYNN!
WHY ARE YOU ALONE?
WHERE'S SOAH?

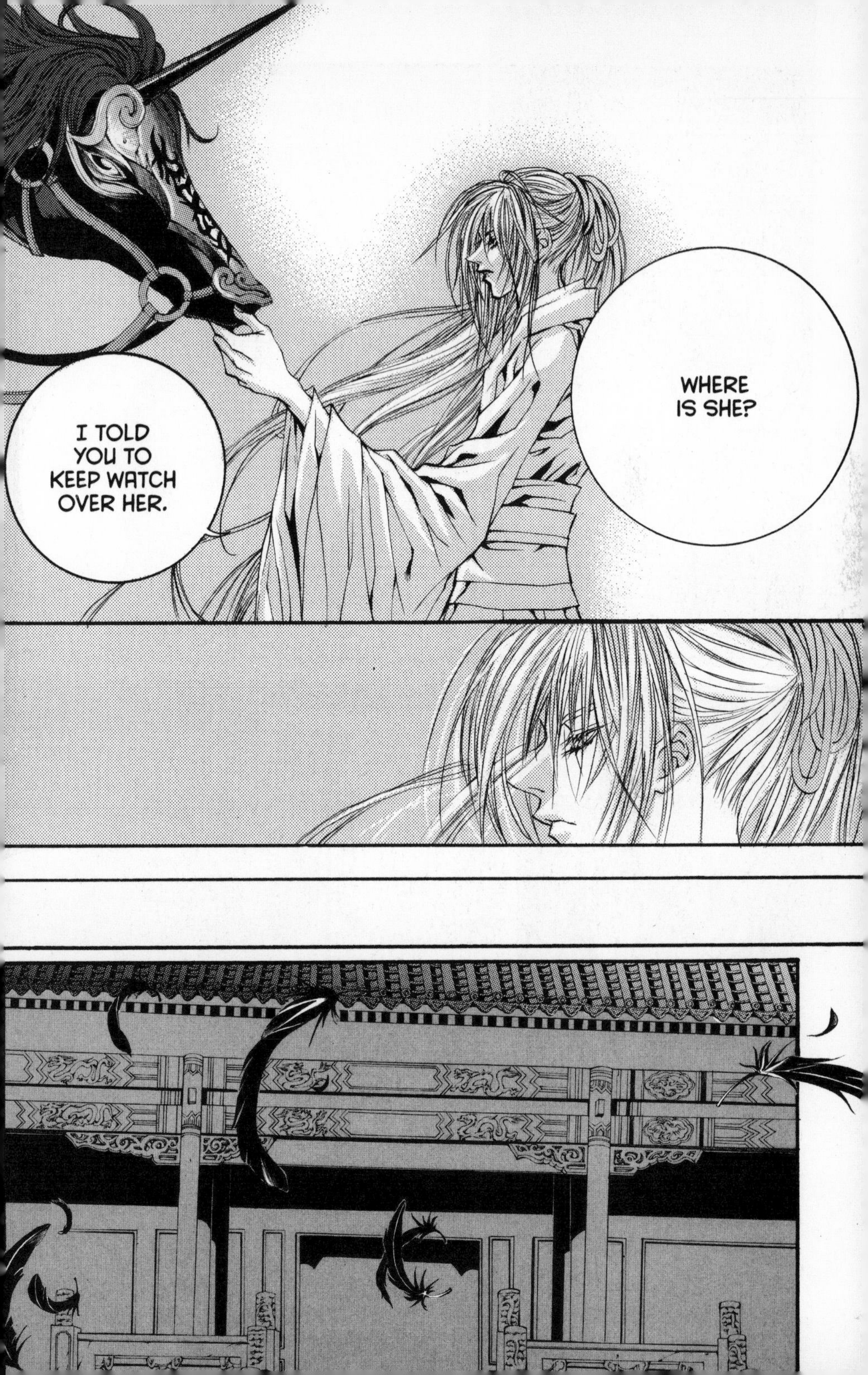
WHERE IS SHE?
I TOLD YOU TO KEEP WATCH OVER HER.

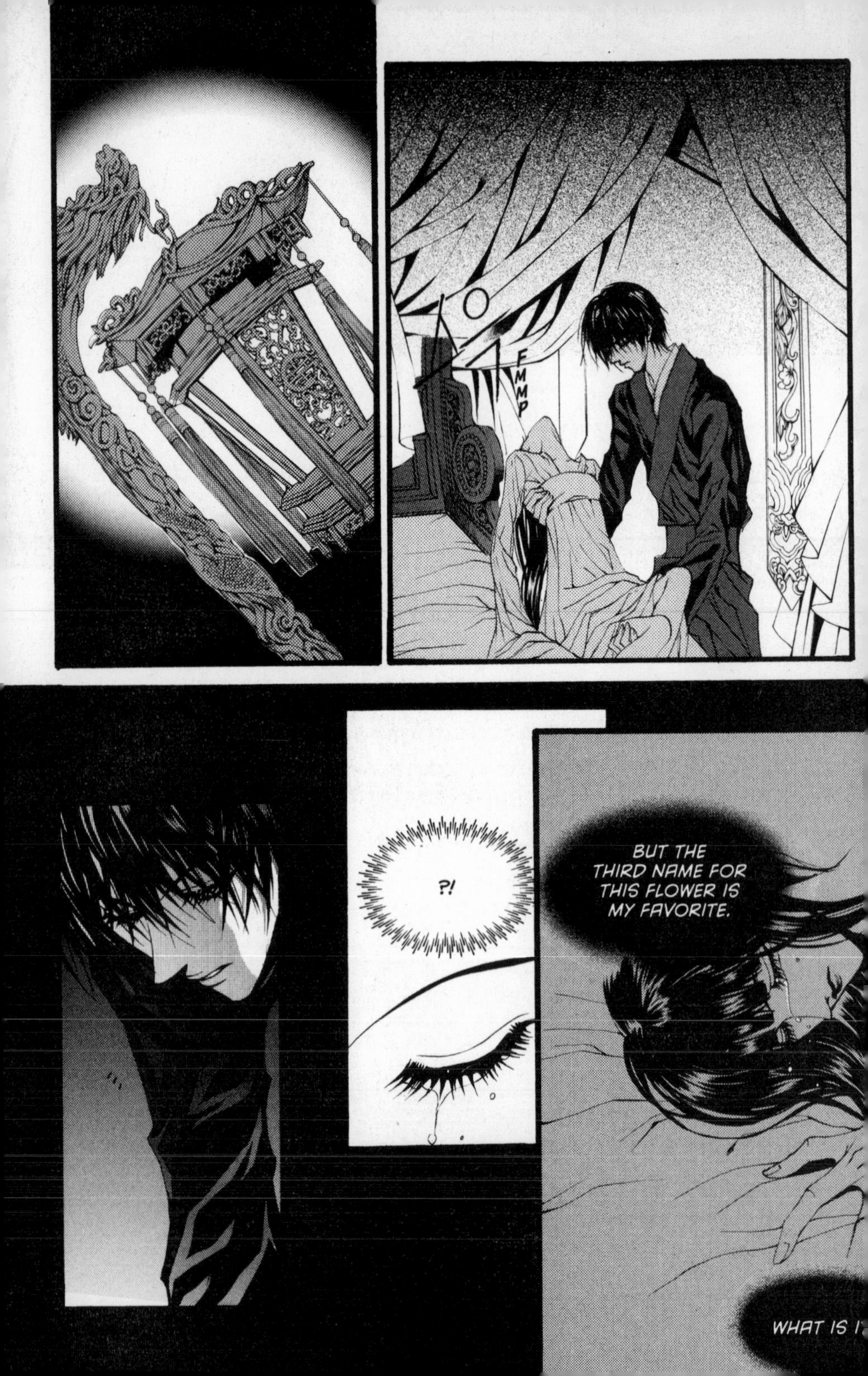
FMMP
?!
BUT THE THIRD NAME FOR THIS FLOWER IS MY FAVORITE.
WHAT IS I

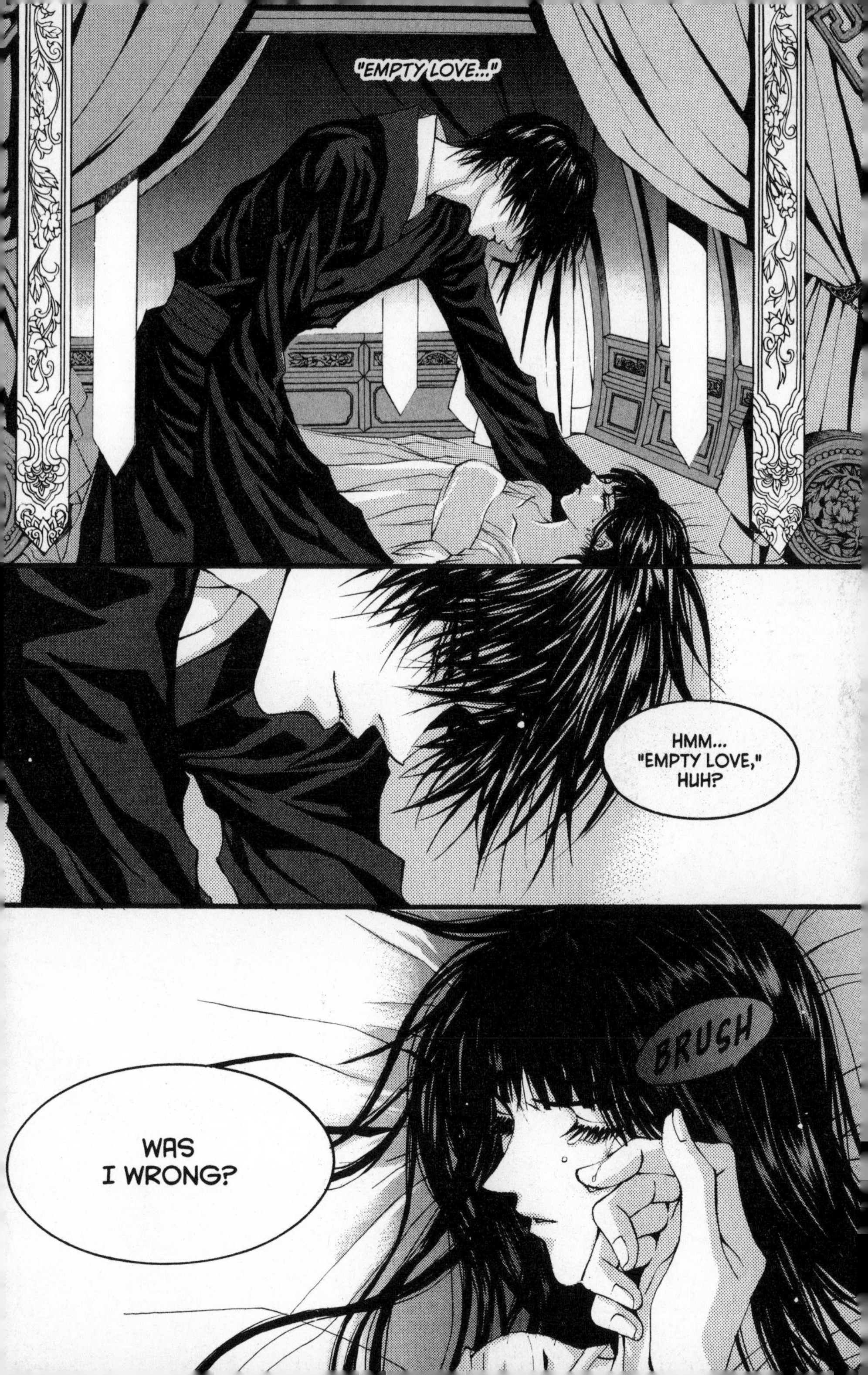
"EMPTY LOVE..."
HMM... "EMPTY LOVE," HUH?
BRUSH
WAS I WRONG?

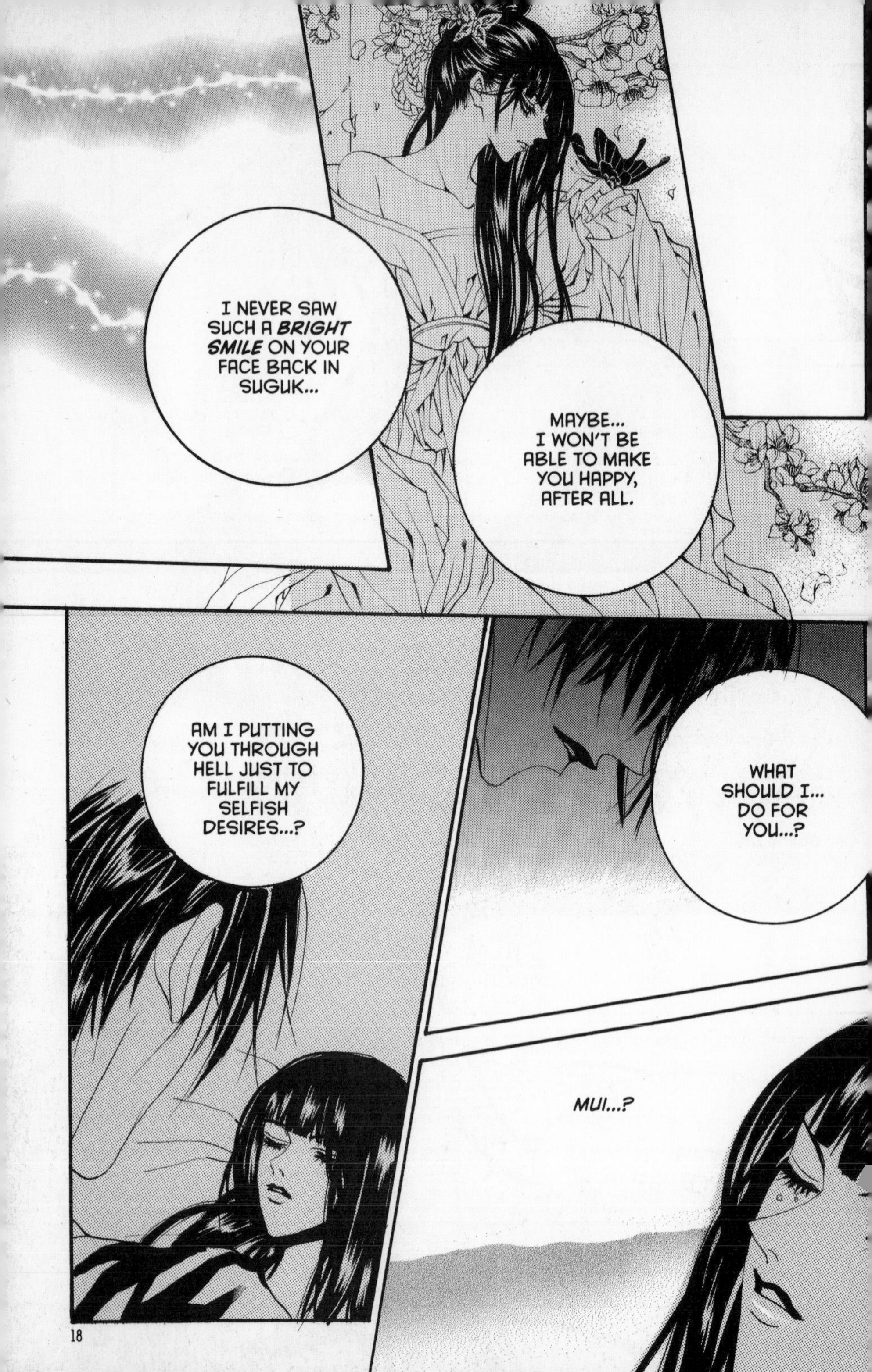
I NEVER SAW SUCH A *BRIGHT SMILE* ON YOUR FACE BACK IN SUGUK...
MAYBE... I WON'T BE ABLE TO MAKE YOU HAPPY, AFTER ALL.
WHAT SHOULD I... DO FOR YOU...?
AM I PUTTING YOU THROUGH HELL JUST TO FULFILL MY SELFISH DESIRES...?
MUI...?

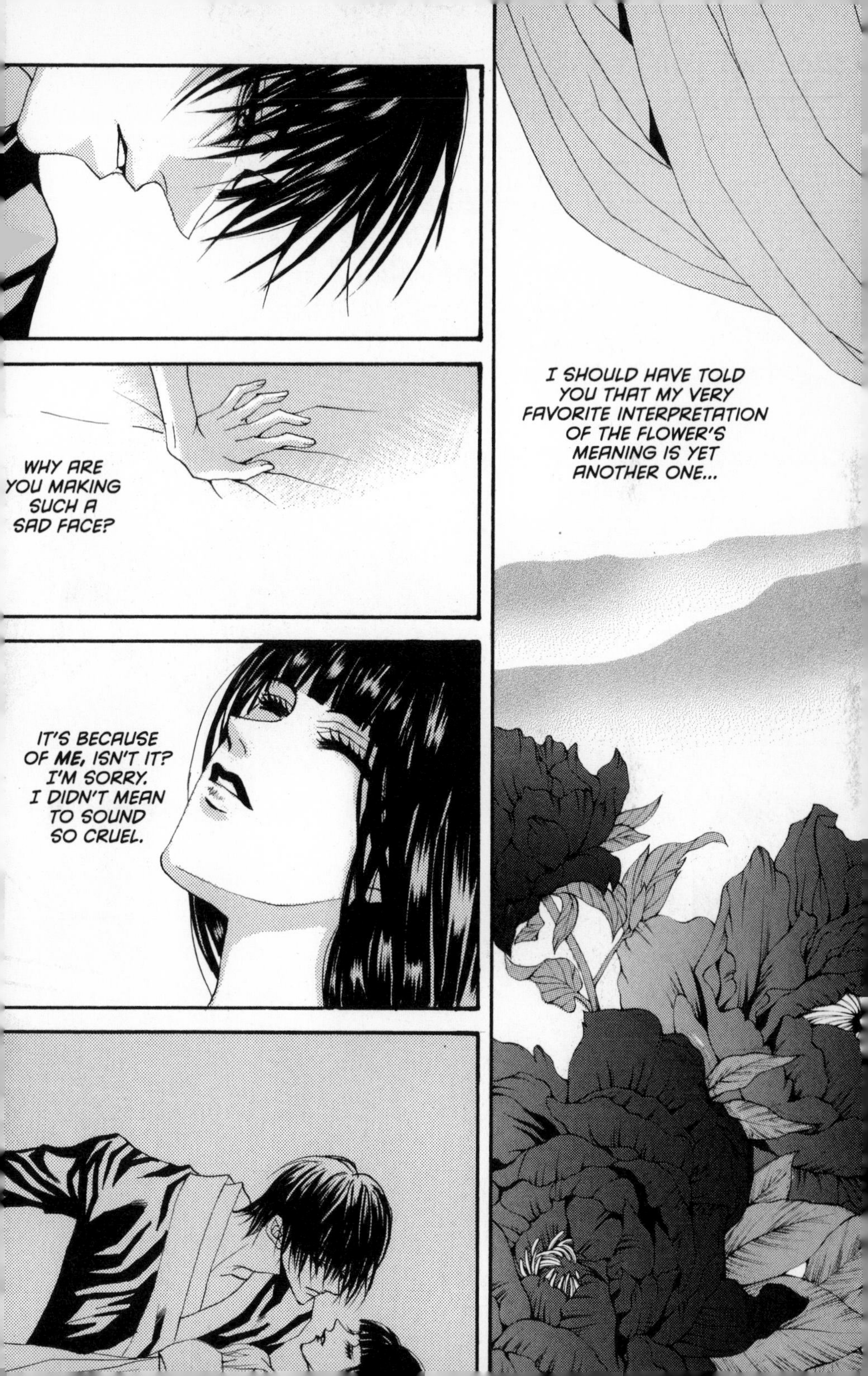
I SHOULD HAVE TOLD YOU THAT MY VERY FAVORITE INTERPRETATION OF THE FLOWER'S MEANING IS YET ANOTHER ONE...
WHY ARE YOU MAKING SUCH A SAD FACE?
IT'S BECAUSE OF ME, ISN'T IT? I'M SORRY. I DIDN'T MEAN TO SOUND SO CRUEL.

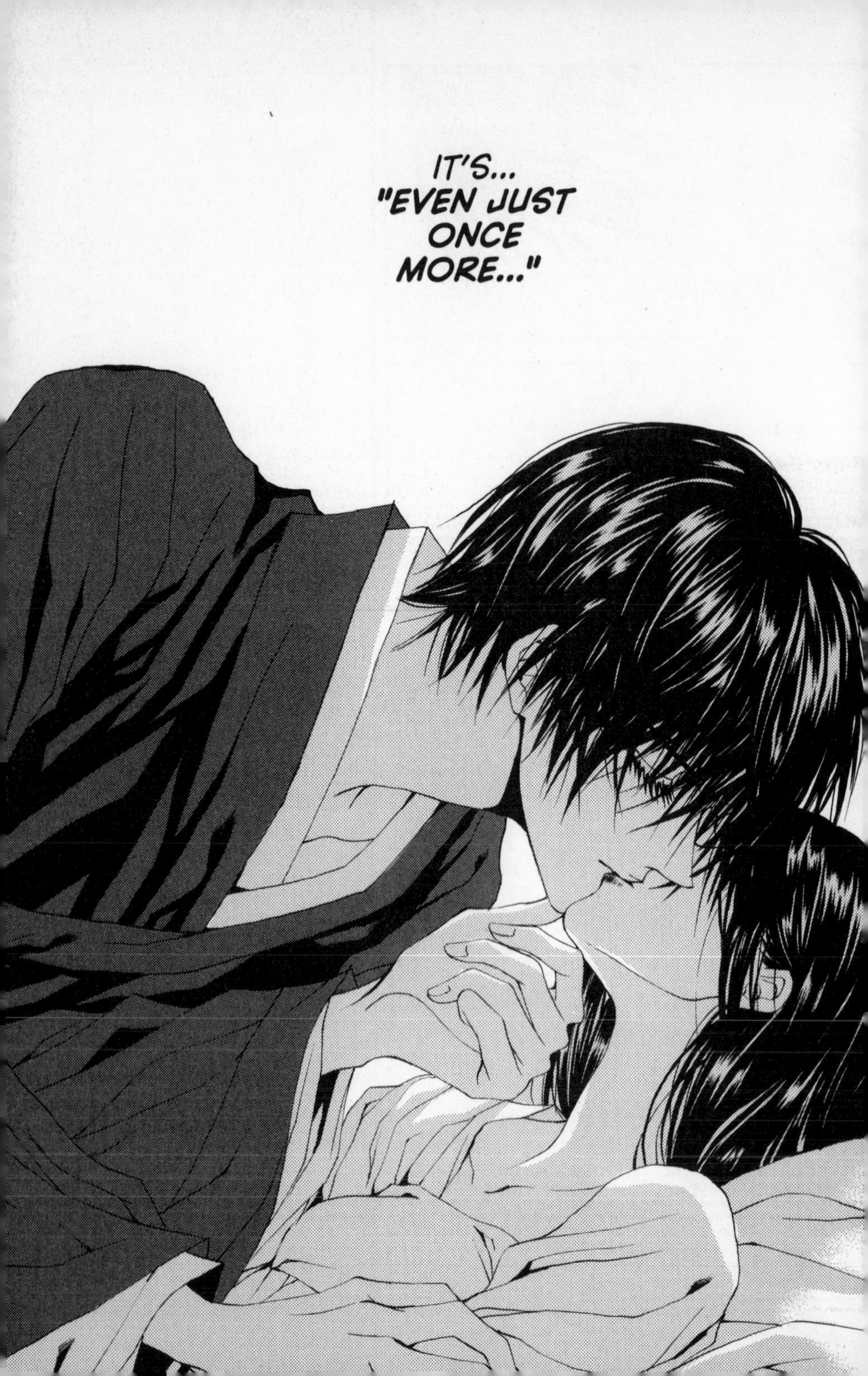
IT'S... "EVEN JUST ONCE MORE..."

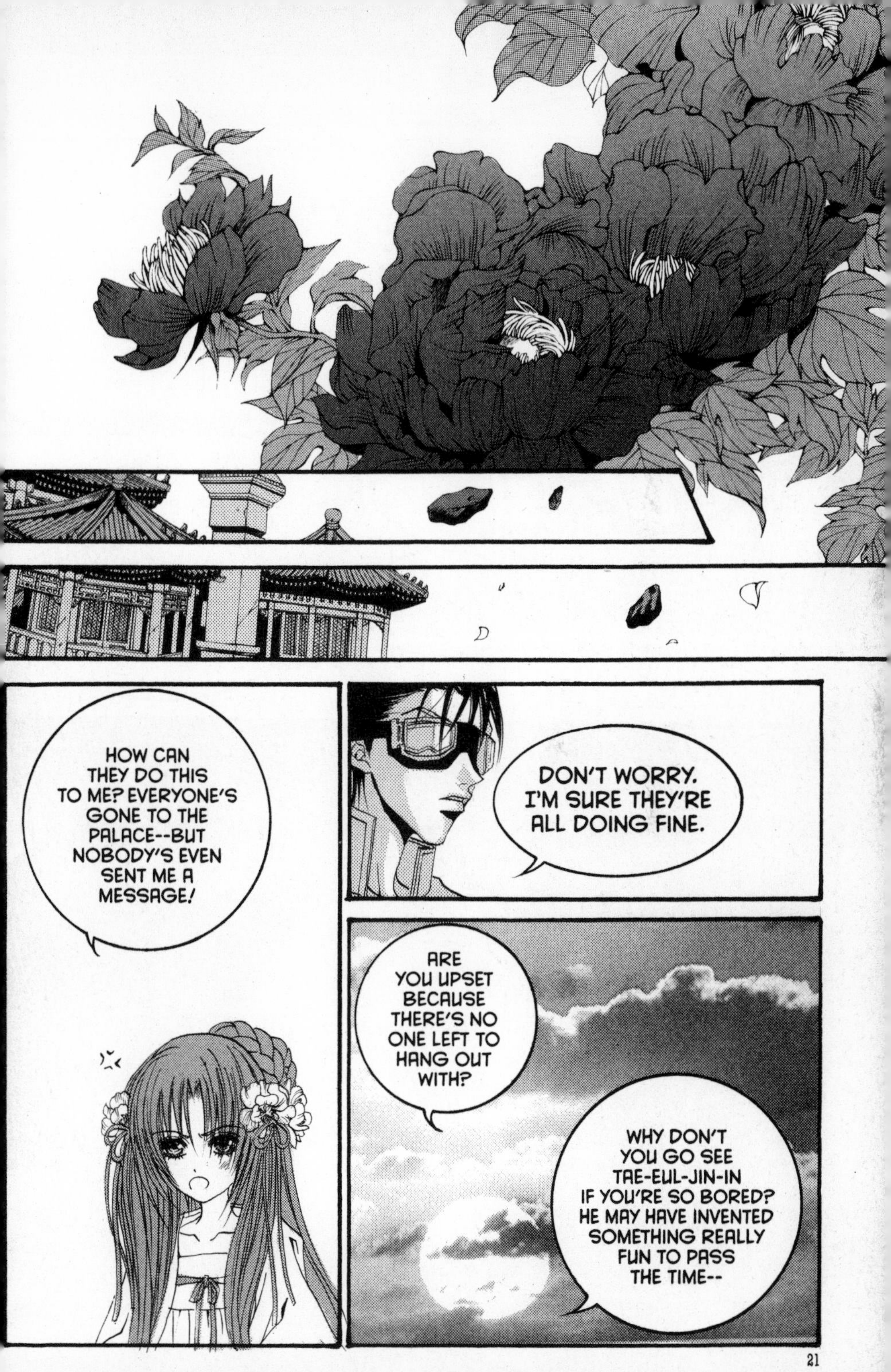

HOW CAN THEY DO THIS TO ME? EVERYONE'S GONE TO THE PALACE--BUT NOBODY'S EVEN SENT ME A MESSAGE!
DON'T WORRY. I'M SURE THEY'RE ALL DOING FINE.
ARE YOU UPSET BECAUSE THERE'S NO ONE LEFT TO HANG OUT WITH?
WHY DON'T YOU GO SEE TAE-EUL-JIN-IN IF YOU'RE SO BORED? HE MAY HAVE INVENTED SOMETHING REALLY FUN TO PASS THE TIME--

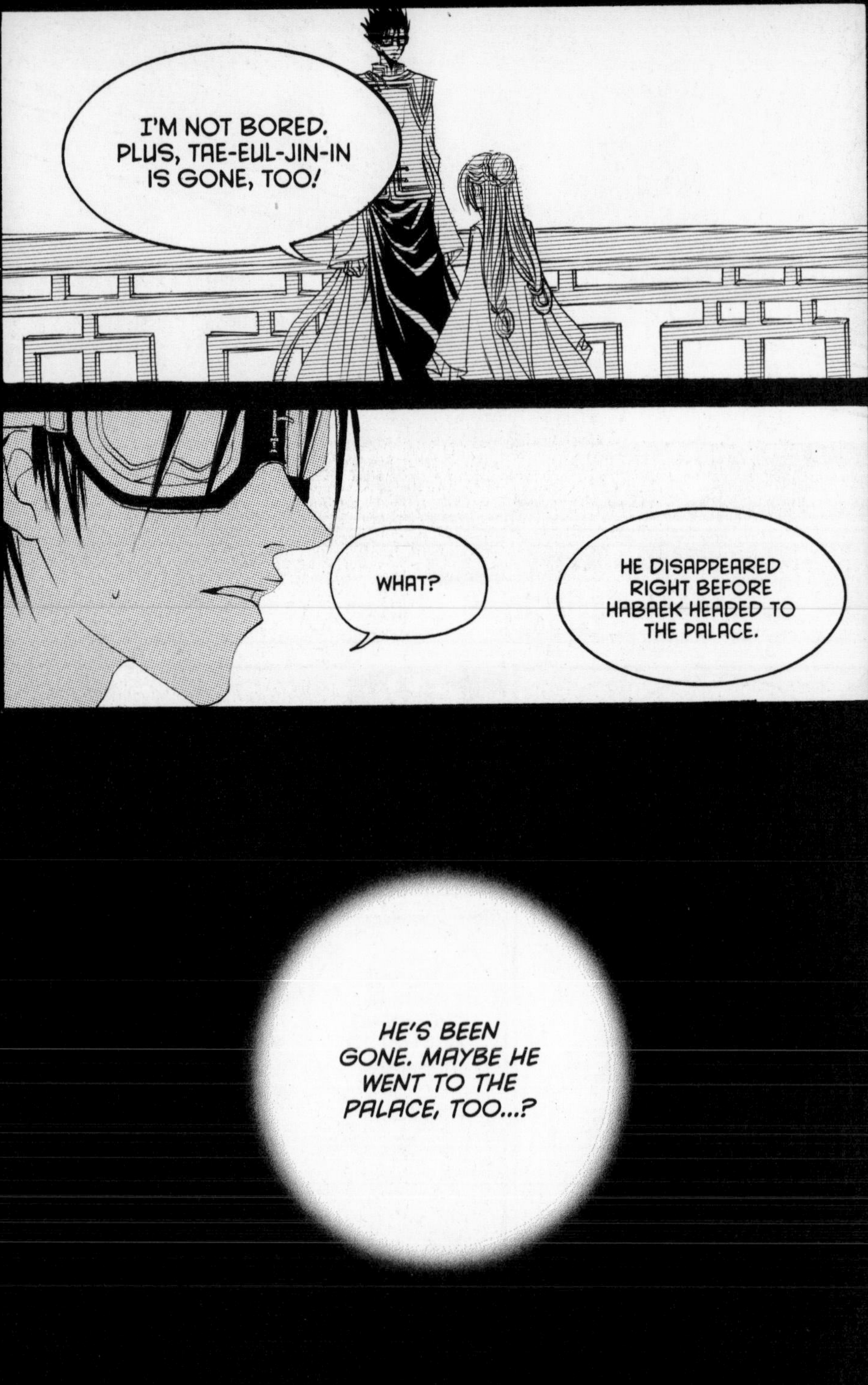
I'M NOT BORED. PLUS, TAE-EUL-JIN-IN IS GONE, TOO!
WHAT?
HE DISAPPEARED RIGHT BEFORE HABAEK HEADED TO THE PALACE.
HE'S BEEN GONE. MAYBE HE WENT TO THE PALACE, TOO...?

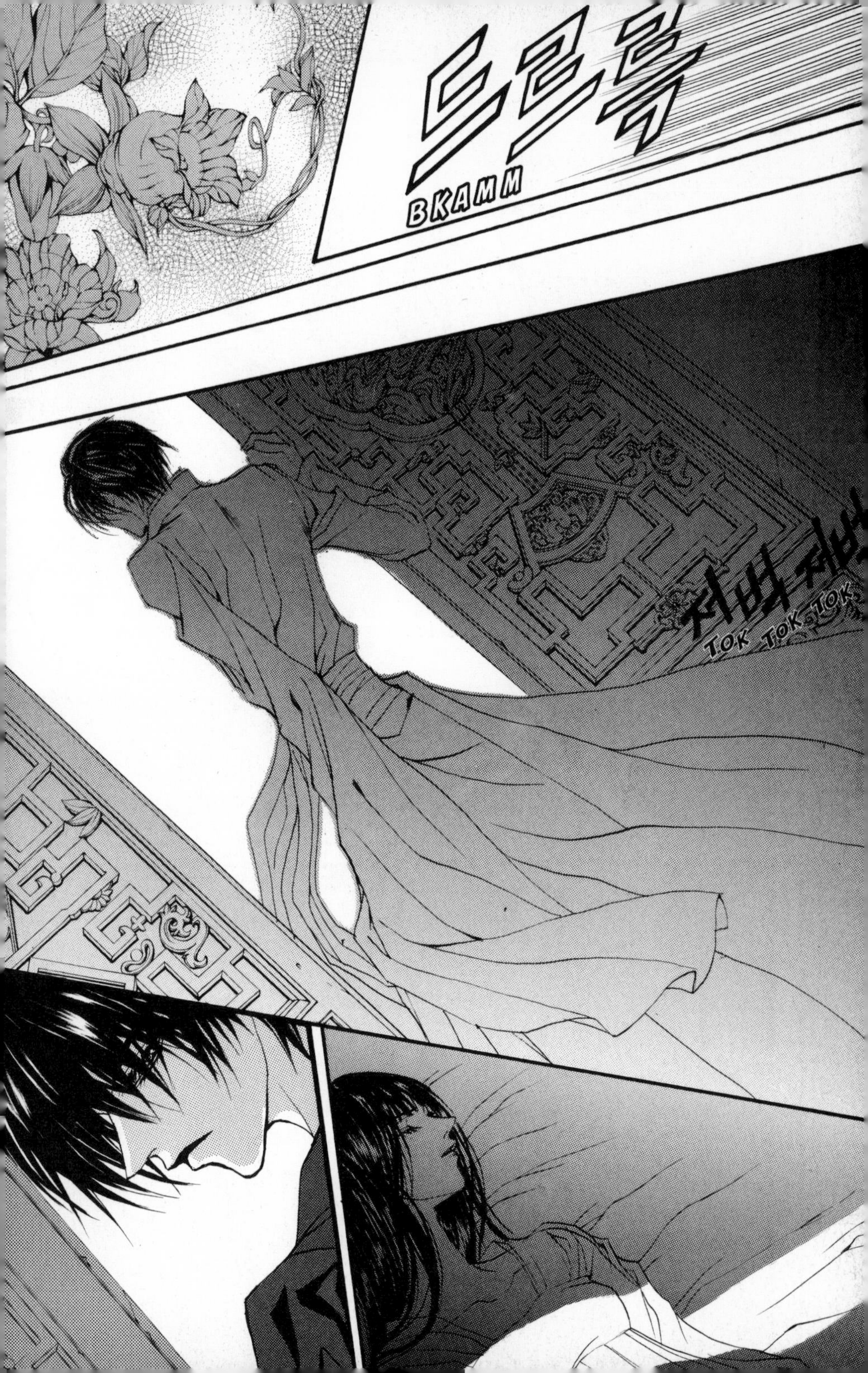

드르륵
BKAMM
저벅 저벅
TOK TOK TOK

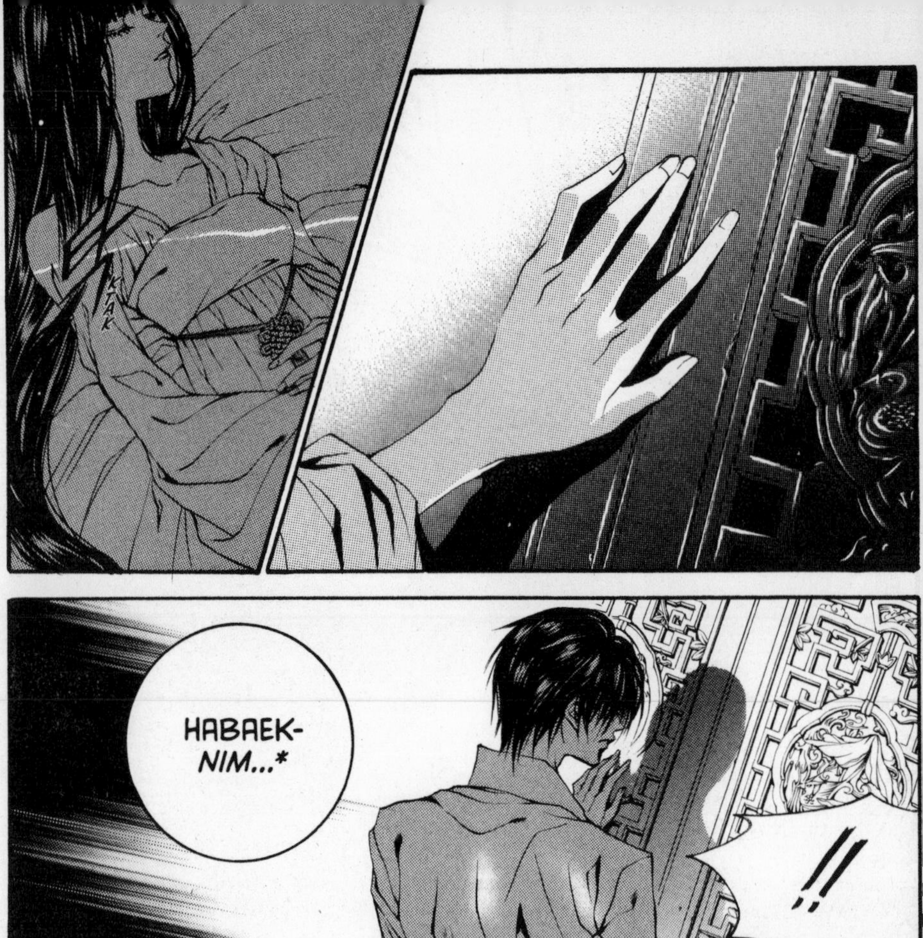
KTAK
HABAEK-NIM...*
!!

*NIM: KOREAN HONORIFIC, USED AFTER NAMES TO SHOW RESPECT.

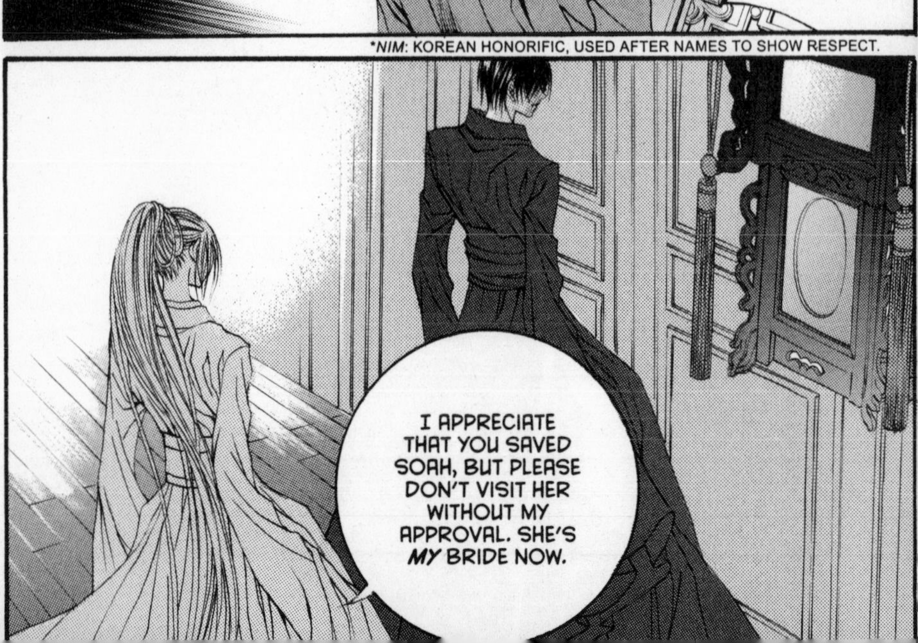
I APPRECIATE THAT YOU SAVED SOAH, BUT PLEASE DON'T VISIT HER WITHOUT MY APPROVAL. SHE'S *MY* BRIDE NOW.

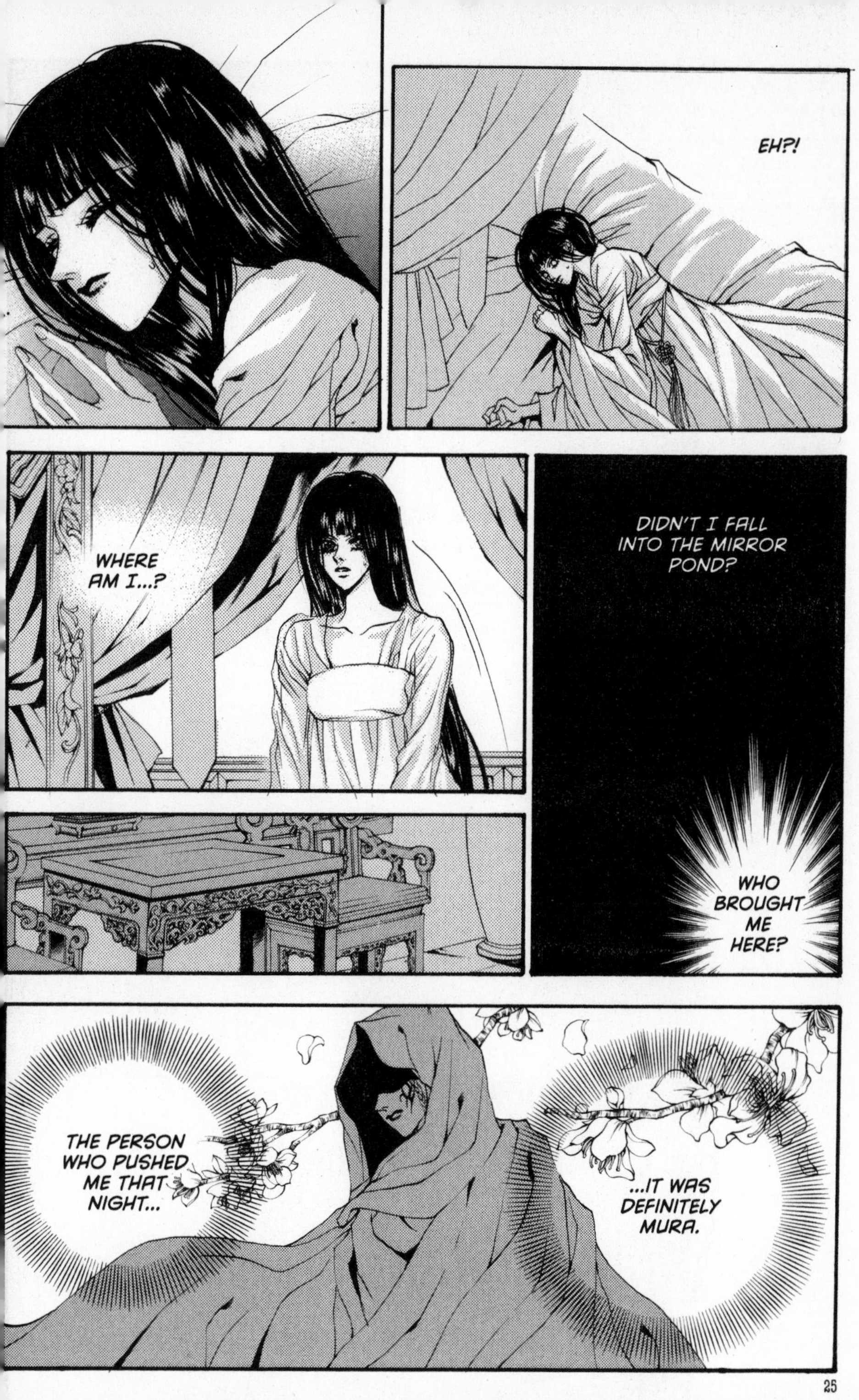
EH?!
WHERE AM I...?
DIDN'T I FALL INTO THE MIRROR POND?
WHO BROUGHT ME HERE?
THE PERSON WHO PUSHED ME THAT NIGHT...
...IT WAS DEFINITELY MURA.

WHY DID SHE DO THAT...?

WELL, THE MORE IMPORTANT QUESTION IS HOW DO I GET BACK TO SUGUK?

THESE FLOWERS ...?

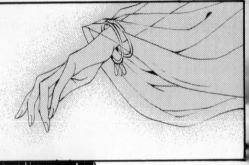

COULD IT HAVE BEEN--

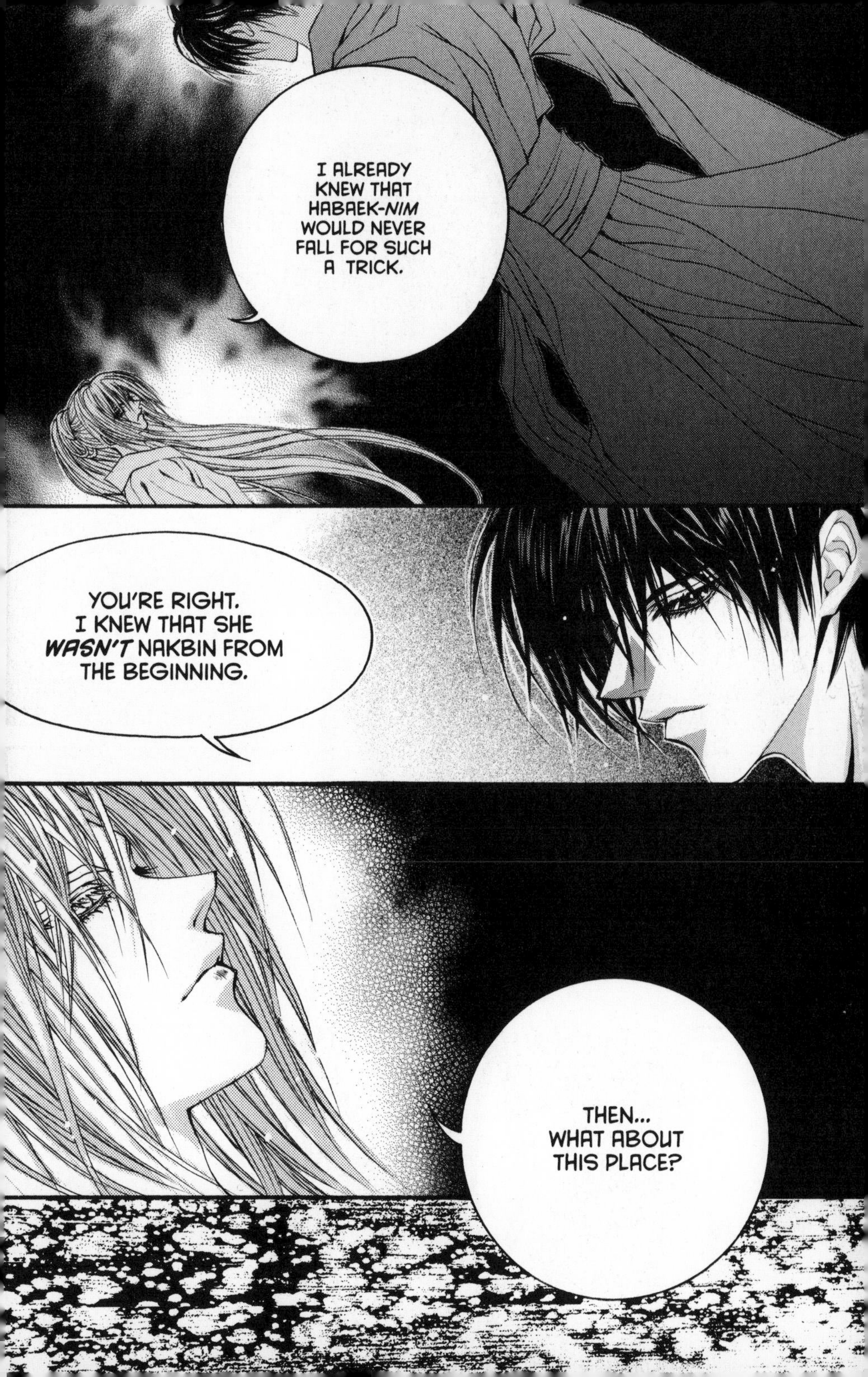
I ALREADY KNEW THAT HABAEK-*NIM* WOULD NEVER FALL FOR SUCH A TRICK.
YOU'RE RIGHT. I KNEW THAT SHE *WASN'T* NAKBIN FROM THE BEGINNING.
THEN... WHAT ABOUT THIS PLACE?

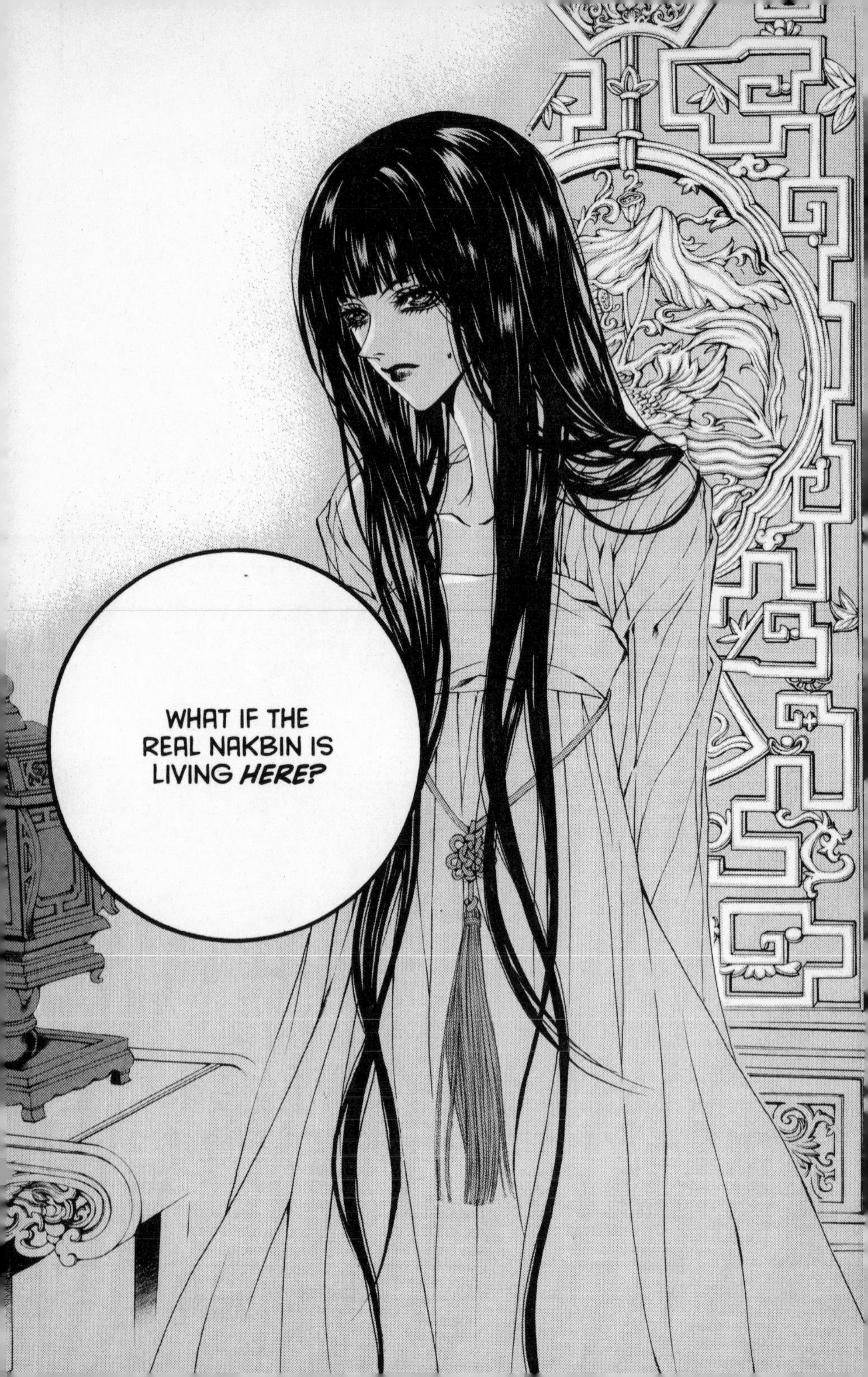
WHAT IF THE REAL NAKBIN IS LIVING *HERE?*

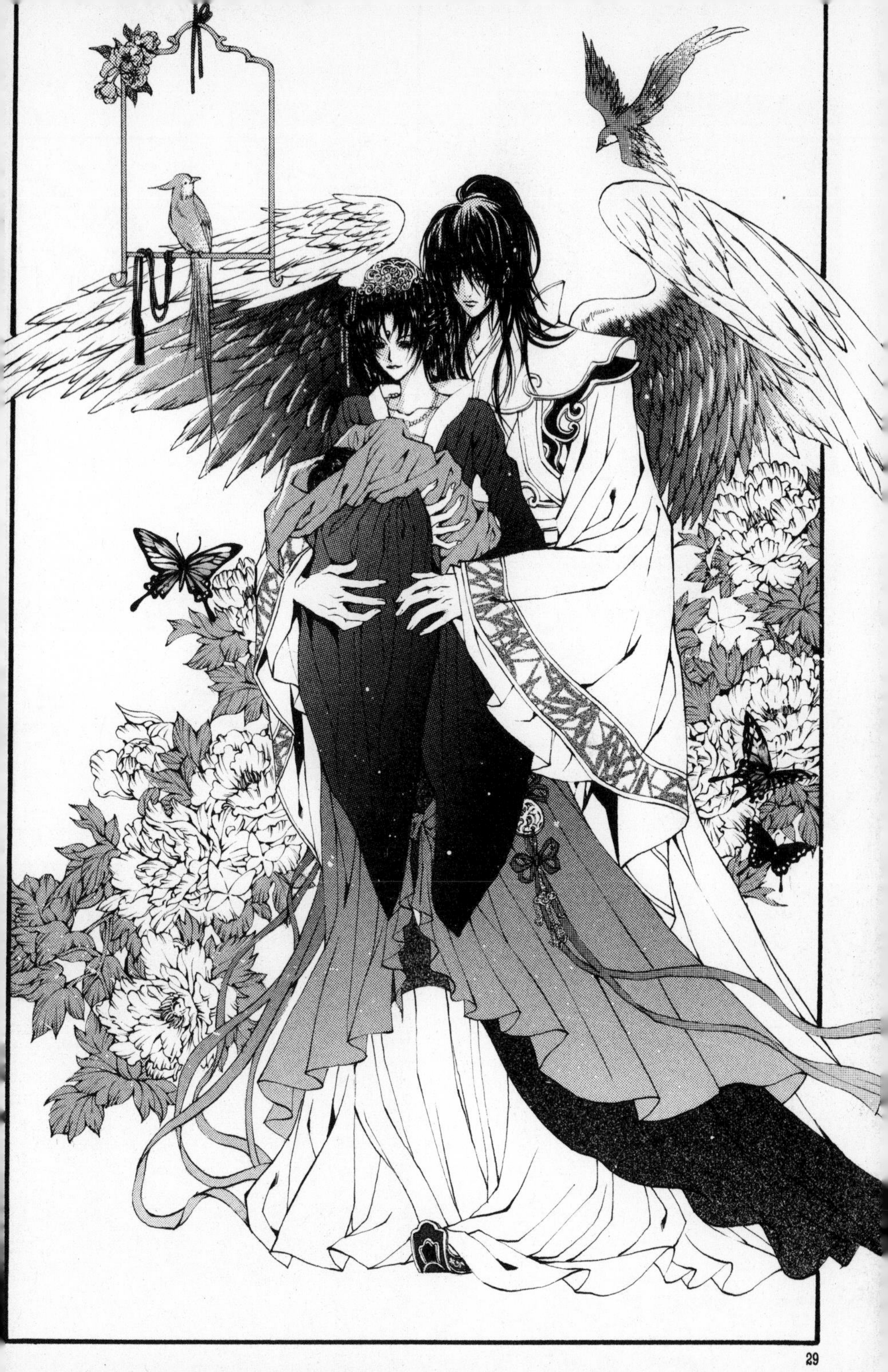

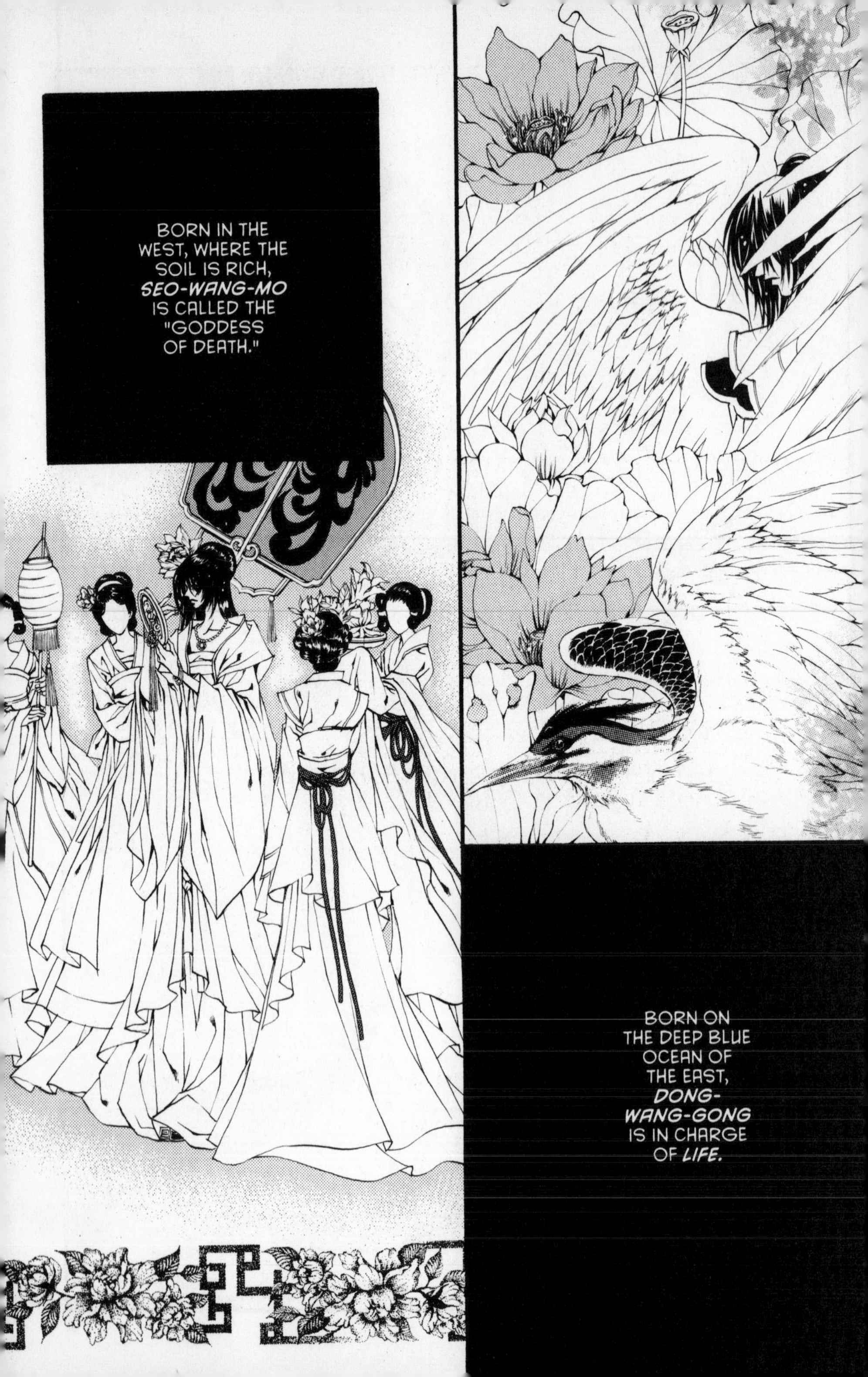
BORN IN THE WEST, WHERE THE SOIL IS RICH, *SEO-WANG-MO* IS CALLED THE "GODDESS OF DEATH."
BORN ON THE DEEP BLUE OCEAN OF THE EAST, *DONG-WANG-GONG* IS IN CHARGE OF *LIFE*.

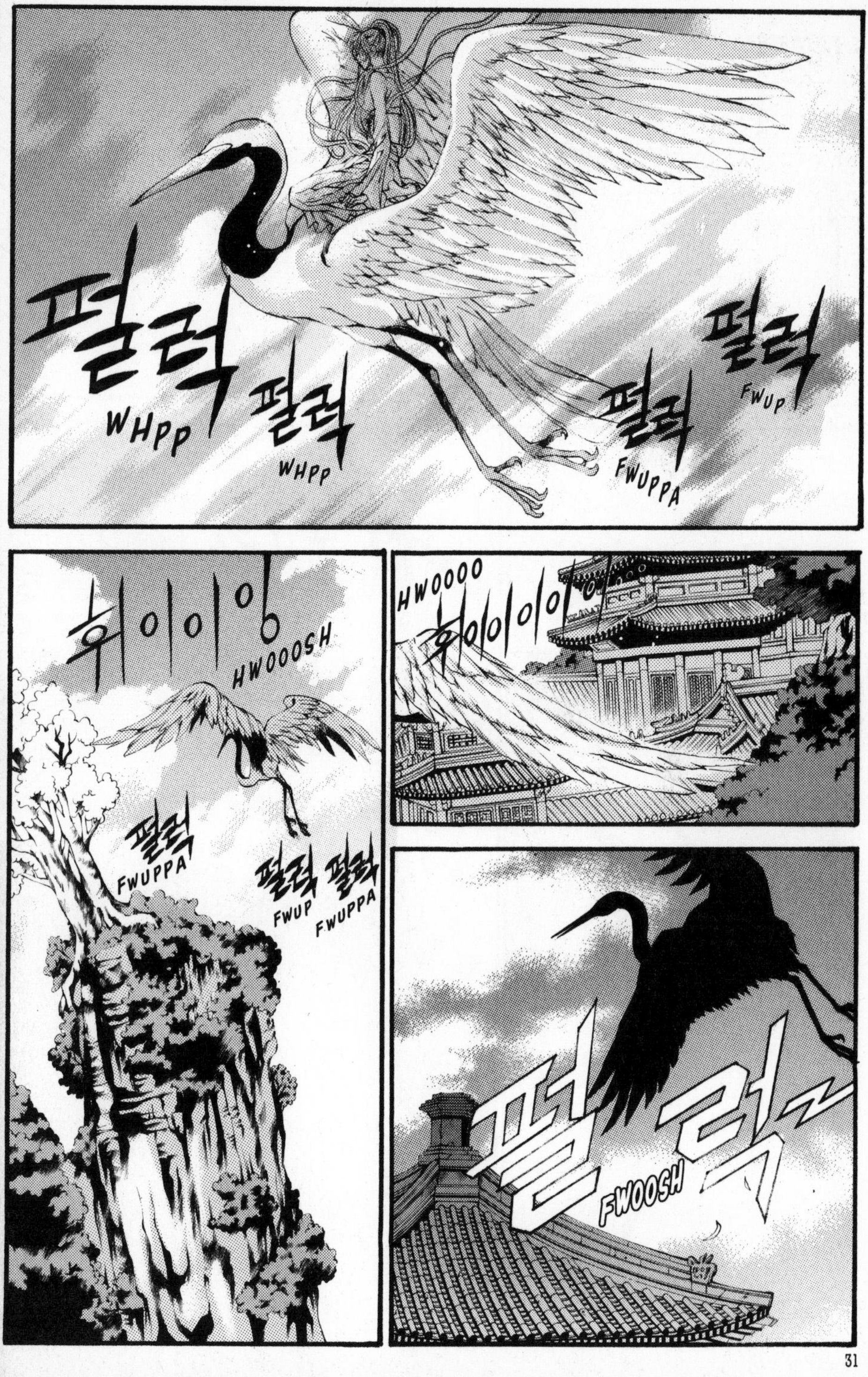
펄럭
WHPP
펄럭
WHPP
펄럭
FWUPPA
펄럭
FWUP
휘이이잉
HWOOOSH
펄럭
FWUPPA
펄럭
FWUP
펄럭
FWUPPA
HWOOOO
휘이이이이
펄럭
FWOOSH

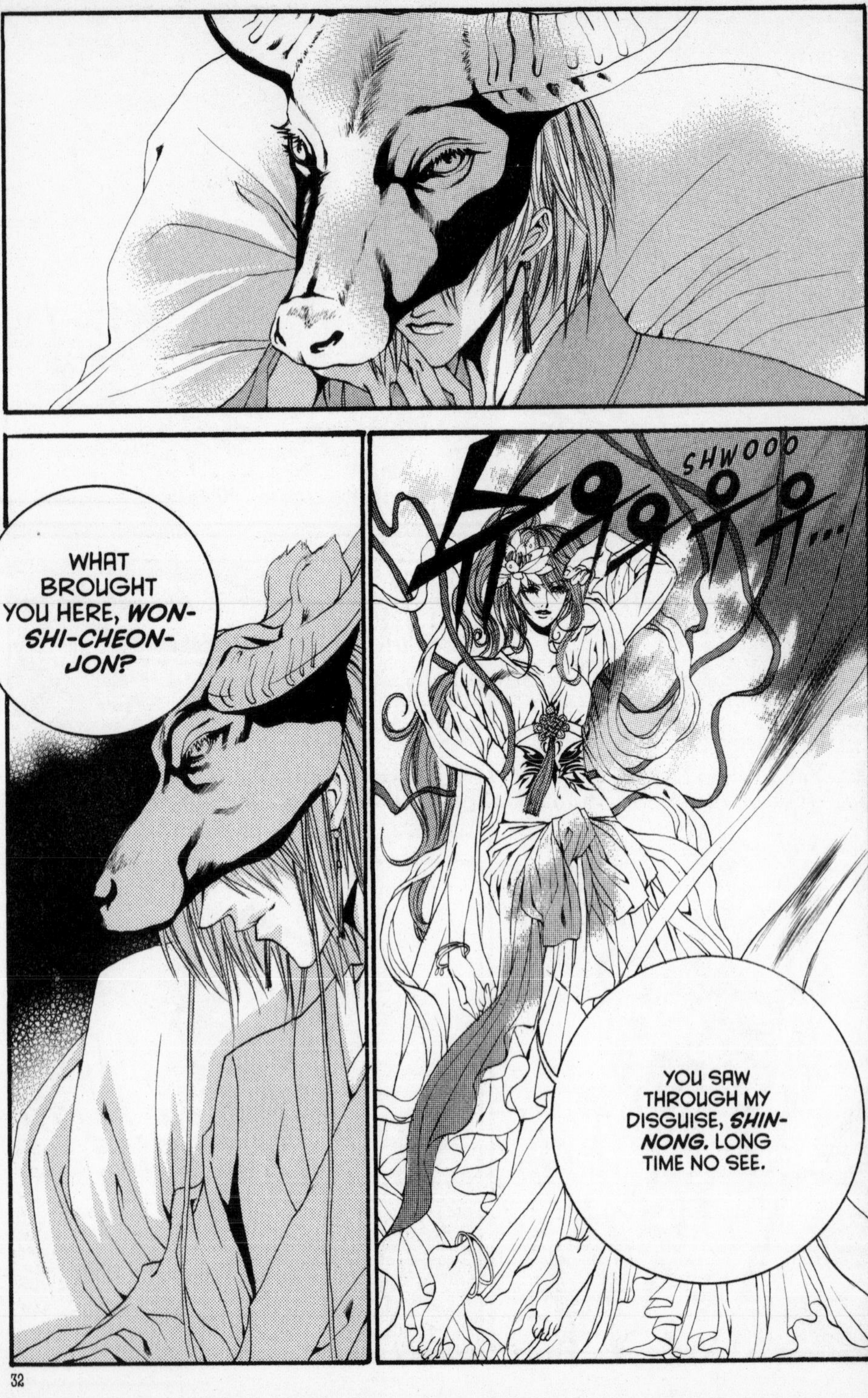
WHAT BROUGHT YOU HERE, WON-SHI-CHEON-JON?
SHWOOO
YOU SAW THROUGH MY DISGUISE, SHIN-NONG. LONG TIME NO SEE.

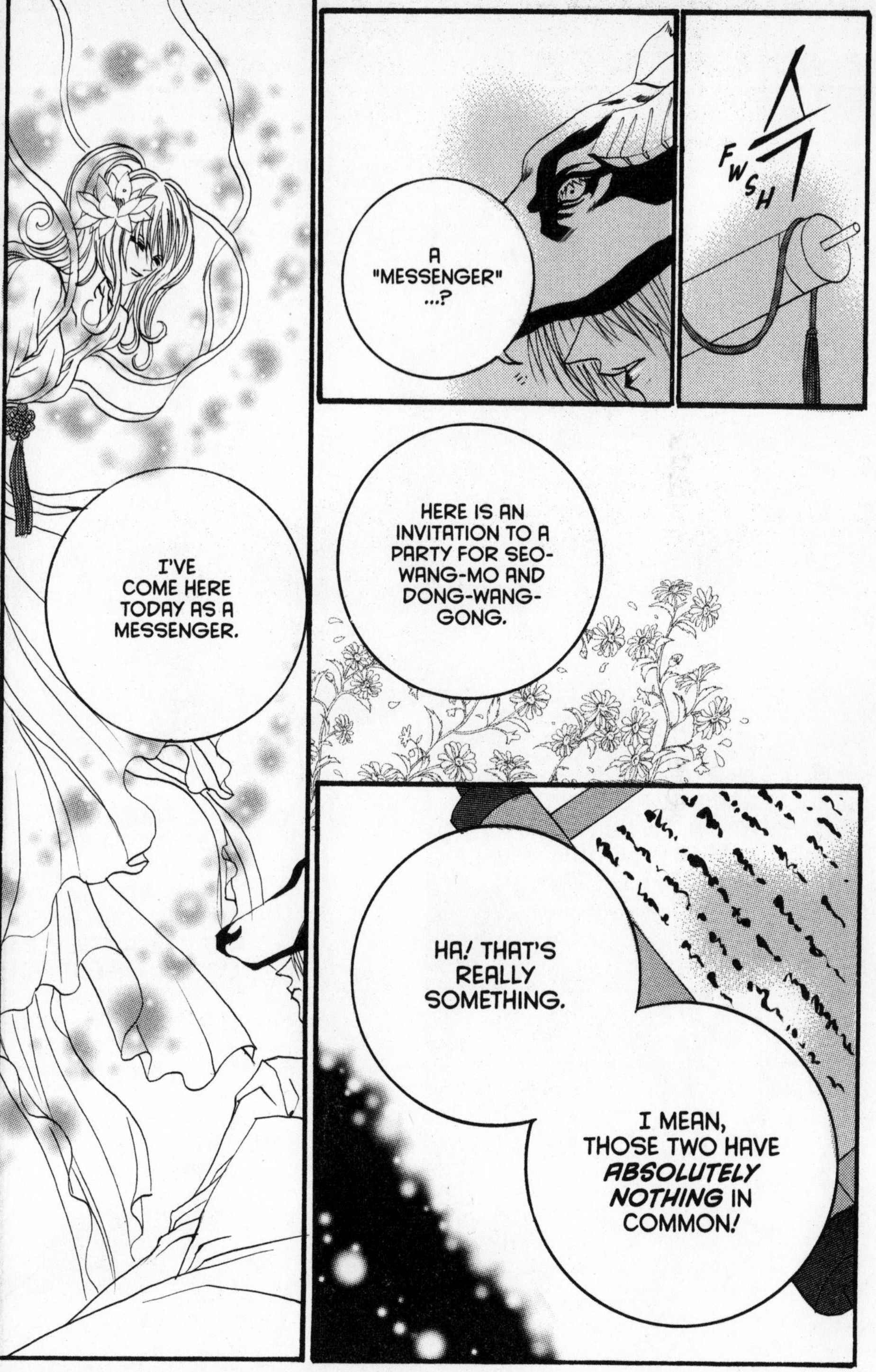
FWSH
A "MESSENGER" ...?
I'VE COME HERE TODAY AS A MESSENGER.
HERE IS AN INVITATION TO A PARTY FOR SEO-WANG-MO AND DONG-WANG-GONG.
HA! THAT'S REALLY SOMETHING.
I MEAN, THOSE TWO HAVE *ABSOLUTELY NOTHING* IN COMMON!

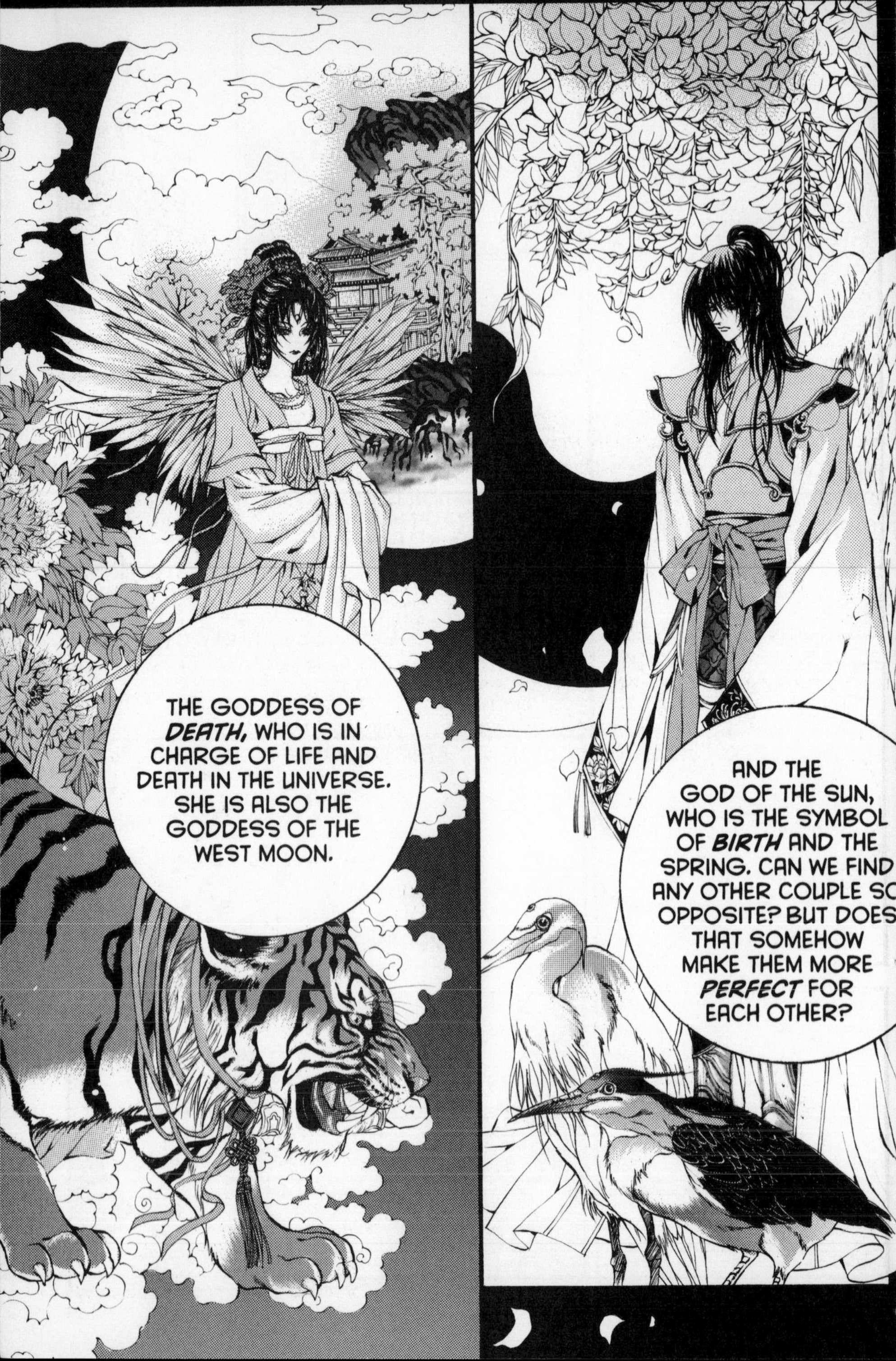
THE GODDESS OF *DEATH,* WHO IS IN CHARGE OF LIFE AND DEATH IN THE UNIVERSE. SHE IS ALSO THE GODDESS OF THE WEST MOON.
AND THE GOD OF THE SUN, WHO IS THE SYMBOL OF *BIRTH* AND THE SPRING. CAN WE FIND ANY OTHER COUPLE SO OPPOSITE? BUT DOES THAT SOMEHOW MAKE THEM MORE *PERFECT* FOR EACH OTHER?

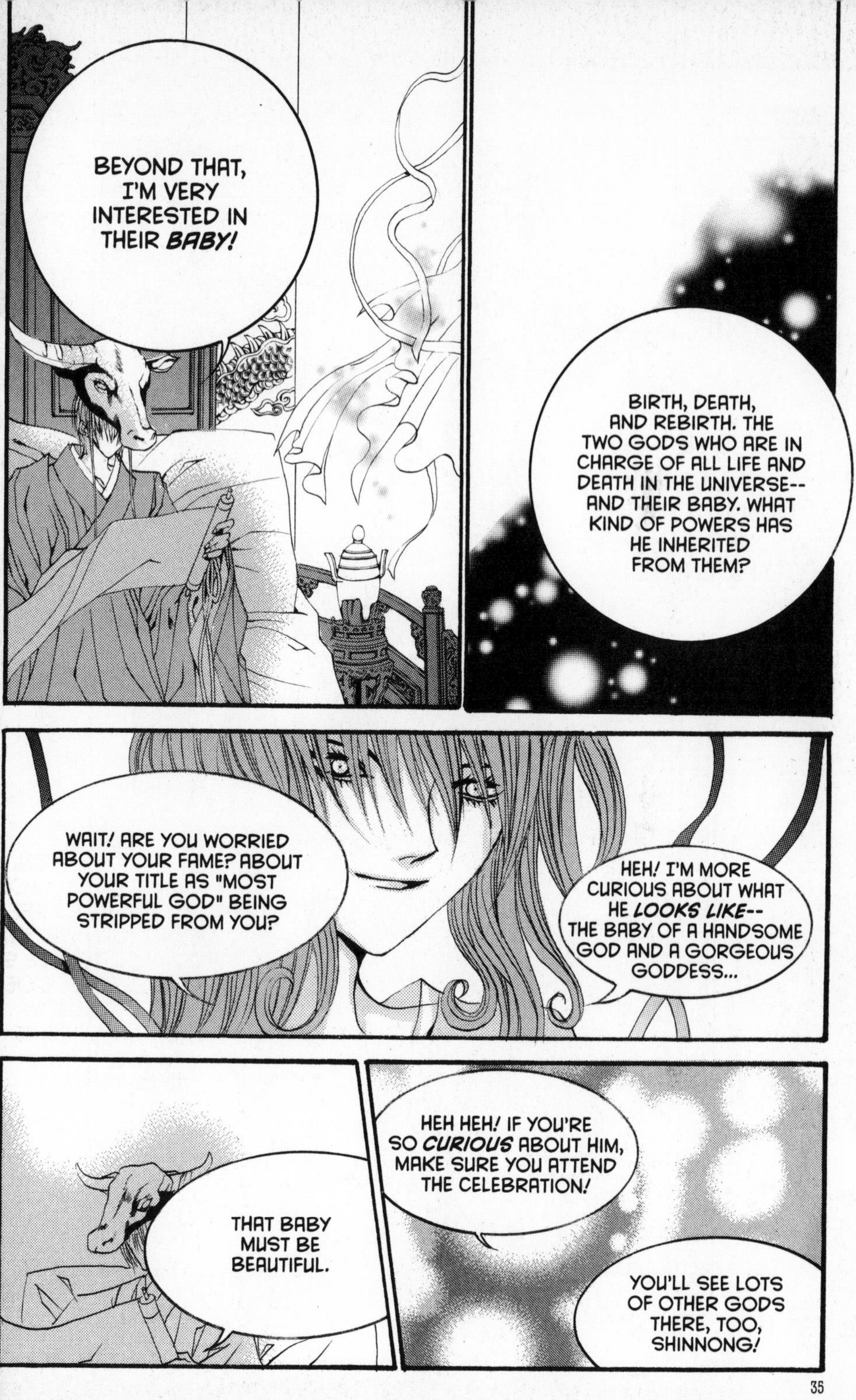
BEYOND THAT, I'M VERY INTERESTED IN THEIR BABY!
BIRTH, DEATH, AND REBIRTH. THE TWO GODS WHO ARE IN CHARGE OF ALL LIFE AND DEATH IN THE UNIVERSE-- AND THEIR BABY. WHAT KIND OF POWERS HAS HE INHERITED FROM THEM?
WAIT! ARE YOU WORRIED ABOUT YOUR FAME? ABOUT YOUR TITLE AS "MOST POWERFUL GOD" BEING STRIPPED FROM YOU?
HEH! I'M MORE CURIOUS ABOUT WHAT HE LOOKS LIKE-- THE BABY OF A HANDSOME GOD AND A GORGEOUS GODDESS...
THAT BABY MUST BE BEAUTIFUL.
HEH HEH! IF YOU'RE SO CURIOUS ABOUT HIM, MAKE SURE YOU ATTEND THE CELEBRATION!
YOU'LL SEE LOTS OF OTHER GODS THERE, TOO, SHINNONG!

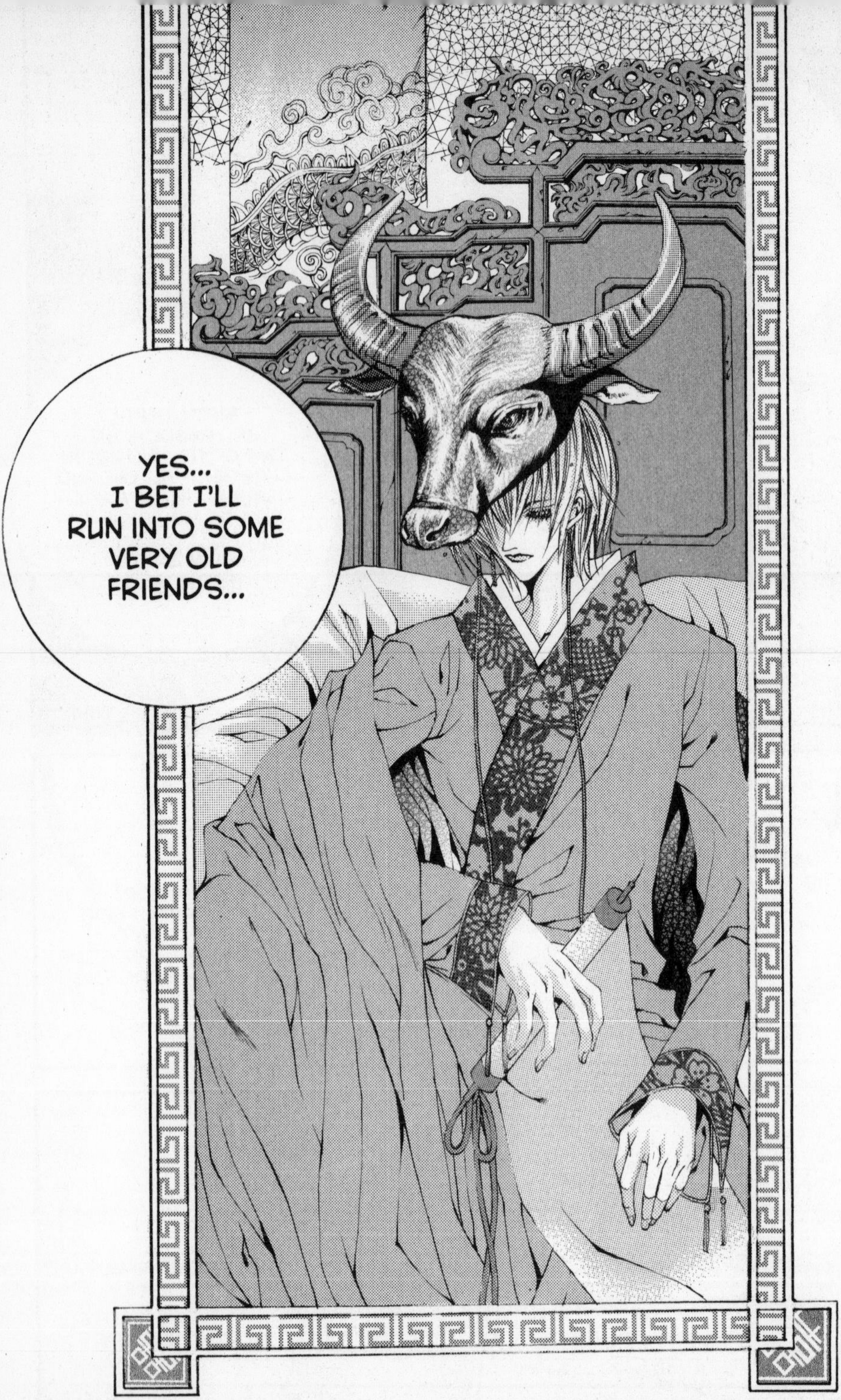
YES... I BET I'LL RUN INTO SOME VERY OLD FRIENDS...

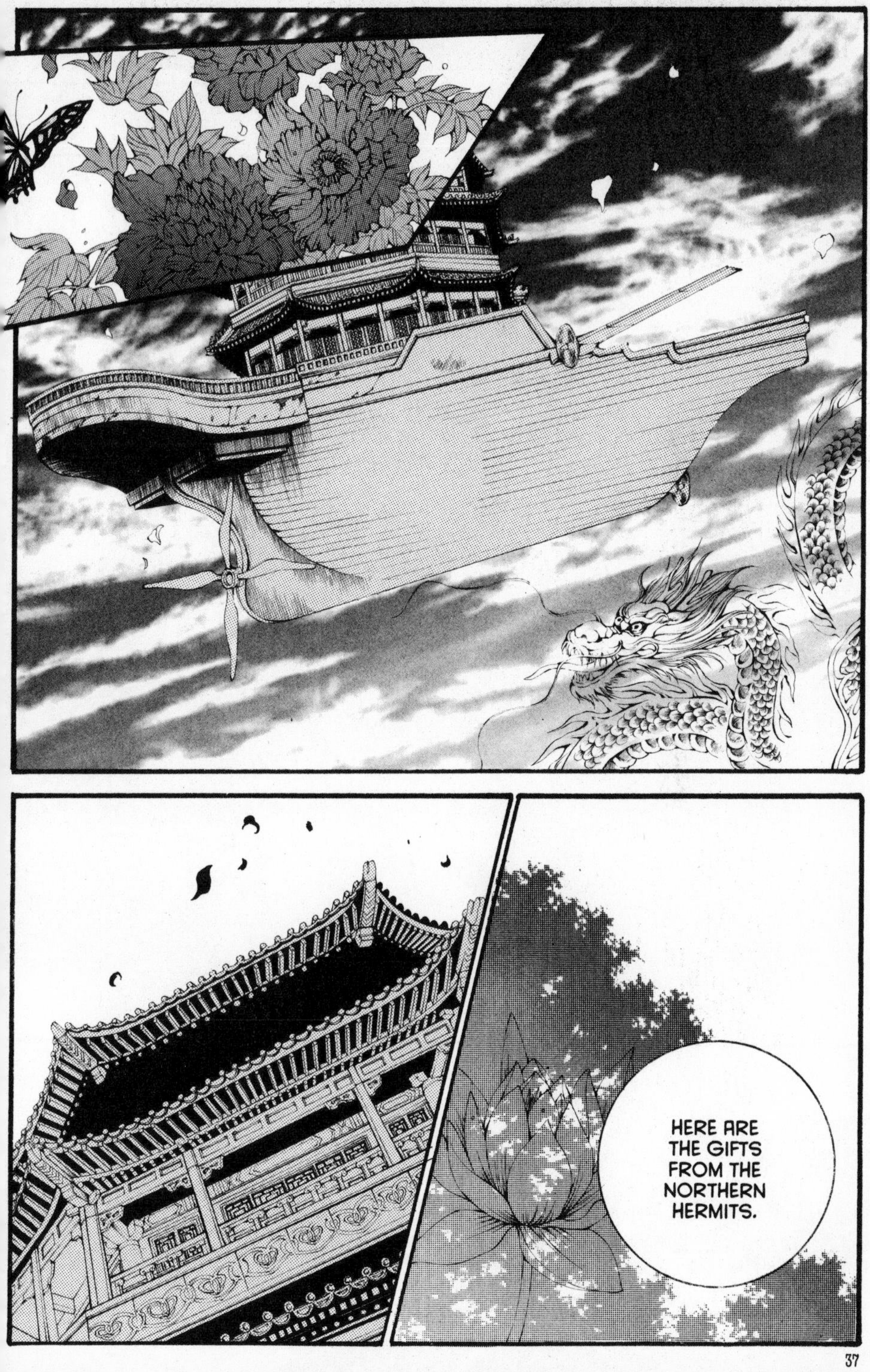
HERE ARE THE GIFTS FROM THE NORTHERN HERMITS.

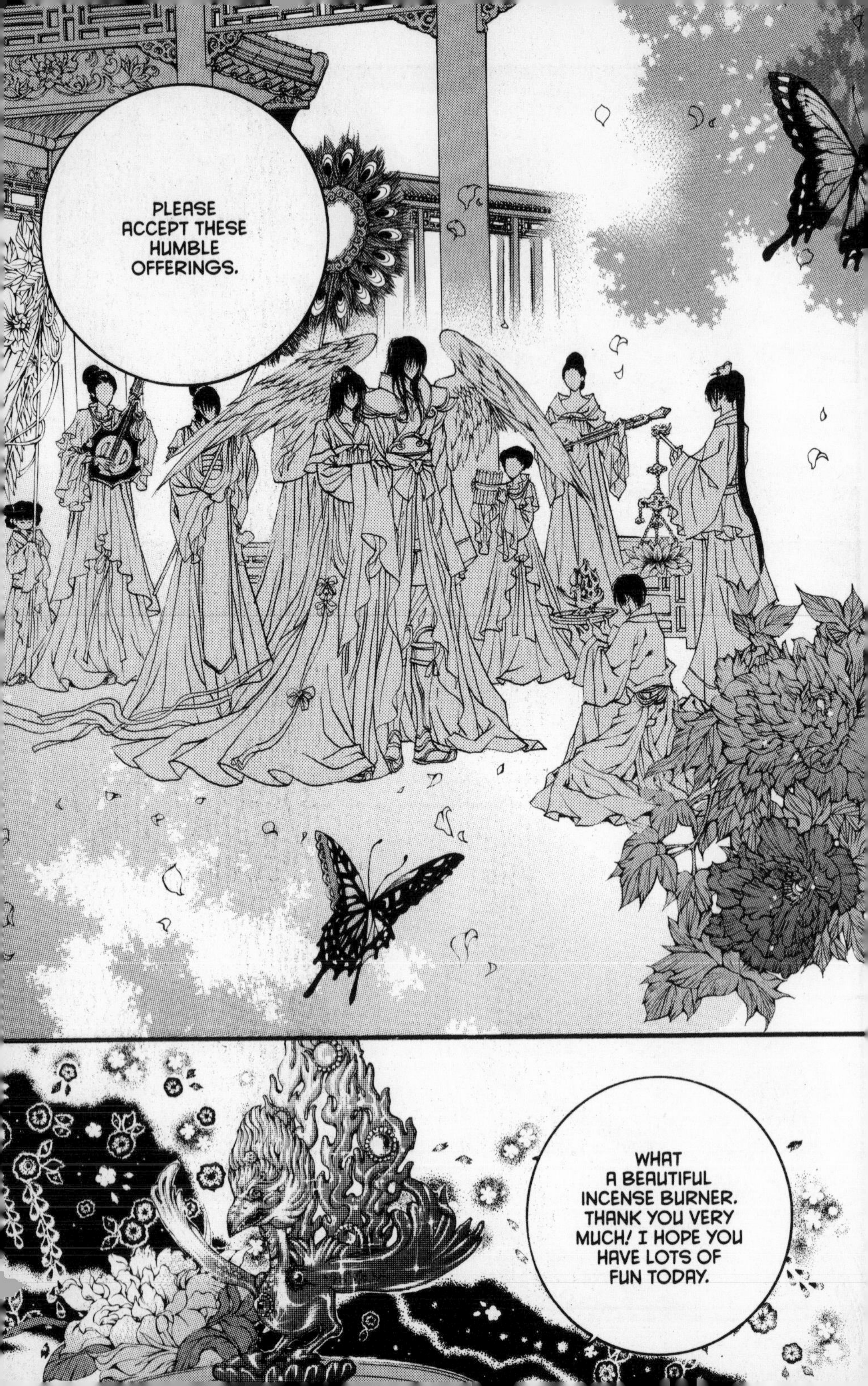
PLEASE ACCEPT THESE HUMBLE OFFERINGS.
WHAT A BEAUTIFUL INCENSE BURNER. THANK YOU VERY MUCH! I HOPE YOU HAVE LOTS OF FUN TODAY.

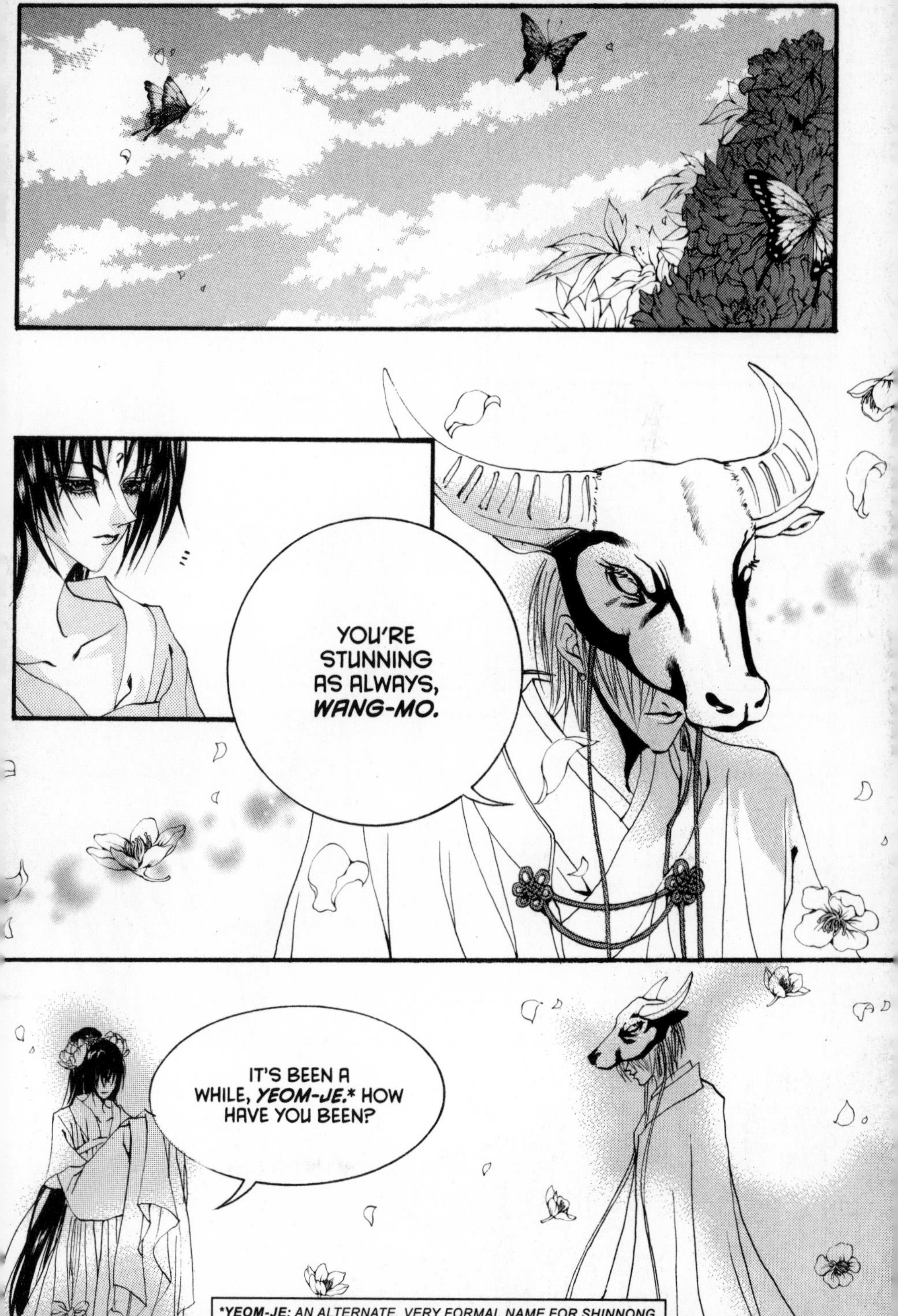
YOU'RE STUNNING AS ALWAYS, *WANG-MO.*
IT'S BEEN A WHILE, *YEOM-JE.** HOW HAVE YOU BEEN?
*YEOM-JE: AN ALTERNATE, VERY FORMAL NAME FOR SHINNONG.

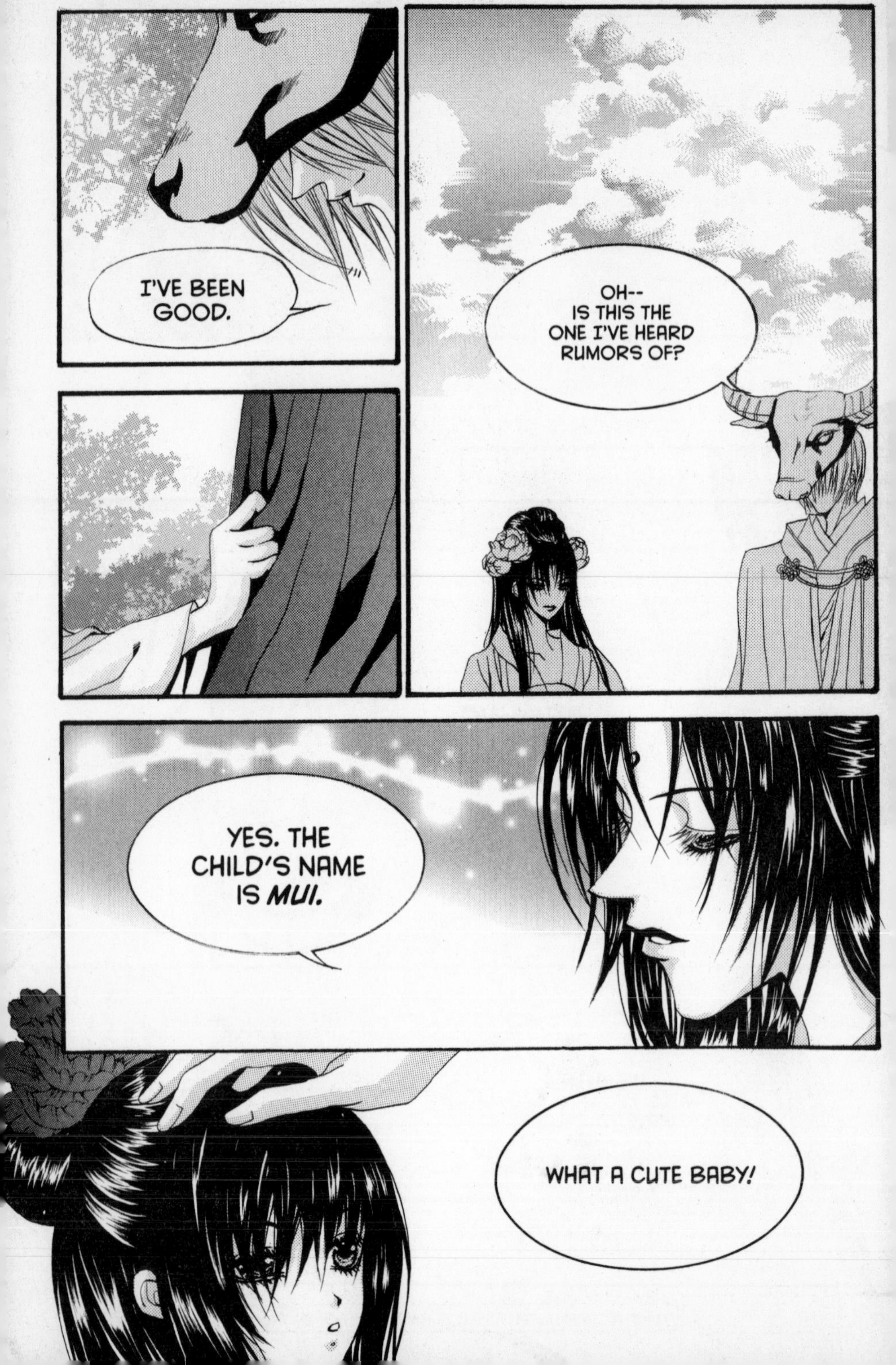
OH-- IS THIS THE ONE I'VE HEARD RUMORS OF?
I'VE BEEN GOOD.
YES. THE CHILD'S NAME IS *MUI.*
WHAT A CUTE BABY!

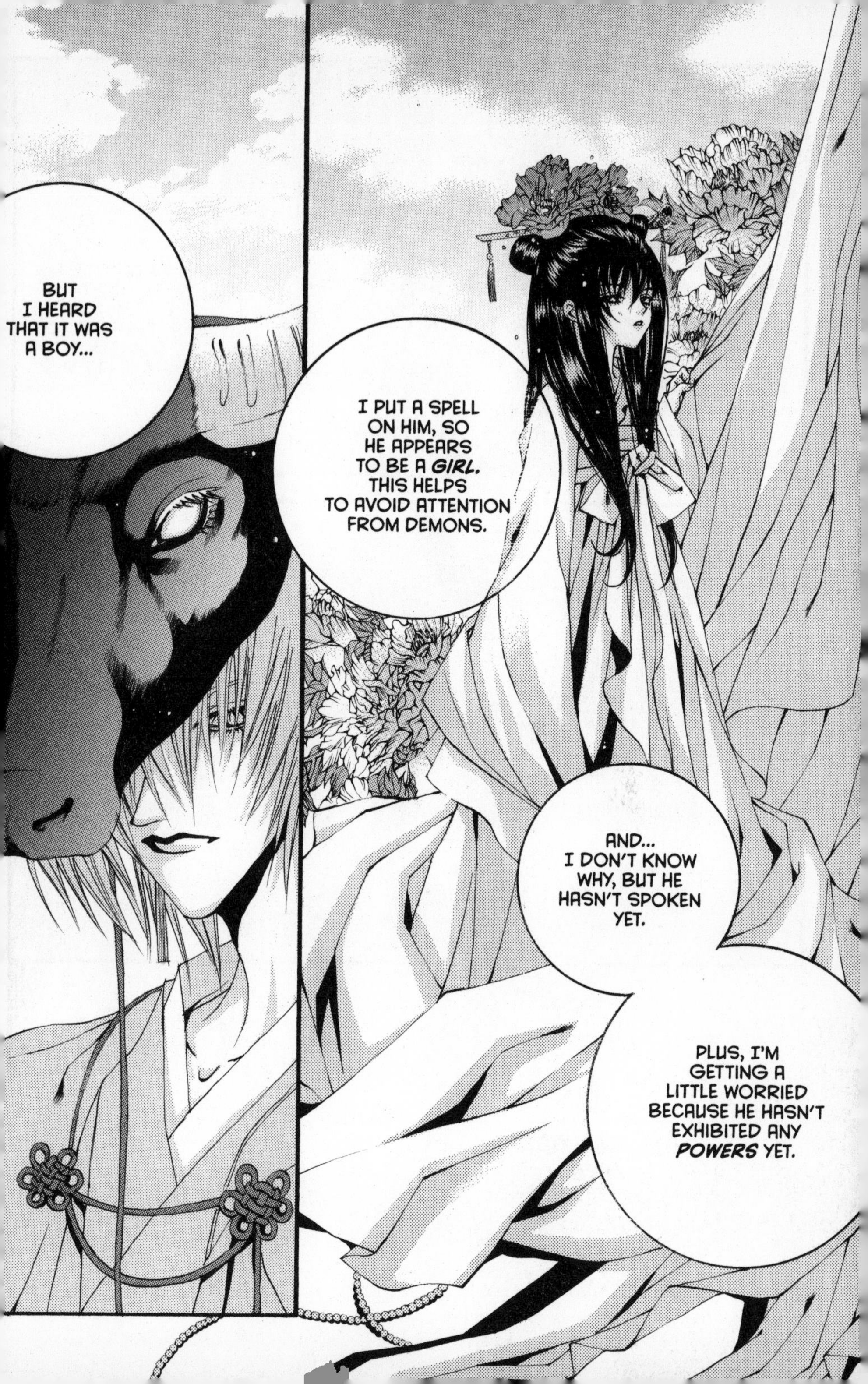
BUT I HEARD THAT IT WAS A BOY...
I PUT A SPELL ON HIM, SO HE APPEARS TO BE A GIRL. THIS HELPS TO AVOID ATTENTION FROM DEMONS.
AND... I DON'T KNOW WHY, BUT HE HASN'T SPOKEN YET.
PLUS, I'M GETTING A LITTLE WORRIED BECAUSE HE HASN'T EXHIBITED ANY POWERS YET.

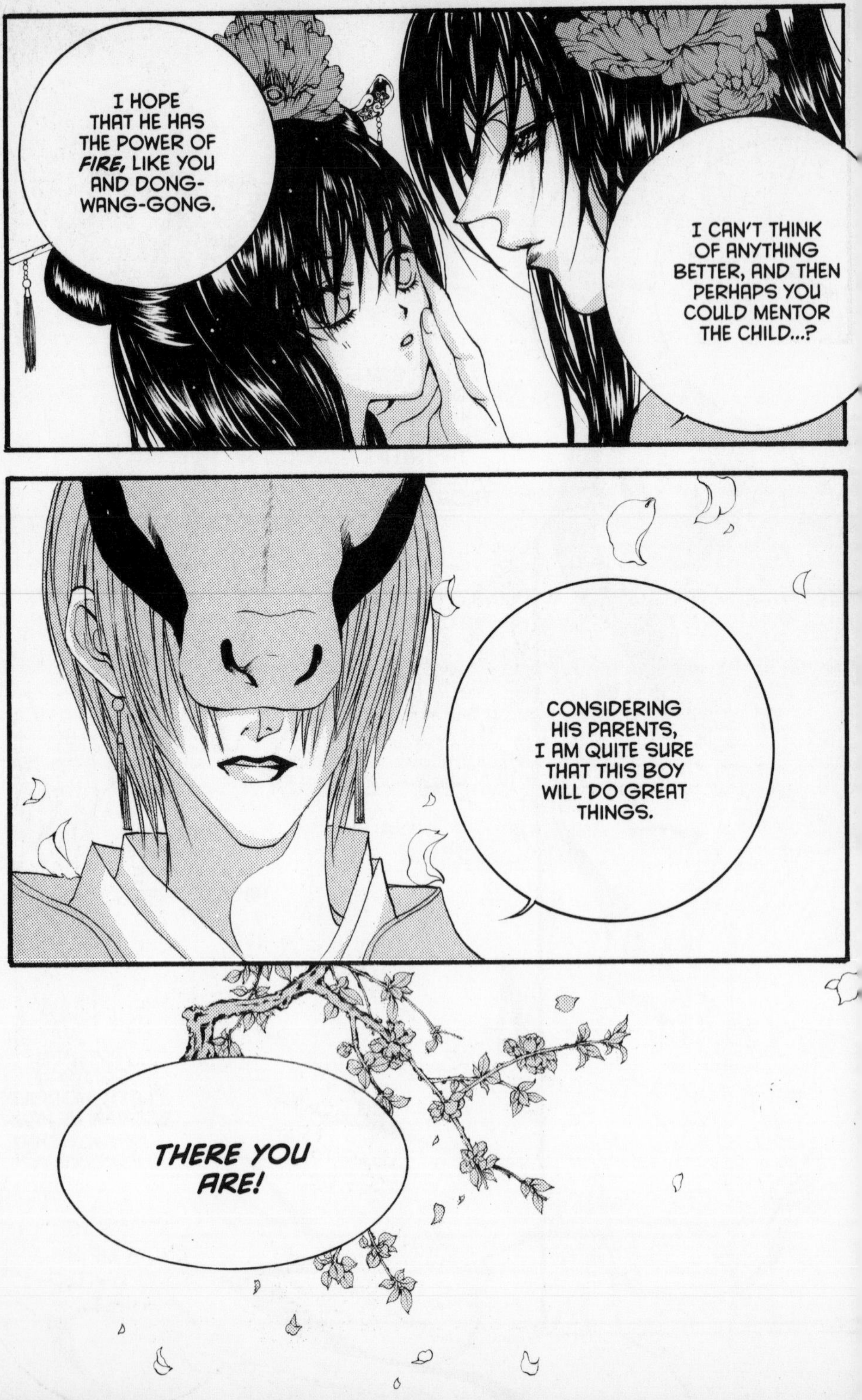
I HOPE THAT HE HAS THE POWER OF *FIRE,* LIKE YOU AND DONG-WANG-GONG.
I CAN'T THINK OF ANYTHING BETTER, AND THEN PERHAPS YOU COULD MENTOR THE CHILD...?
CONSIDERING HIS PARENTS, I AM QUITE SURE THAT THIS BOY WILL DO GREAT THINGS.
THERE YOU ARE!

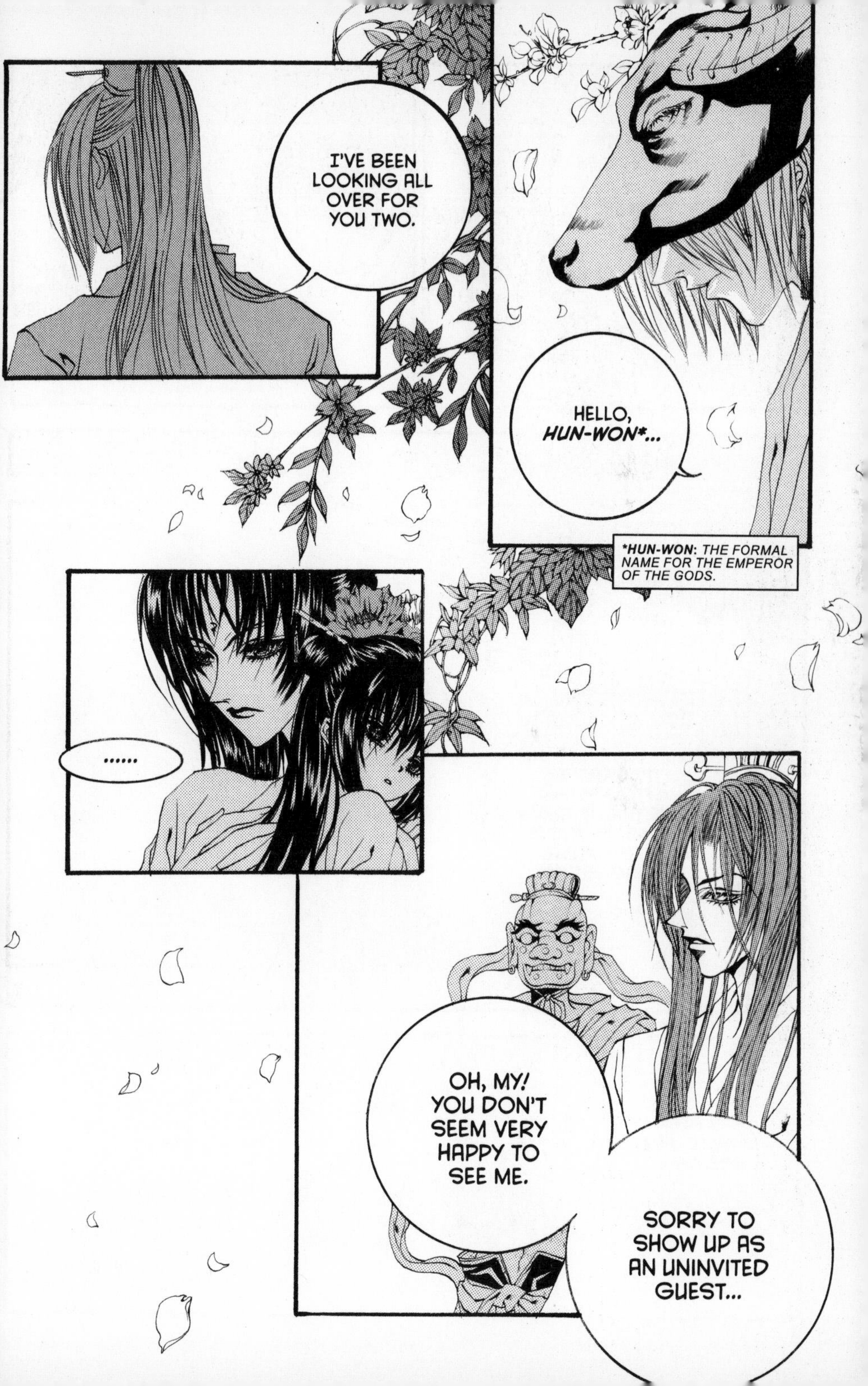

I'VE BEEN LOOKING ALL OVER FOR YOU TWO.
HELLO, *HUN-WON**...
***HUN-WON**: THE FORMAL NAME FOR THE EMPEROR OF THE GODS.
......
OH, MY! YOU DON'T SEEM VERY HAPPY TO SEE ME.
SORRY TO SHOW UP AS AN UNINVITED GUEST...

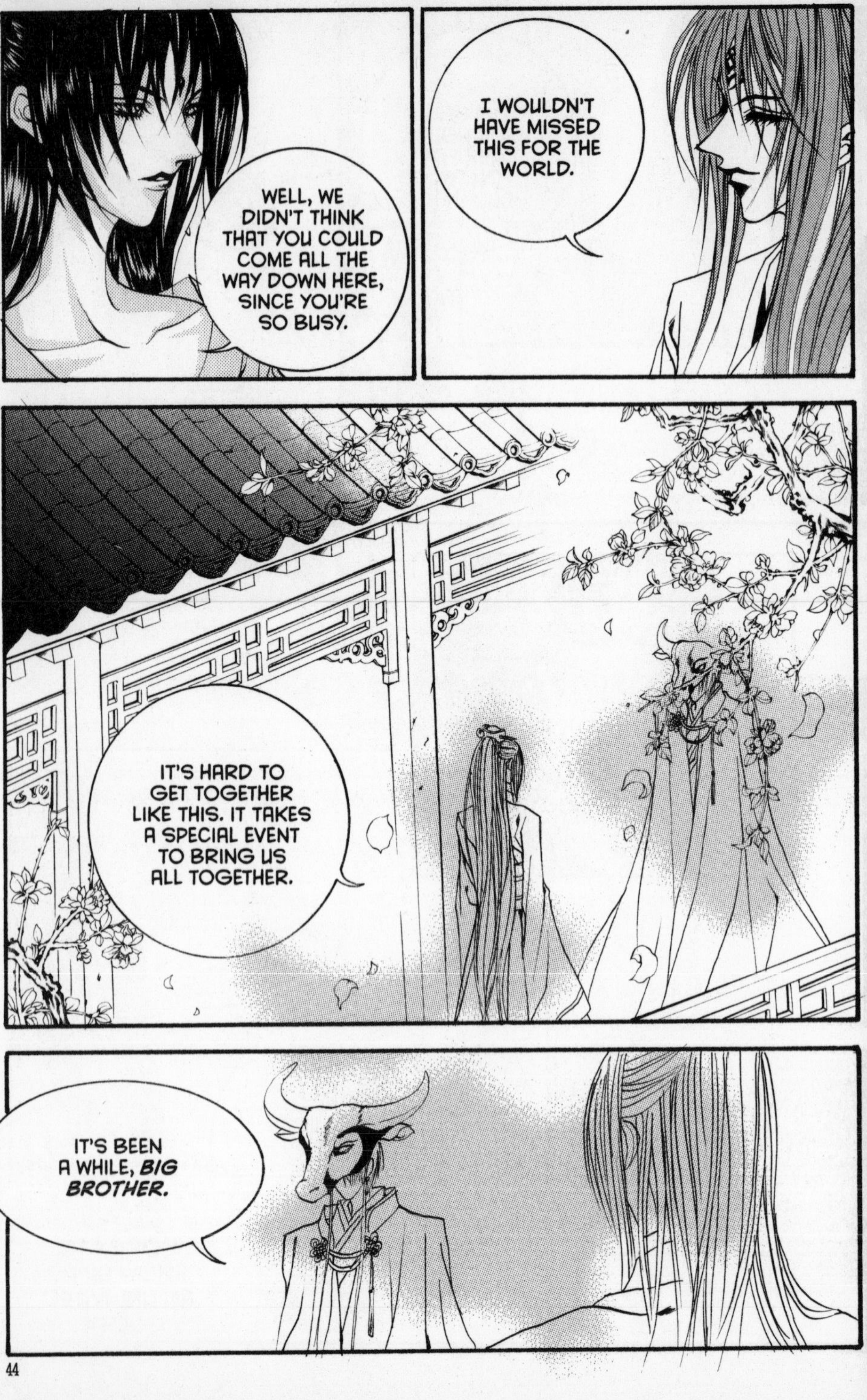
WELL, WE DIDN'T THINK THAT YOU COULD COME ALL THE WAY DOWN HERE, SINCE YOU'RE SO BUSY.
I WOULDN'T HAVE MISSED THIS FOR THE WORLD.
IT'S HARD TO GET TOGETHER LIKE THIS. IT TAKES A SPECIAL EVENT TO BRING US ALL TOGETHER.
IT'S BEEN A WHILE, *BIG BROTHER.*

IT HAS BEEN A LONG TIME. I THOUGHT YOU WERE TRYING TO AVOID ME ON PURPOSE.

I'VE HEARD SOME VERY NASTY RUMORS.

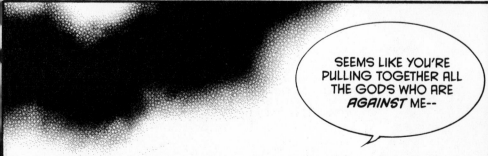

SEEMS LIKE YOU'RE PULLING TOGETHER ALL THE GODS WHO ARE *AGAINST* ME--

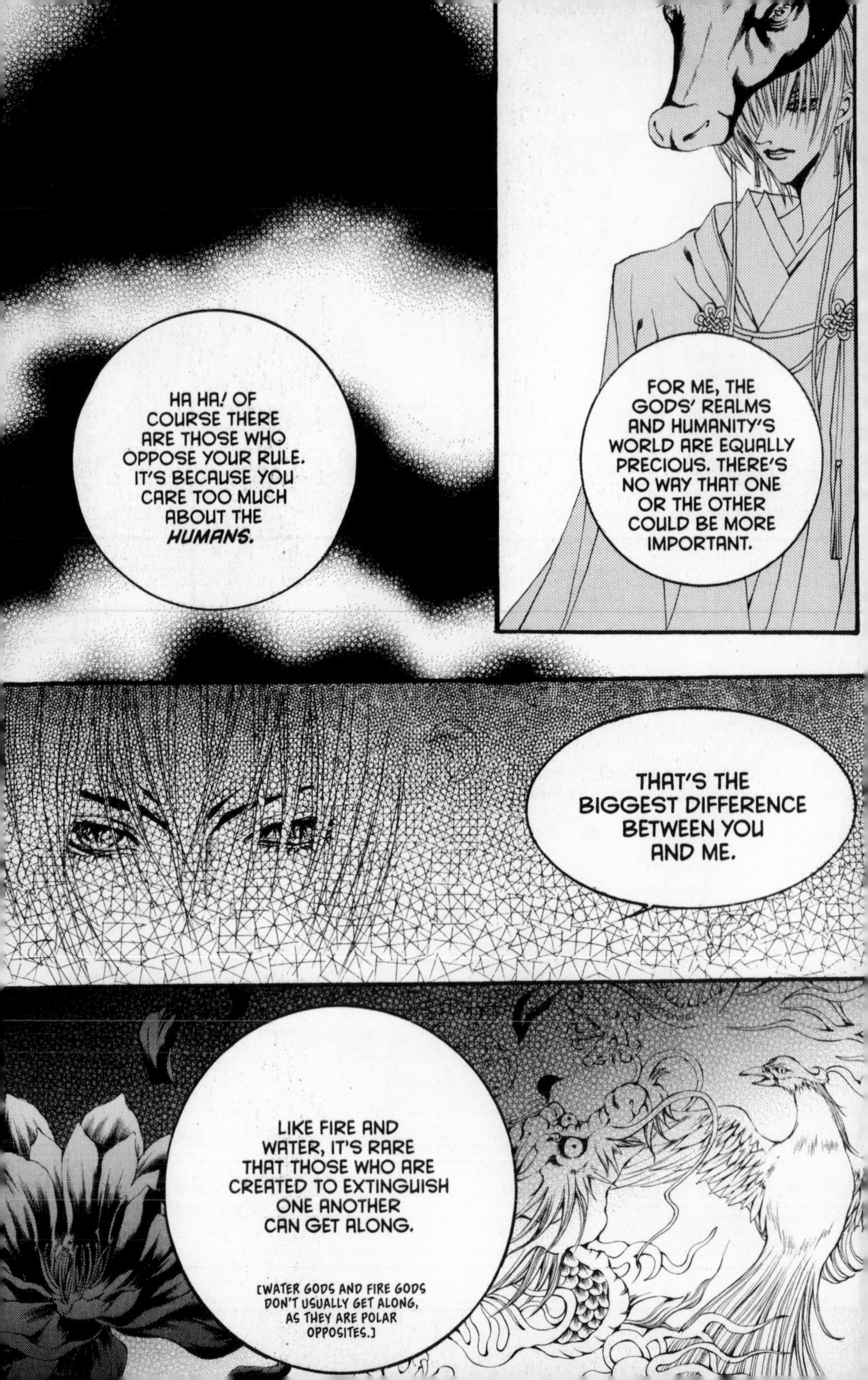
FOR ME, THE GODS' REALMS AND HUMANITY'S WORLD ARE EQUALLY PRECIOUS. THERE'S NO WAY THAT ONE OR THE OTHER COULD BE MORE IMPORTANT.
HA HA! OF COURSE THERE ARE THOSE WHO OPPOSE YOUR RULE. IT'S BECAUSE YOU CARE TOO MUCH ABOUT THE *HUMANS.*
THAT'S THE BIGGEST DIFFERENCE BETWEEN YOU AND ME.
LIKE FIRE AND WATER, IT'S RARE THAT THOSE WHO ARE CREATED TO EXTINGUISH ONE ANOTHER CAN GET ALONG.
[WATER GODS AND FIRE GODS DON'T USUALLY GET ALONG, AS THEY ARE POLAR OPPOSITES.]

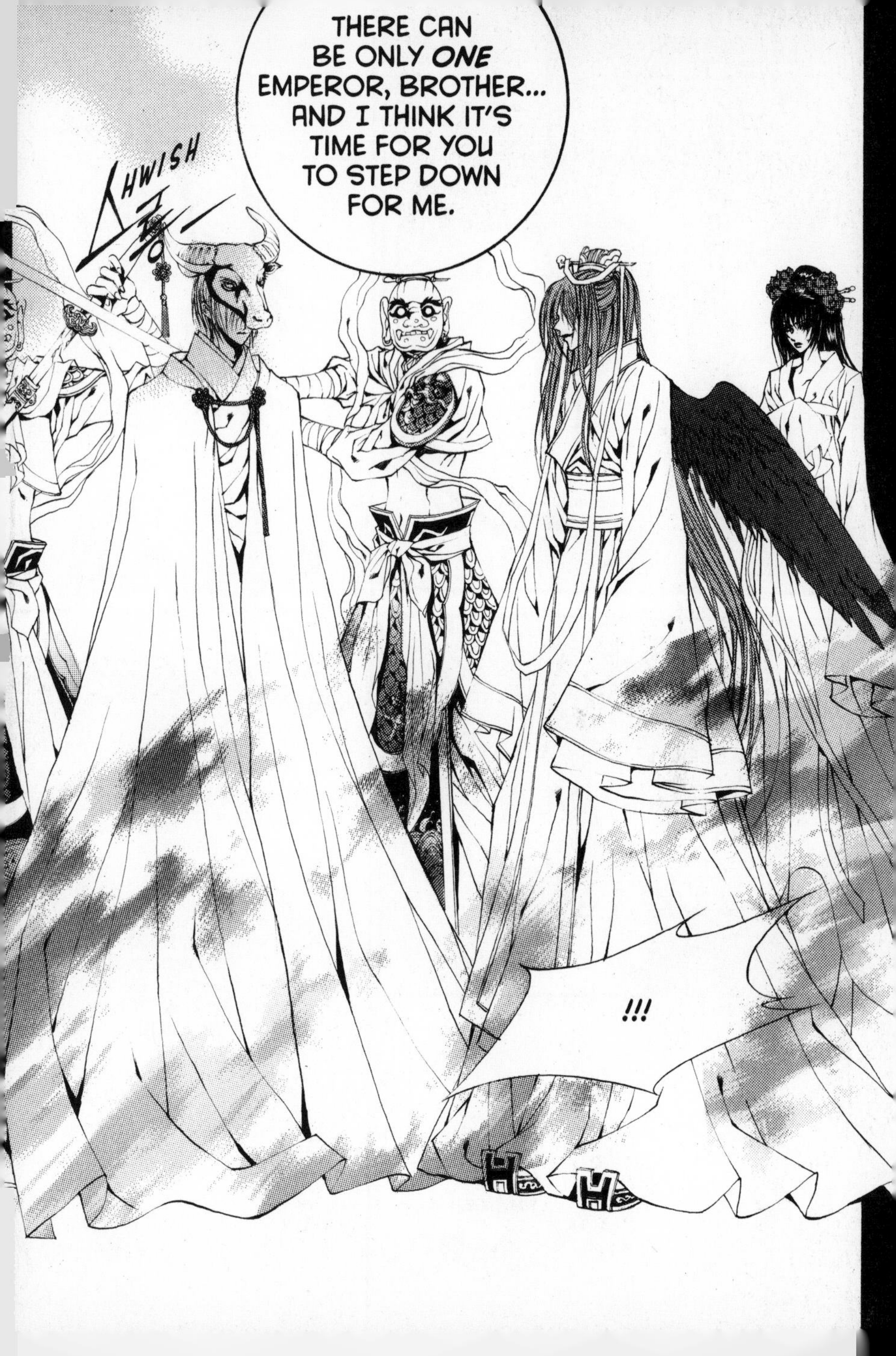
THERE CAN BE ONLY *ONE* EMPEROR, BROTHER... AND I THINK IT'S TIME FOR YOU TO STEP DOWN FOR ME.
KHWISH
!!!

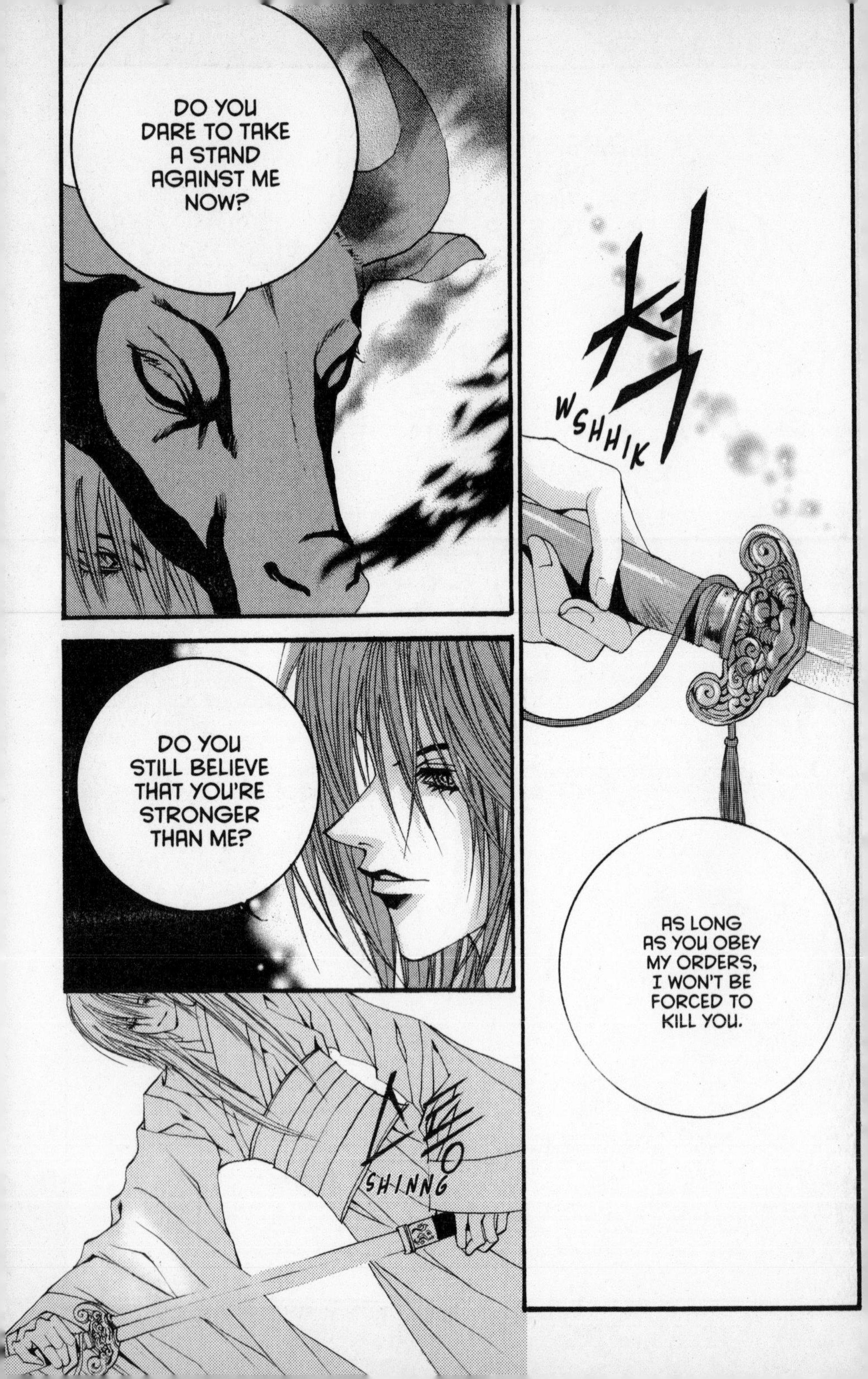
DO YOU DARE TO TAKE A STAND AGAINST ME NOW?
DO YOU STILL BELIEVE THAT YOU'RE STRONGER THAN ME?
SHINNG
WSHHIK
AS LONG AS YOU OBEY MY ORDERS, I WON'T BE FORCED TO KILL YOU.

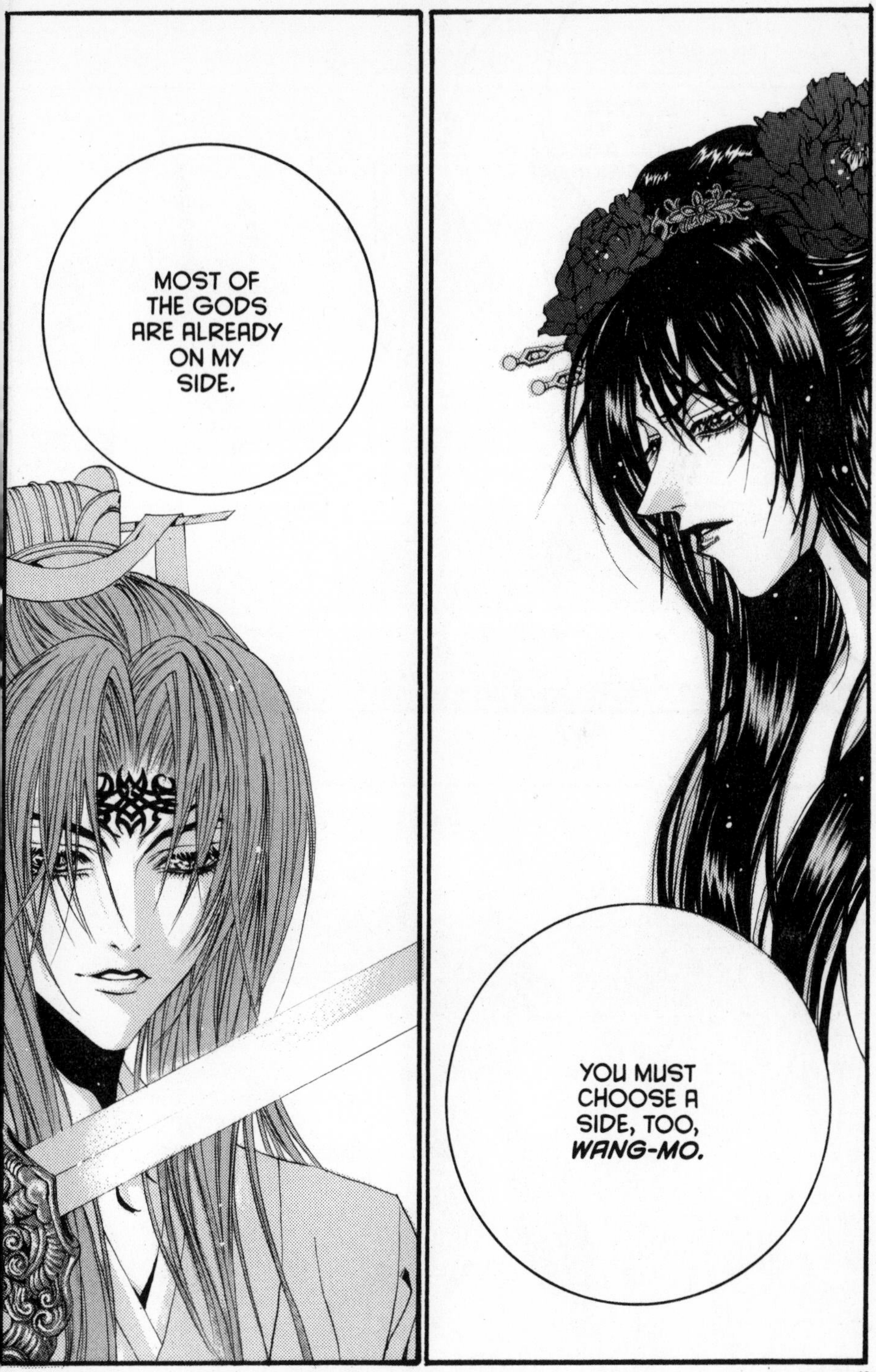
MOST OF THE GODS ARE ALREADY ON MY SIDE.
YOU MUST CHOOSE A SIDE, TOO, *WANG-MO.*

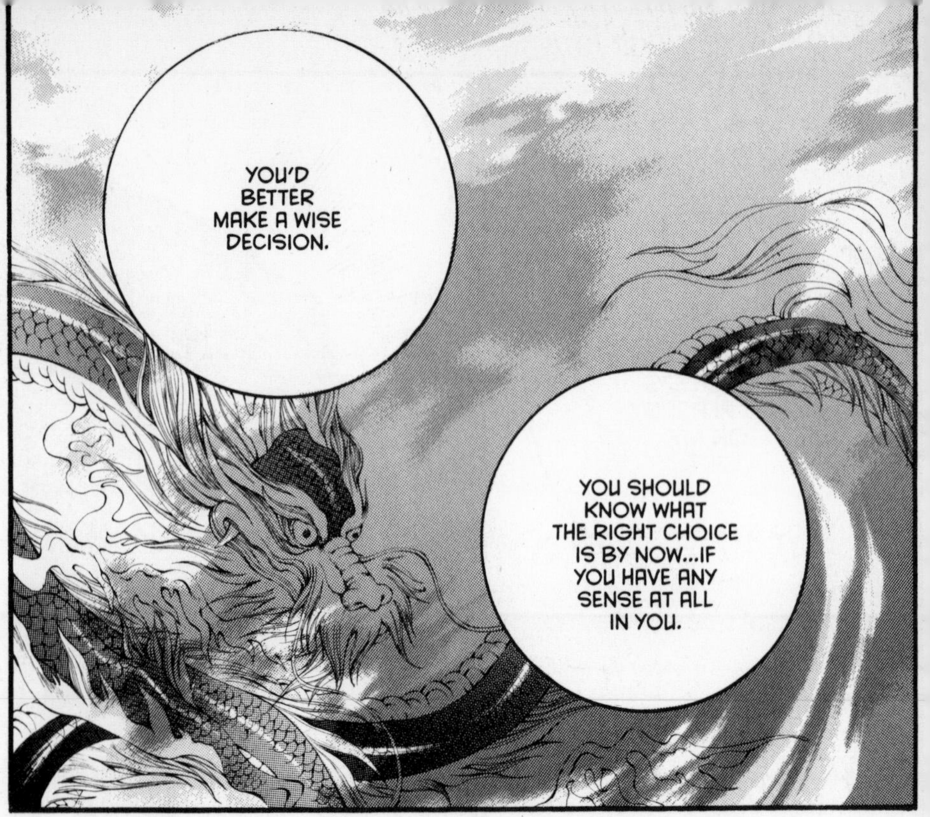
YOU'D BETTER MAKE A WISE DECISION.
YOU SHOULD KNOW WHAT THE RIGHT CHOICE IS BY NOW...IF YOU HAVE ANY SENSE AT ALL IN YOU.

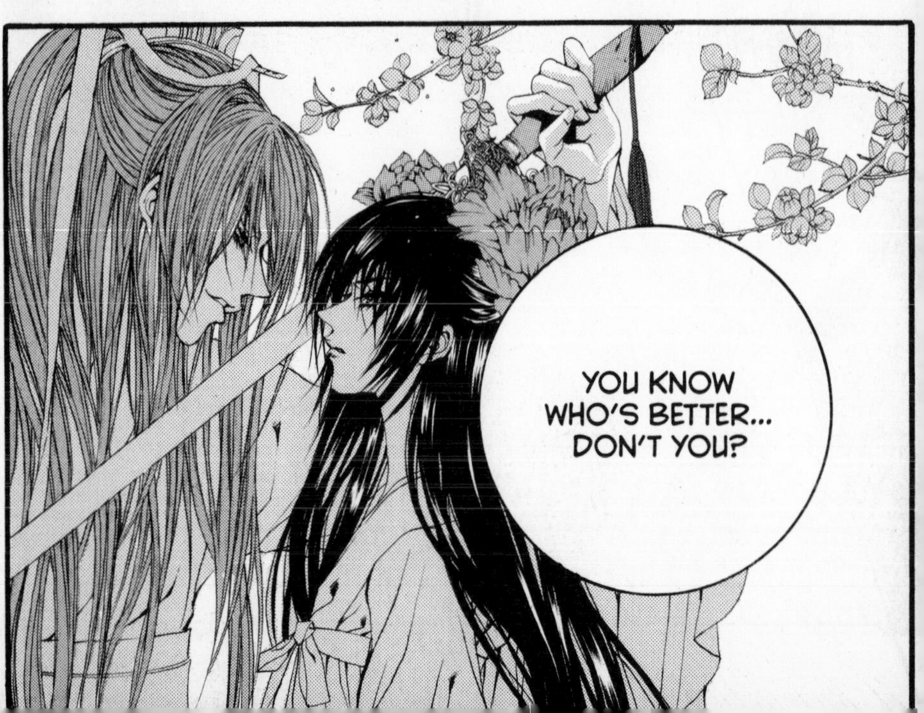
YOU KNOW WHO'S BETTER... DON'T YOU?

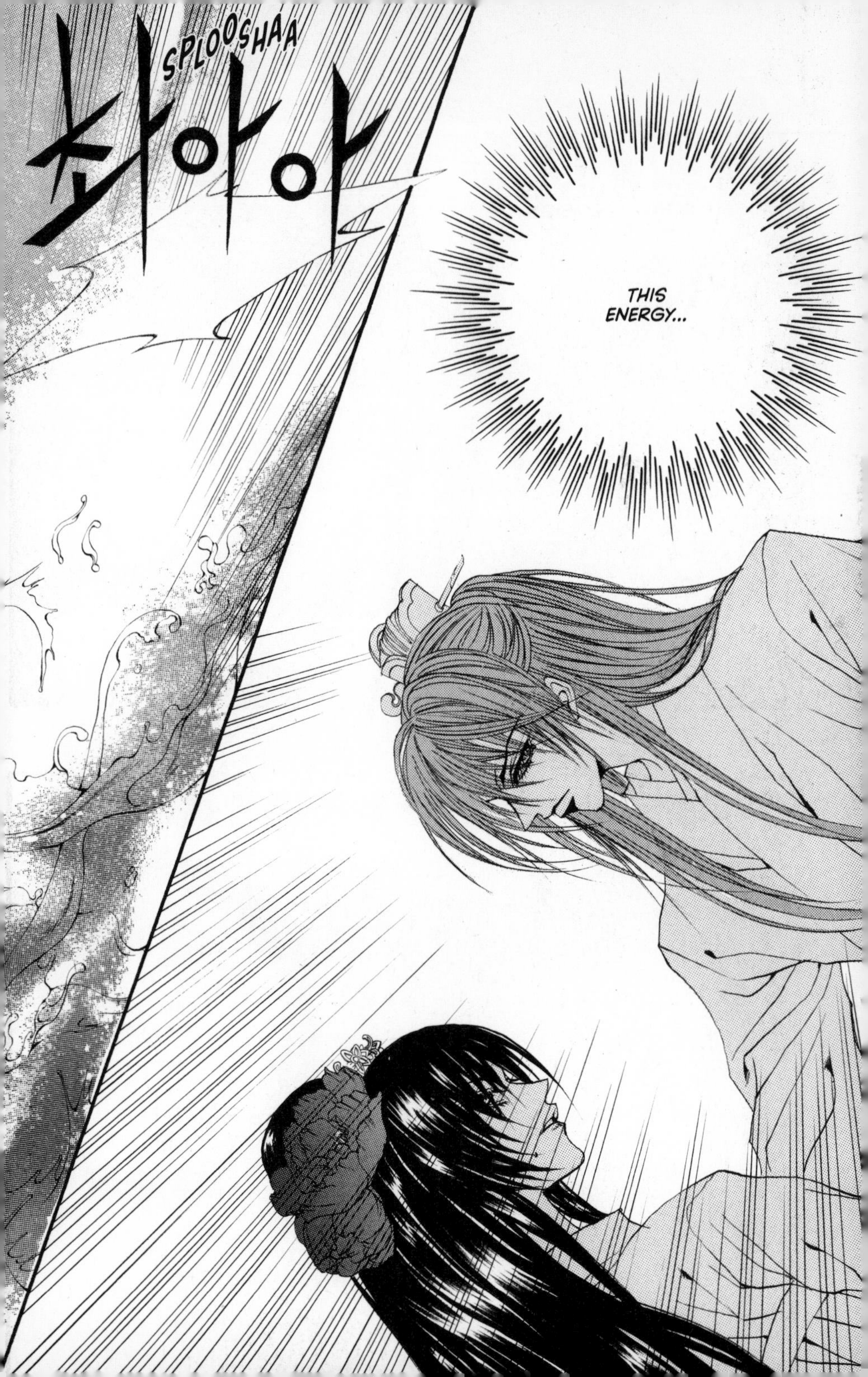

SPLOOSHAA
촤아아
THIS ENERGY...

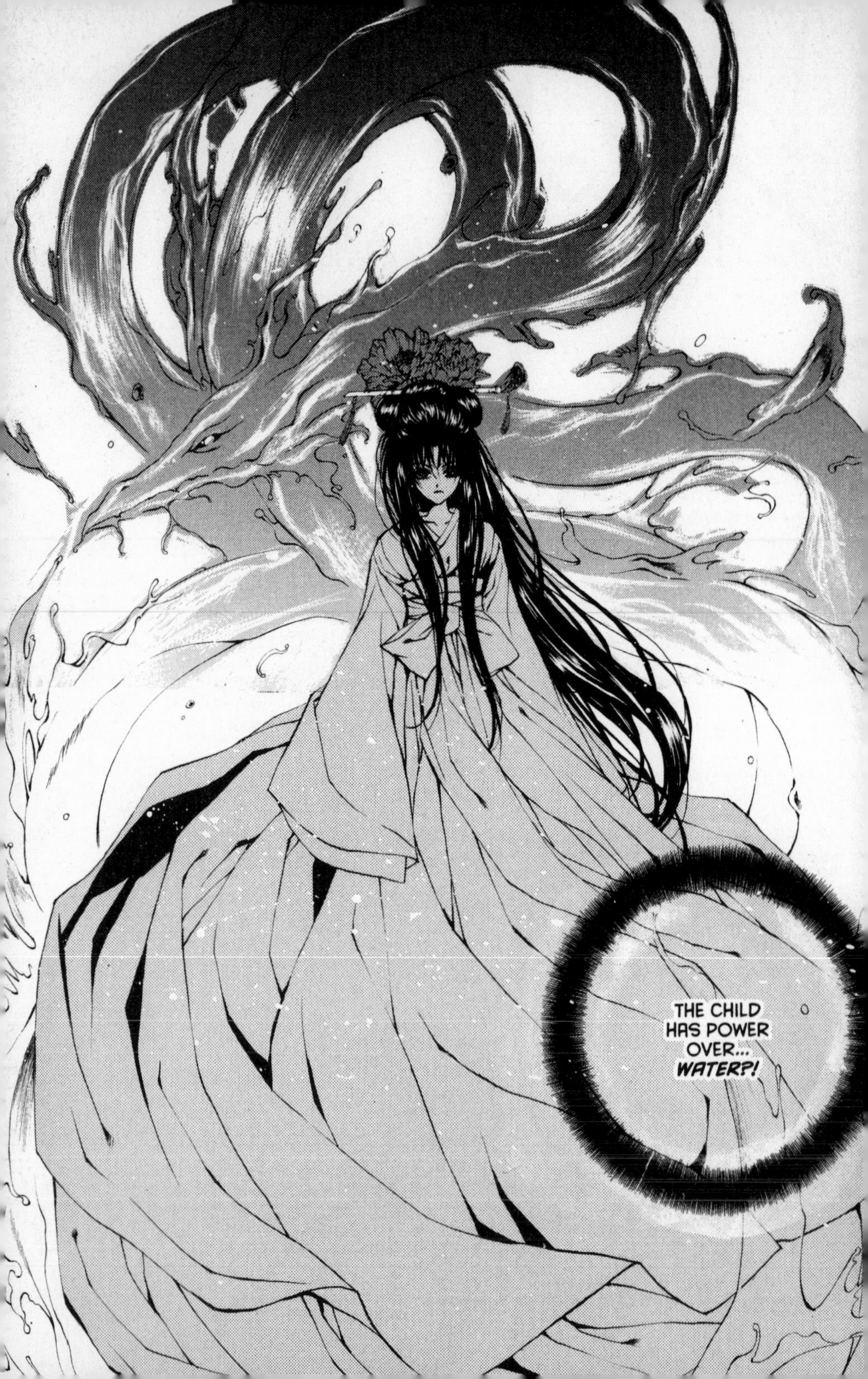
THE CHILD HAS POWER OVER... WATER?!

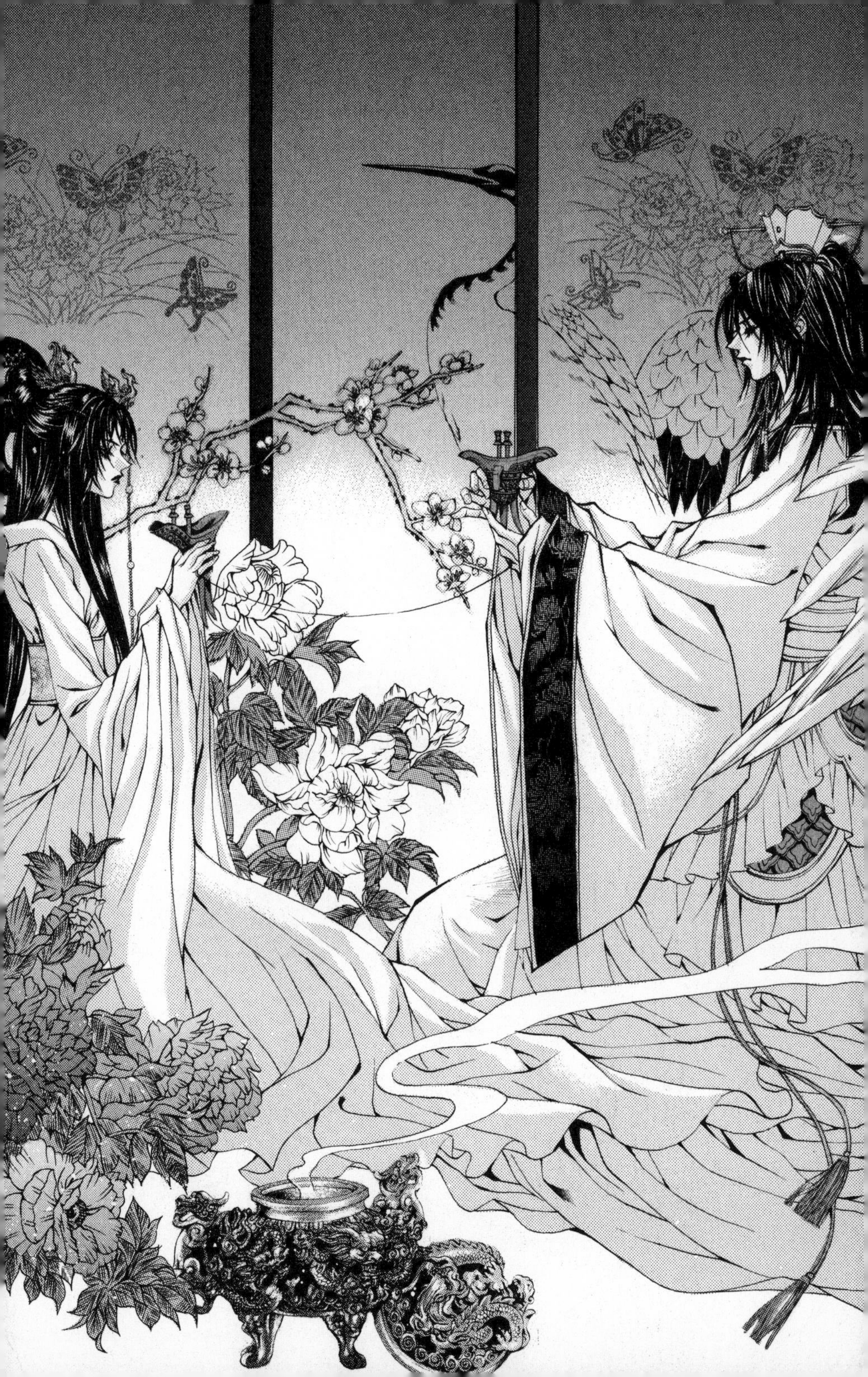

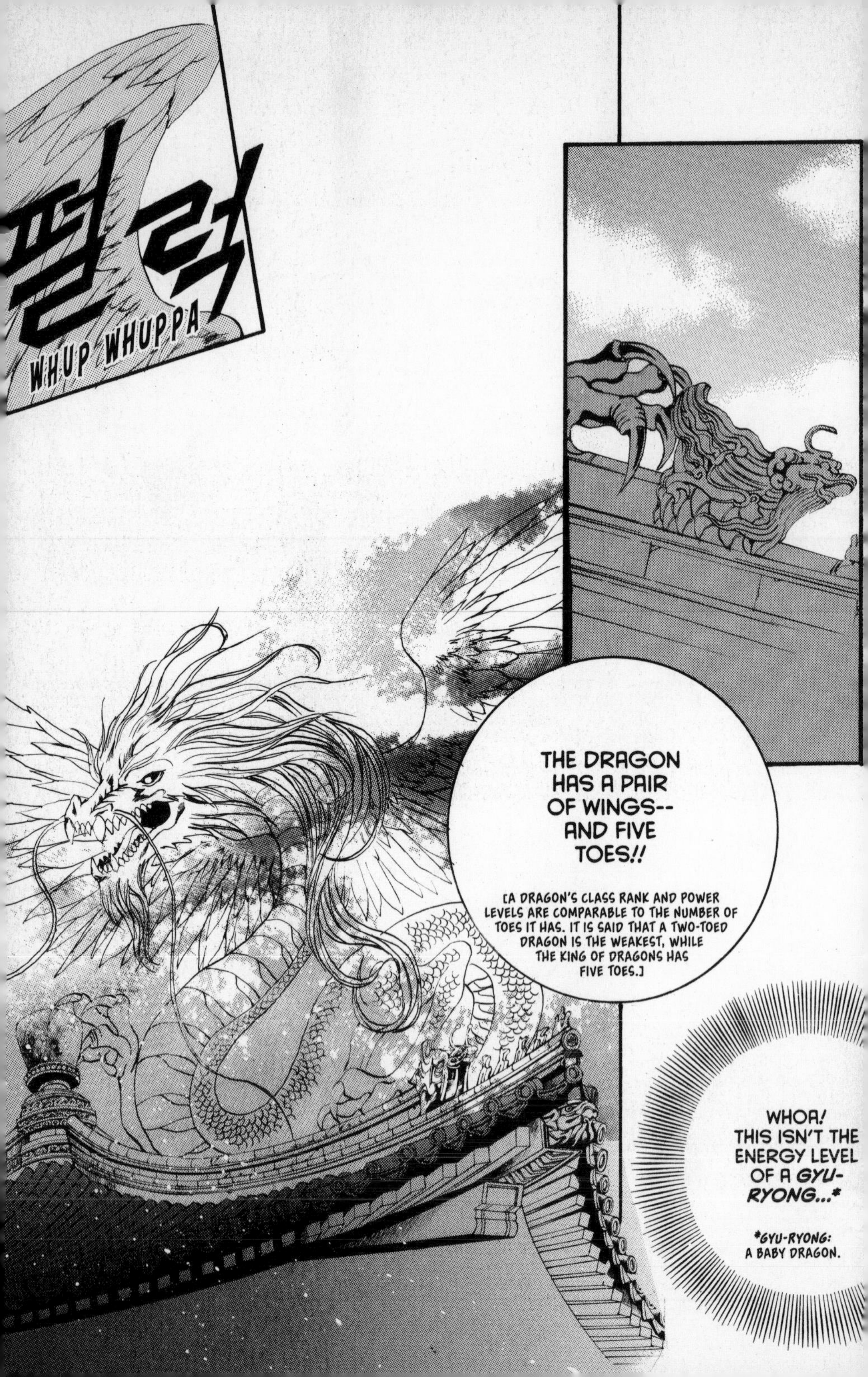
펄럭
WHUP WHUPPA
THE DRAGON HAS A PAIR OF WINGS-- AND FIVE TOES!!
[A DRAGON'S CLASS RANK AND POWER LEVELS ARE COMPARABLE TO THE NUMBER OF TOES IT HAS. IT IS SAID THAT A TWO-TOED DRAGON IS THE WEAKEST, WHILE THE KING OF DRAGONS HAS FIVE TOES.]
WHOA! THIS ISN'T THE ENERGY LEVEL OF A *GYU-RYONG*...*
*GYU-RYONG: A BABY DRAGON.

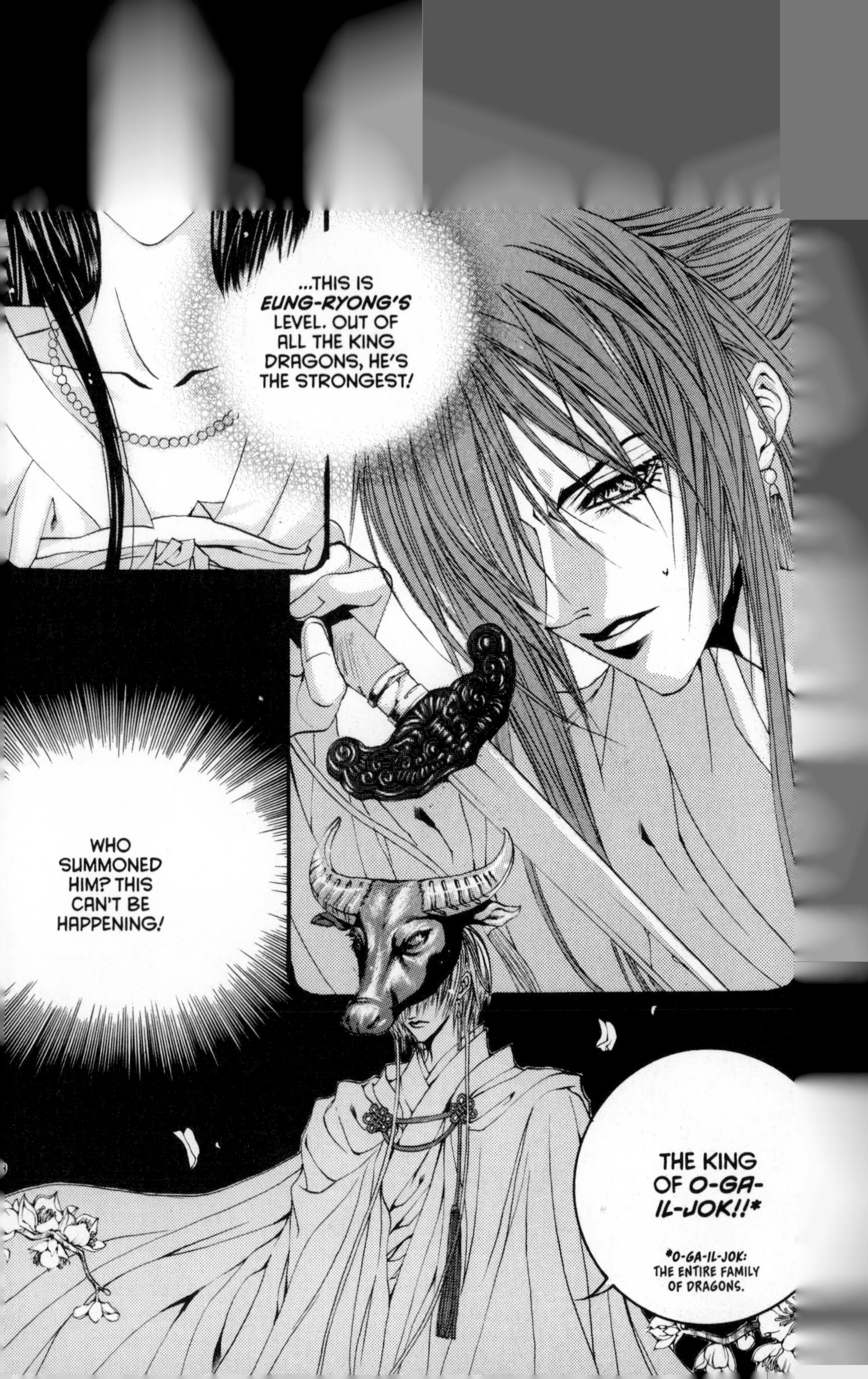
...THIS IS EUNG-RYONG'S LEVEL. OUT OF ALL THE KING DRAGONS, HE'S THE STRONGEST!
WHO SUMMONED HIM? THIS CAN'T BE HAPPENING!
THE KING OF O-GA-IL-JOK!!*
*O-GA-IL-JOK: THE ENTIRE FAMILY OF DRAGONS.

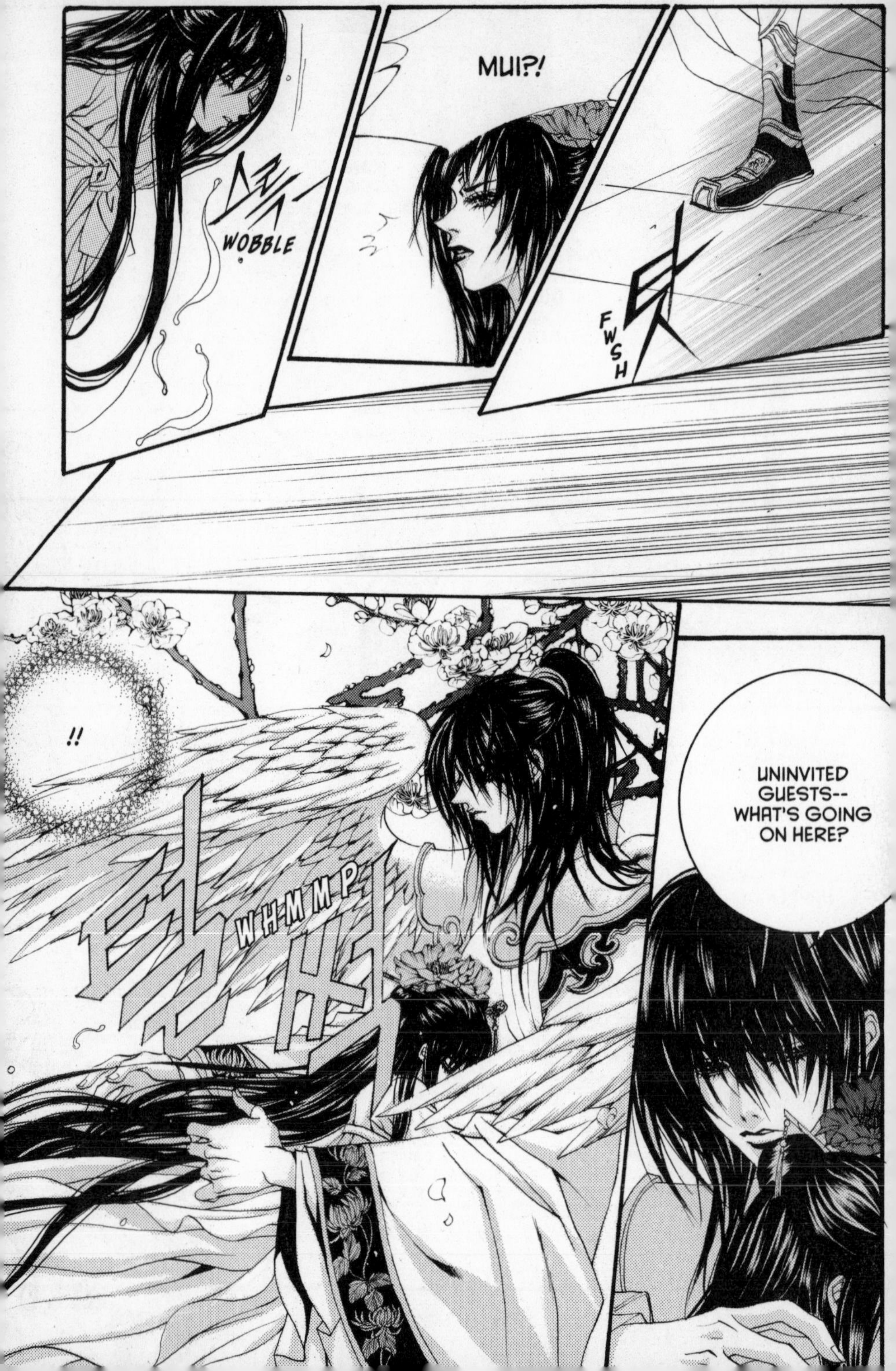
WOBBLE
MUI?!
FWSH
UNINVITED GUESTS-- WHAT'S GOING ON HERE?
!!
WHMMP

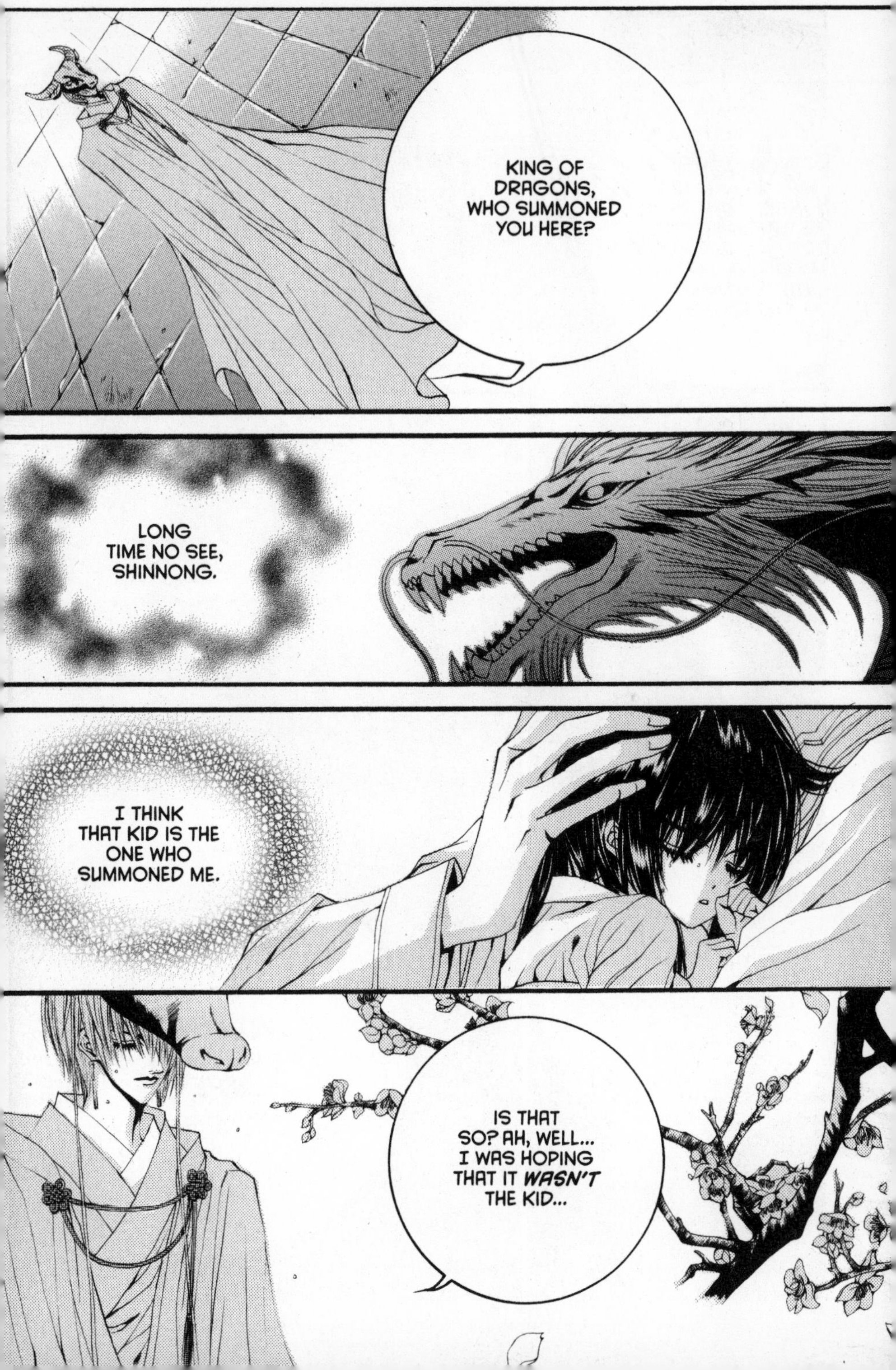
KING OF DRAGONS, WHO SUMMONED YOU HERE?
LONG TIME NO SEE, SHINNONG.
I THINK THAT KID IS THE ONE WHO SUMMONED ME.
IS THAT SO? AH, WELL... I WAS HOPING THAT IT *WASN'T* THE KID...

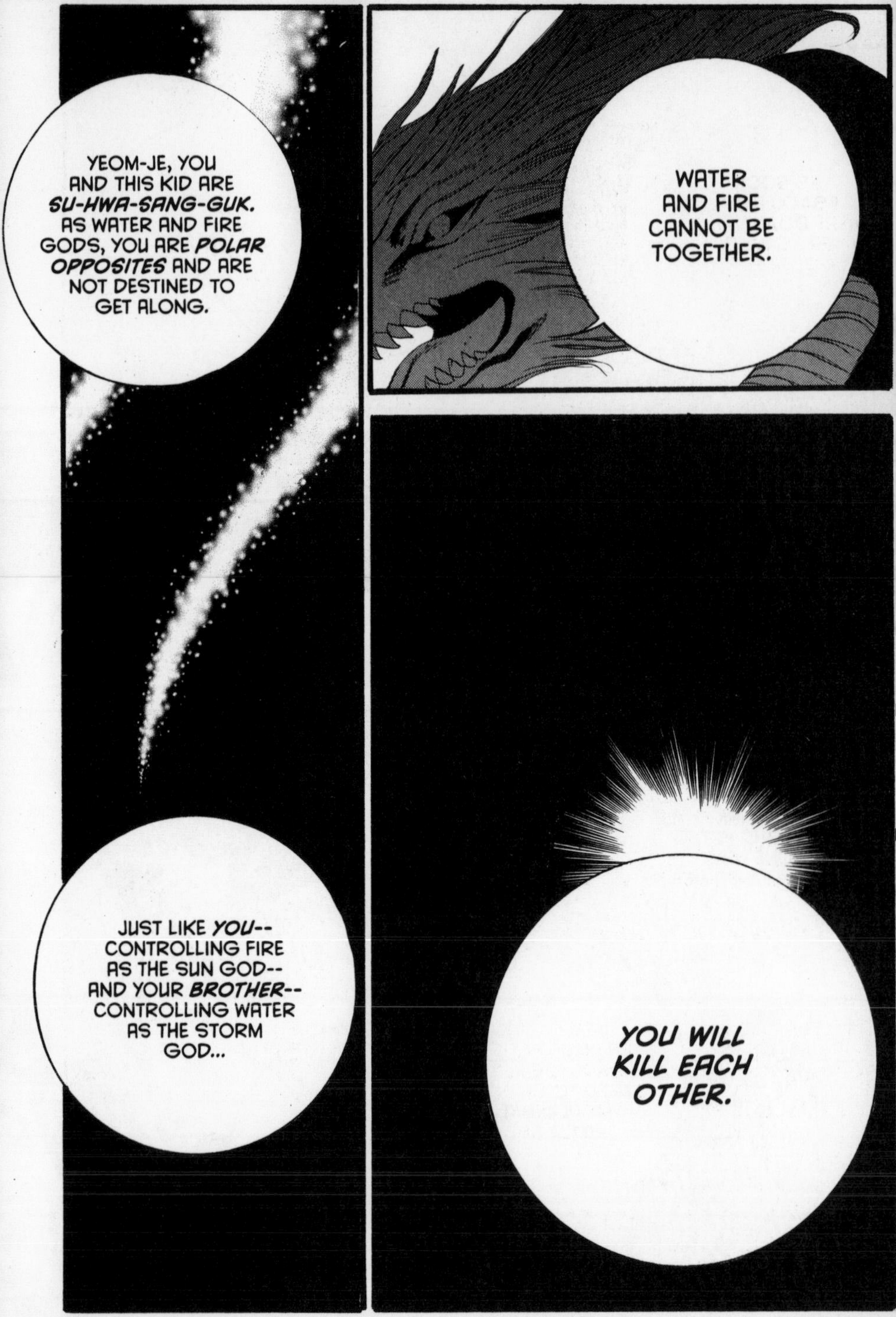
YEOM-JE, YOU AND THIS KID ARE *SU-HWA-SANG-GUK.* AS WATER AND FIRE GODS, YOU ARE *POLAR OPPOSITES* AND ARE NOT DESTINED TO GET ALONG.
WATER AND FIRE CANNOT BE TOGETHER.
JUST LIKE *YOU*--CONTROLLING FIRE AS THE SUN GOD--AND YOUR *BROTHER*--CONTROLLING WATER AS THE STORM GOD...
YOU WILL KILL EACH OTHER.

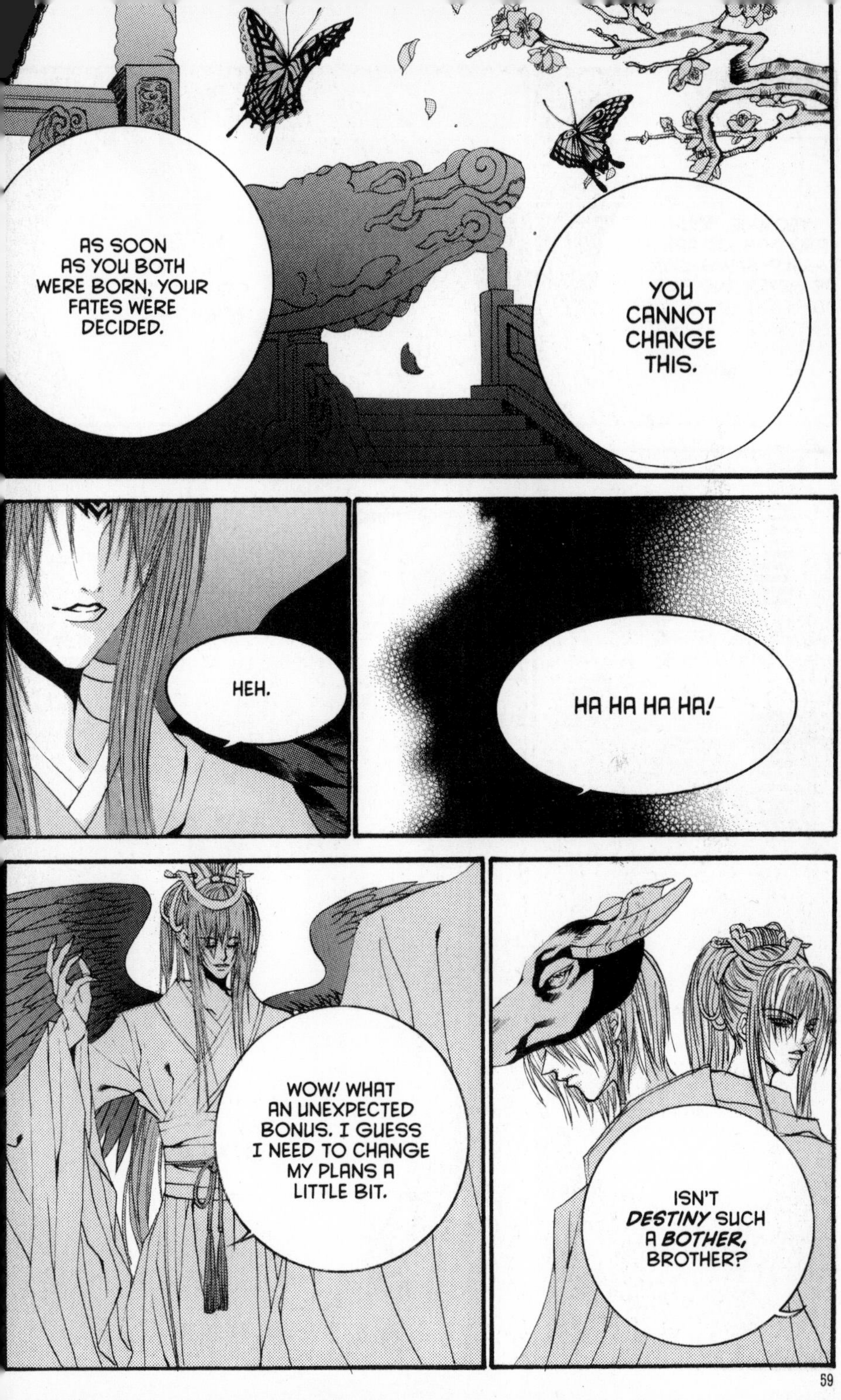
AS SOON AS YOU BOTH WERE BORN, YOUR FATES WERE DECIDED.
YOU CANNOT CHANGE THIS.
HEH.
HA HA HA HA!
WOW! WHAT AN UNEXPECTED BONUS. I GUESS I NEED TO CHANGE MY PLANS A LITTLE BIT.
ISN'T *DESTINY* SUCH A *BOTHER*, BROTHER?

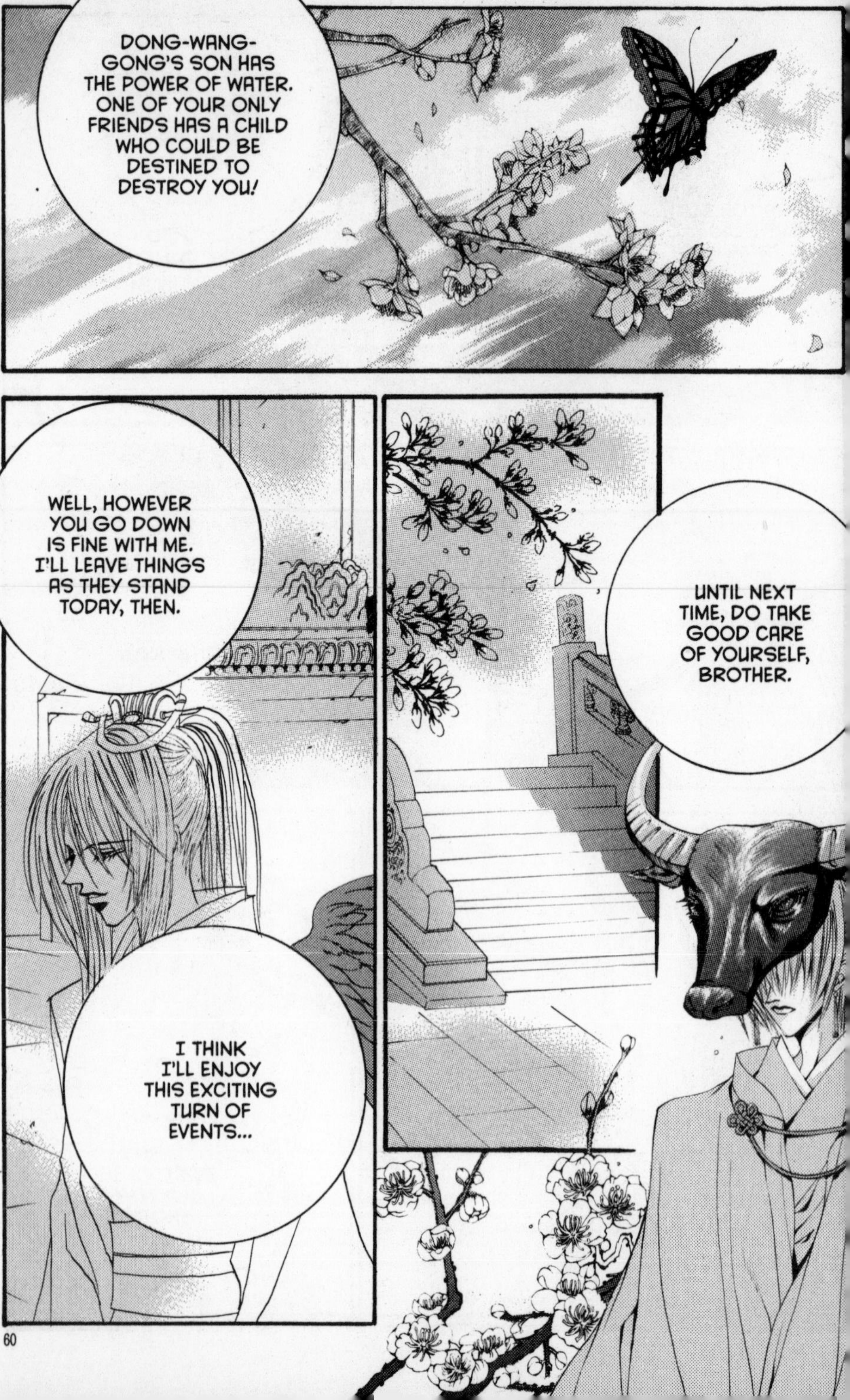
DONG-WANG-GONG'S SON HAS THE POWER OF WATER. ONE OF YOUR ONLY FRIENDS HAS A CHILD WHO COULD BE DESTINED TO DESTROY YOU!
UNTIL NEXT TIME, DO TAKE GOOD CARE OF YOURSELF, BROTHER.
WELL, HOWEVER YOU GO DOWN IS FINE WITH ME. I'LL LEAVE THINGS AS THEY STAND TODAY, THEN.
I THINK I'LL ENJOY THIS EXCITING TURN OF EVENTS...

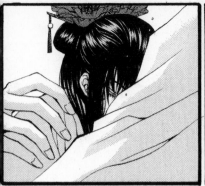

MUI! MUI! WAKE UP!

UH... MOTHER?

MUI!

TOK TOK

SHIN-NONG.

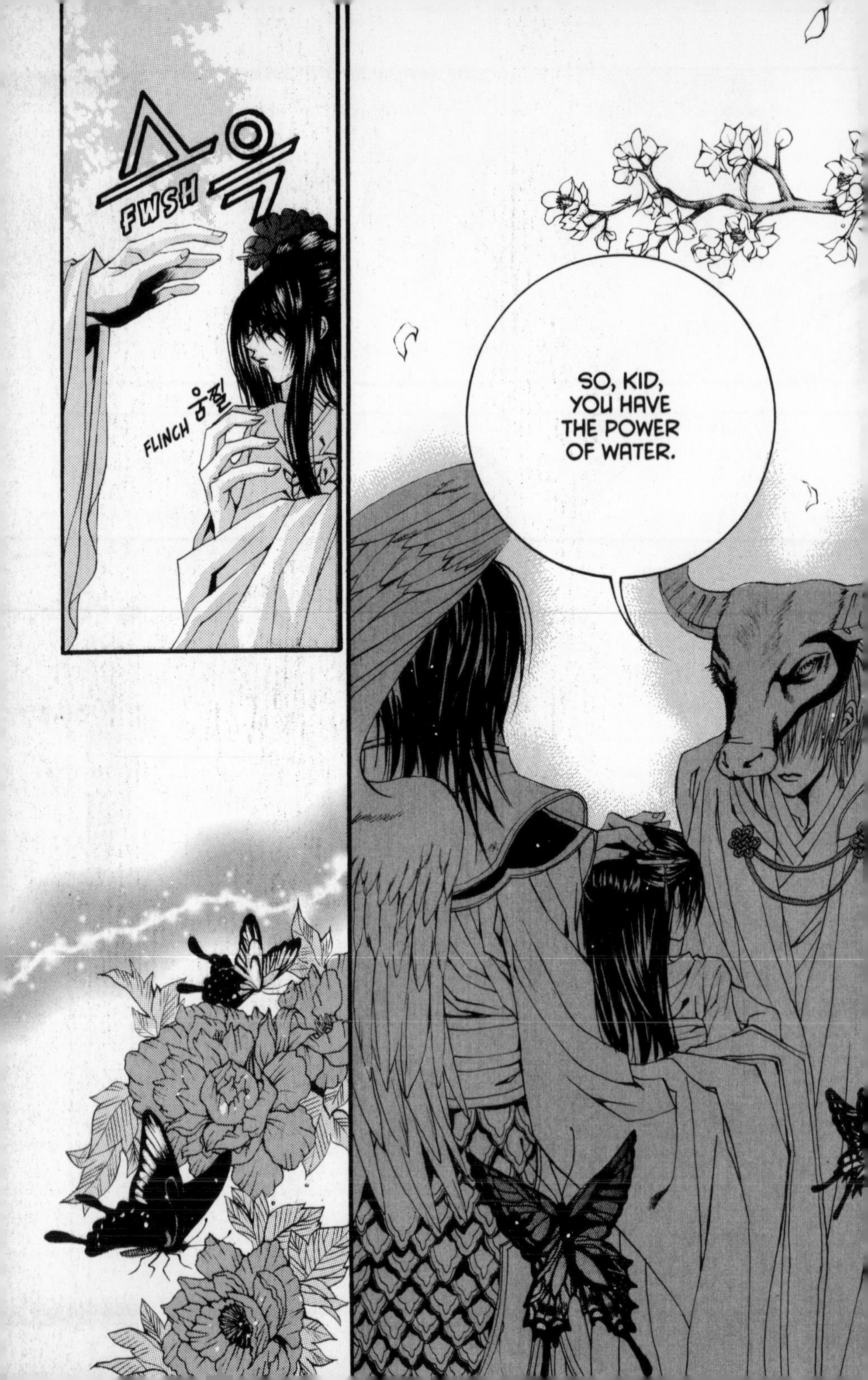
스응
FWSH
움찔
FLINCH
SO, KID, YOU HAVE THE POWER OF WATER.

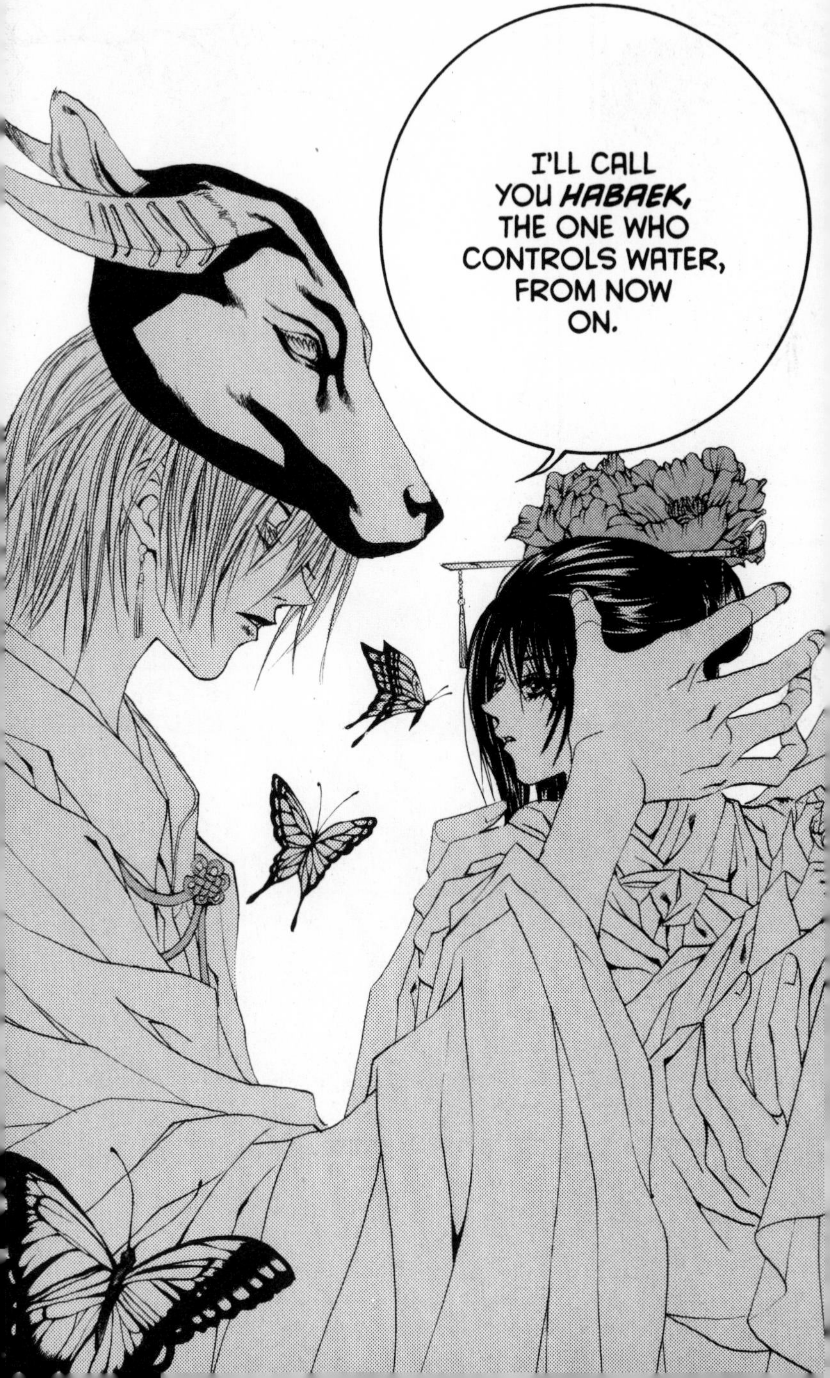
I'LL CALL YOU *HABAEK,* THE ONE WHO CONTROLS WATER, FROM NOW ON.

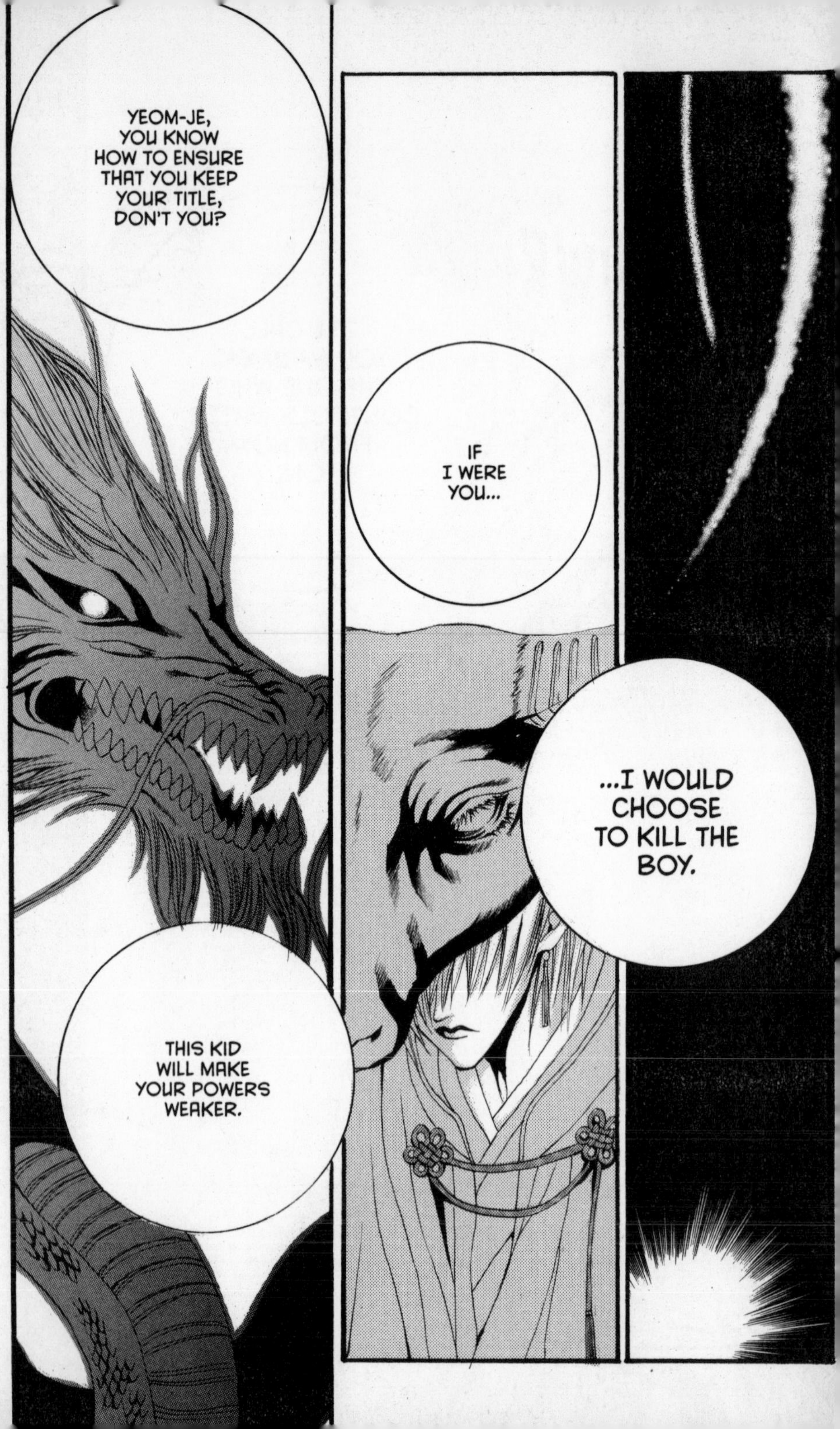
YEOM-JE, YOU KNOW HOW TO ENSURE THAT YOU KEEP YOUR TITLE, DON'T YOU?
THIS KID WILL MAKE YOUR POWERS WEAKER.
IF I WERE YOU...
...I WOULD CHOOSE TO KILL THE BOY.

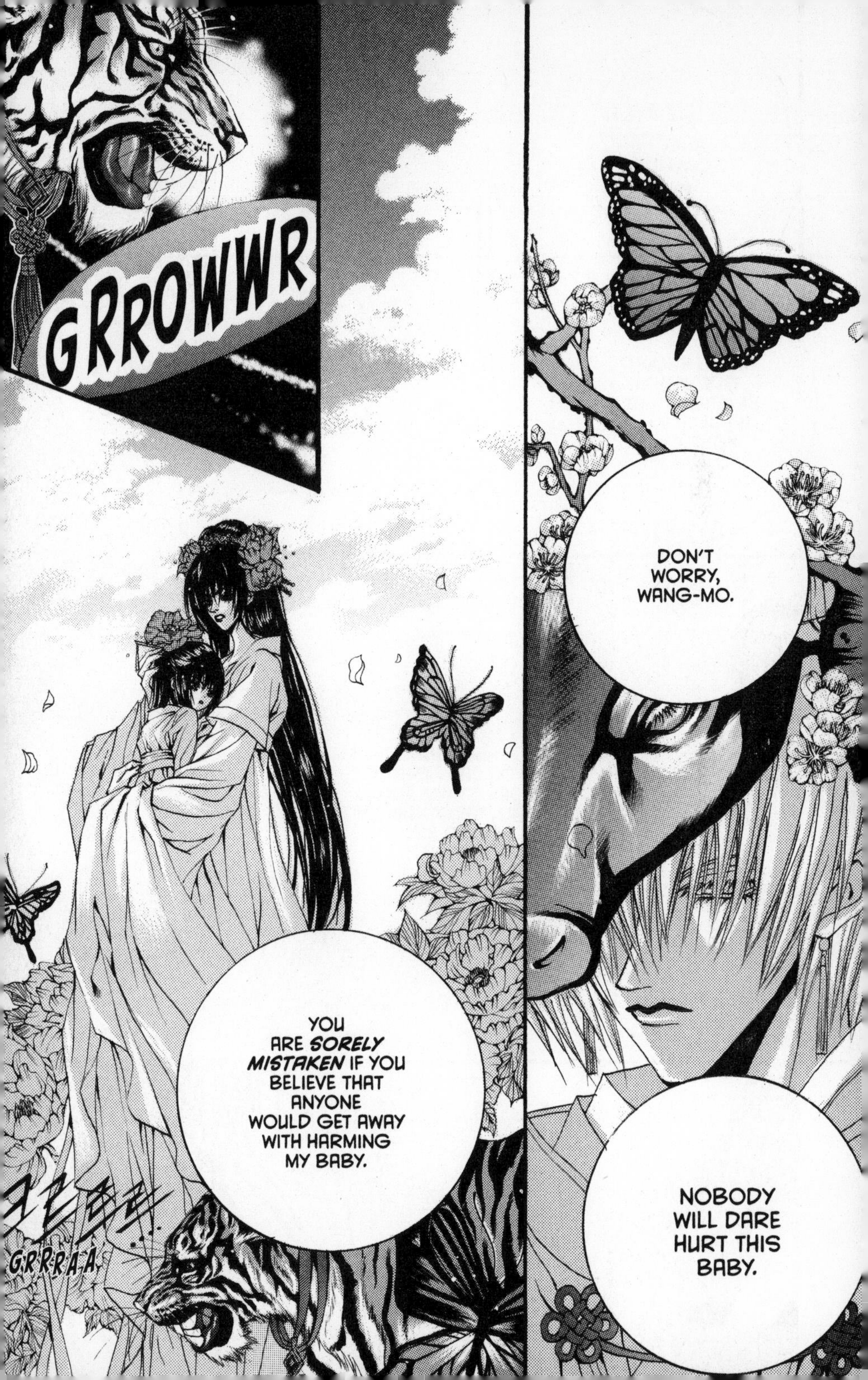

GRROWWR
YOU ARE ***SORELY MISTAKEN*** IF YOU BELIEVE THAT ANYONE WOULD GET AWAY WITH HARMING MY BABY.
GRRRAA
DON'T WORRY, WANG-MO.
NOBODY WILL DARE HURT THIS BABY.

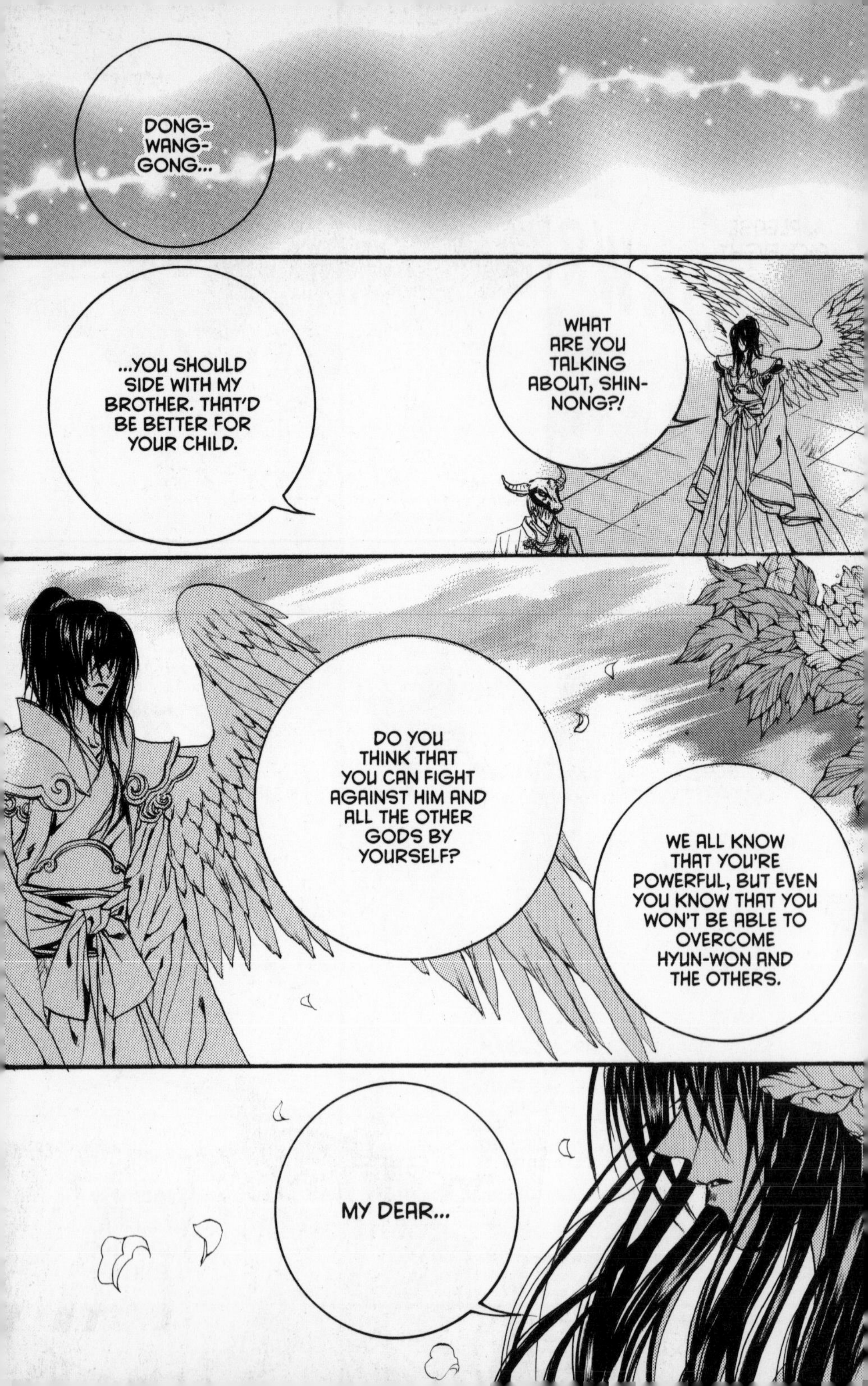
DONG-WANG-GONG...
WHAT ARE YOU TALKING ABOUT, SHIN-NONG?!
...YOU SHOULD SIDE WITH MY BROTHER. THAT'D BE BETTER FOR YOUR CHILD.
WE ALL KNOW THAT YOU'RE POWERFUL, BUT EVEN YOU KNOW THAT YOU WON'T BE ABLE TO OVERCOME HYUN-WON AND THE OTHERS.
DO YOU THINK THAT YOU CAN FIGHT AGAINST HIM AND ALL THE OTHER GODS BY YOURSELF?
MY DEAR...

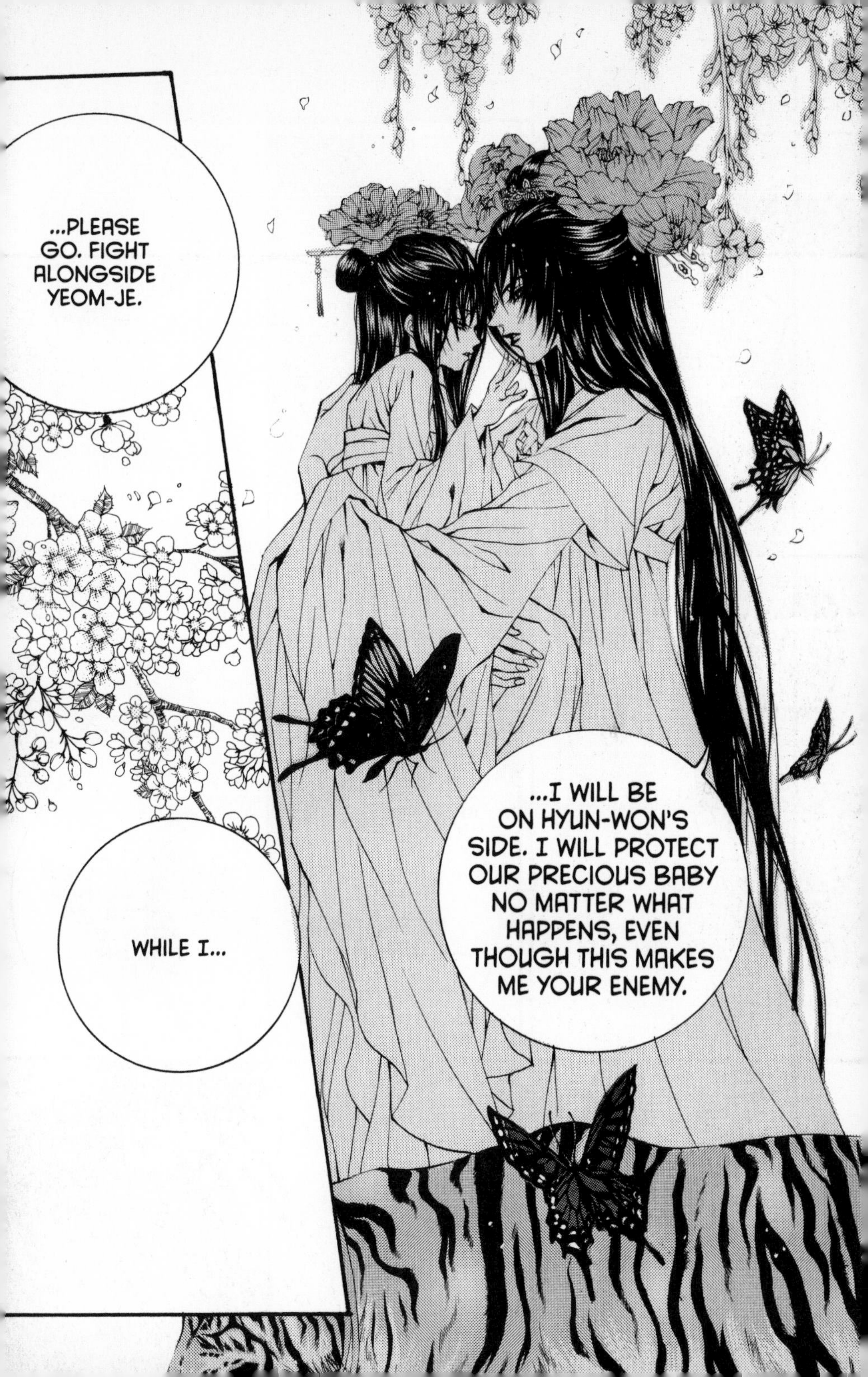
...PLEASE GO. FIGHT ALONGSIDE YEOM-JE.
WHILE I...
...I WILL BE ON HYUN-WON'S SIDE. I WILL PROTECT OUR PRECIOUS BABY NO MATTER WHAT HAPPENS, EVEN THOUGH THIS MAKES ME YOUR ENEMY.

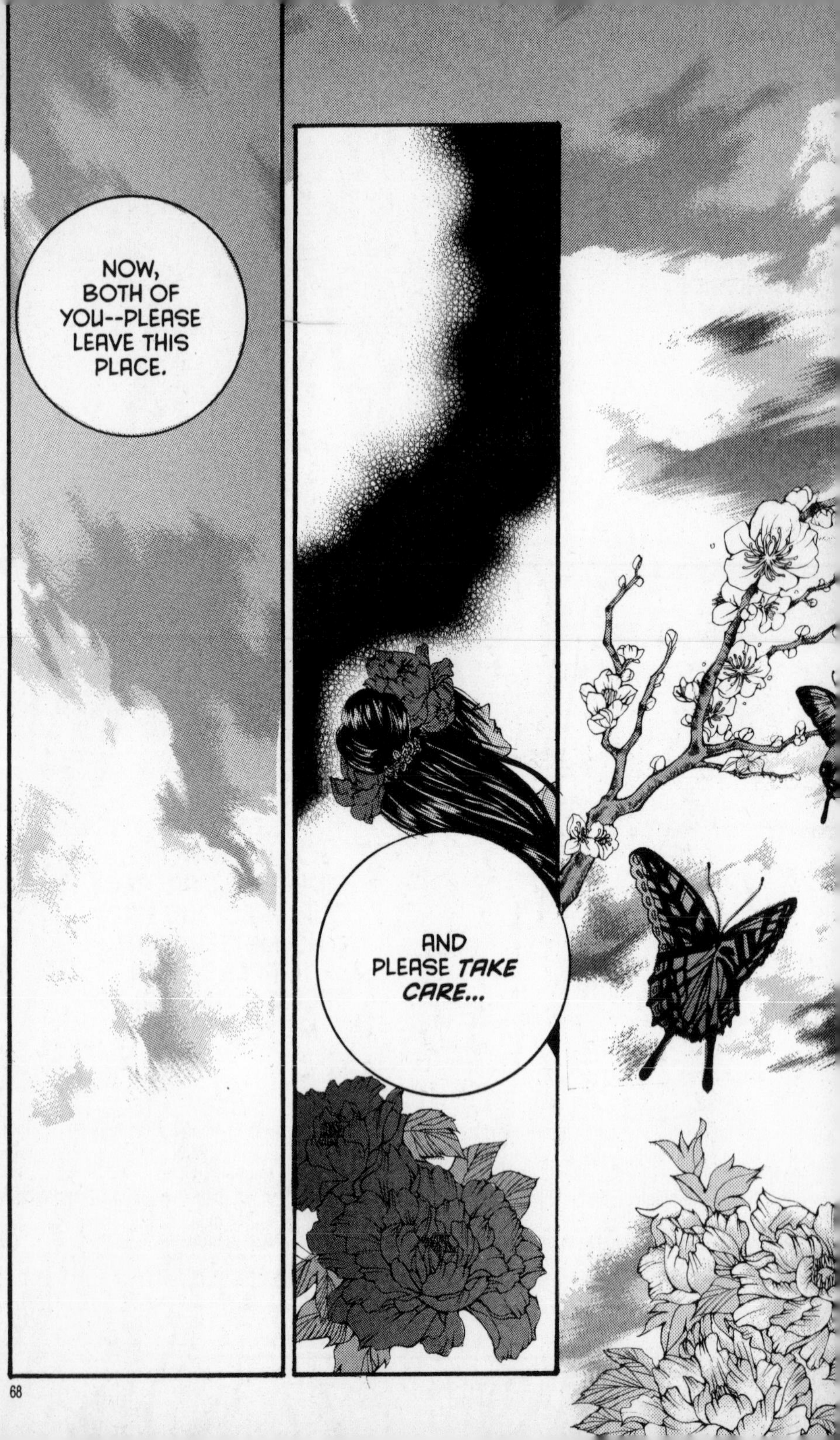
NOW, BOTH OF YOU--PLEASE LEAVE THIS PLACE.
AND PLEASE *TAKE CARE...*

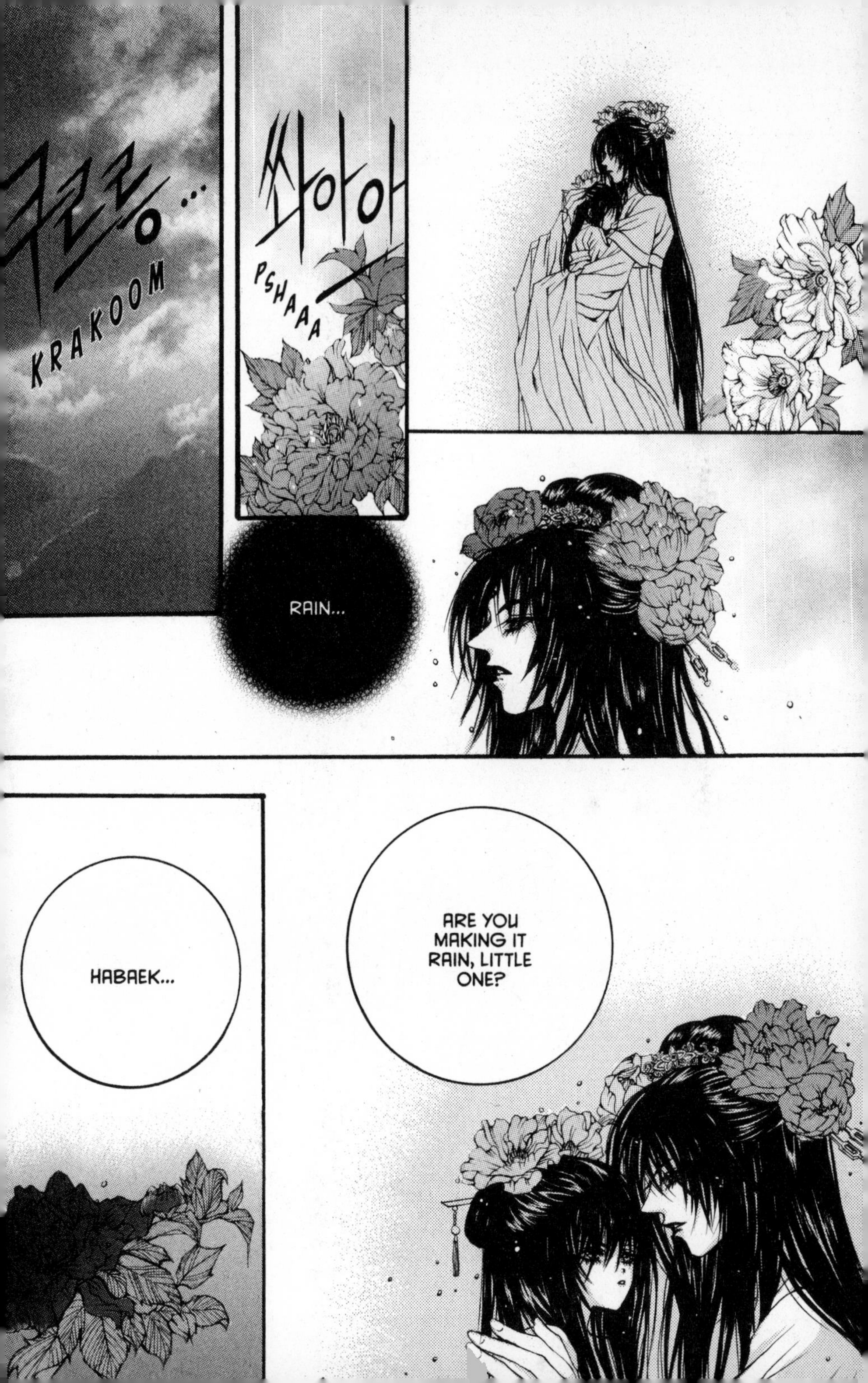

쏴아아
PSHAAA
쿠르릉 …
KRAKOOM
RAIN...
ARE YOU MAKING IT RAIN, LITTLE ONE?
HABAEK...

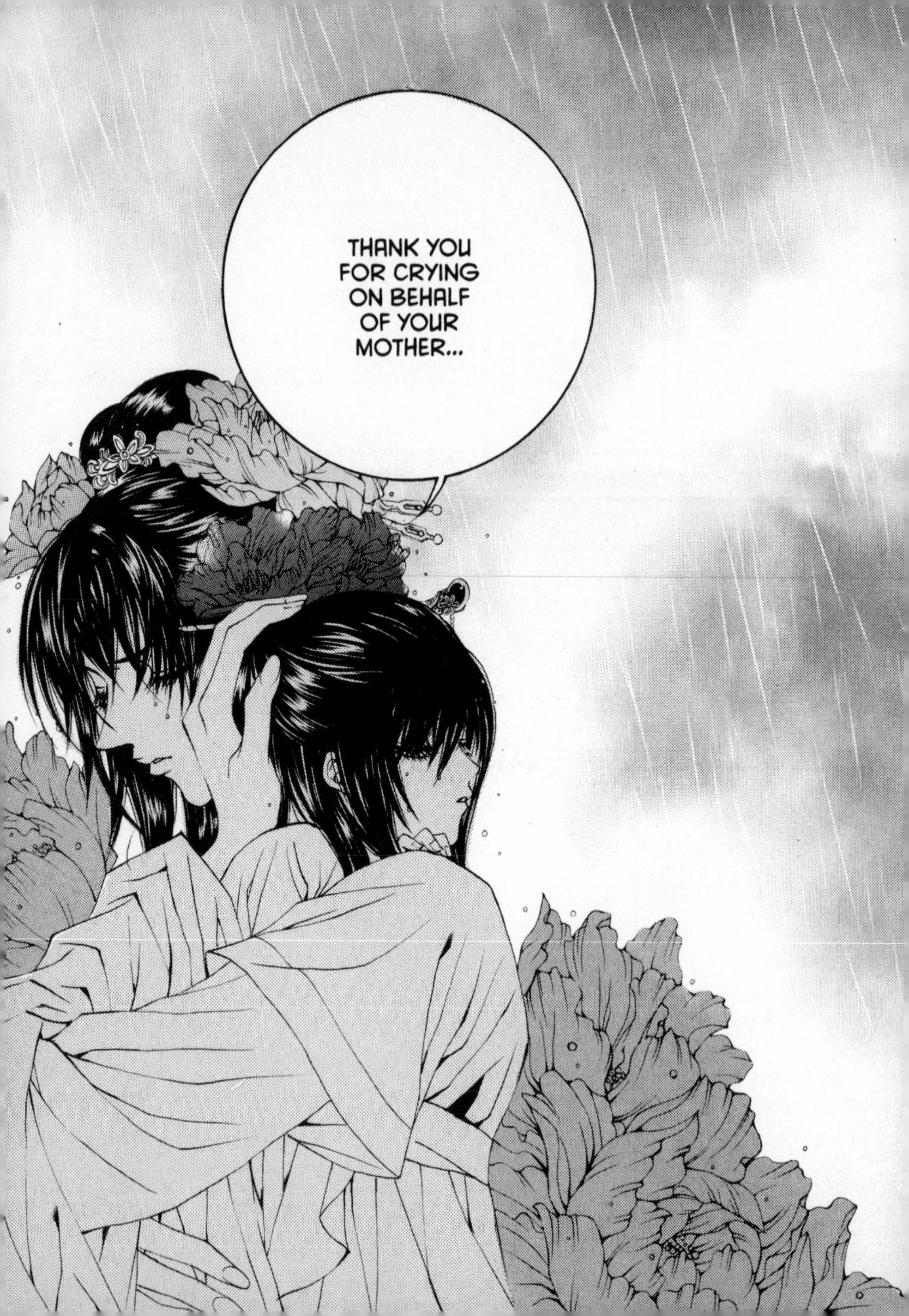
THANK YOU FOR CRYING ON BEHALF OF YOUR MOTHER...

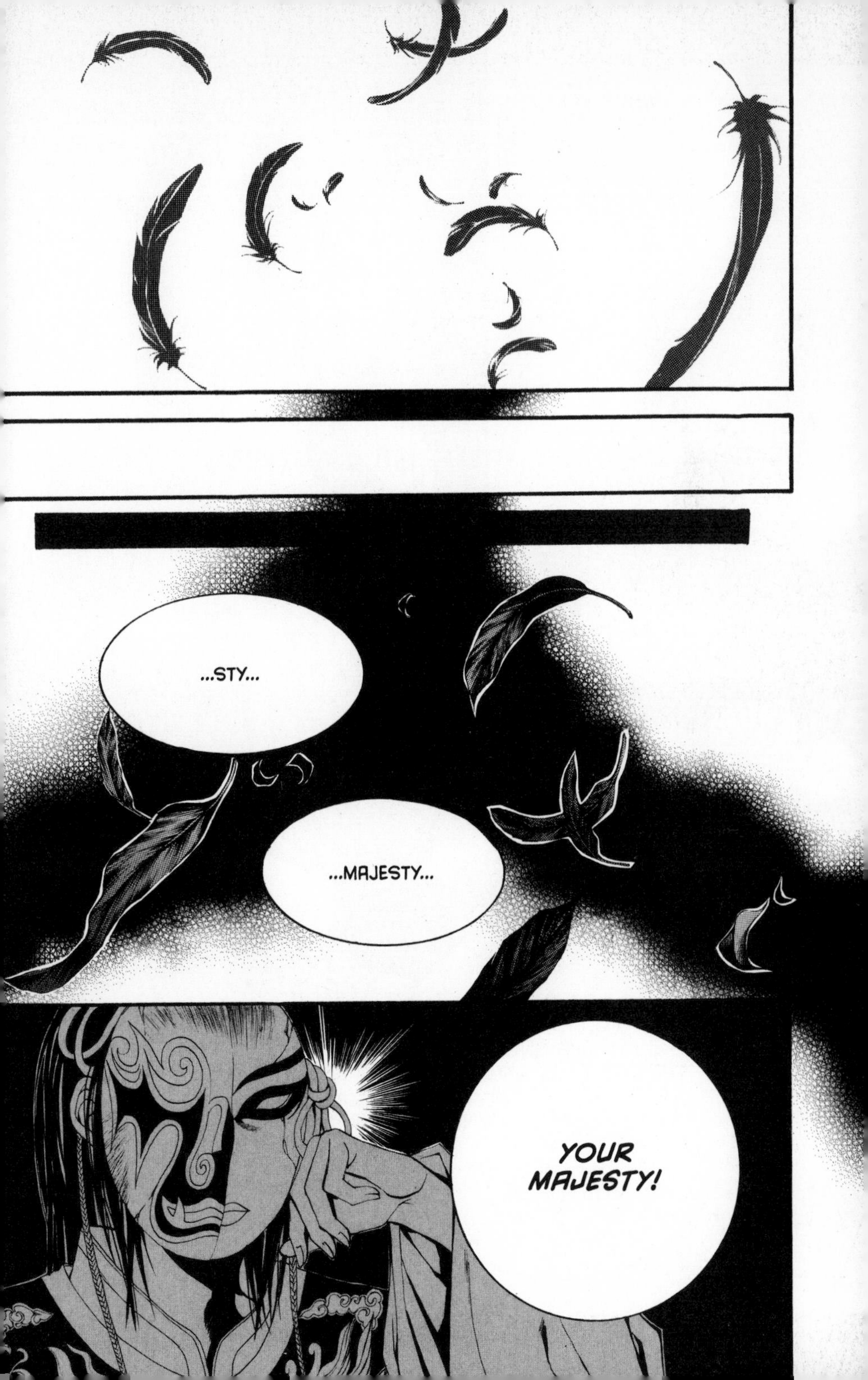
...STY...
...MAJESTY...
YOUR MAJESTY!

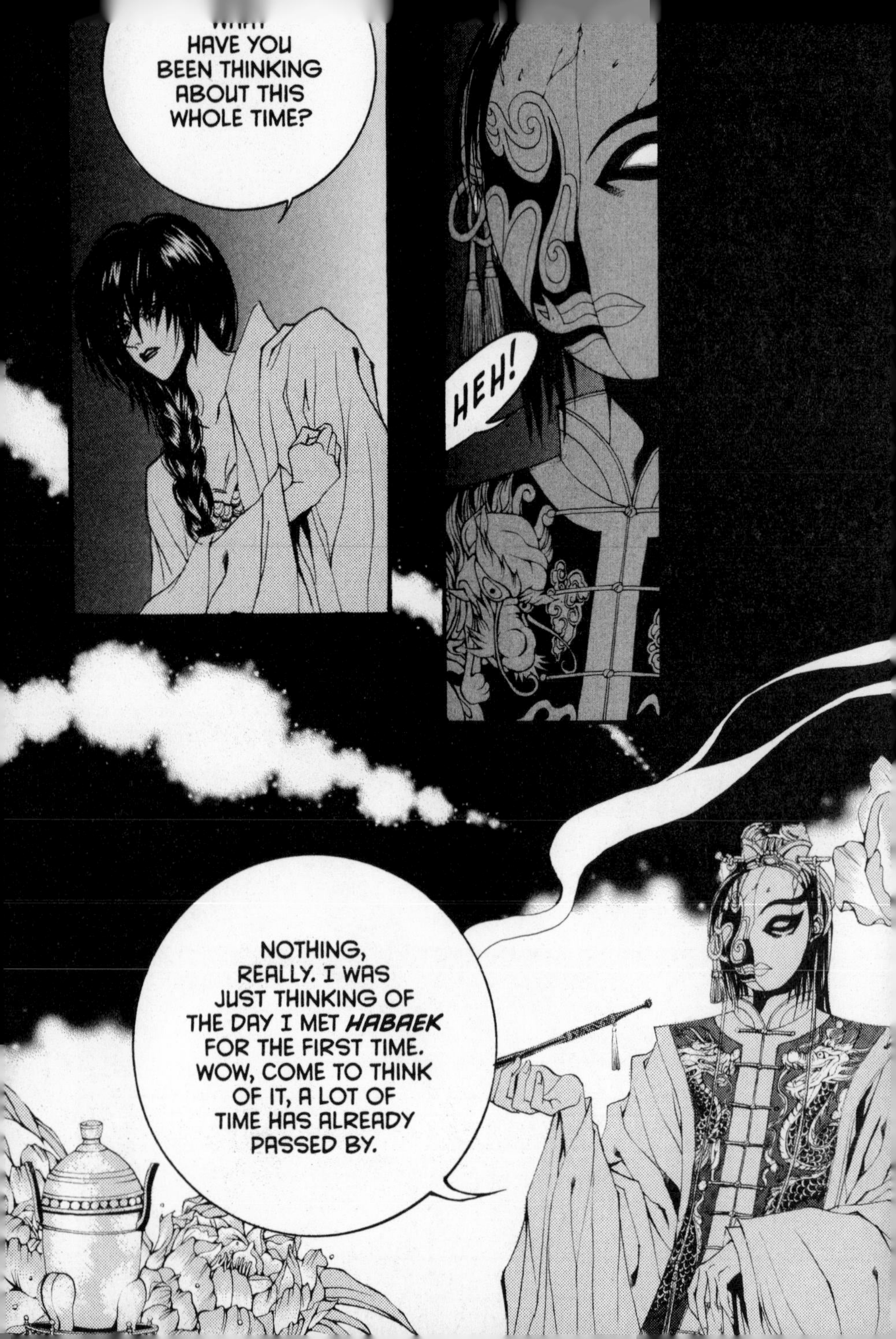
HAVE YOU BEEN THINKING ABOUT THIS WHOLE TIME?
HEH!
NOTHING, REALLY. I WAS JUST THINKING OF THE DAY I MET *HABAEK* FOR THE FIRST TIME. WOW, COME TO THINK OF IT, A LOT OF TIME HAS ALREADY PASSED BY.

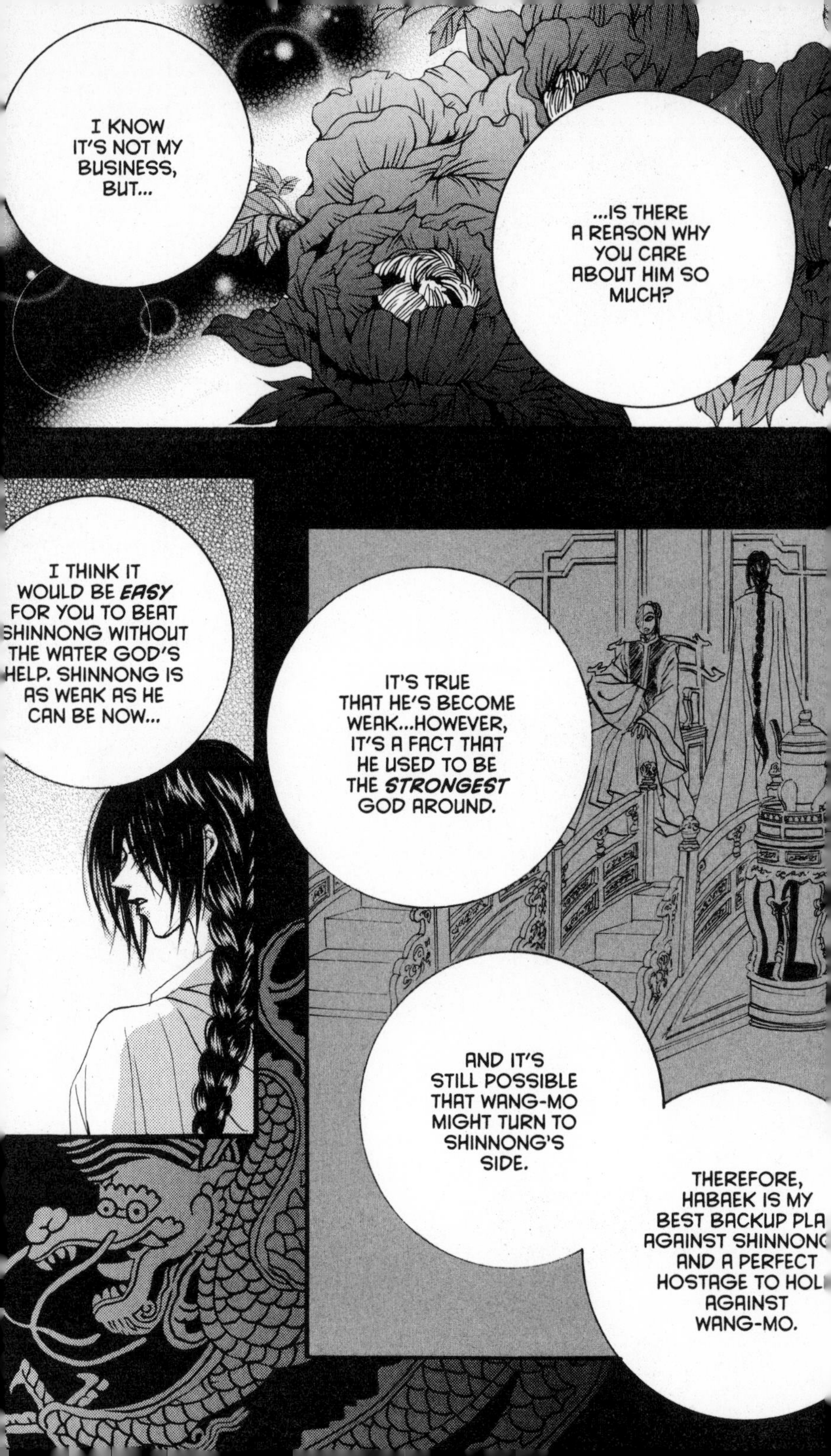
I KNOW IT'S NOT MY BUSINESS, BUT...
...IS THERE A REASON WHY YOU CARE ABOUT HIM SO MUCH?
I THINK IT WOULD BE *EASY* FOR YOU TO BEAT SHINNONG WITHOUT THE WATER GOD'S HELP. SHINNONG IS AS WEAK AS HE CAN BE NOW...
IT'S TRUE THAT HE'S BECOME WEAK...HOWEVER, IT'S A FACT THAT HE USED TO BE THE *STRONGEST* GOD AROUND.
AND IT'S STILL POSSIBLE THAT WANG-MO MIGHT TURN TO SHINNONG'S SIDE.
THEREFORE, HABAEK IS MY BEST BACKUP PLA AGAINST SHINNONG AND A PERFECT HOSTAGE TO HOL AGAINST WANG-MO.

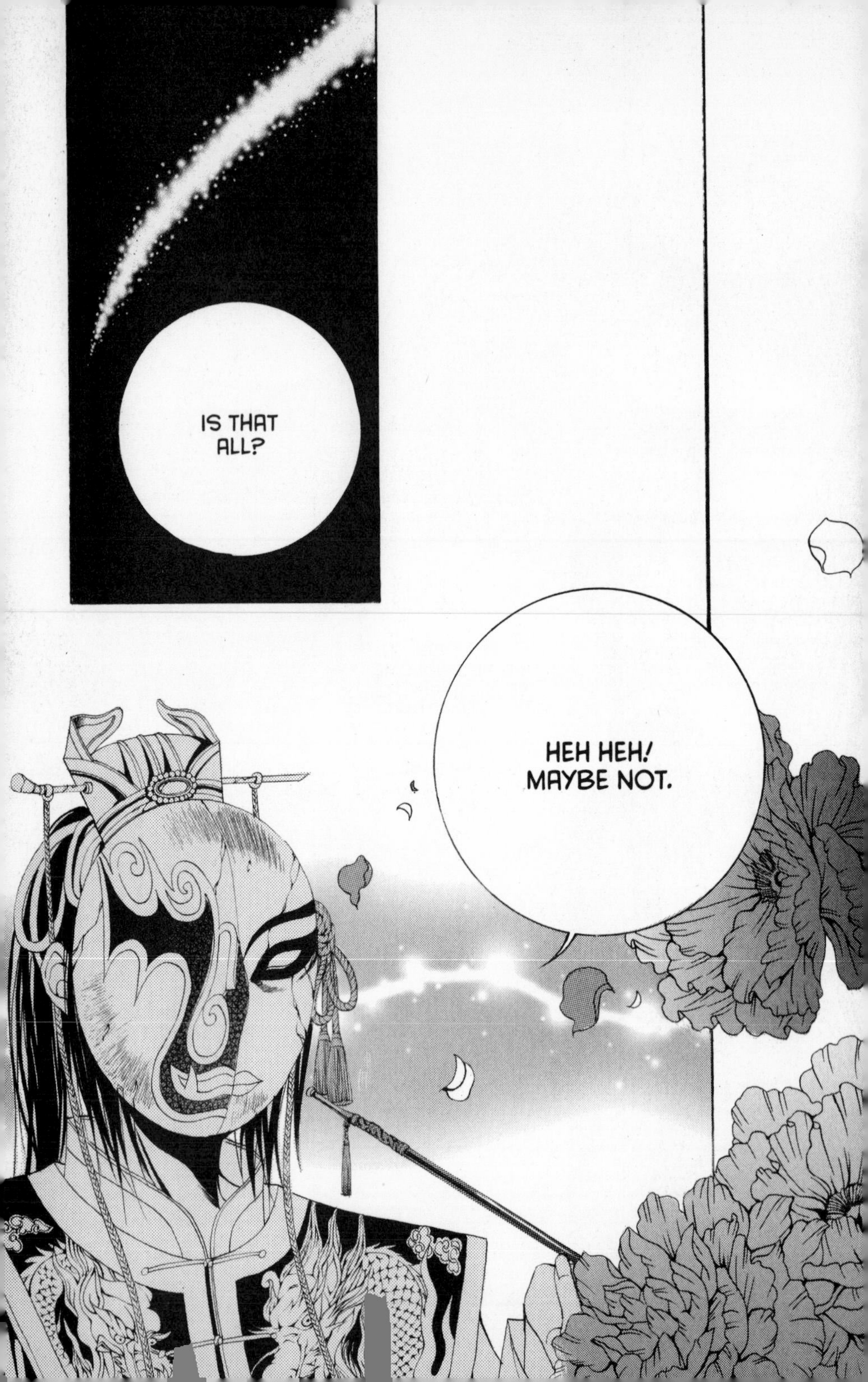
IS THAT ALL?
HEH HEH! MAYBE NOT.

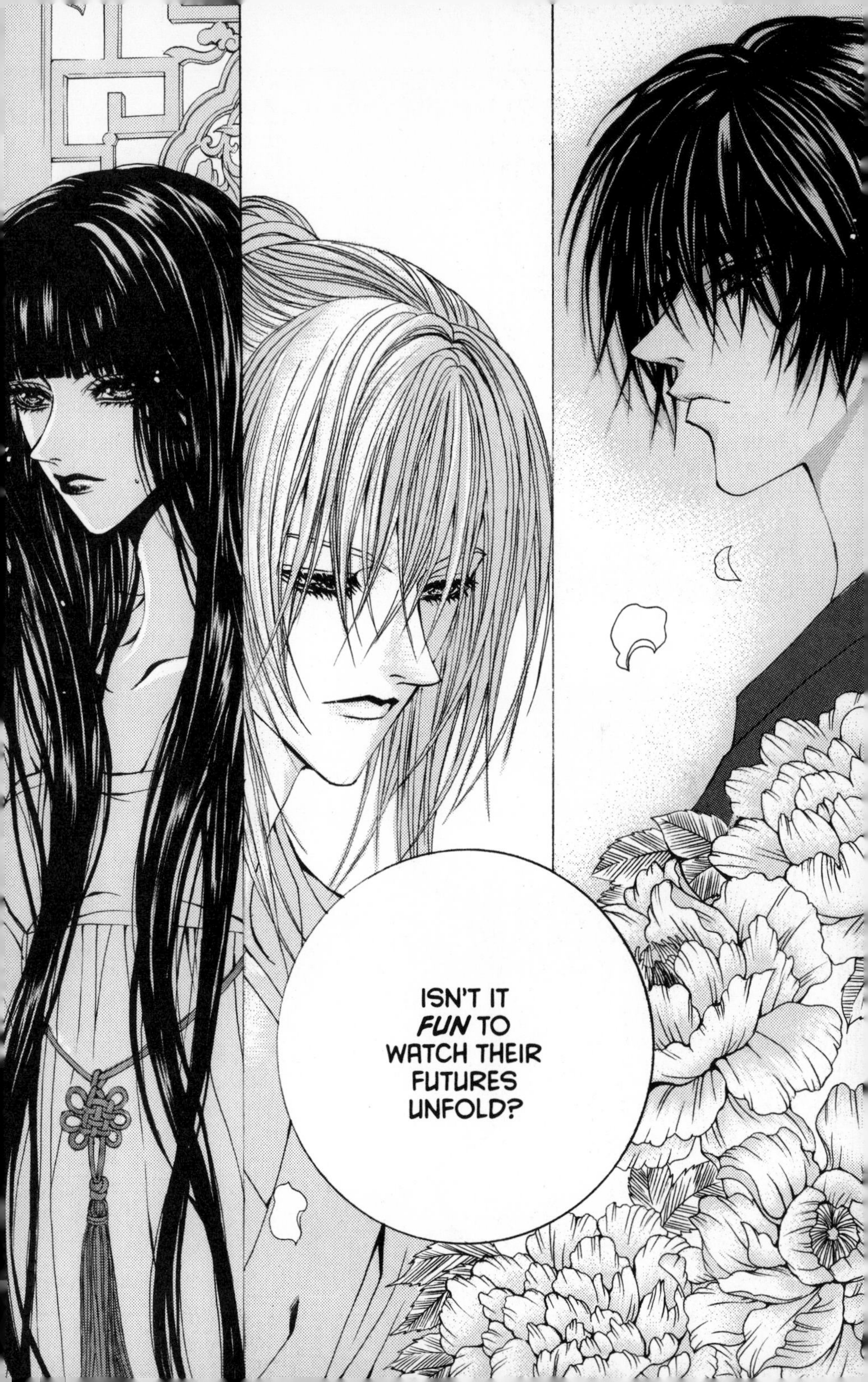
ISN'T IT *FUN* TO WATCH THEIR FUTURES UNFOLD?

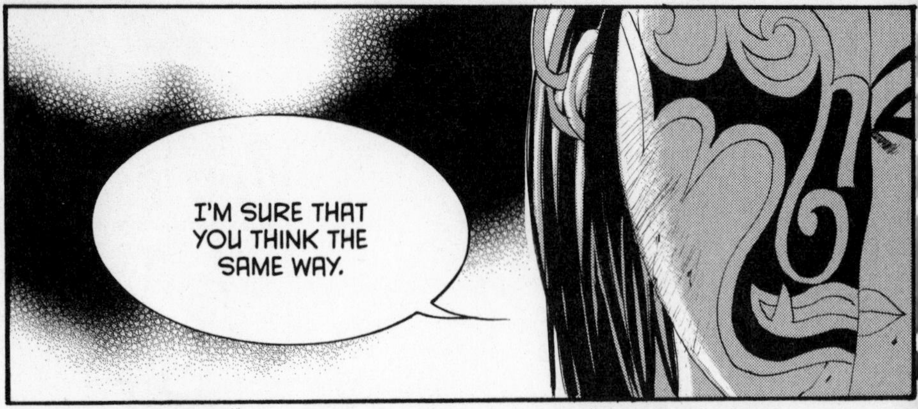
I'M SURE THAT YOU THINK THE SAME WAY.

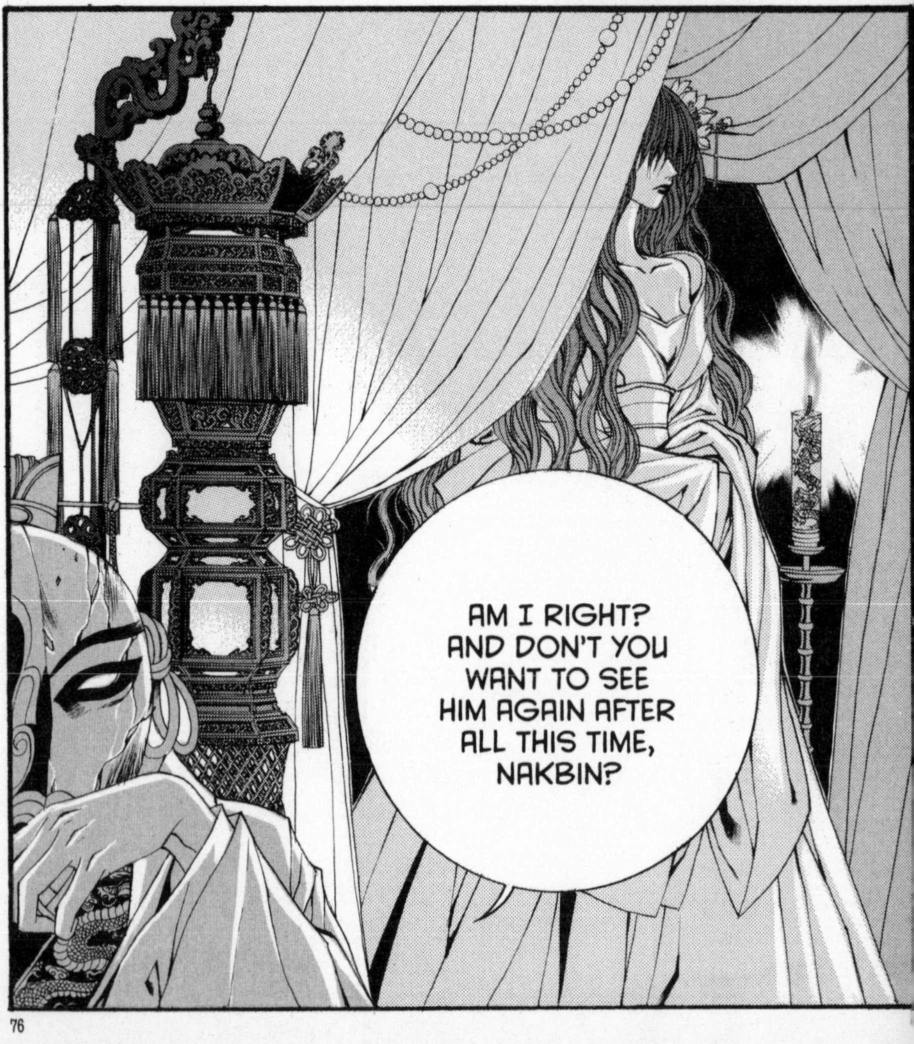
AM I RIGHT? AND DON'T YOU WANT TO SEE HIM AGAIN AFTER ALL THIS TIME, NAKBIN?

BRIDE of the WATER GOD

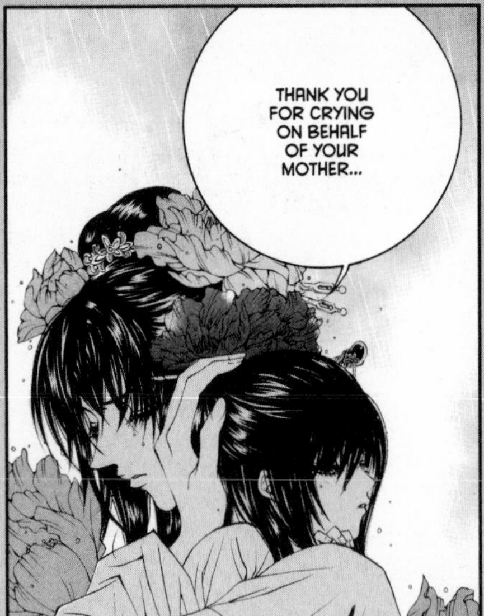
THANK YOU FOR CRYING ON BEHALF OF YOUR MOTHER...

"Thank you for crying on behalf of your mother . . ."

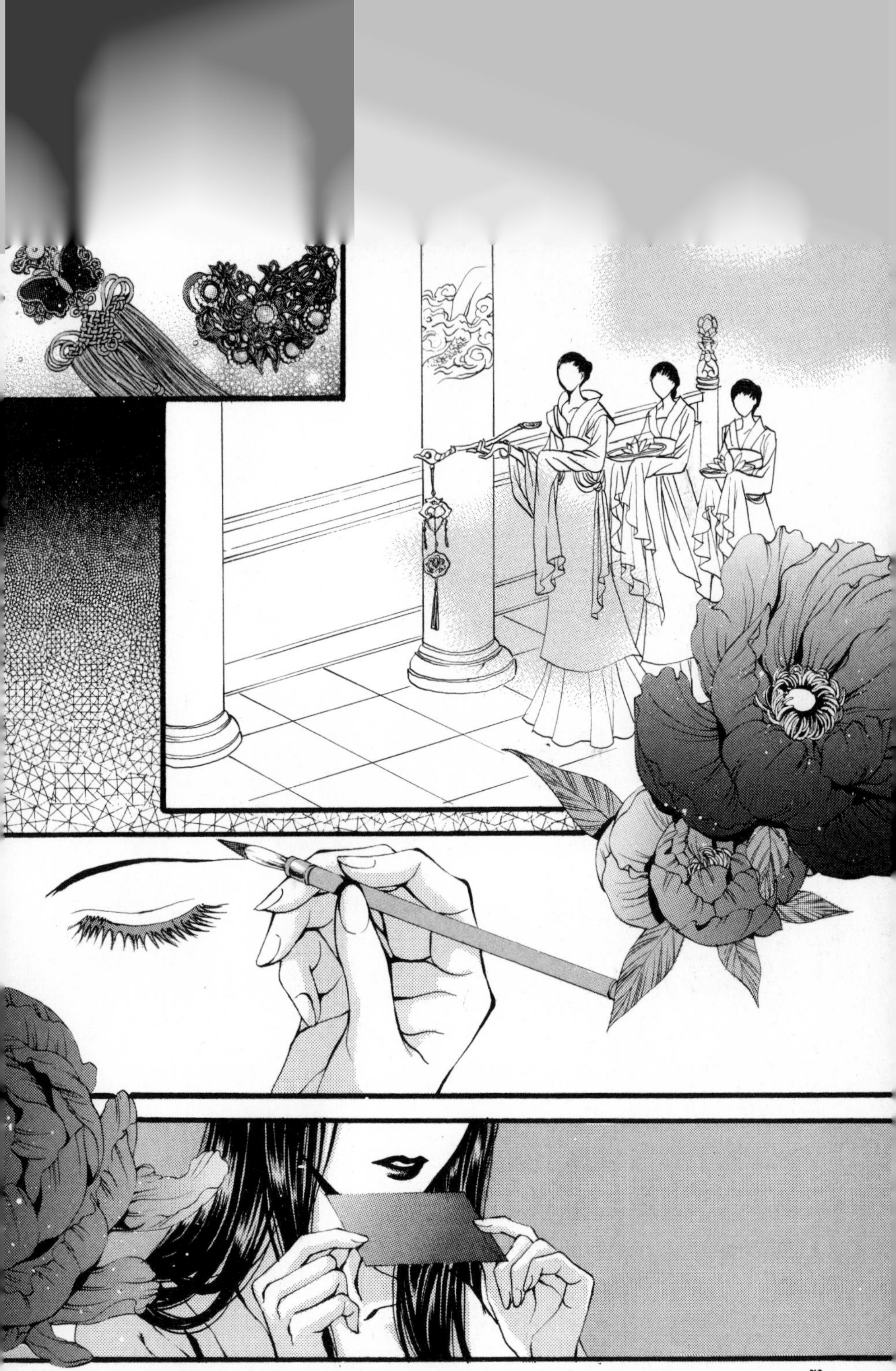

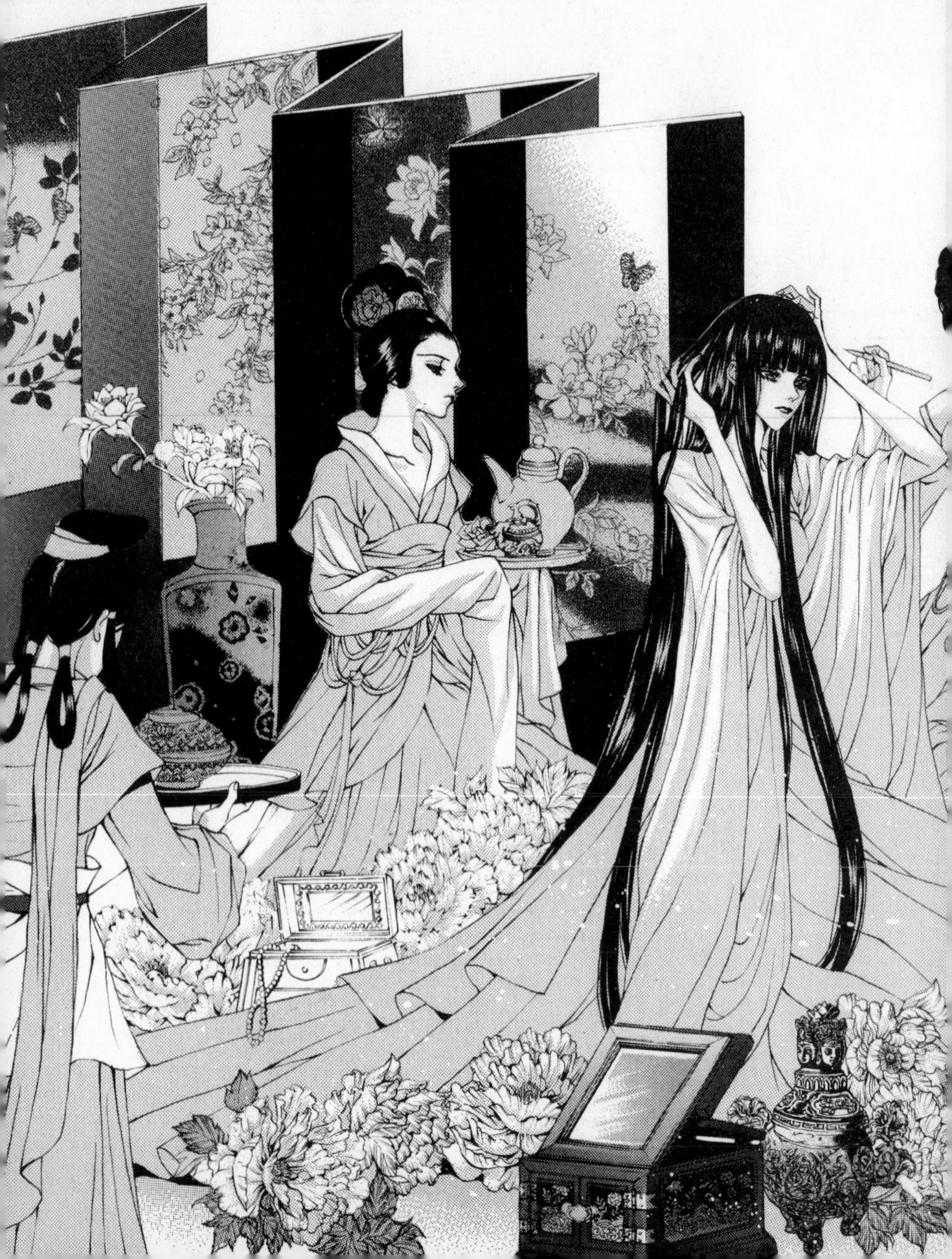

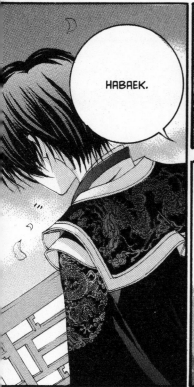

HABAEK.

MURA.

YOU DON'T SEEM SURPRISED. I GUESS YOU KNEW THAT I WAS HERE.

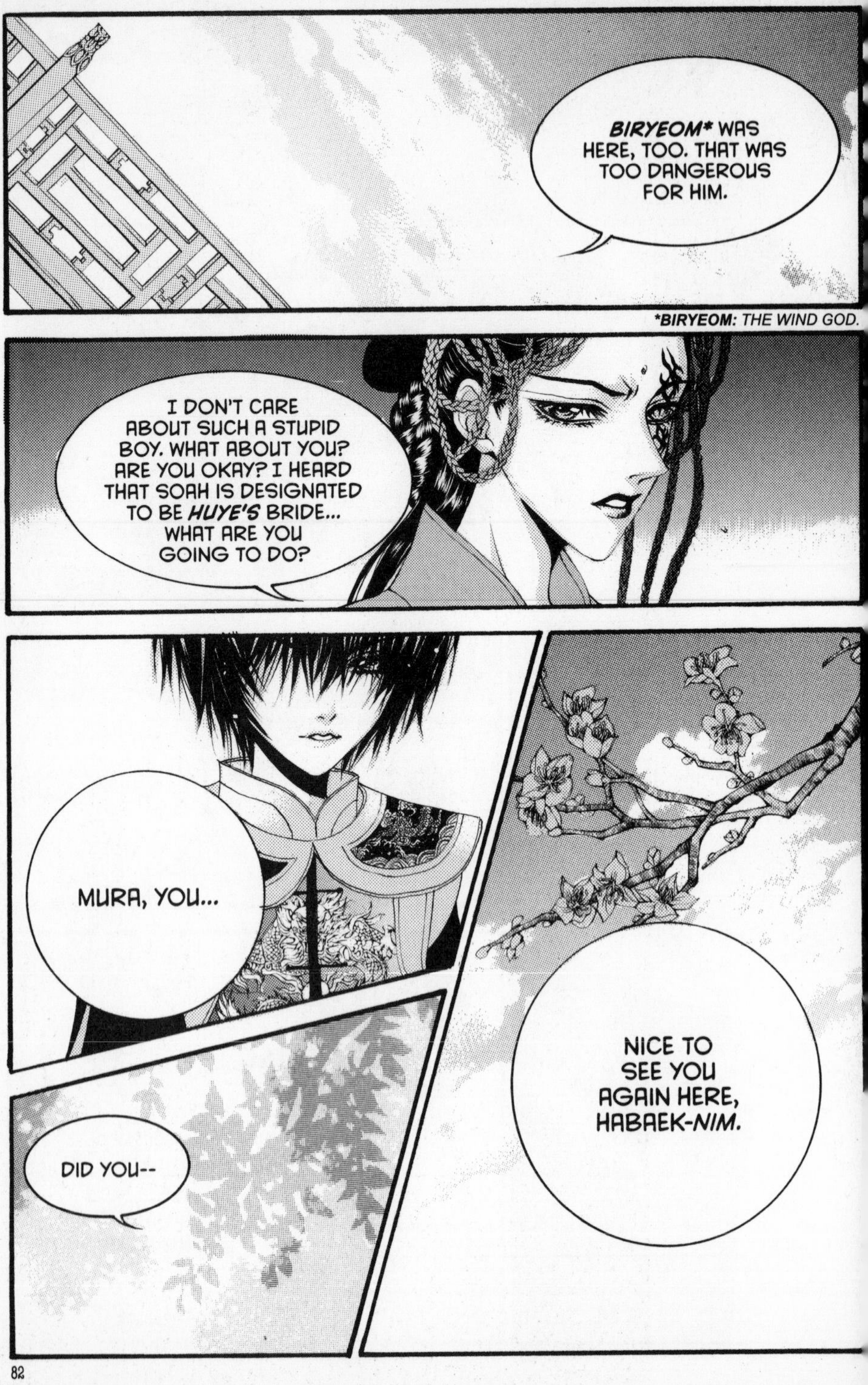
BIRYEOM* WAS HERE, TOO. THAT WAS TOO DANGEROUS FOR HIM.
*BIRYEOM: THE WIND GOD.
I DON'T CARE ABOUT SUCH A STUPID BOY. WHAT ABOUT YOU? ARE YOU OKAY? I HEARD THAT SOAH IS DESIGNATED TO BE HUYE'S BRIDE... WHAT ARE YOU GOING TO DO?
MURA, YOU...
DID YOU--
NICE TO SEE YOU AGAIN HERE, HABAEK-NIM.

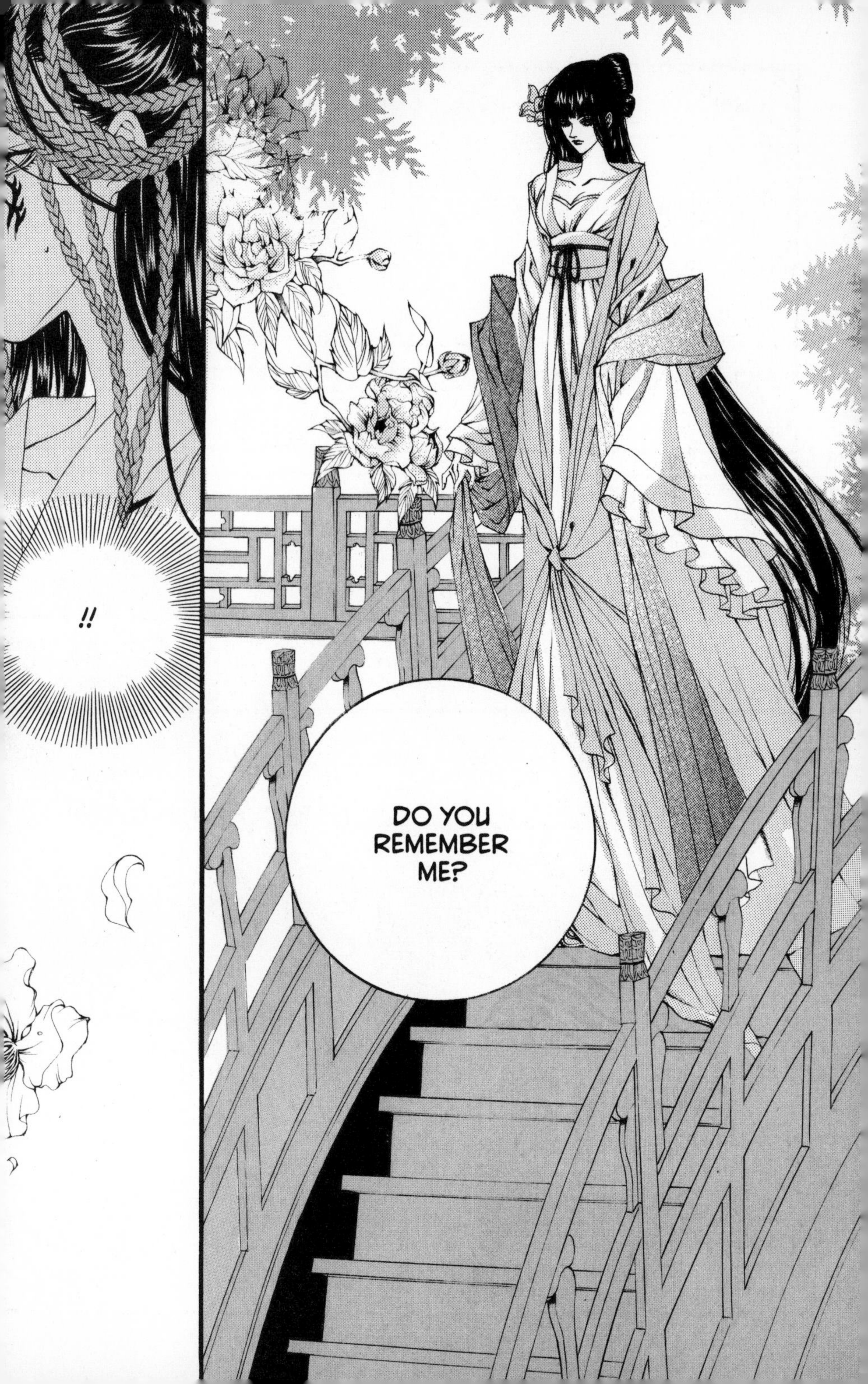
!!
DO YOU REMEMBER ME?

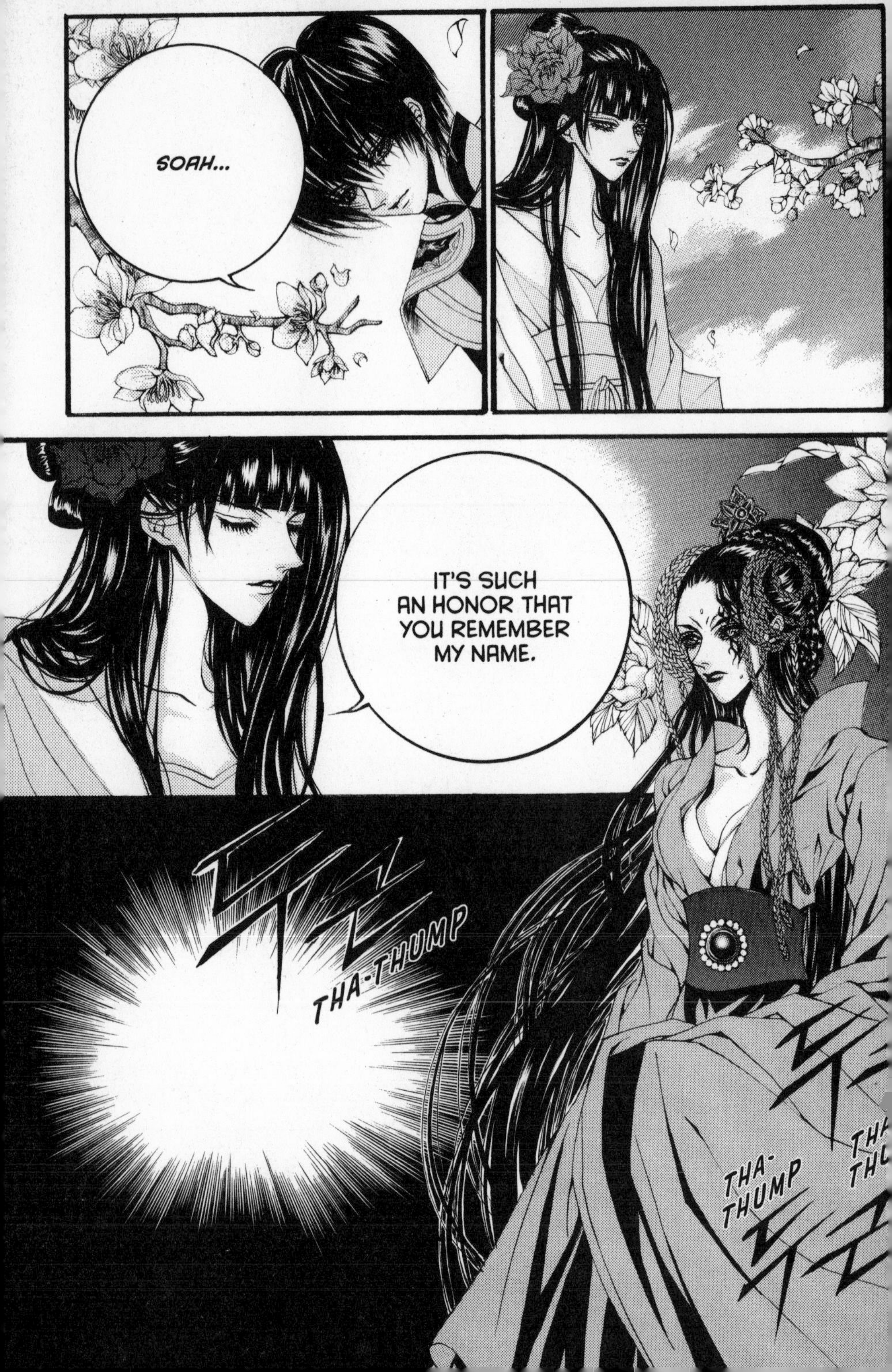
SOAH...
IT'S SUCH AN HONOR THAT YOU REMEMBER MY NAME.
THA-THUMP
THA-THUMP

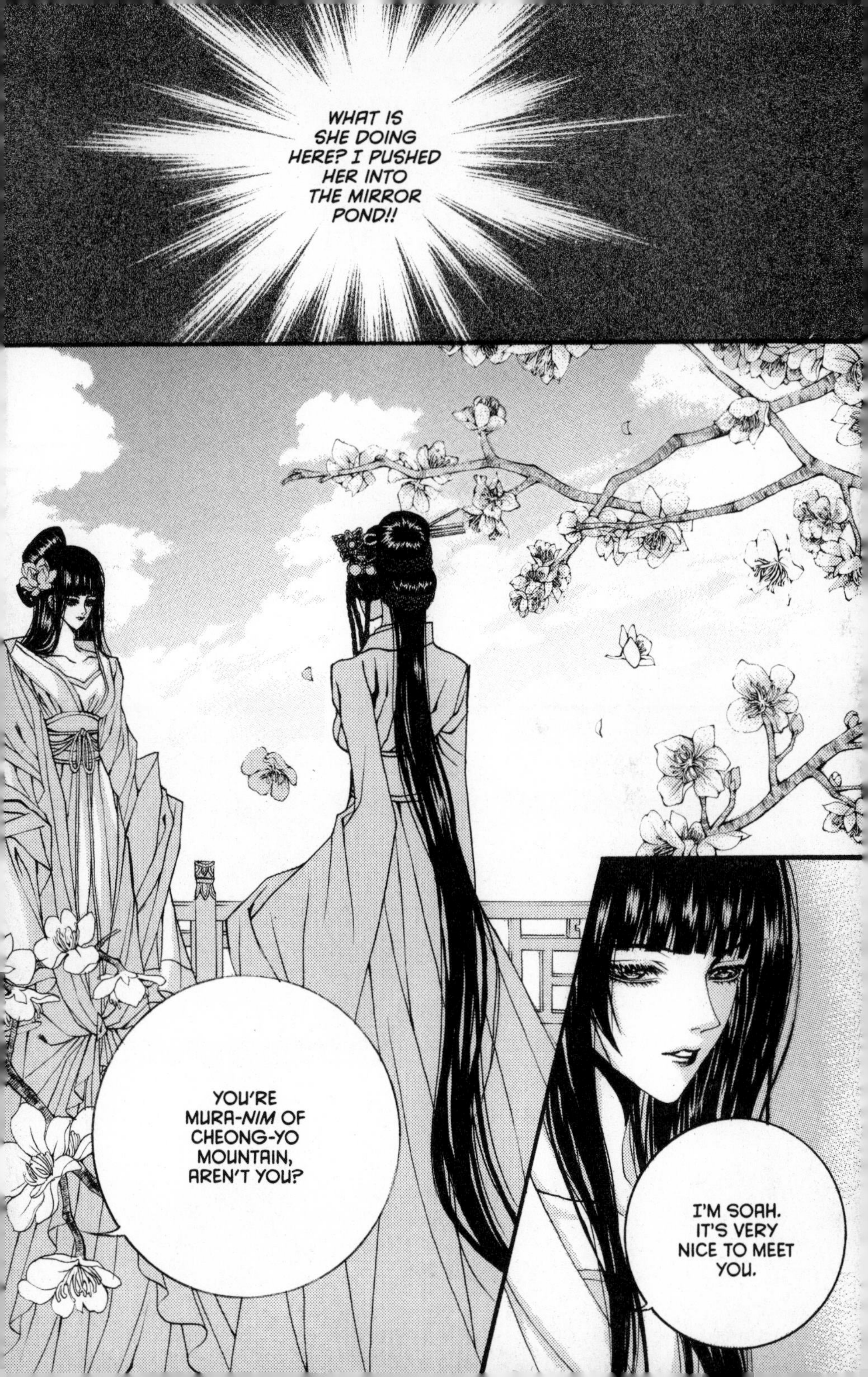
WHAT IS SHE DOING HERE? I PUSHED HER INTO THE MIRROR POND!!
YOU'RE MURA-*NIM* OF CHEONG-YO MOUNTAIN, AREN'T YOU?
I'M SOAH. IT'S VERY NICE TO MEET YOU.

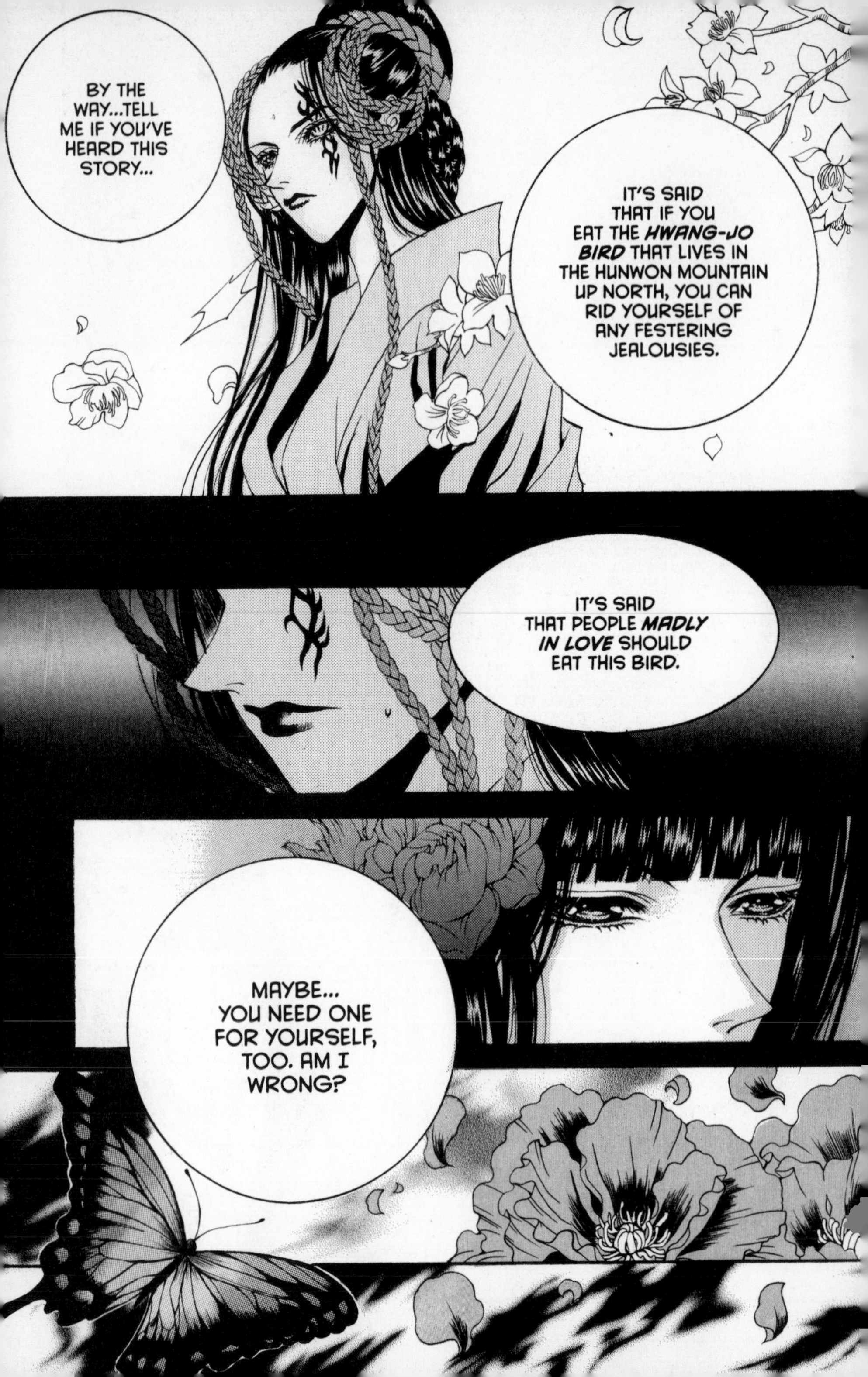
BY THE WAY...TELL ME IF YOU'VE HEARD THIS STORY...
IT'S SAID THAT IF YOU EAT THE *HWANG-JO BIRD* THAT LIVES IN THE HUNWON MOUNTAIN UP NORTH, YOU CAN RID YOURSELF OF ANY FESTERING JEALOUSIES.
IT'S SAID THAT PEOPLE *MADLY IN LOVE* SHOULD EAT THIS BIRD.
MAYBE... YOU NEED ONE FOR YOURSELF, TOO. AM I WRONG?

OH!
EVERYONE'S
HERE!

YOUR MAJESTY.

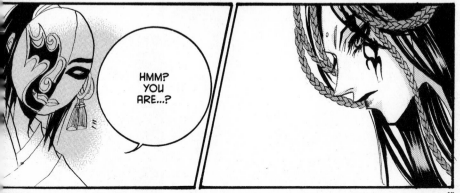

HMM?
YOU
ARE...?

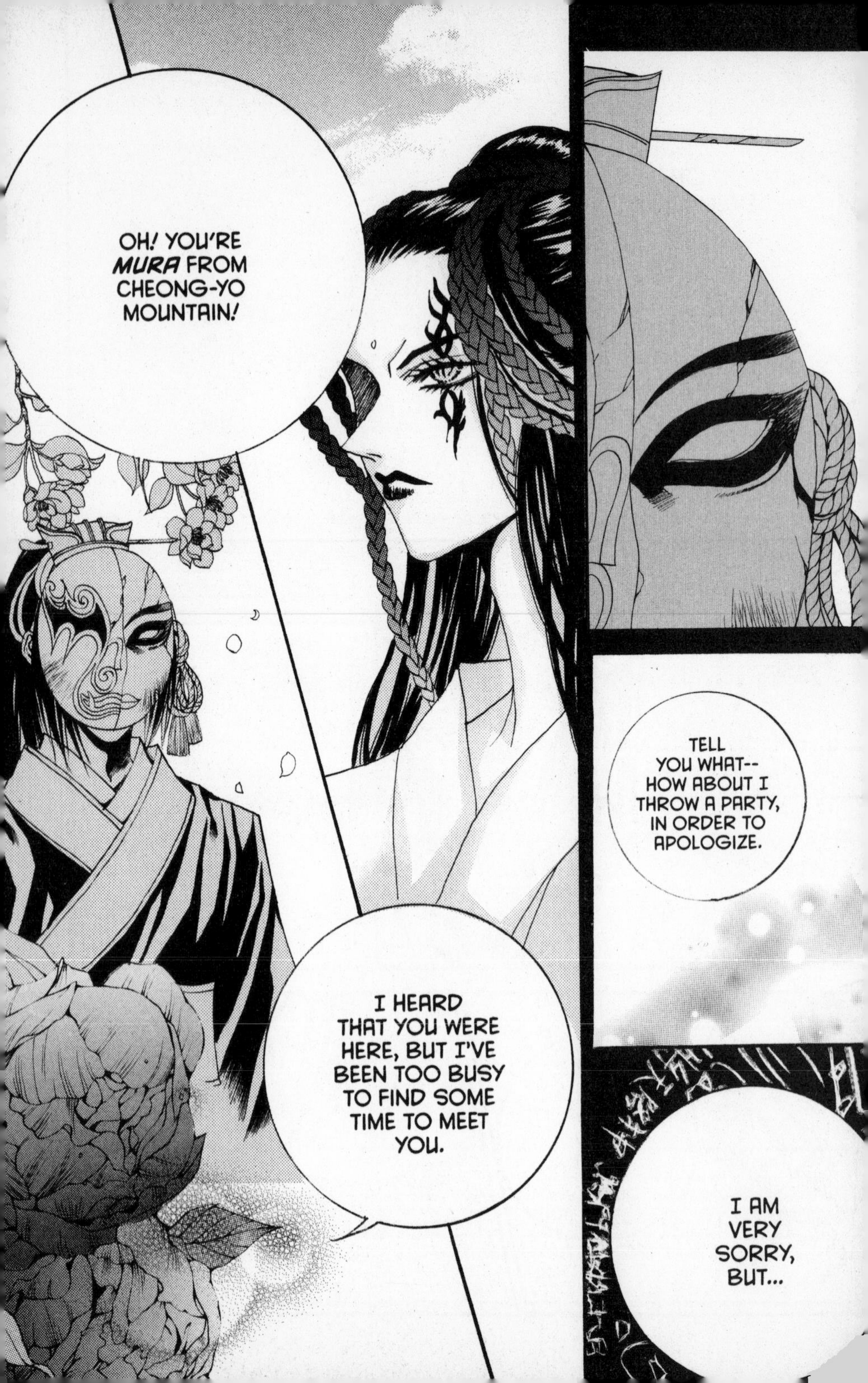
OH! YOU'RE *MURA* FROM CHEONG-YO MOUNTAIN!
I HEARD THAT YOU WERE HERE, BUT I'VE BEEN TOO BUSY TO FIND SOME TIME TO MEET YOU.
TELL YOU WHAT-- HOW ABOUT I THROW A PARTY, IN ORDER TO APOLOGIZE.
I AM VERY SORRY, BUT...

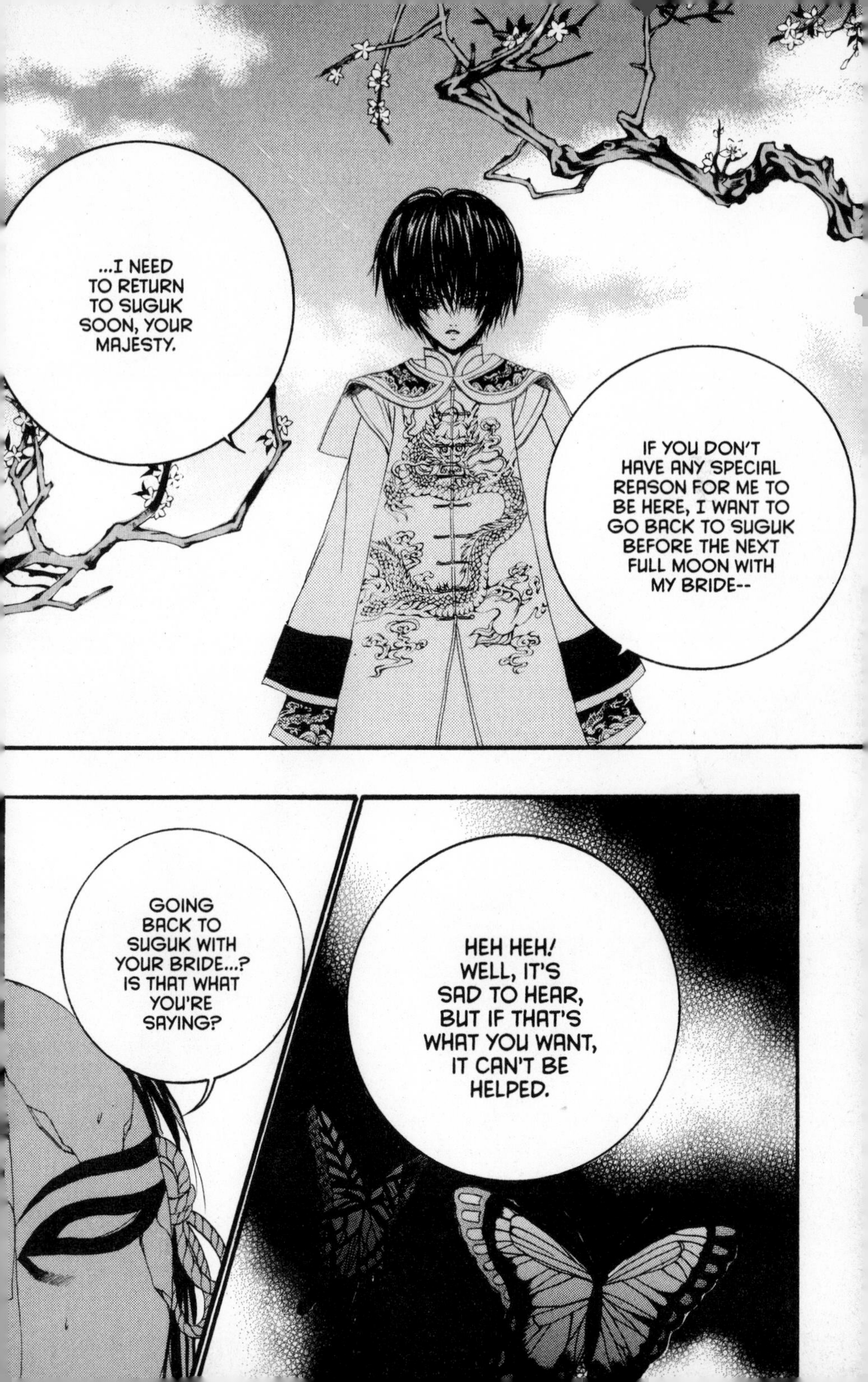
...I NEED TO RETURN TO SUGUK SOON, YOUR MAJESTY.
IF YOU DON'T HAVE ANY SPECIAL REASON FOR ME TO BE HERE, I WANT TO GO BACK TO SUGUK BEFORE THE NEXT FULL MOON WITH MY BRIDE--
GOING BACK TO SUGUK WITH YOUR BRIDE...? IS THAT WHAT YOU'RE SAYING?
HEH HEH! WELL, IT'S SAD TO HEAR, BUT IF THAT'S WHAT YOU WANT, IT CAN'T BE HELPED.

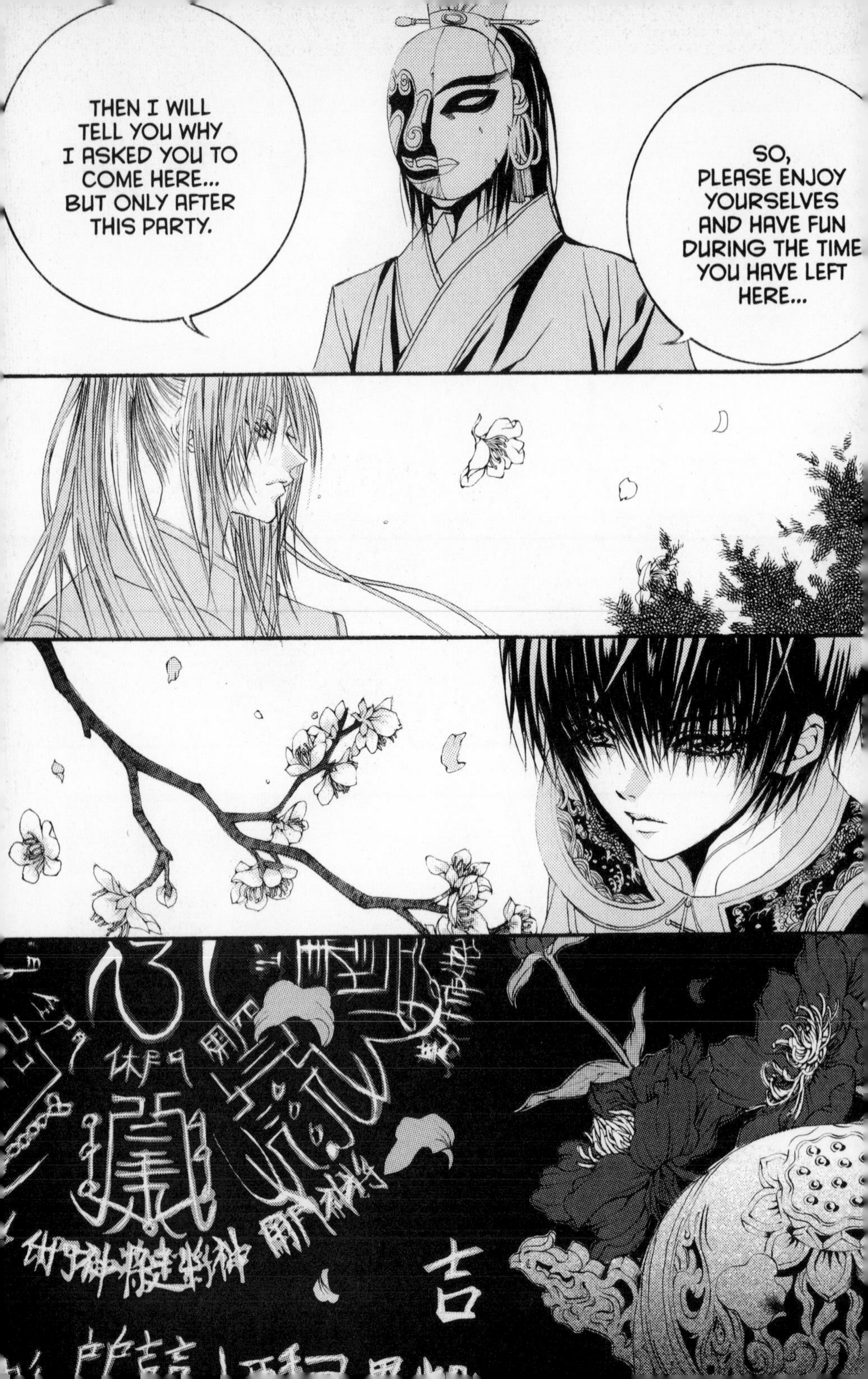
SO, PLEASE ENJOY YOURSELVES AND HAVE FUN DURING THE TIME YOU HAVE LEFT HERE...
THEN I WILL TELL YOU WHY I ASKED YOU TO COME HERE... BUT ONLY AFTER THIS PARTY.

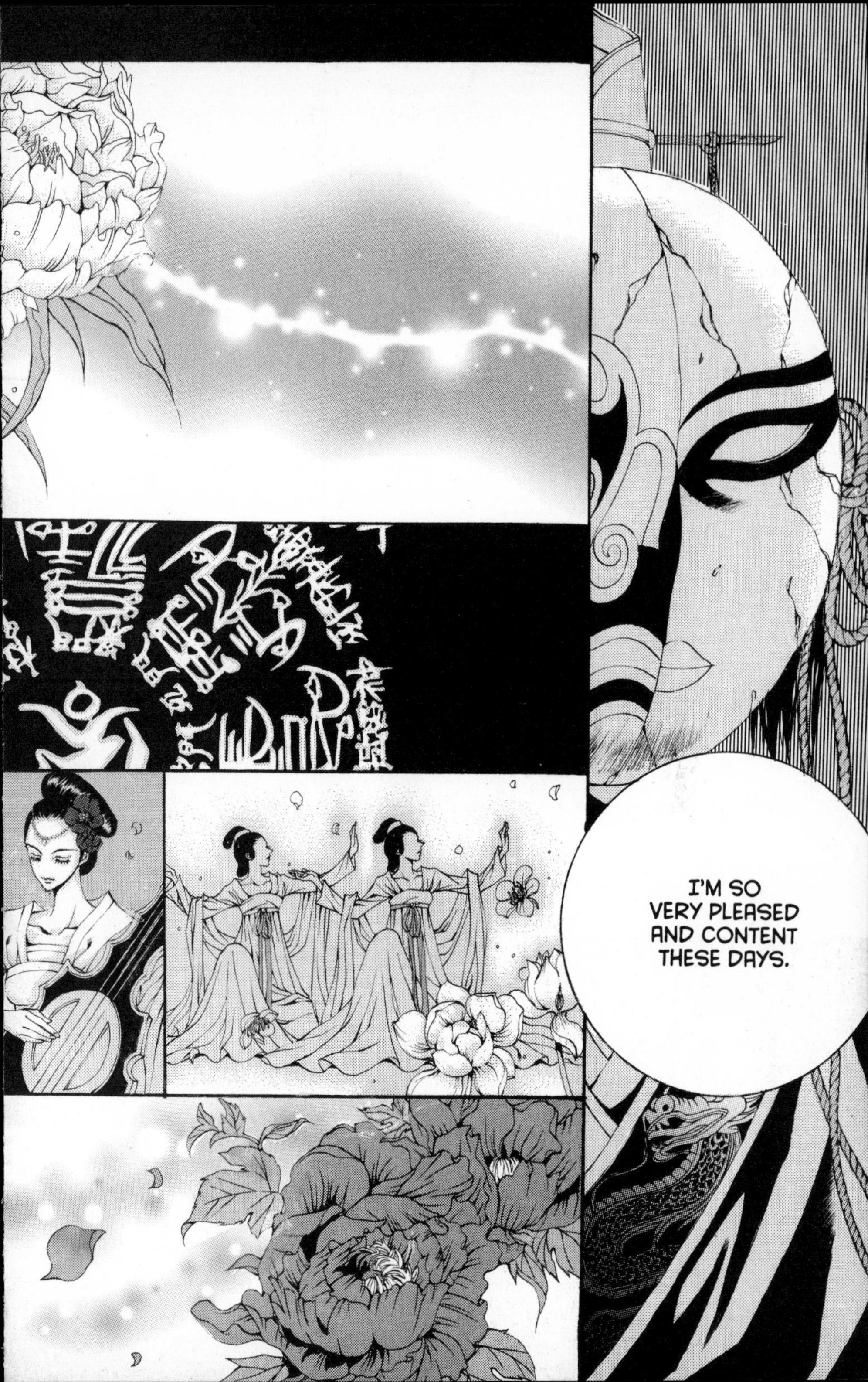
I'M SO VERY PLEASED AND CONTENT THESE DAYS.

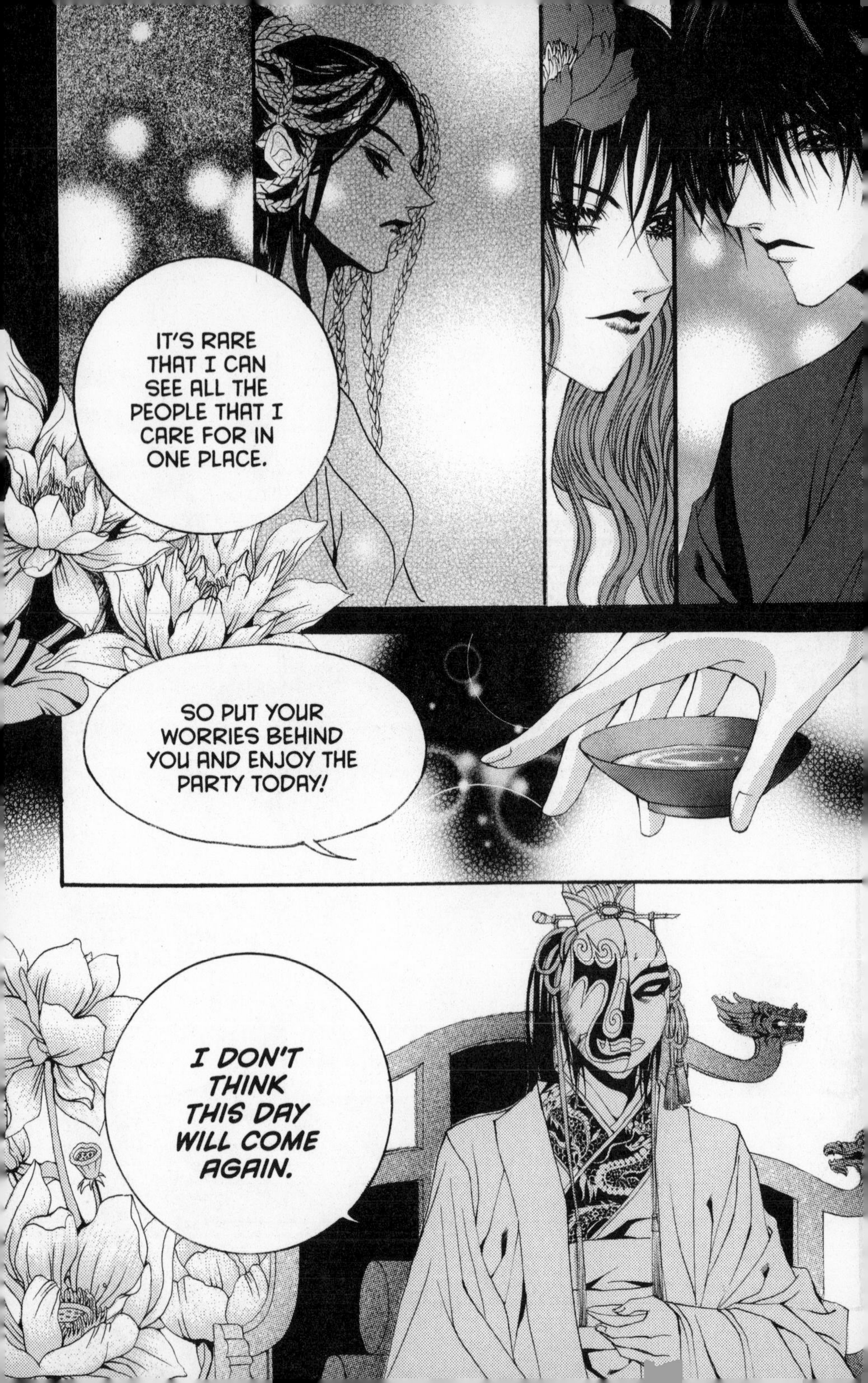
IT'S RARE THAT I CAN SEE ALL THE PEOPLE THAT I CARE FOR IN ONE PLACE.
SO PUT YOUR WORRIES BEHIND YOU AND ENJOY THE PARTY TODAY!
I DON'T THINK THIS DAY WILL COME AGAIN.

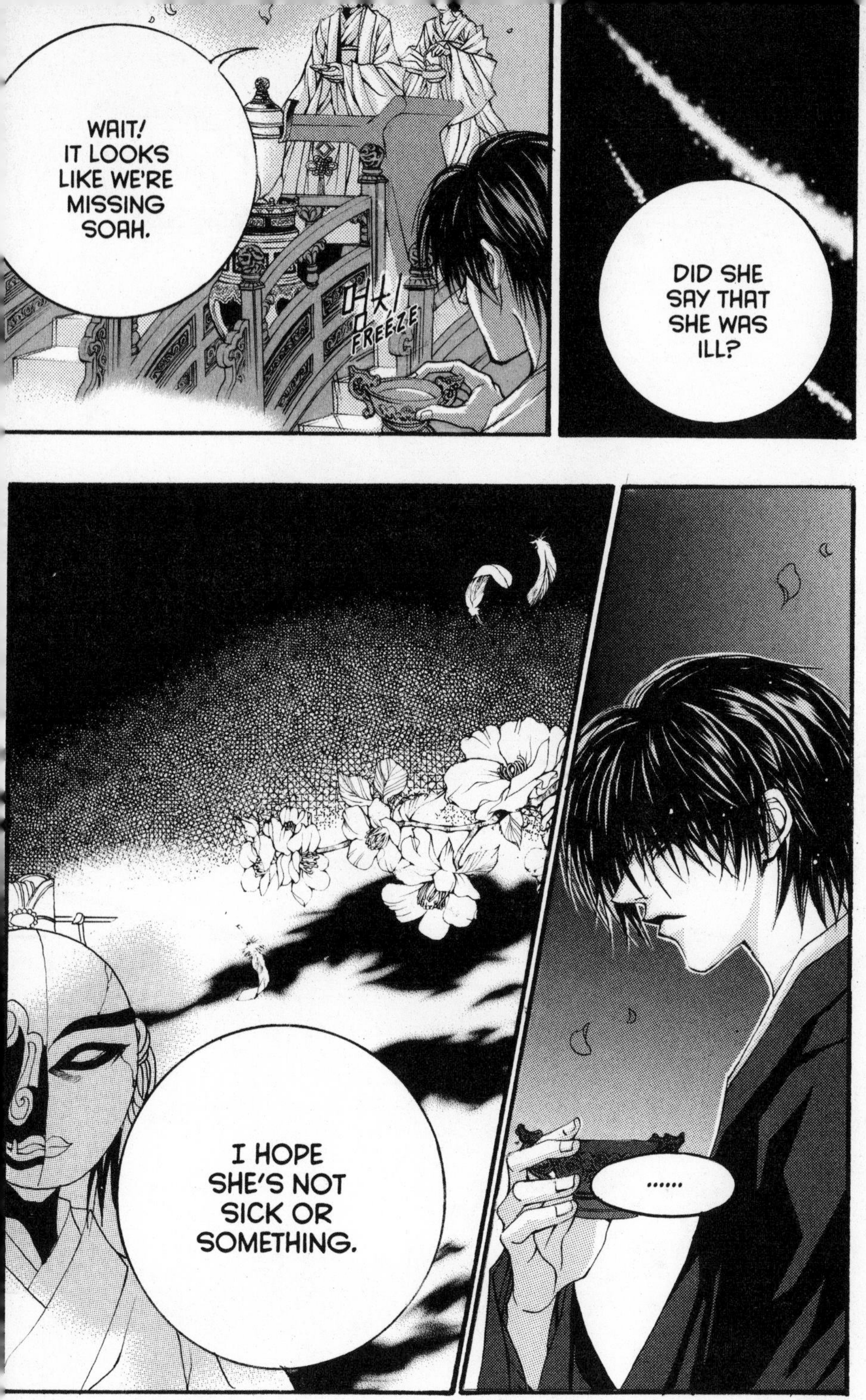
WAIT! IT LOOKS LIKE WE'RE MISSING SOAH.
FREEZE
DID SHE SAY THAT SHE WAS ILL?
I HOPE SHE'S NOT SICK OR SOMETHING.
......

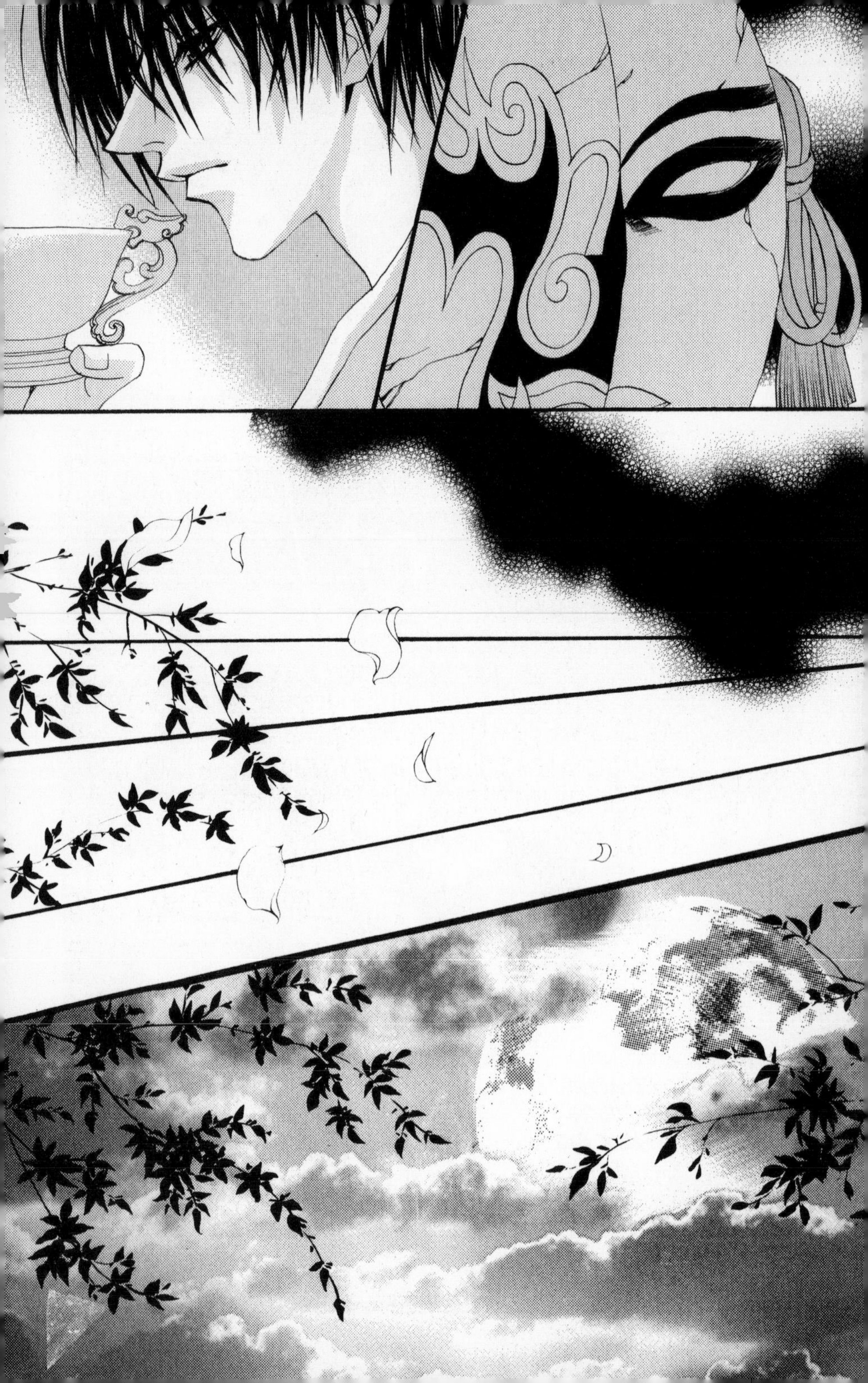

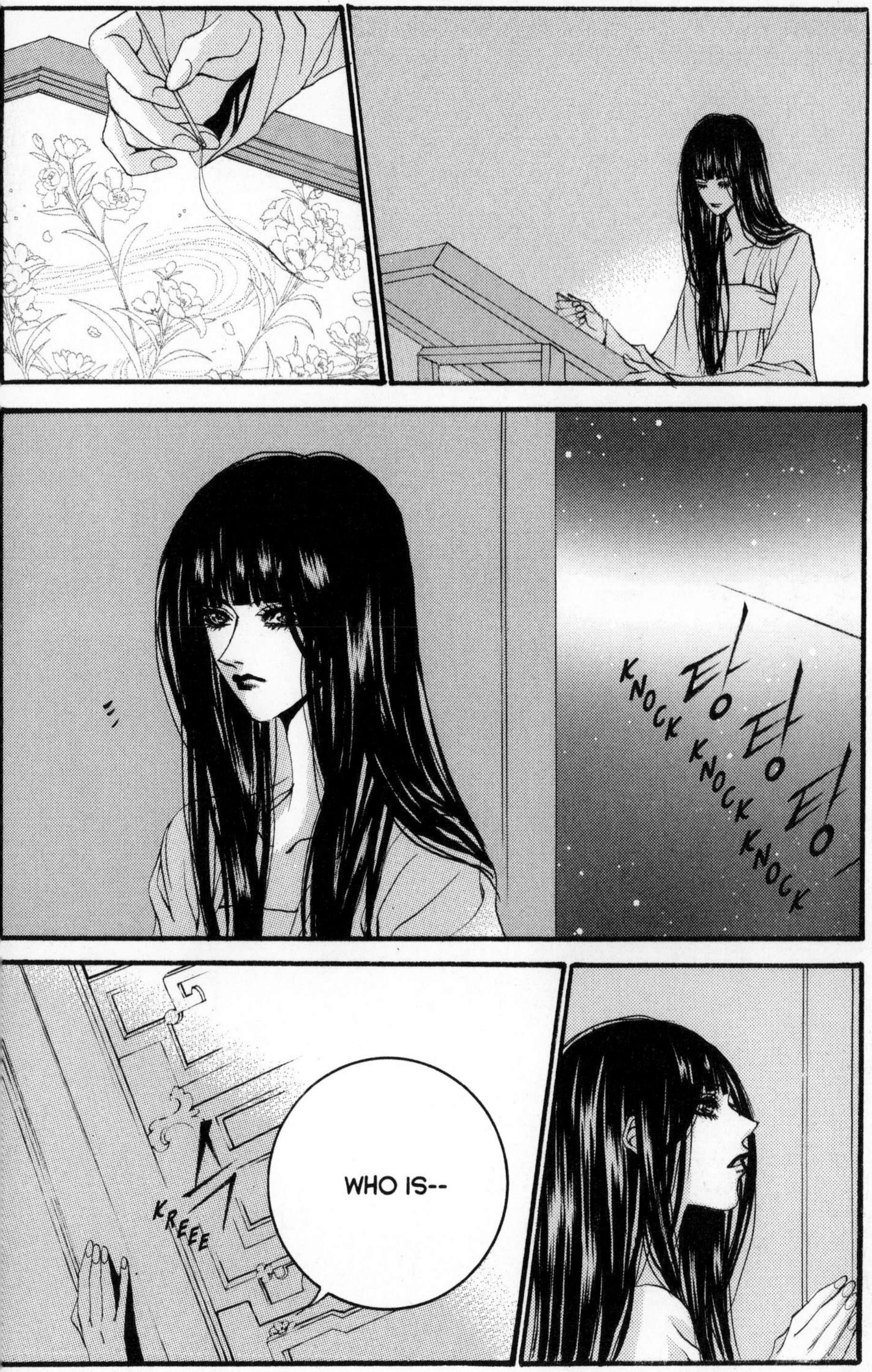
KNOCK KNOCK KNOCK
KREEE
WHO IS--

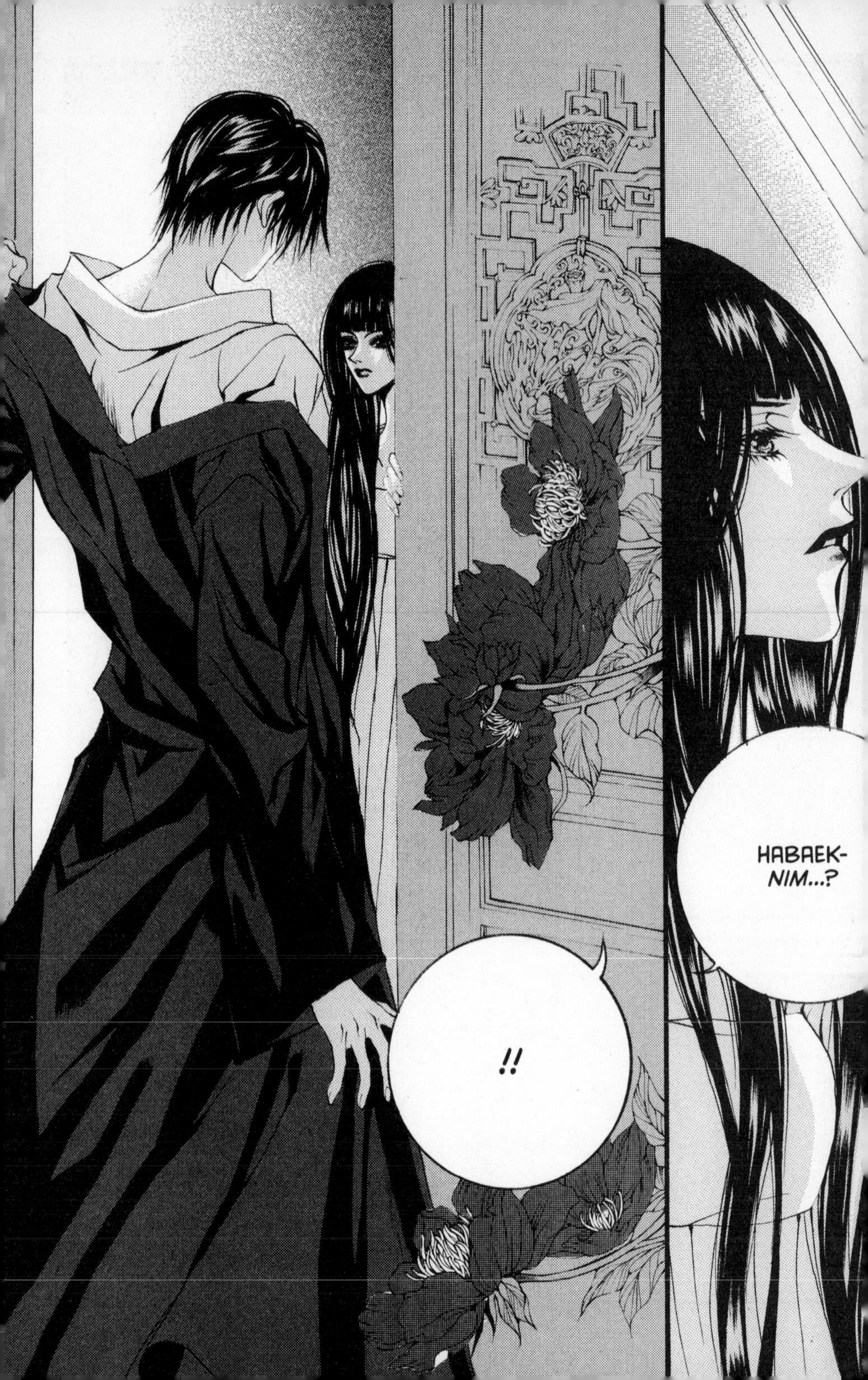
!!
HABAEK-NIM...?

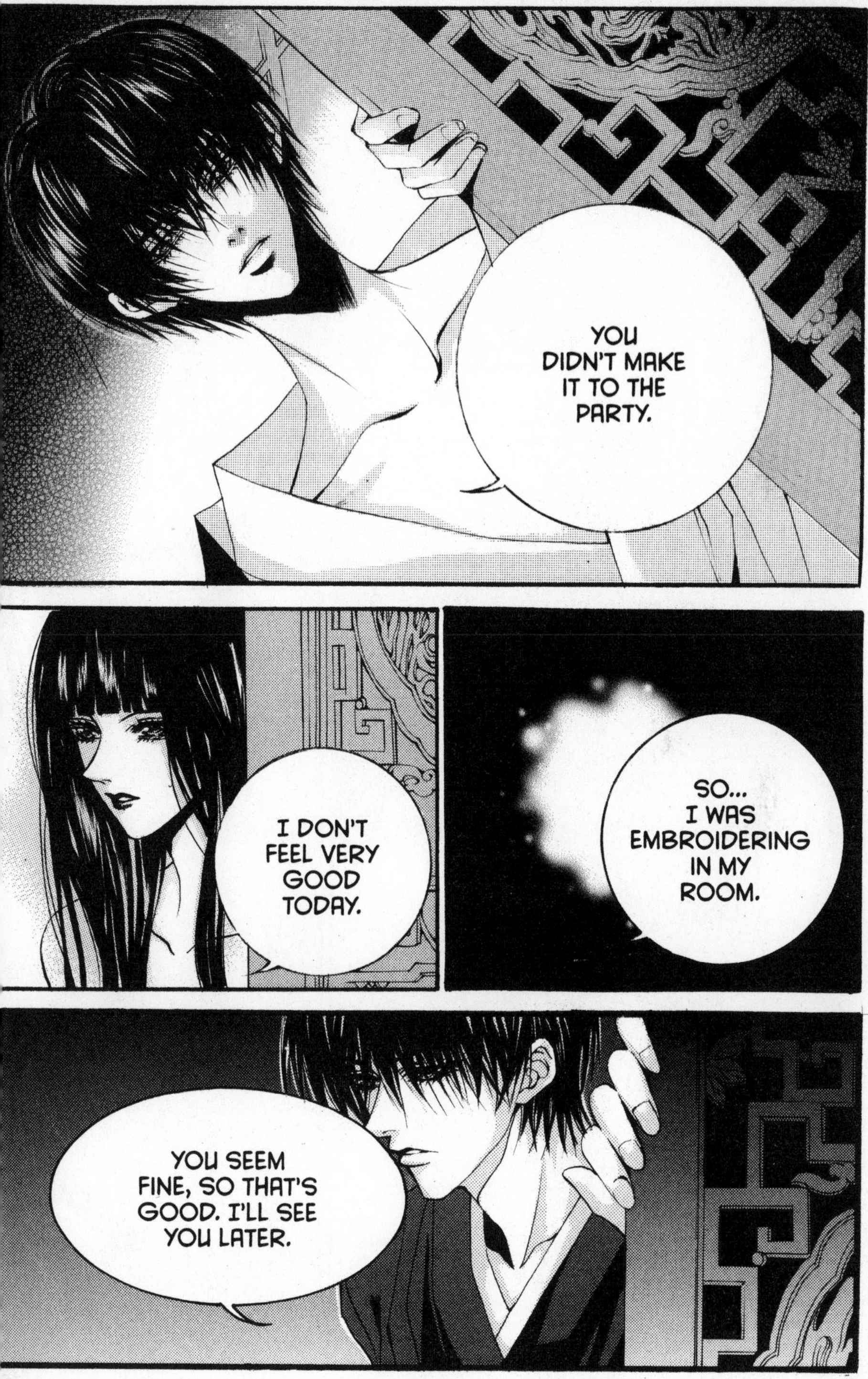
YOU DIDN'T MAKE IT TO THE PARTY.
I DON'T FEEL VERY GOOD TODAY.
SO... I WAS EMBROIDERING IN MY ROOM.
YOU SEEM FINE, SO THAT'S GOOD. I'LL SEE YOU LATER.

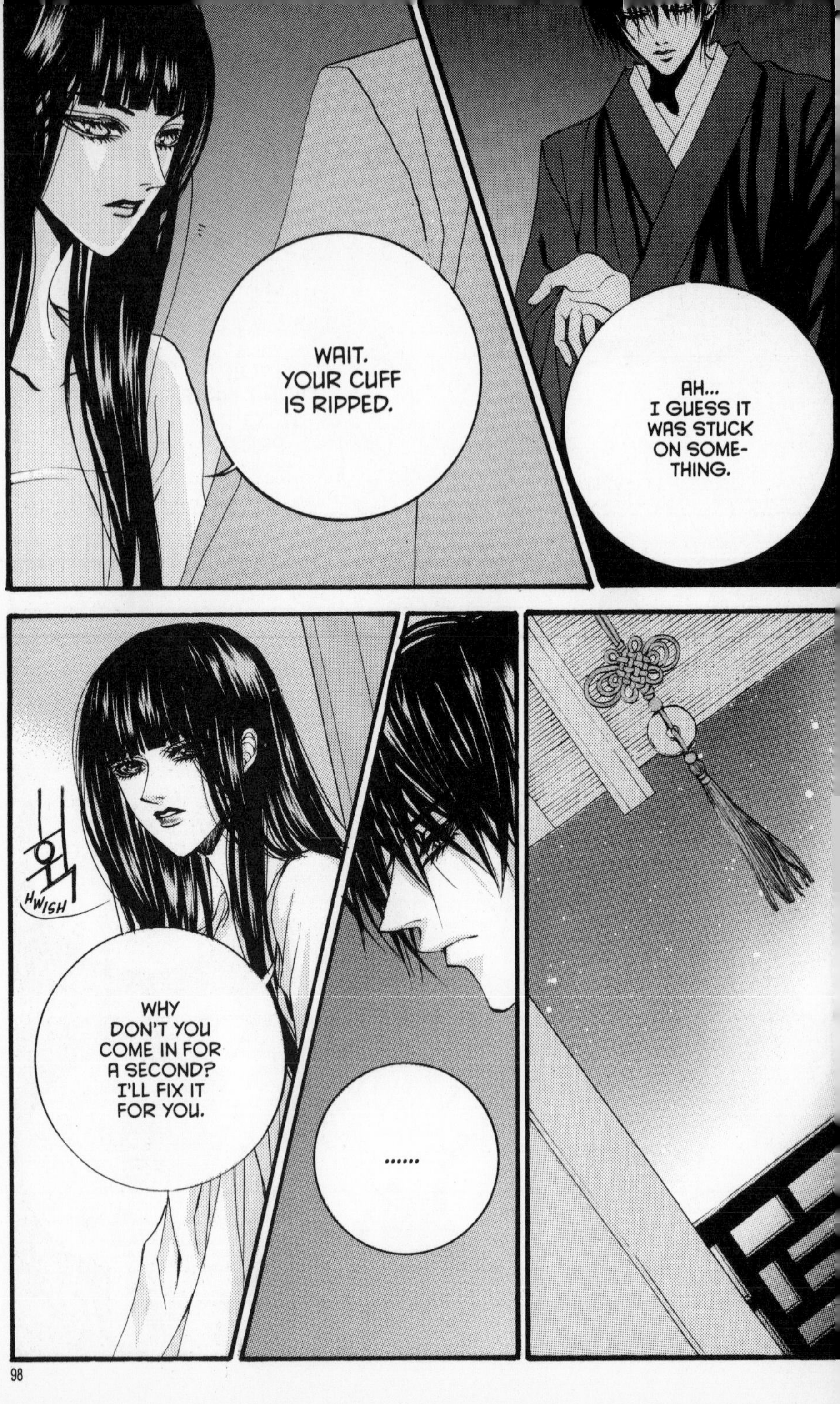
WAIT. YOUR CUFF IS RIPPED.
AH... I GUESS IT WAS STUCK ON SOME-THING.
HWISH
WHY DON'T YOU COME IN FOR A SECOND? I'LL FIX IT FOR YOU.
......

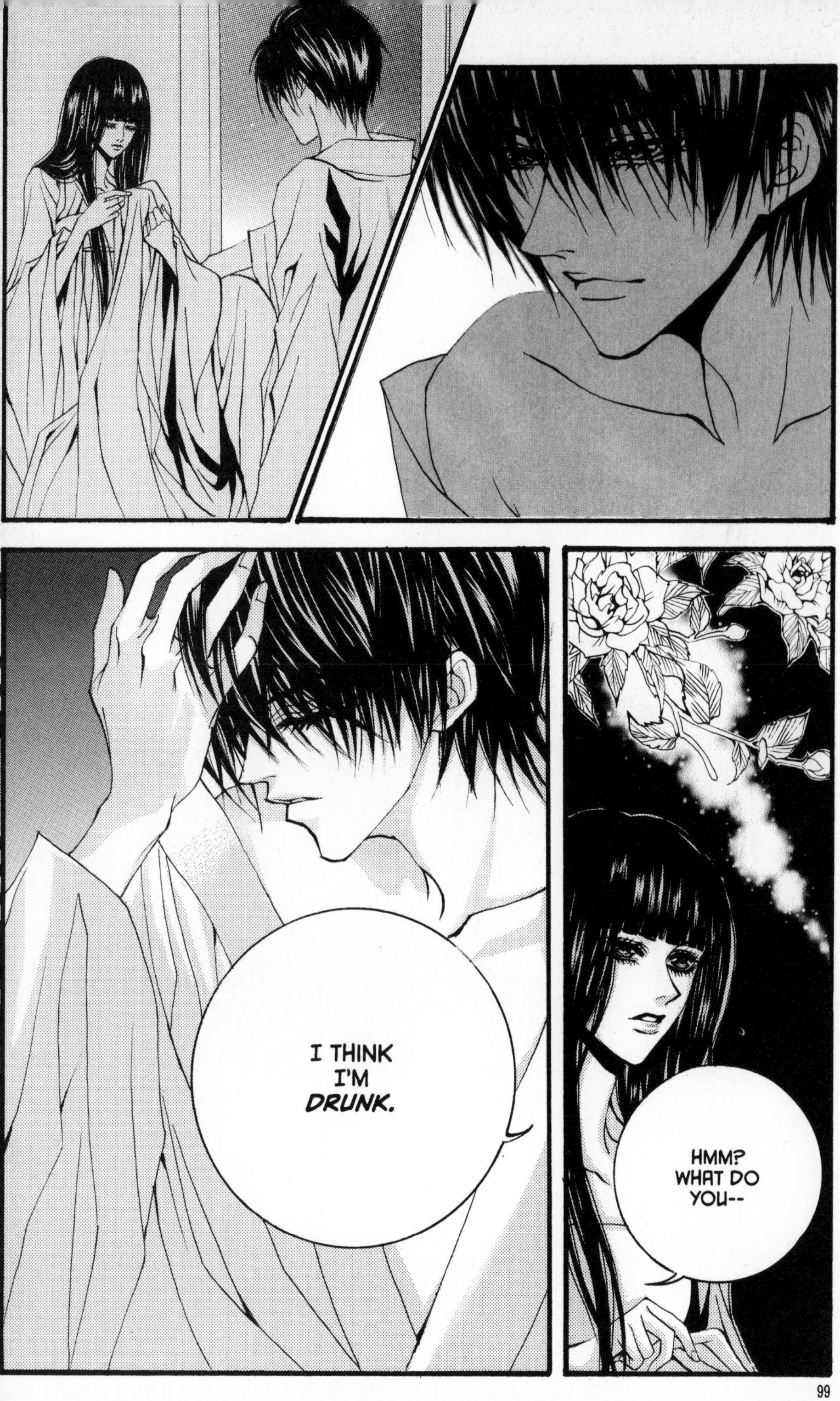
I THINK I'M *DRUNK.*
HMM? WHAT DO YOU--

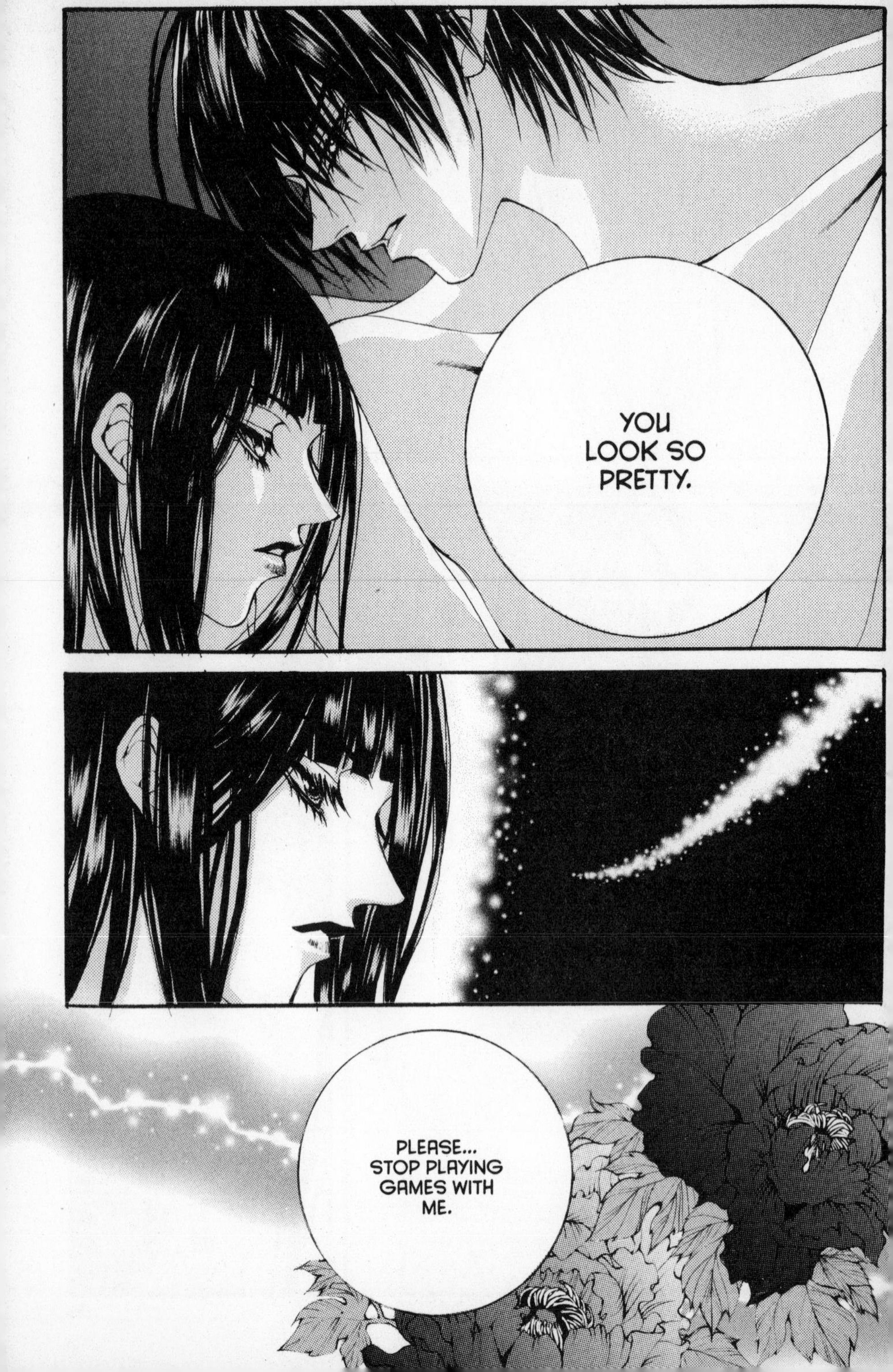
YOU LOOK SO PRETTY.
PLEASE... STOP PLAYING GAMES WITH ME.

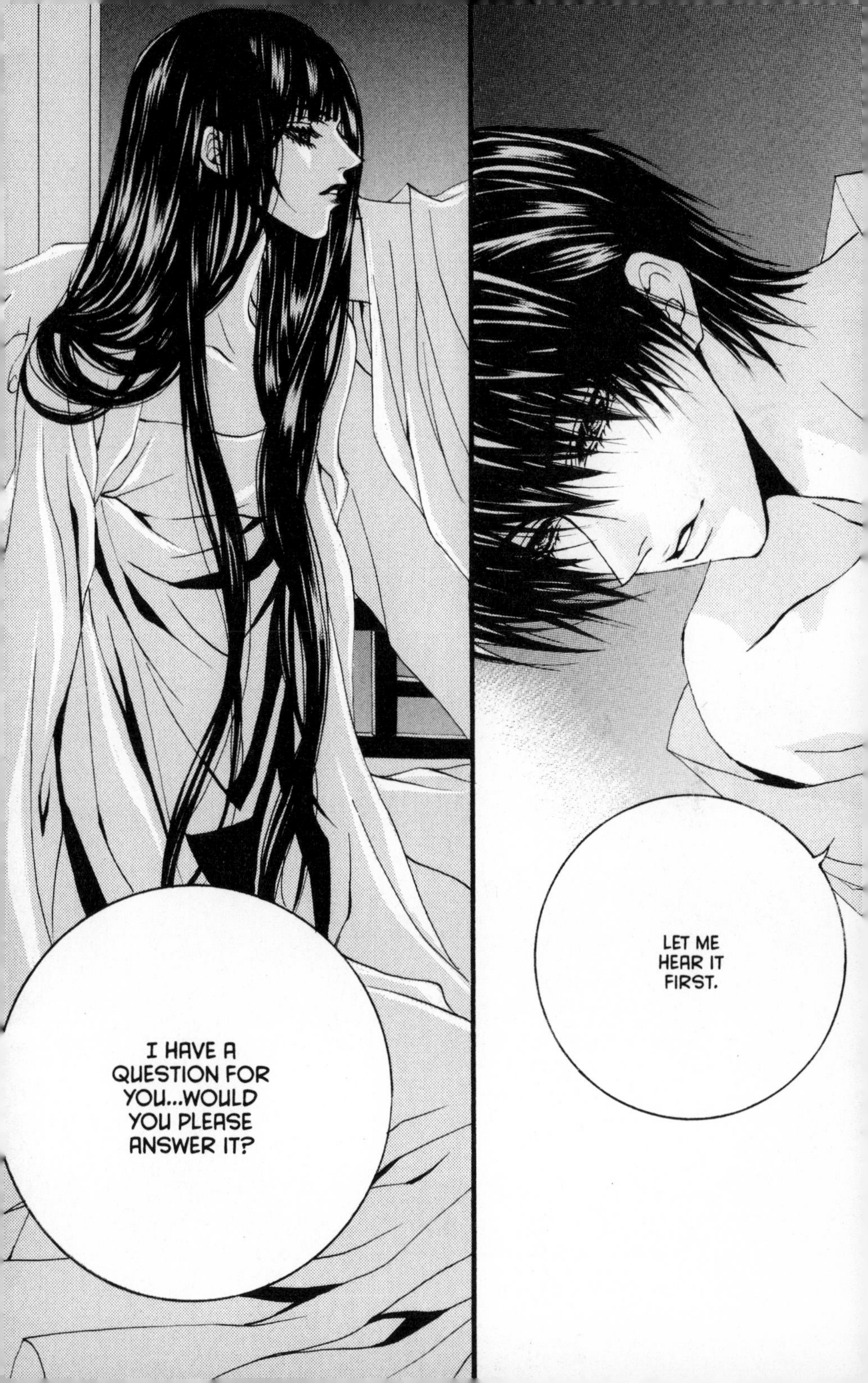

I HAVE A QUESTION FOR YOU...WOULD YOU PLEASE ANSWER IT?
LET ME HEAR IT FIRST.

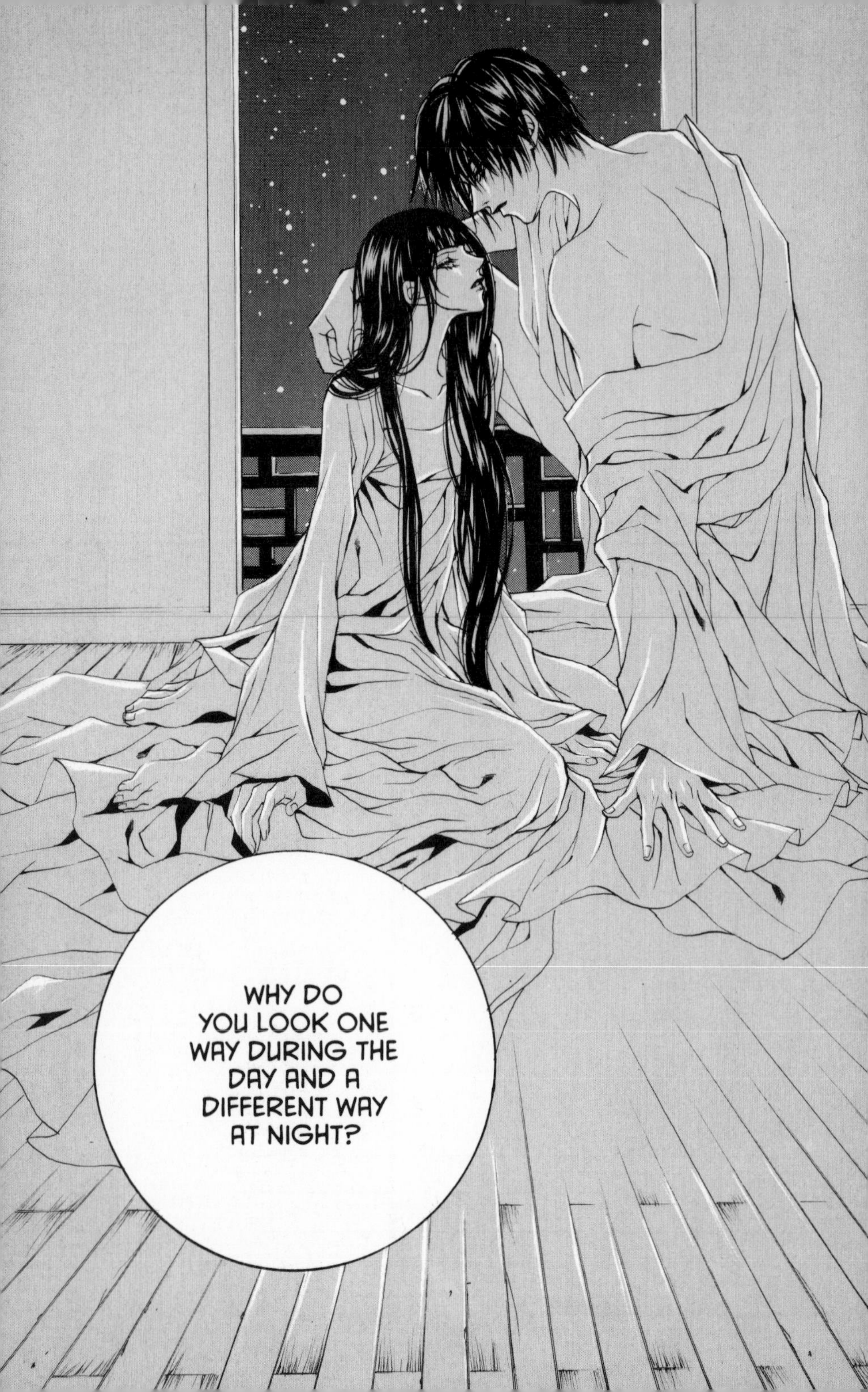
WHY DO YOU LOOK ONE WAY DURING THE DAY AND A DIFFERENT WAY AT NIGHT?

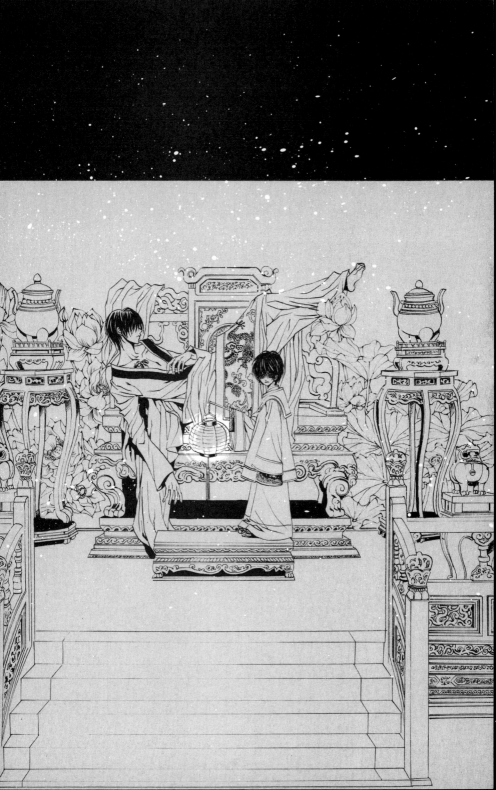

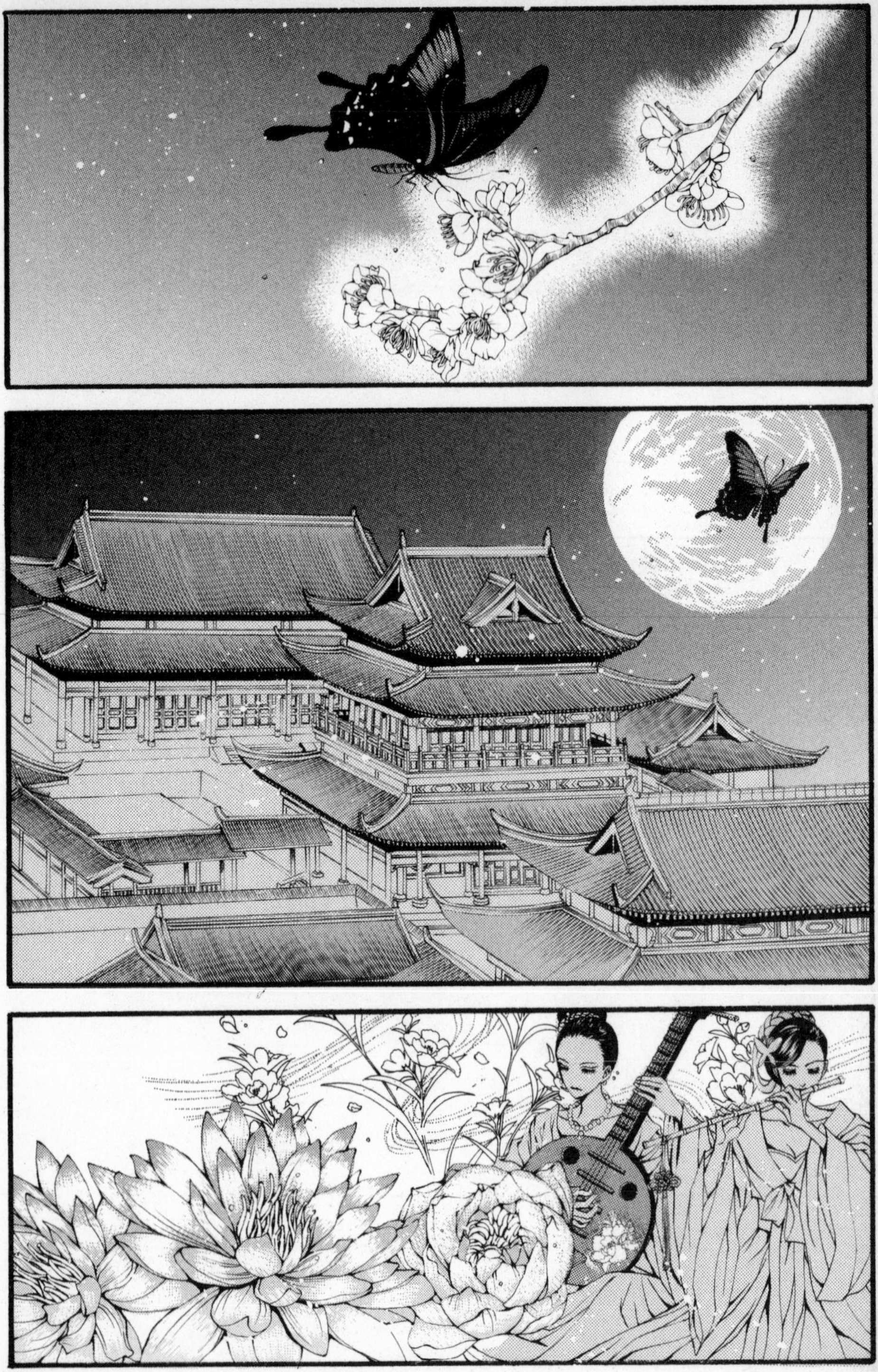

DRRUMM
DRRUMM

DRRUMM DRRUMM DRRUMM

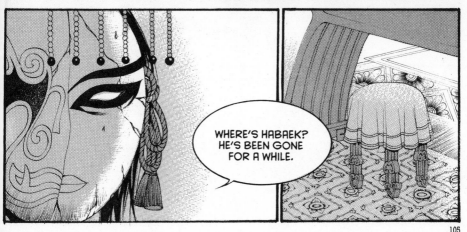

WHERE'S HABAEK?
HE'S BEEN GONE
FOR A WHILE.

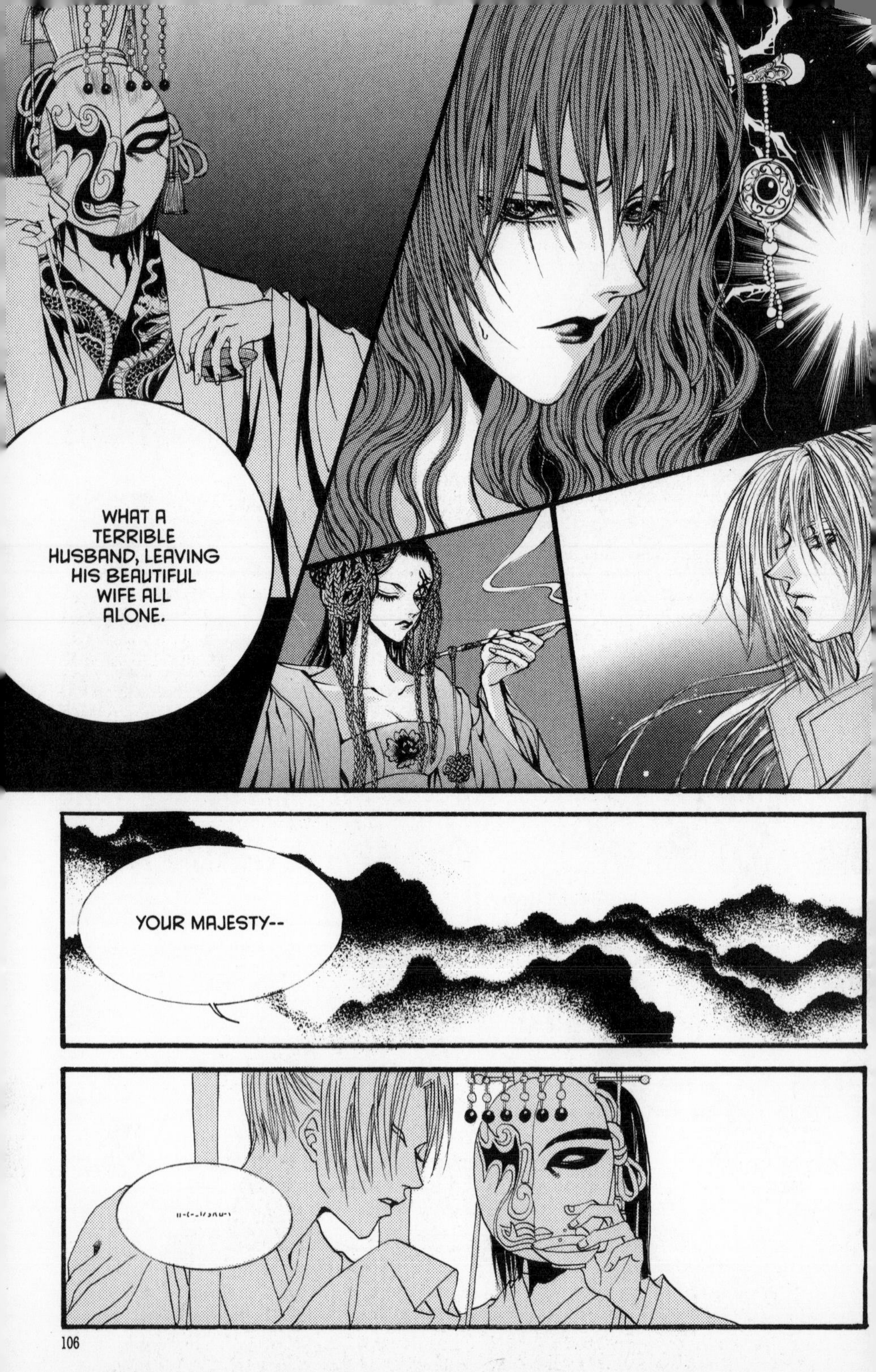
WHAT A TERRIBLE HUSBAND, LEAVING HIS BEAUTIFUL WIFE ALL ALONE.
YOUR MAJESTY--

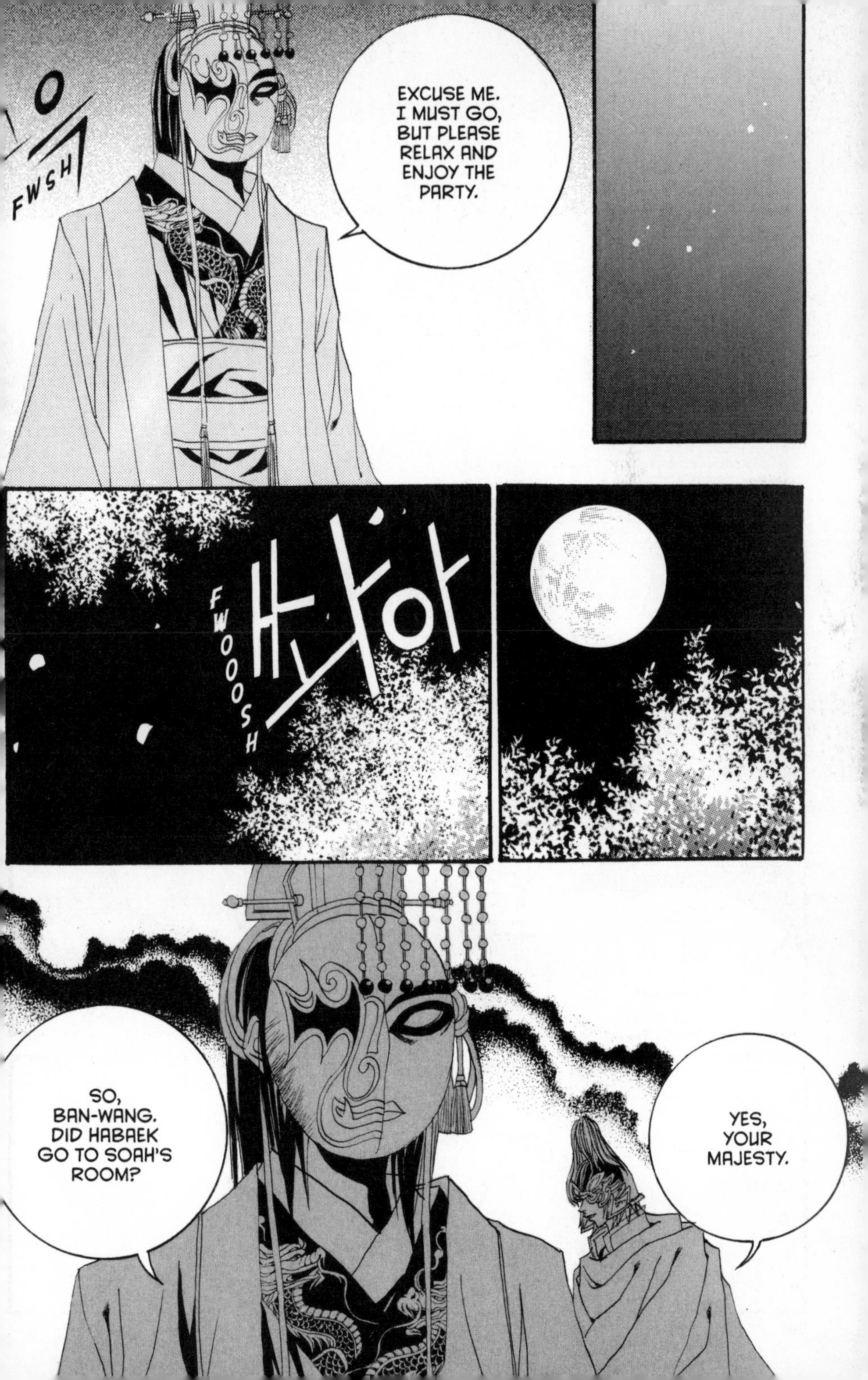
FWSH
EXCUSE ME. I MUST GO, BUT PLEASE RELAX AND ENJOY THE PARTY.
FWOOOOSH
SO, BAN-WANG. DID HABAEK GO TO SOAH'S ROOM?
YES, YOUR MAJESTY.

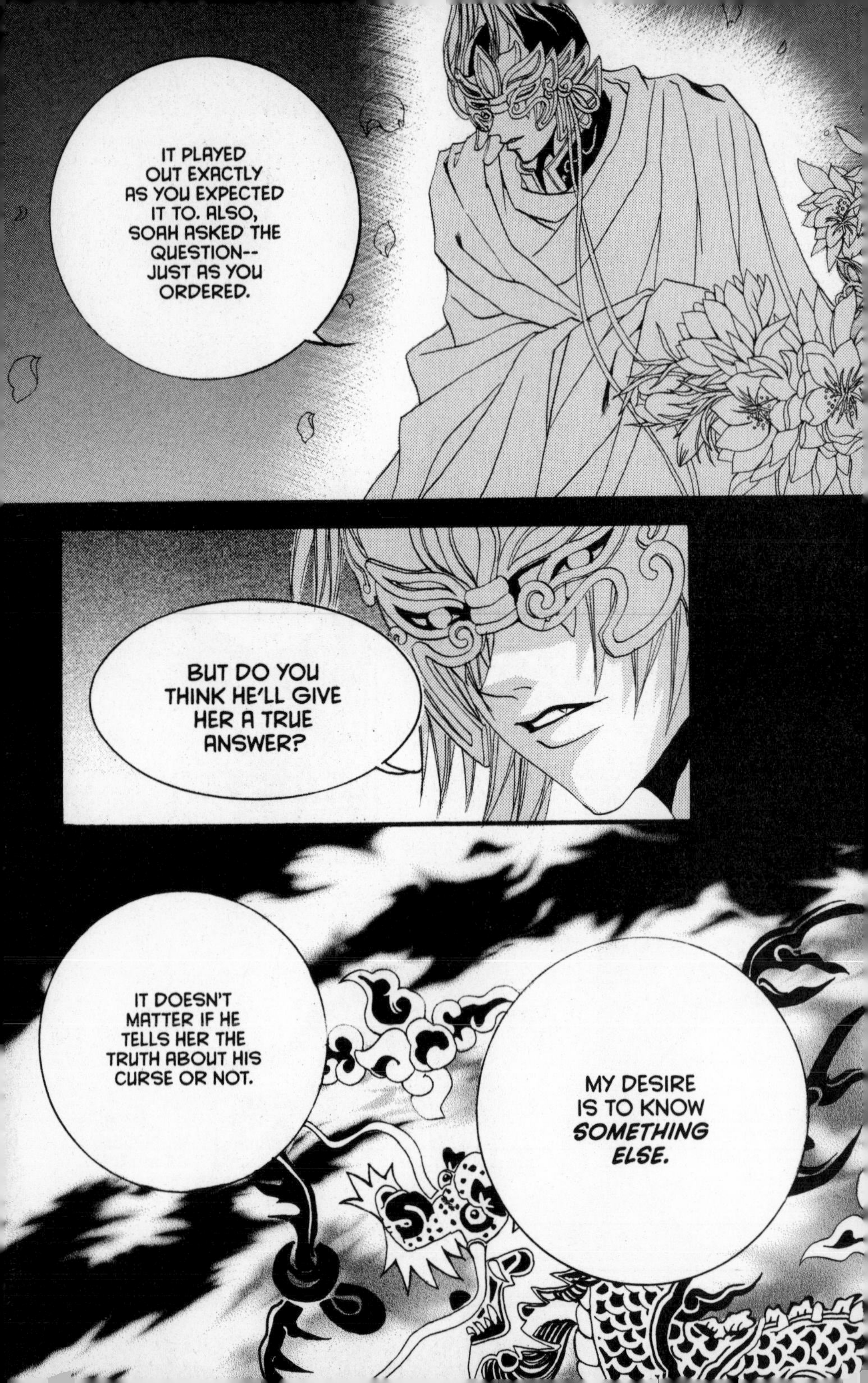
IT PLAYED OUT EXACTLY AS YOU EXPECTED IT TO. ALSO, SOAH ASKED THE QUESTION-- JUST AS YOU ORDERED.
BUT DO YOU THINK HE'LL GIVE HER A TRUE ANSWER?
IT DOESN'T MATTER IF HE TELLS HER THE TRUTH ABOUT HIS CURSE OR NOT.
MY DESIRE IS TO KNOW *SOMETHING ELSE.*

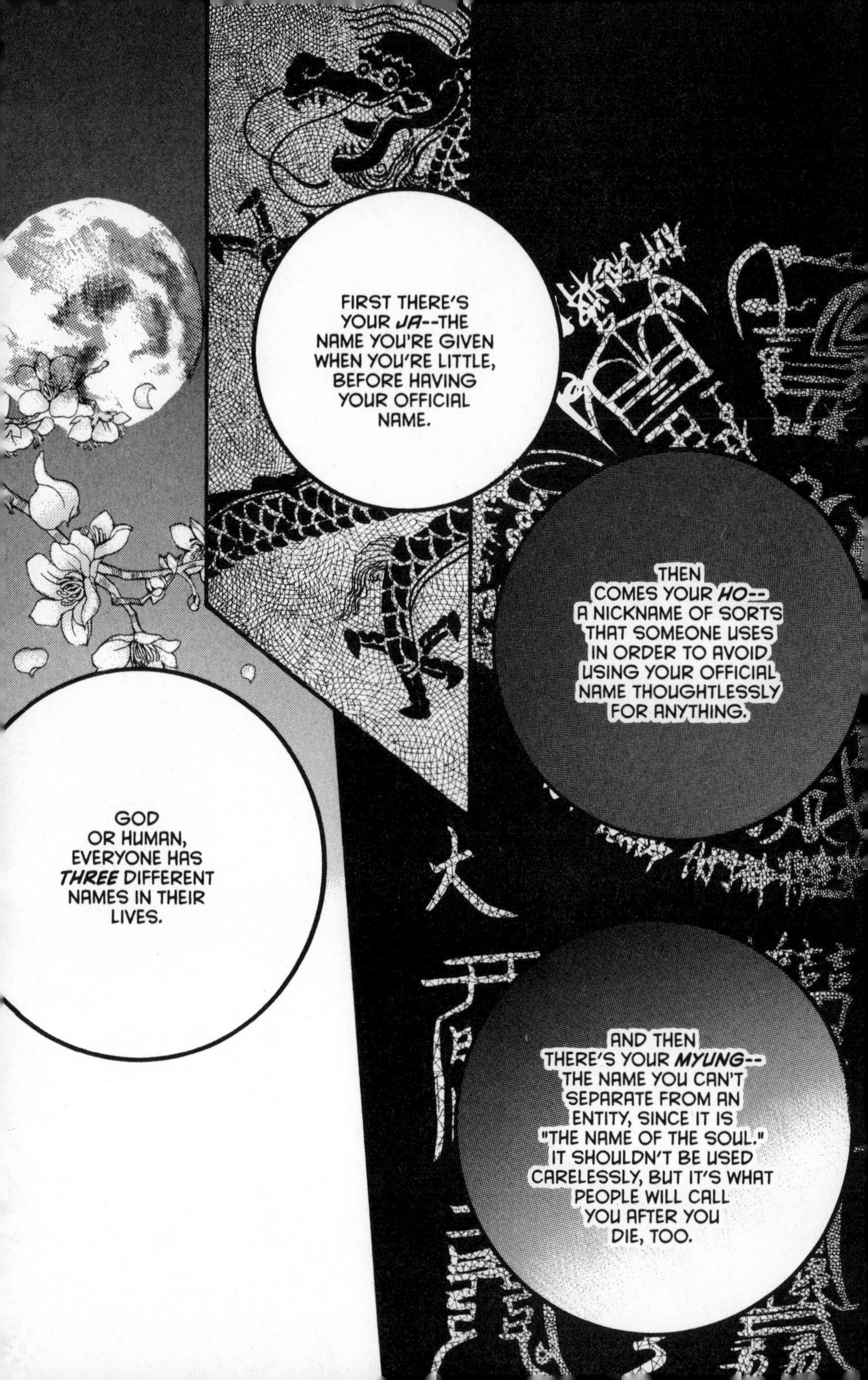
FIRST THERE'S YOUR *JA*--THE NAME YOU'RE GIVEN WHEN YOU'RE LITTLE, BEFORE HAVING YOUR OFFICIAL NAME.
GOD OR HUMAN, EVERYONE HAS *THREE* DIFFERENT NAMES IN THEIR LIVES.
THEN COMES YOUR *HO*-- A NICKNAME OF SORTS THAT SOMEONE USES IN ORDER TO AVOID USING YOUR OFFICIAL NAME THOUGHTLESSLY FOR ANYTHING.
AND THEN THERE'S YOUR *MYUNG*-- THE NAME YOU CAN'T SEPARATE FROM AN ENTITY, SINCE IT IS "THE NAME OF THE SOUL." IT SHOULDN'T BE USED CARELESSLY, BUT IT'S WHAT PEOPLE WILL CALL YOU AFTER YOU DIE, TOO.

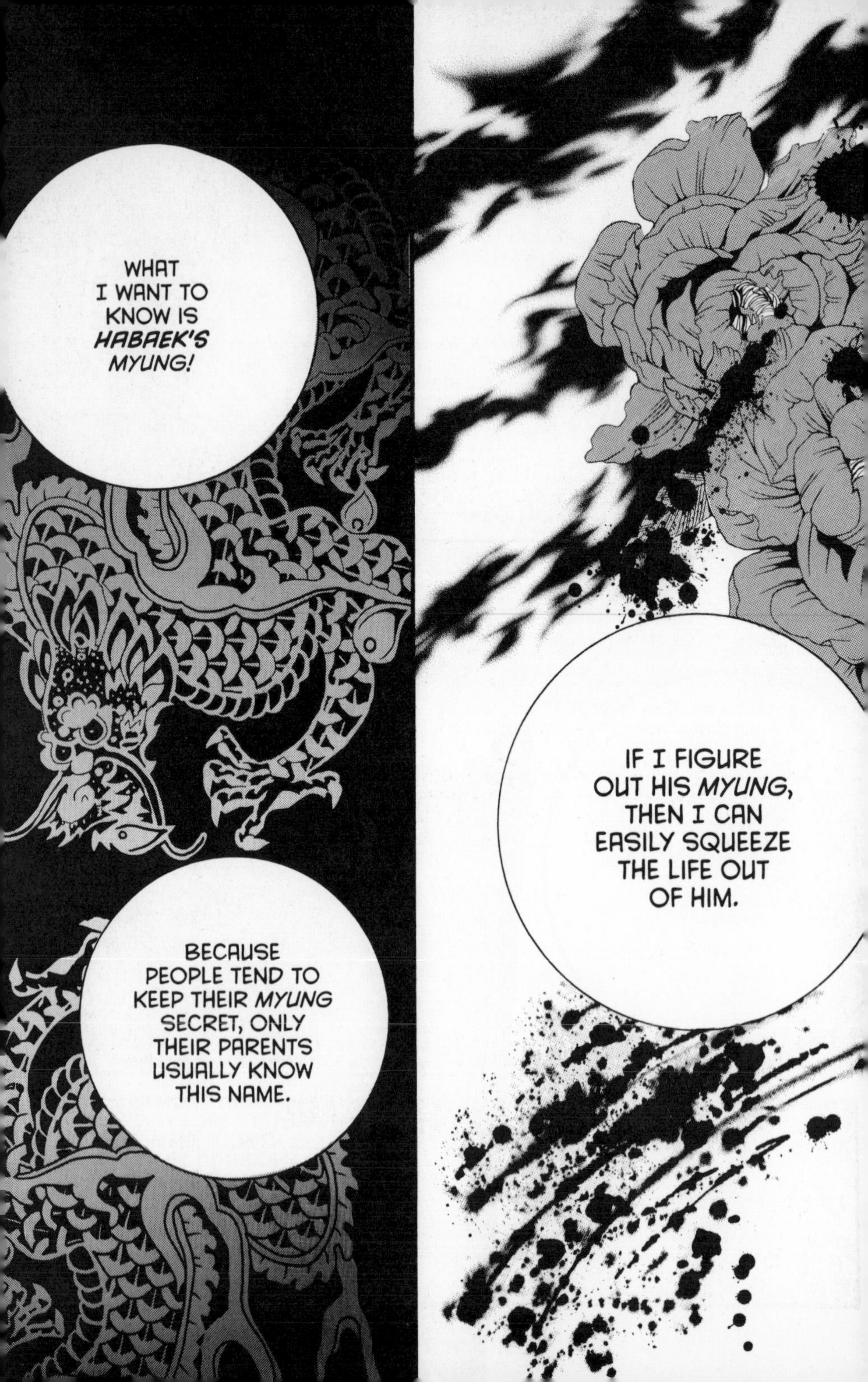
WHAT I WANT TO KNOW IS *HABAEK'S MYUNG!*
BECAUSE PEOPLE TEND TO KEEP THEIR *MYUNG* SECRET, ONLY THEIR PARENTS USUALLY KNOW THIS NAME.
IF I FIGURE OUT HIS *MYUNG*, THEN I CAN EASILY SQUEEZE THE LIFE OUT OF HIM.

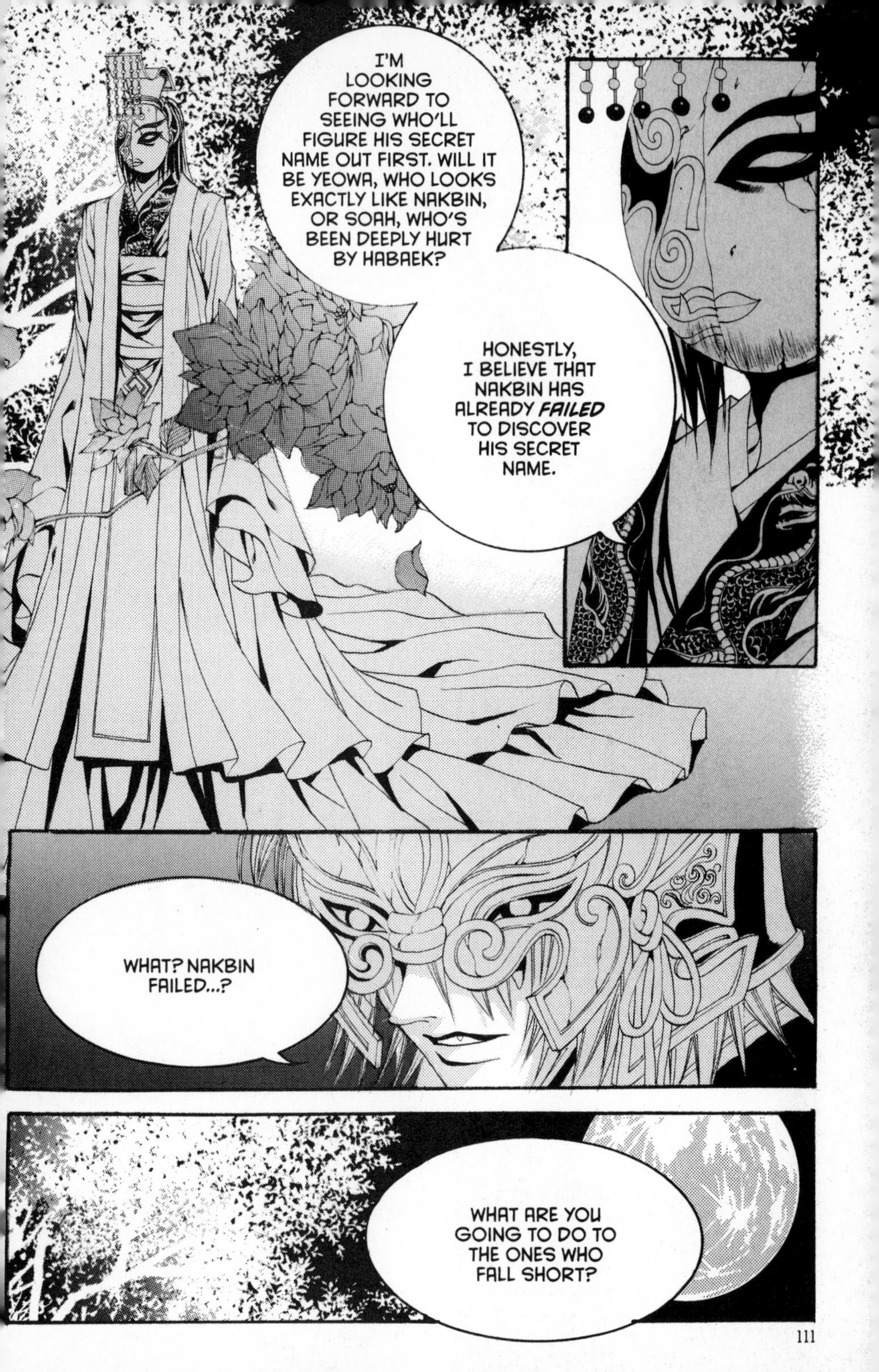
I'M LOOKING FORWARD TO SEEING WHO'LL FIGURE HIS SECRET NAME OUT FIRST. WILL IT BE YEOWA, WHO LOOKS EXACTLY LIKE NAKBIN, OR SOAH, WHO'S BEEN DEEPLY HURT BY HABAEK?
HONESTLY, I BELIEVE THAT NAKBIN HAS ALREADY *FAILED* TO DISCOVER HIS SECRET NAME.
WHAT? NAKBIN FAILED...?
WHAT ARE YOU GOING TO DO TO THE ONES WHO FALL SHORT?

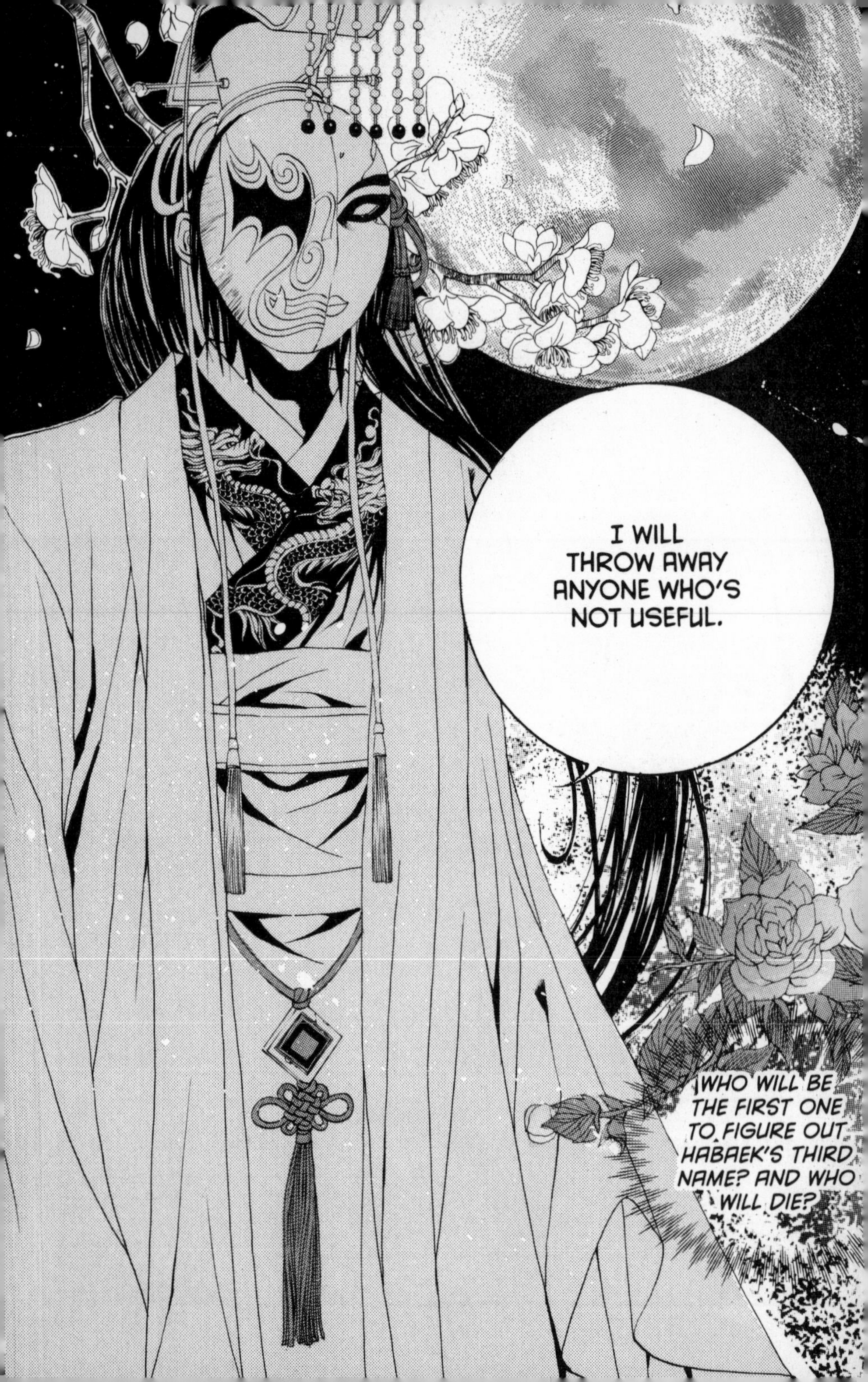
I WILL THROW AWAY ANYONE WHO'S NOT USEFUL.
WHO WILL BE THE FIRST ONE TO FIGURE OUT HABAEK'S THIRD NAME? AND WHO WILL DIE?

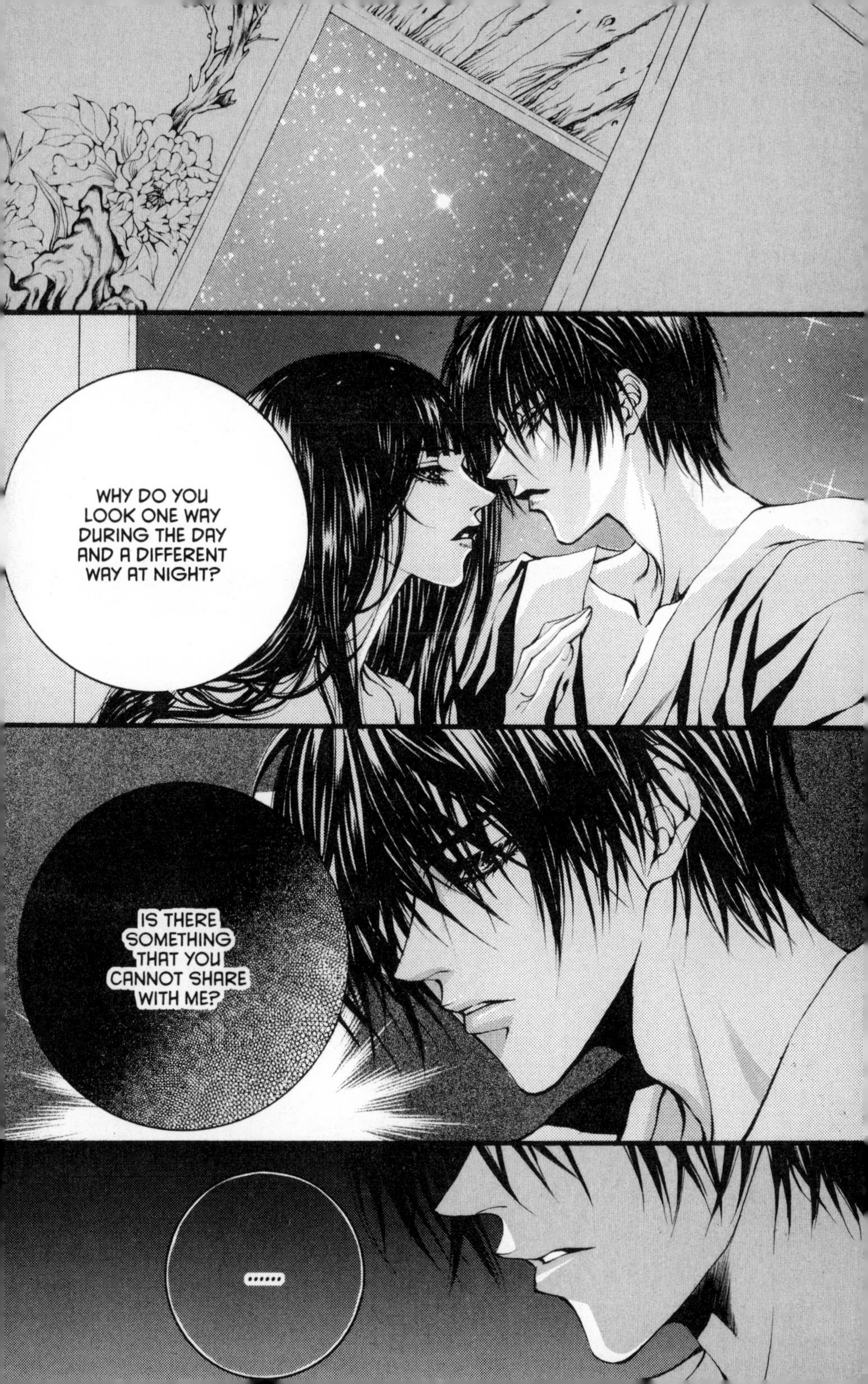
WHY DO YOU LOOK ONE WAY DURING THE DAY AND A DIFFERENT WAY AT NIGHT?
IS THERE SOMETHING THAT YOU CANNOT SHARE WITH ME?
......

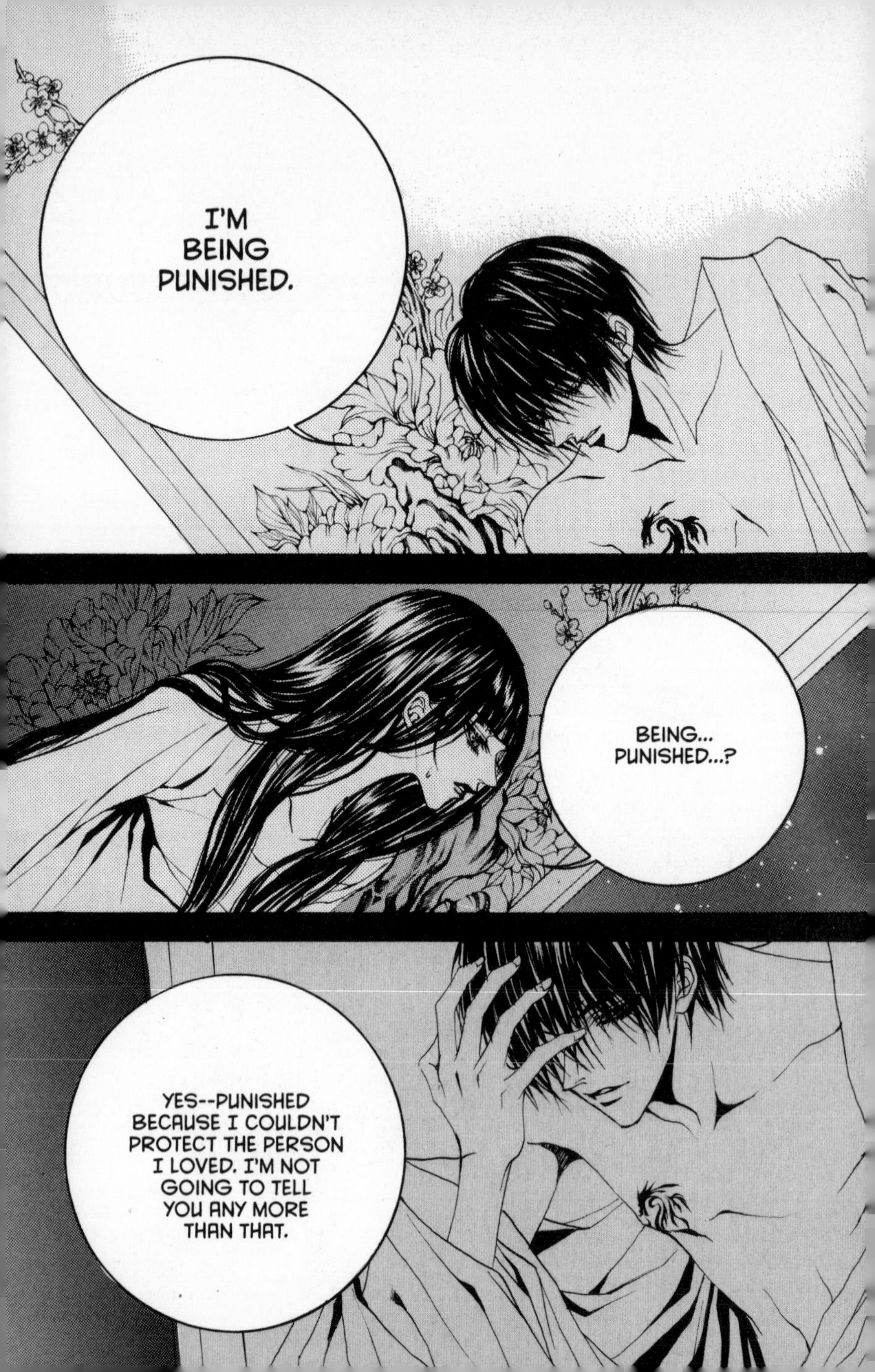
I'M BEING PUNISHED.
BEING... PUNISHED...?
YES--PUNISHED BECAUSE I COULDN'T PROTECT THE PERSON I LOVED. I'M NOT GOING TO TELL YOU ANY MORE THAN THAT.

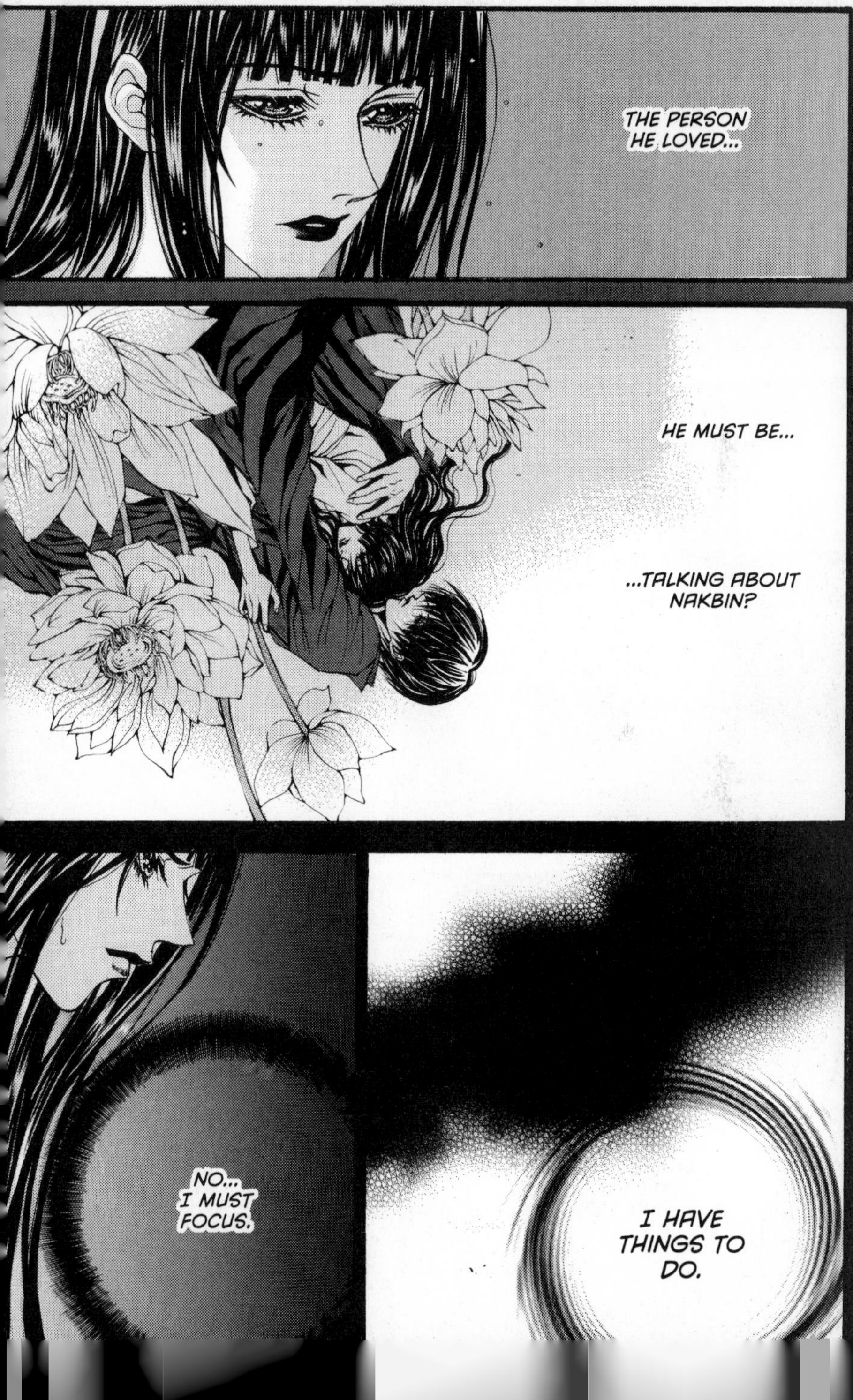
THE PERSON HE LOVED...
HE MUST BE...
...TALKING ABOUT NAKBIN?
NO... I MUST FOCUS.
I HAVE THINGS TO DO.

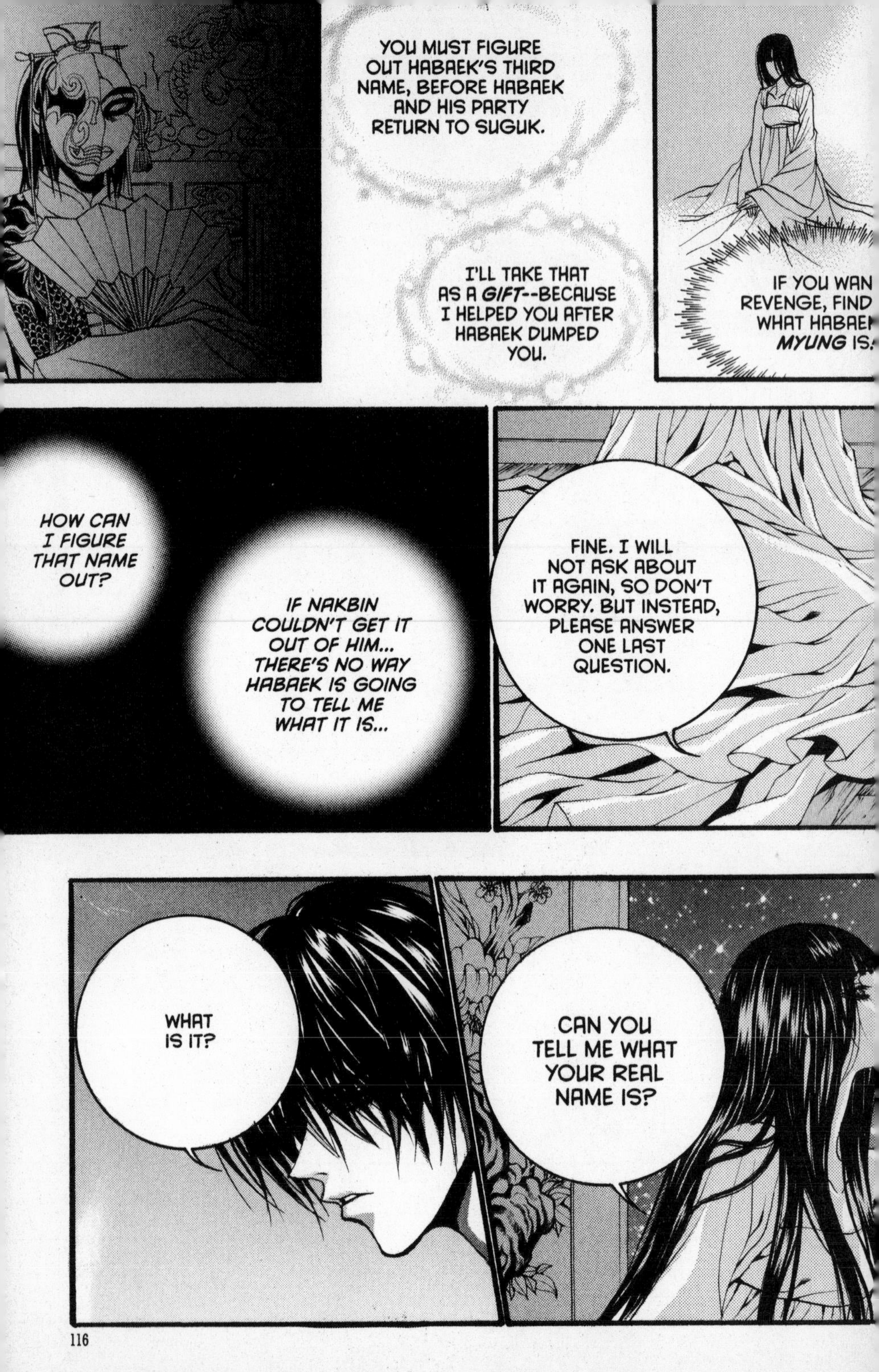
YOU MUST FIGURE OUT HABAEK'S THIRD NAME, BEFORE HABAEK AND HIS PARTY RETURN TO SUGUK.
I'LL TAKE THAT AS A *GIFT*--BECAUSE I HELPED YOU AFTER HABAEK DUMPED YOU.
IF YOU WAN REVENGE, FIND WHAT HABAE *MYUNG* IS.
HOW CAN I FIGURE THAT NAME OUT?
IF NAKBIN COULDN'T GET IT OUT OF HIM... THERE'S NO WAY HABAEK IS GOING TO TELL ME WHAT IT IS...
FINE. I WILL NOT ASK ABOUT IT AGAIN, SO DON'T WORRY. BUT INSTEAD, PLEASE ANSWER ONE LAST QUESTION.
WHAT IS IT?
CAN YOU TELL ME WHAT YOUR REAL NAME IS?

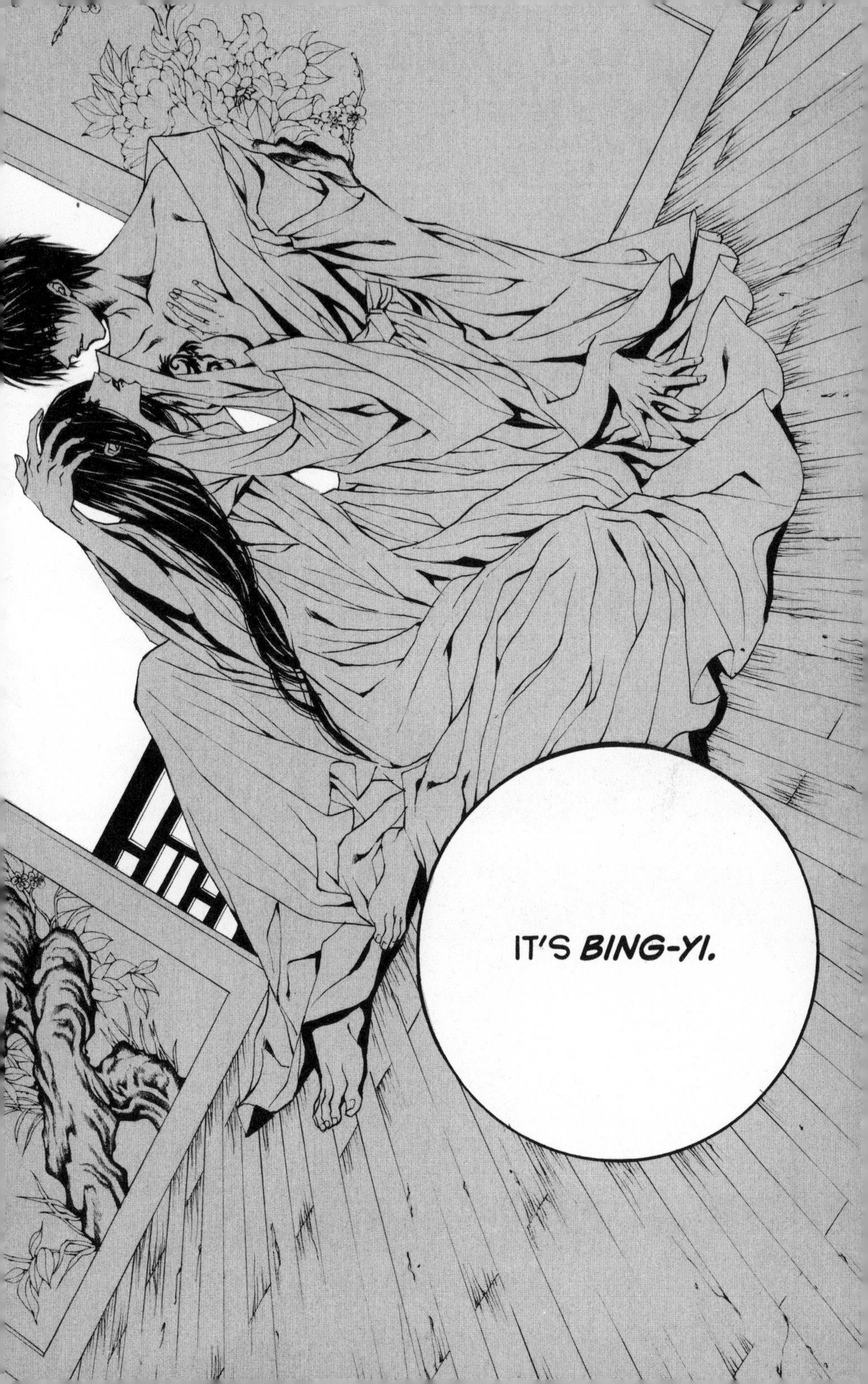
IT'S *BING-YI.*

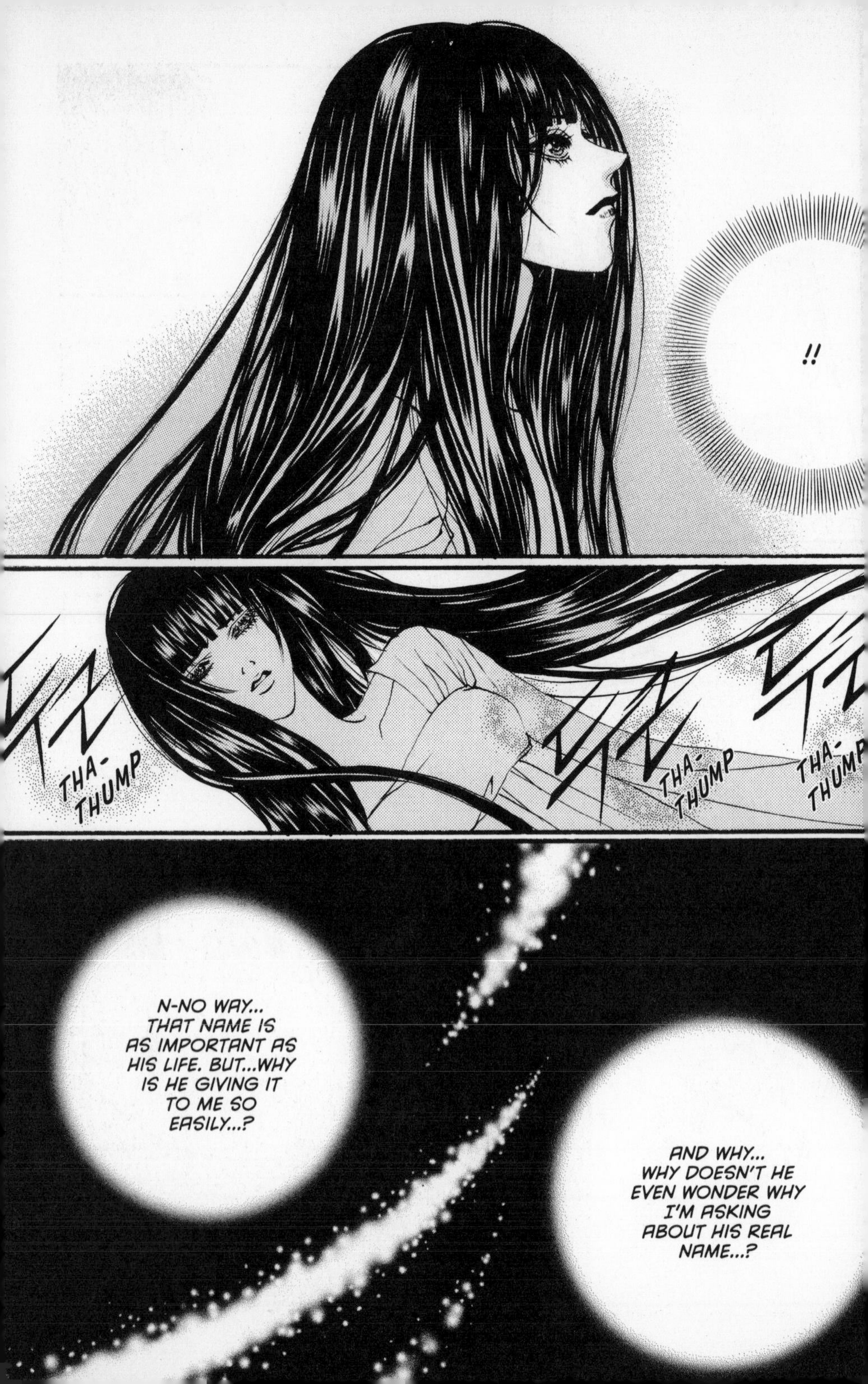
!!
THA-THUMP
THA-THUMP
THA-THUMP
N-NO WAY... THAT NAME IS AS IMPORTANT AS HIS LIFE. BUT...WHY IS HE GIVING IT TO ME SO EASILY...?
AND WHY... WHY DOESN'T HE EVEN WONDER WHY I'M ASKING ABOUT HIS REAL NAME...?

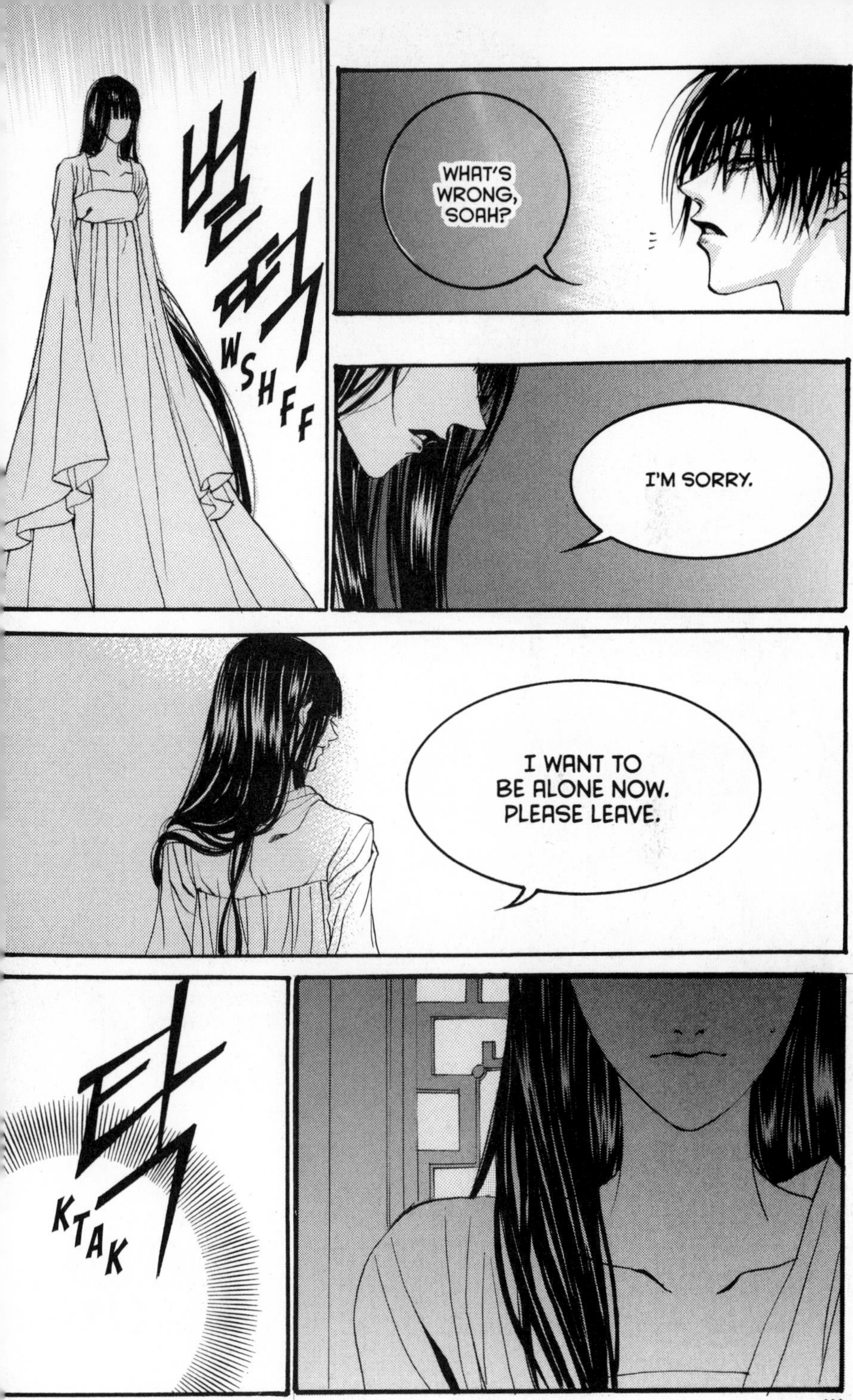
벌떡
WSHFF
WHAT'S WRONG, SOAH?
I'M SORRY.
I WANT TO BE ALONE NOW. PLEASE LEAVE.
턱
KTAK

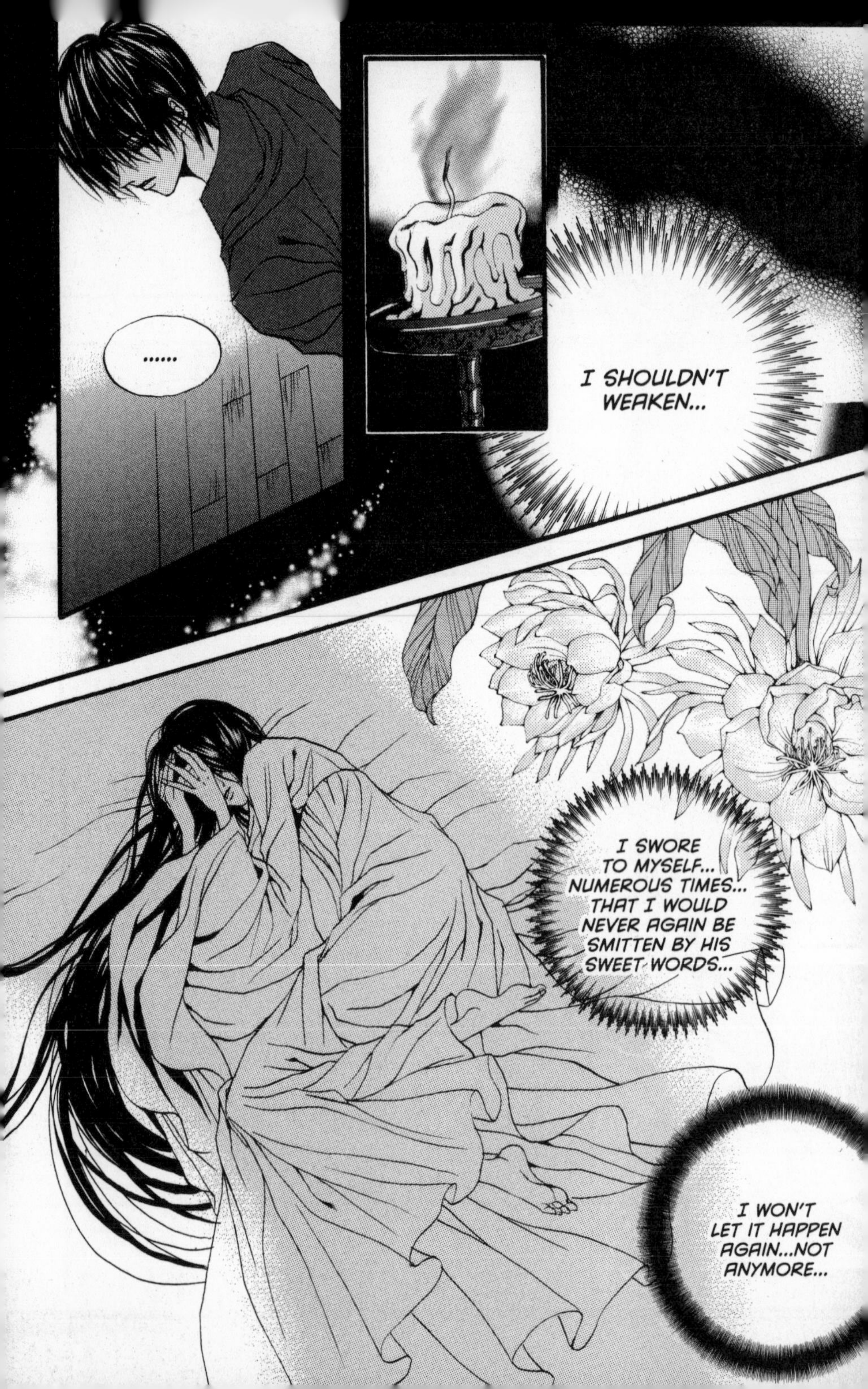
......
I SHOULDN'T WEAKEN...
I SWORE TO MYSELF... NUMEROUS TIMES... THAT I WOULD NEVER AGAIN BE SMITTEN BY HIS SWEET WORDS...
I WON'T LET IT HAPPEN AGAIN...NOT ANYMORE...

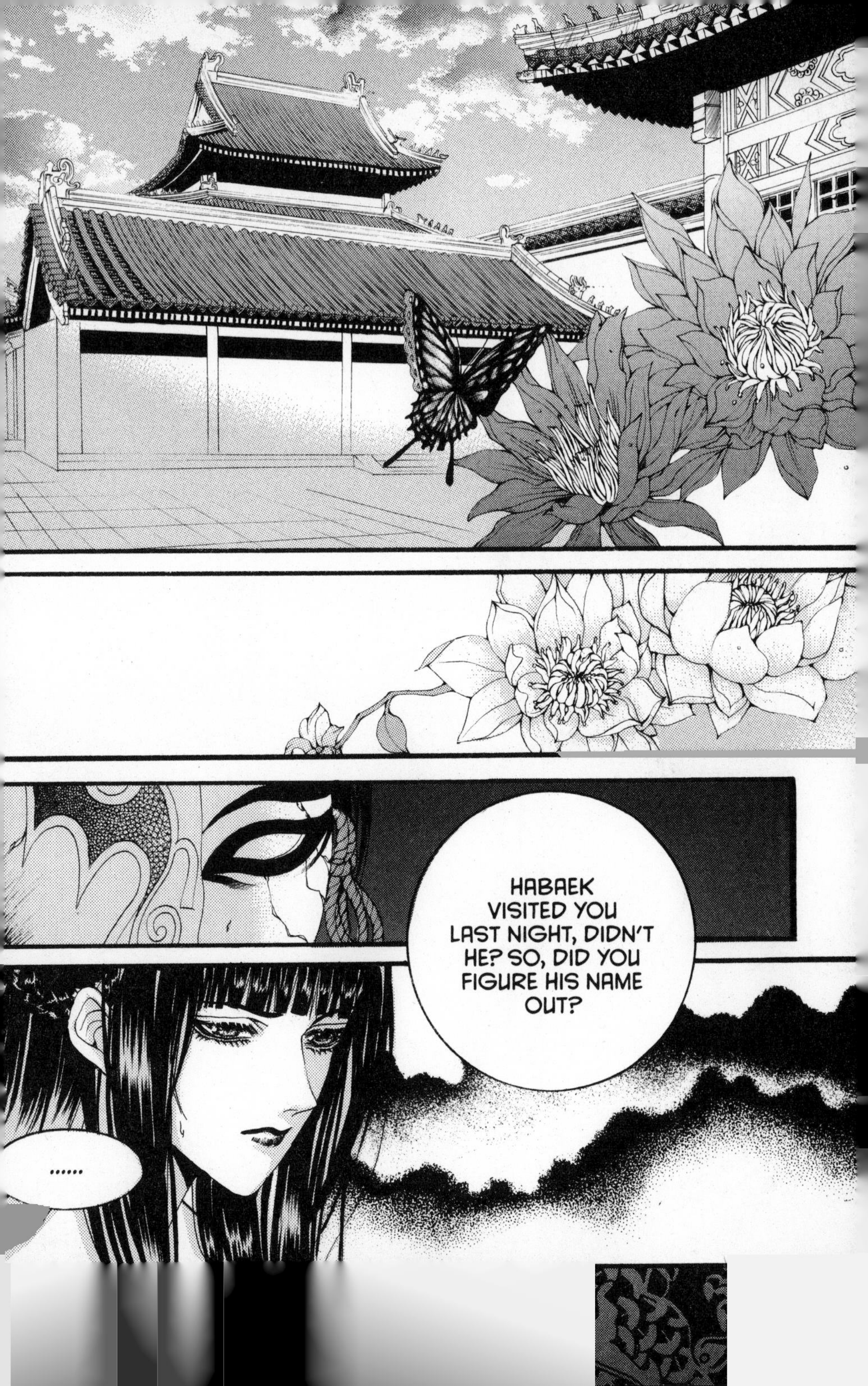

HABAEK VISITED YOU LAST NIGHT, DIDN'T HE? SO, DID YOU FIGURE HIS NAME OUT?
......

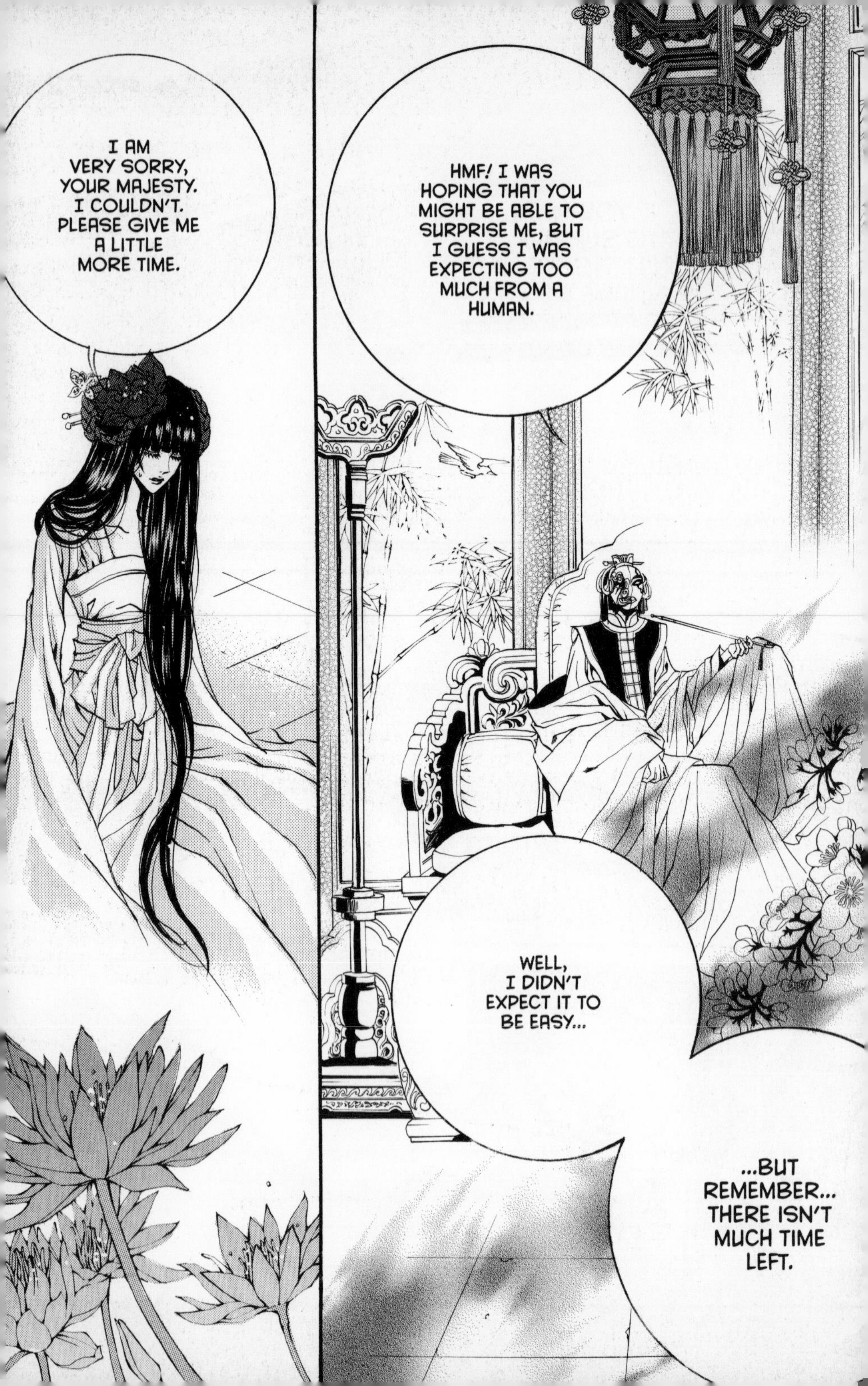
I AM VERY SORRY, YOUR MAJESTY. I COULDN'T. PLEASE GIVE ME A LITTLE MORE TIME.
HMF! I WAS HOPING THAT YOU MIGHT BE ABLE TO SURPRISE ME, BUT I GUESS I WAS EXPECTING TOO MUCH FROM A HUMAN.
WELL, I DIDN'T EXPECT IT TO BE EASY...
...BUT REMEMBER... THERE ISN'T MUCH TIME LEFT.

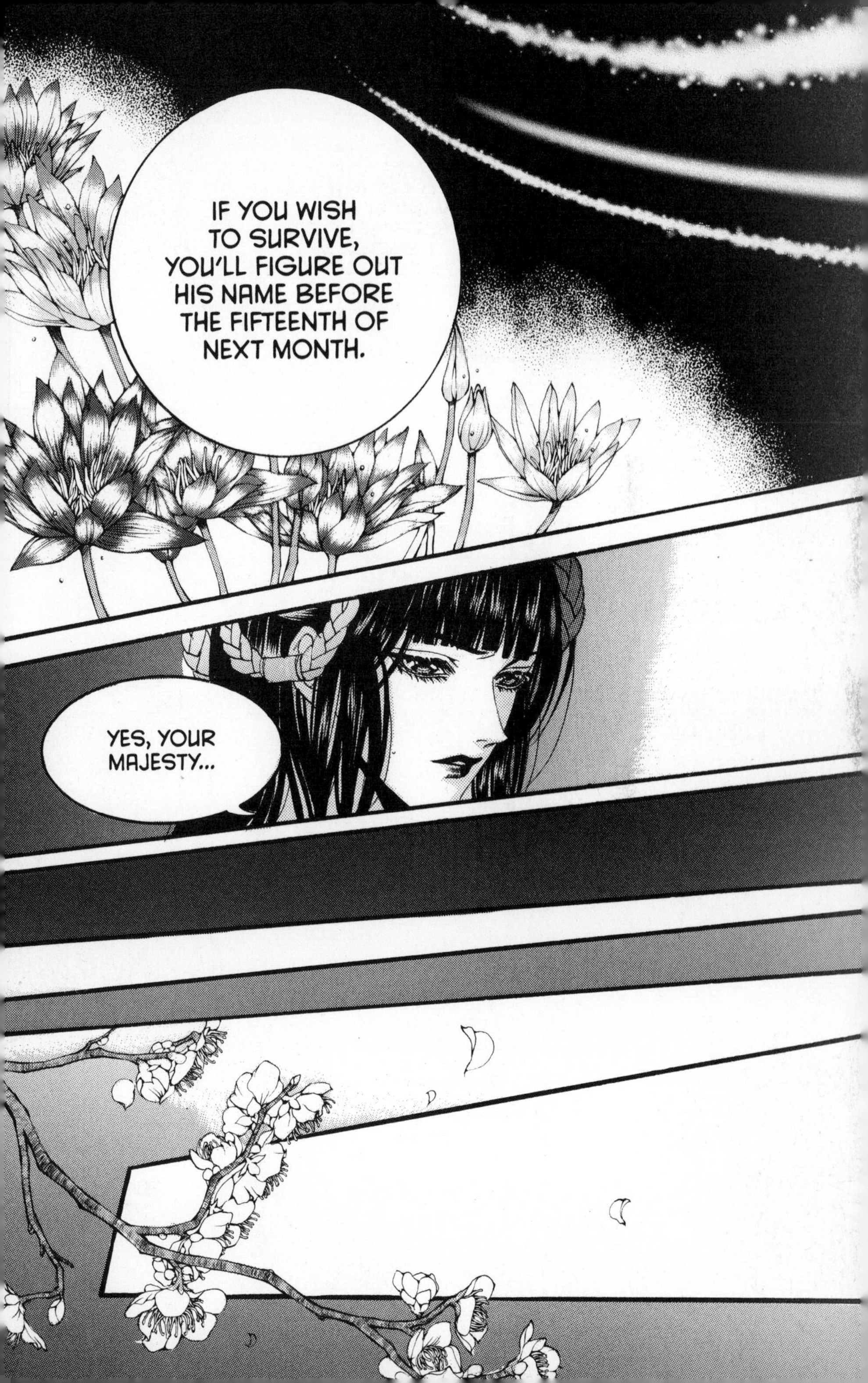
IF YOU WISH TO SURVIVE, YOU'LL FIGURE OUT HIS NAME BEFORE THE FIFTEENTH OF NEXT MONTH.
YES, YOUR MAJESTY...

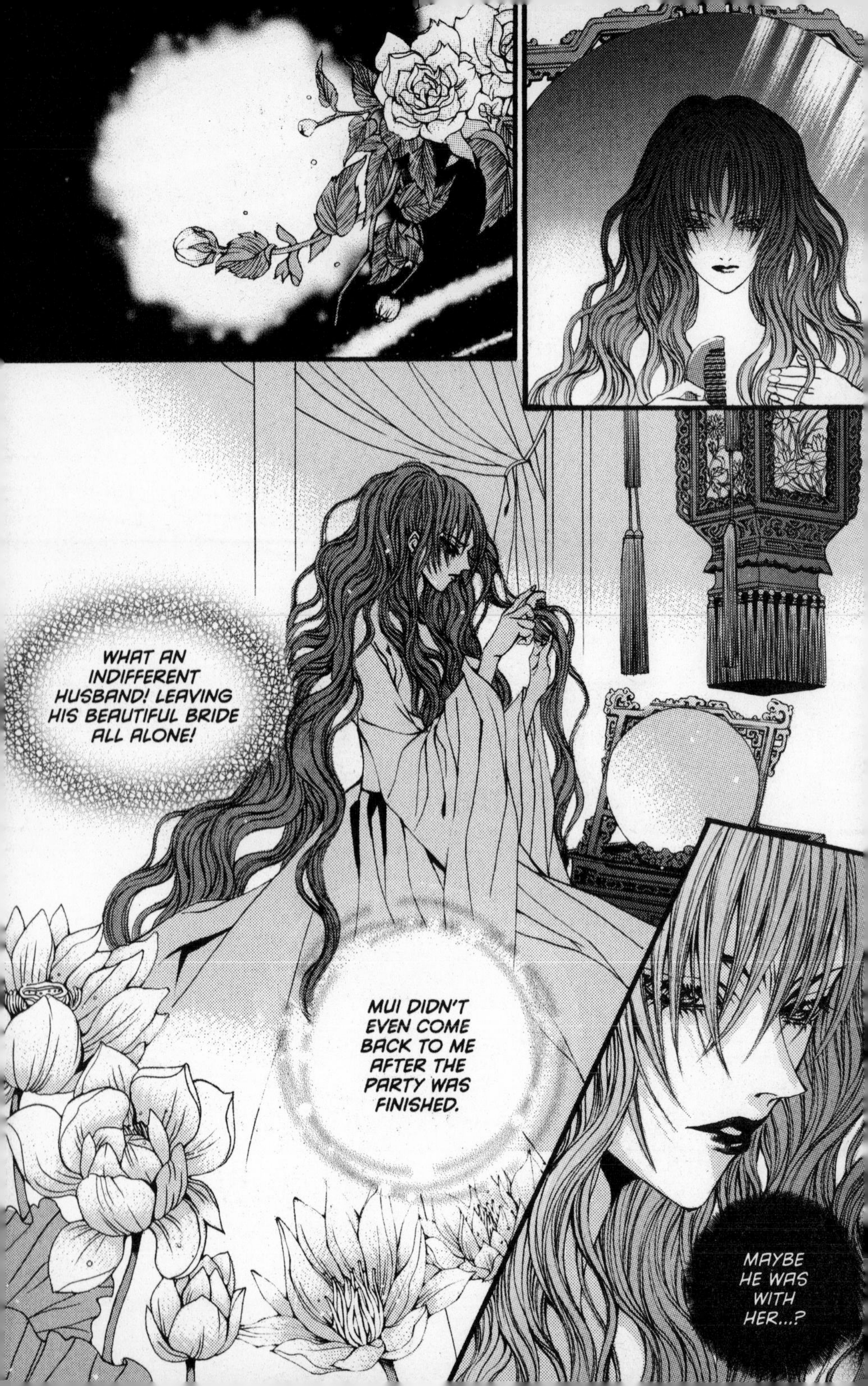
WHAT AN INDIFFERENT HUSBAND! LEAVING HIS BEAUTIFUL BRIDE ALL ALONE!
MUI DIDN'T EVEN COME BACK TO ME AFTER THE PARTY WAS FINISHED.
MAYBE HE WAS WITH HER...?

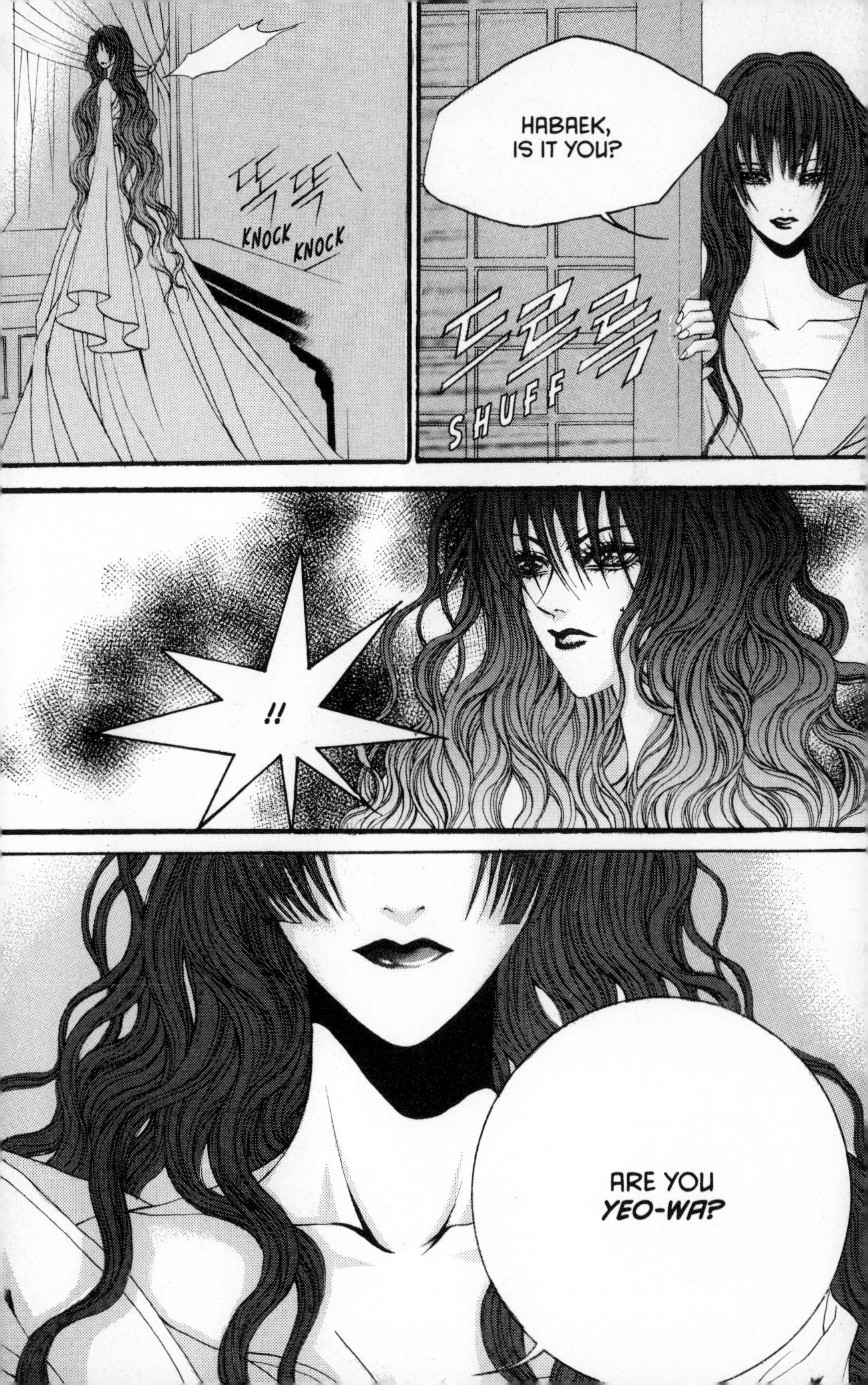
똑똑
KNOCK KNOCK
HABAEK, IS IT YOU?
드르륵
SHUFF
!!
ARE YOU *YEO-WA?*

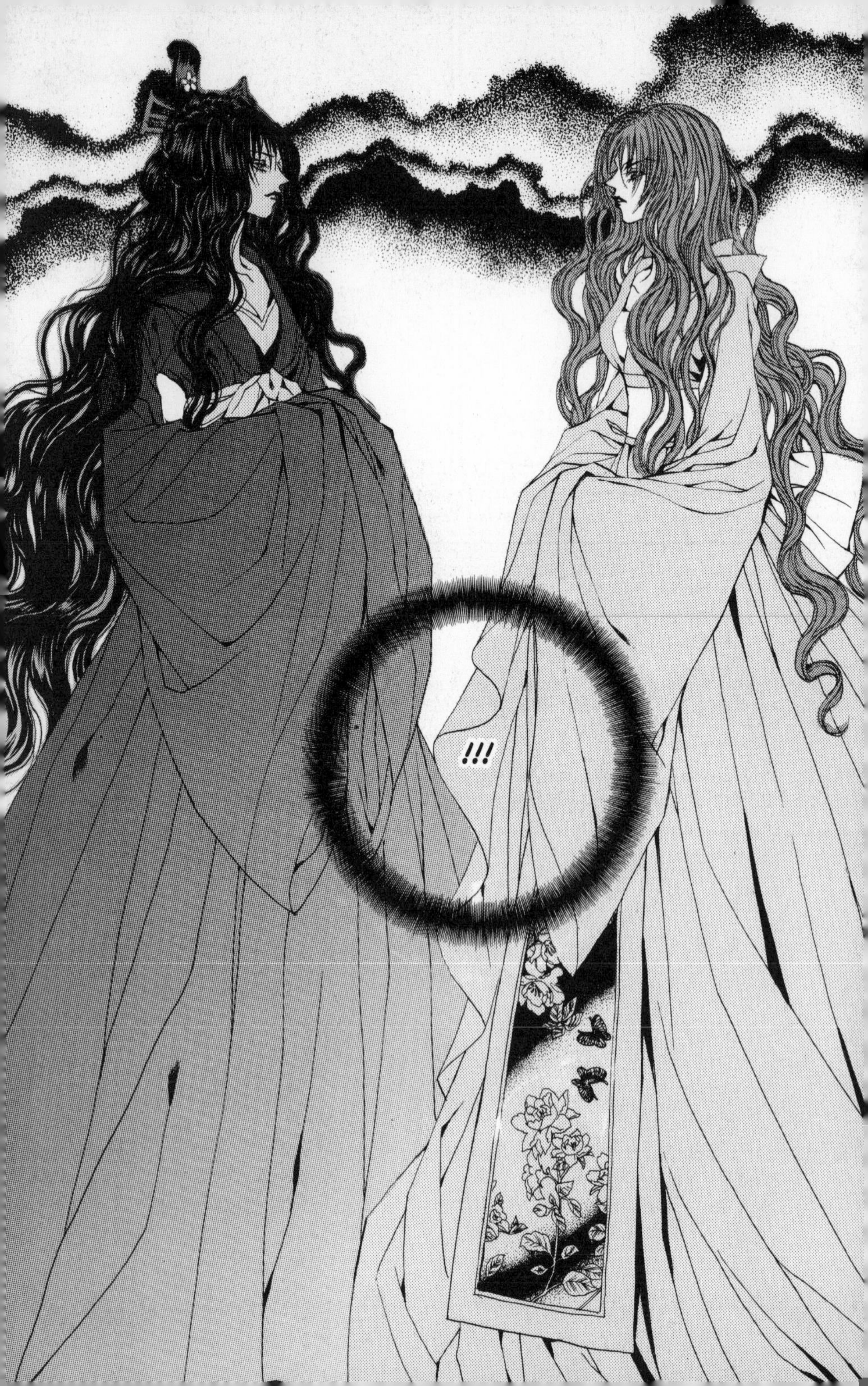
!!!

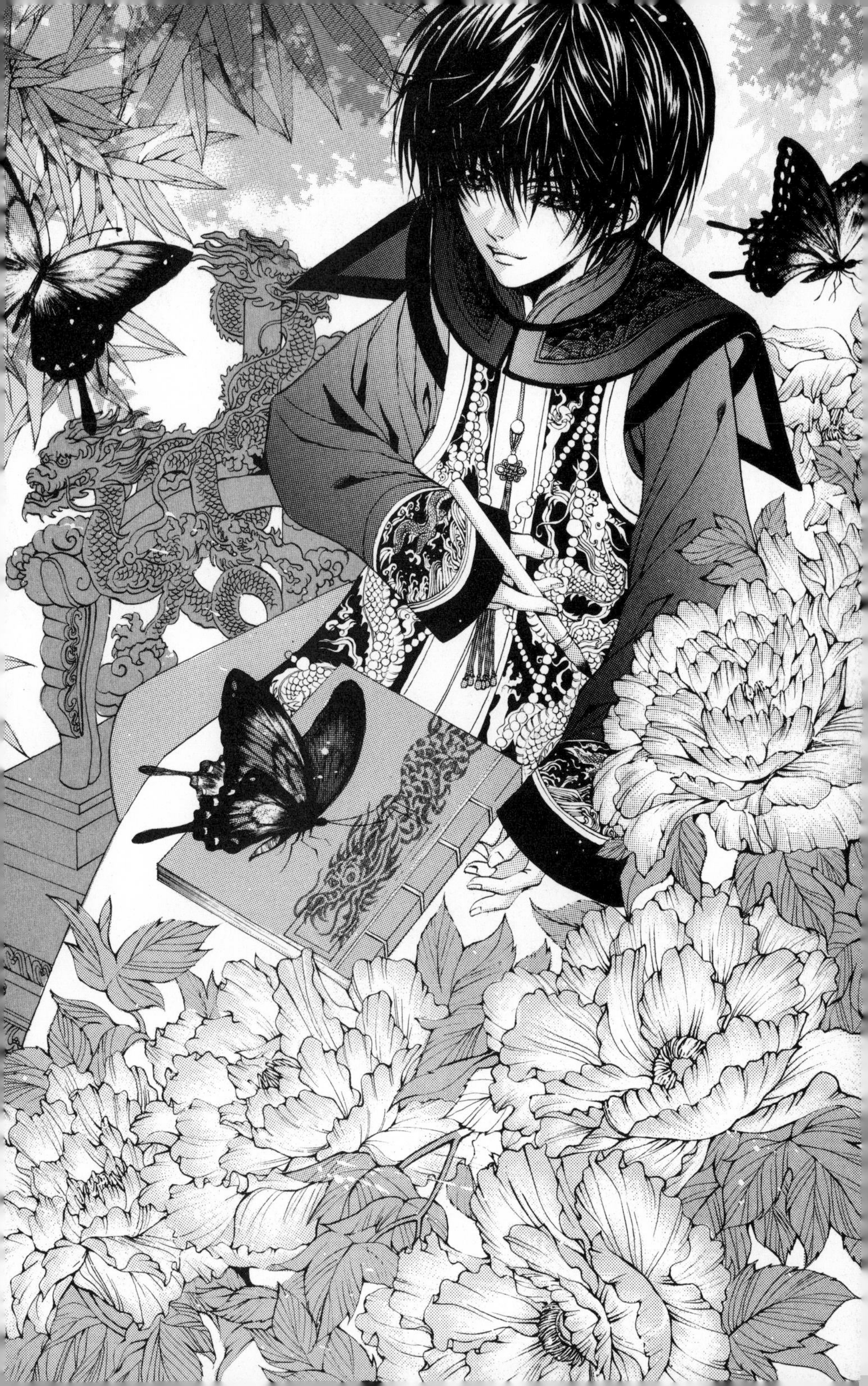

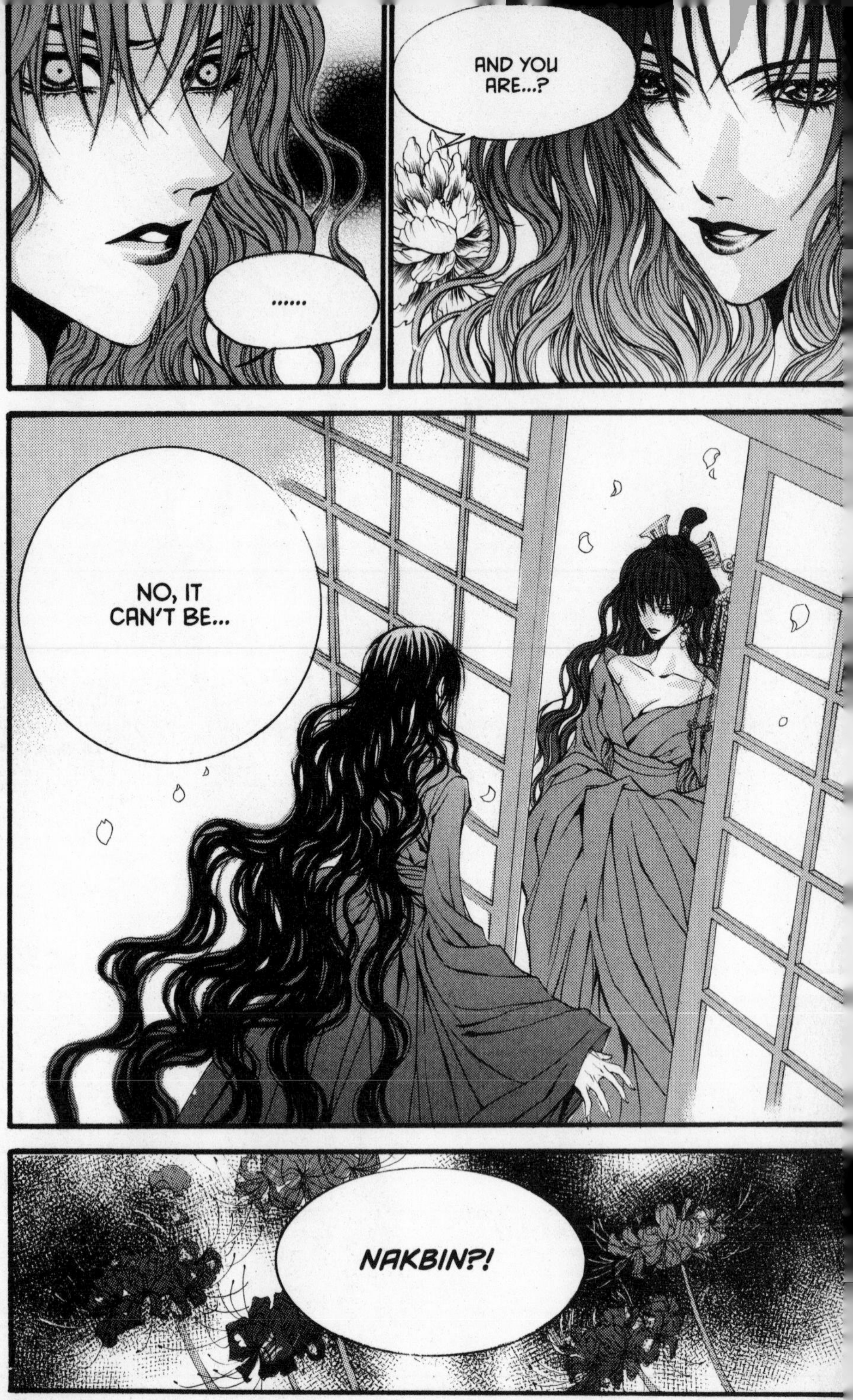
AND YOU ARE...?
......
NO, IT CAN'T BE...
NAKBIN?!

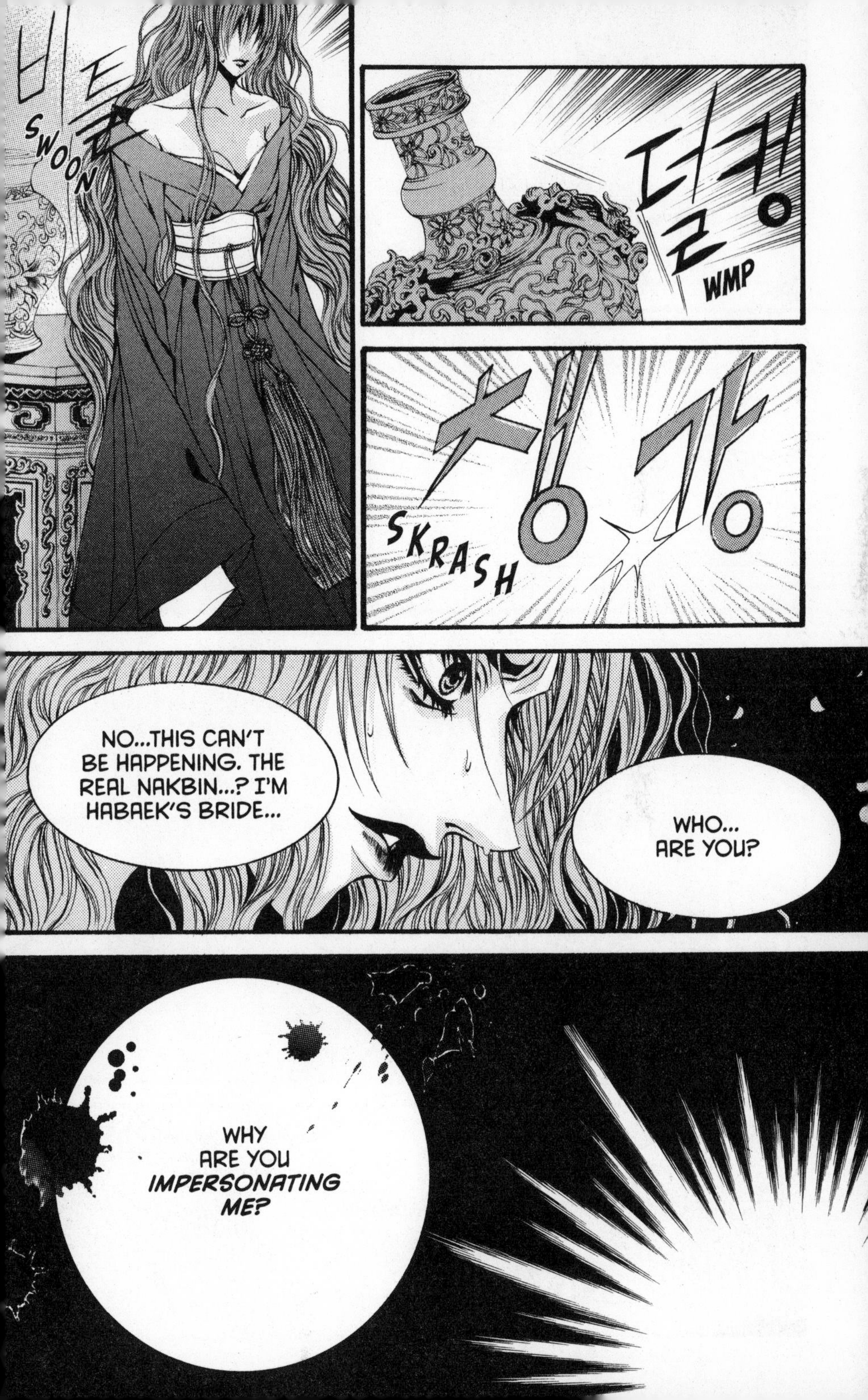
SWOON
WMP
SKRASH
NO...THIS CAN'T BE HAPPENING. THE REAL NAKBIN...? I'M HABAEK'S BRIDE...
WHO... ARE YOU?
WHY ARE YOU *IMPERSONATING* *ME?*

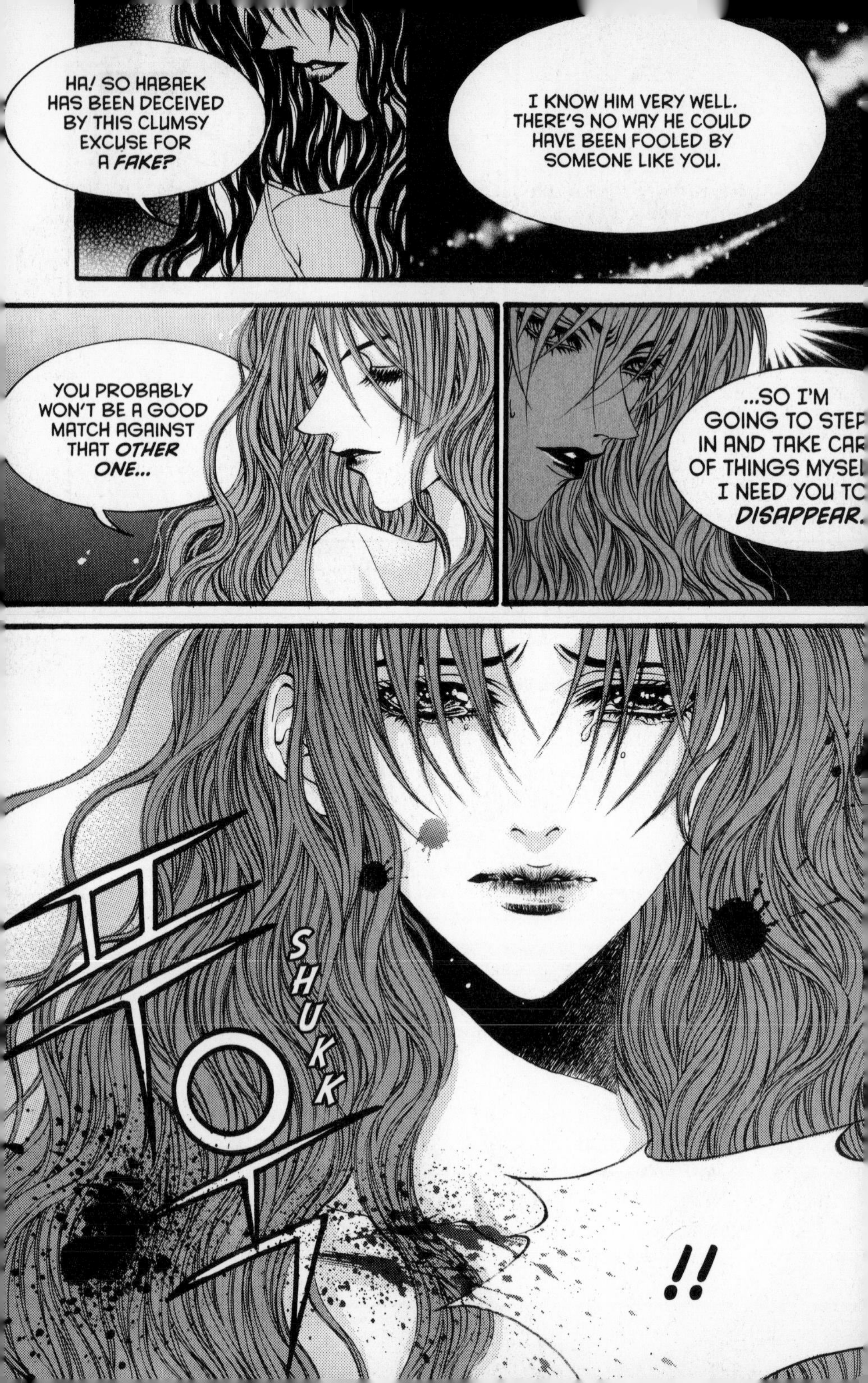
HA! SO HABAEK HAS BEEN DECEIVED BY THIS CLUMSY EXCUSE FOR A *FAKE?*
I KNOW HIM VERY WELL. THERE'S NO WAY HE COULD HAVE BEEN FOOLED BY SOMEONE LIKE YOU.
YOU PROBABLY WON'T BE A GOOD MATCH AGAINST THAT *OTHER ONE...*
...SO I'M GOING TO STE IN AND TAKE CAR OF THINGS MYSEL I NEED YOU T *DISAPPEAR.*
SHUKK
!!

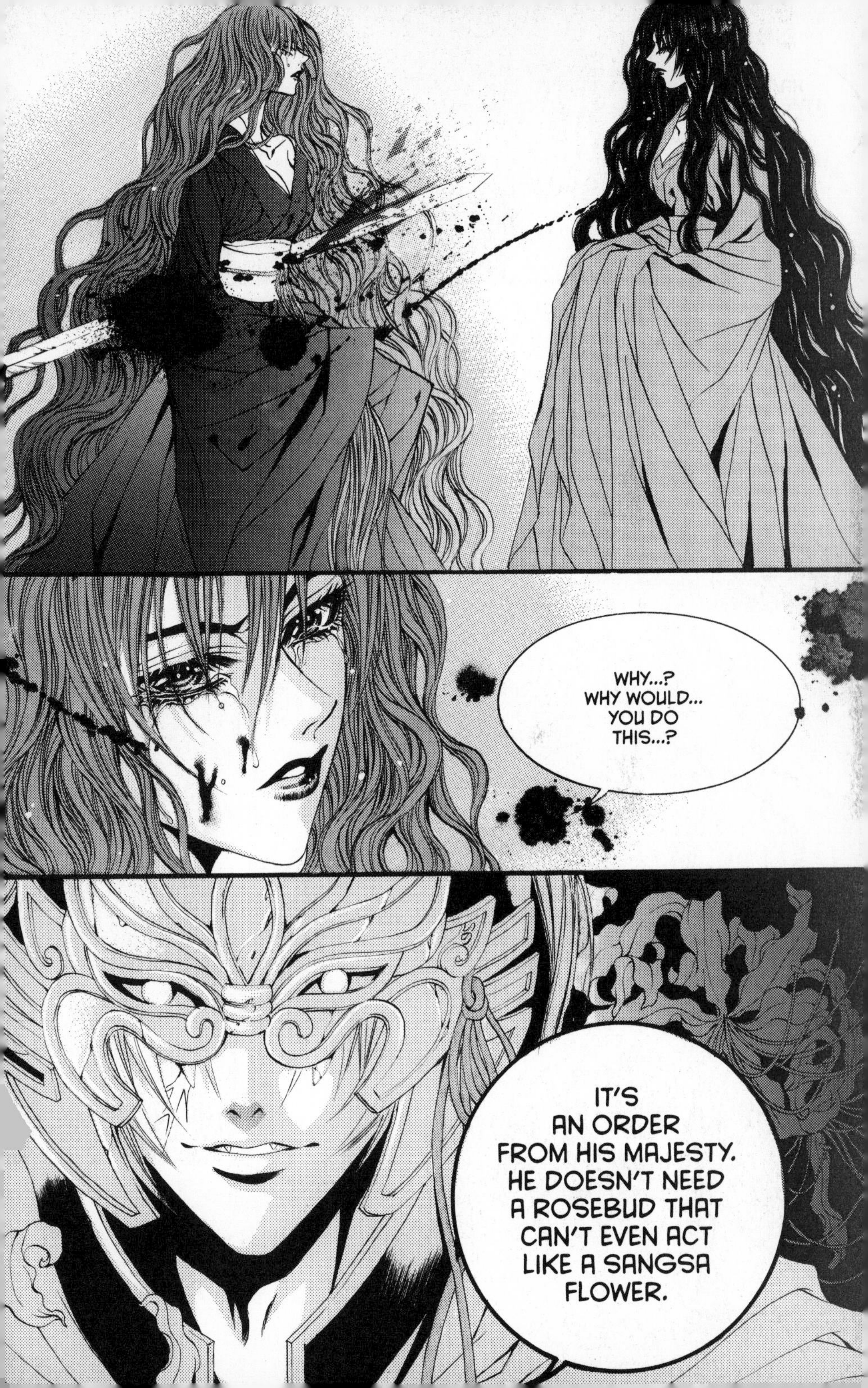
WHY...? WHY WOULD... YOU DO THIS...?
IT'S AN ORDER FROM HIS MAJESTY. HE DOESN'T NEED A ROSEBUD THAT CAN'T EVEN ACT LIKE A SANGSA FLOWER.

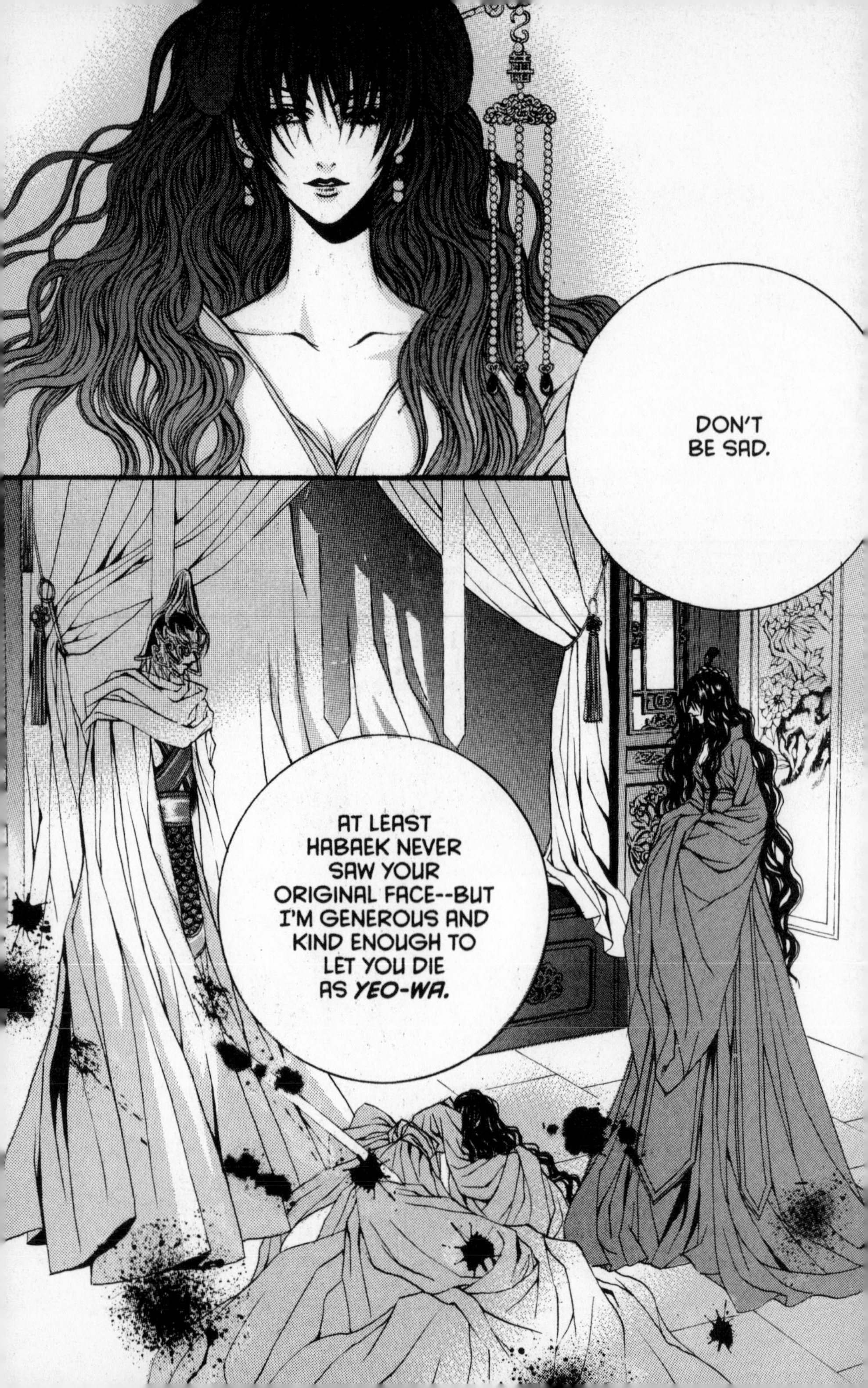
DON'T BE SAD.
AT LEAST HABAEK NEVER SAW YOUR ORIGINAL FACE--BUT I'M GENEROUS AND KIND ENOUGH TO LET YOU DIE AS *YEO-WA.*

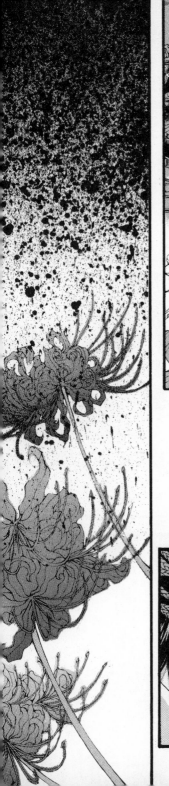

HABAEK--

WHERE WERE YOU YESTERDAY?

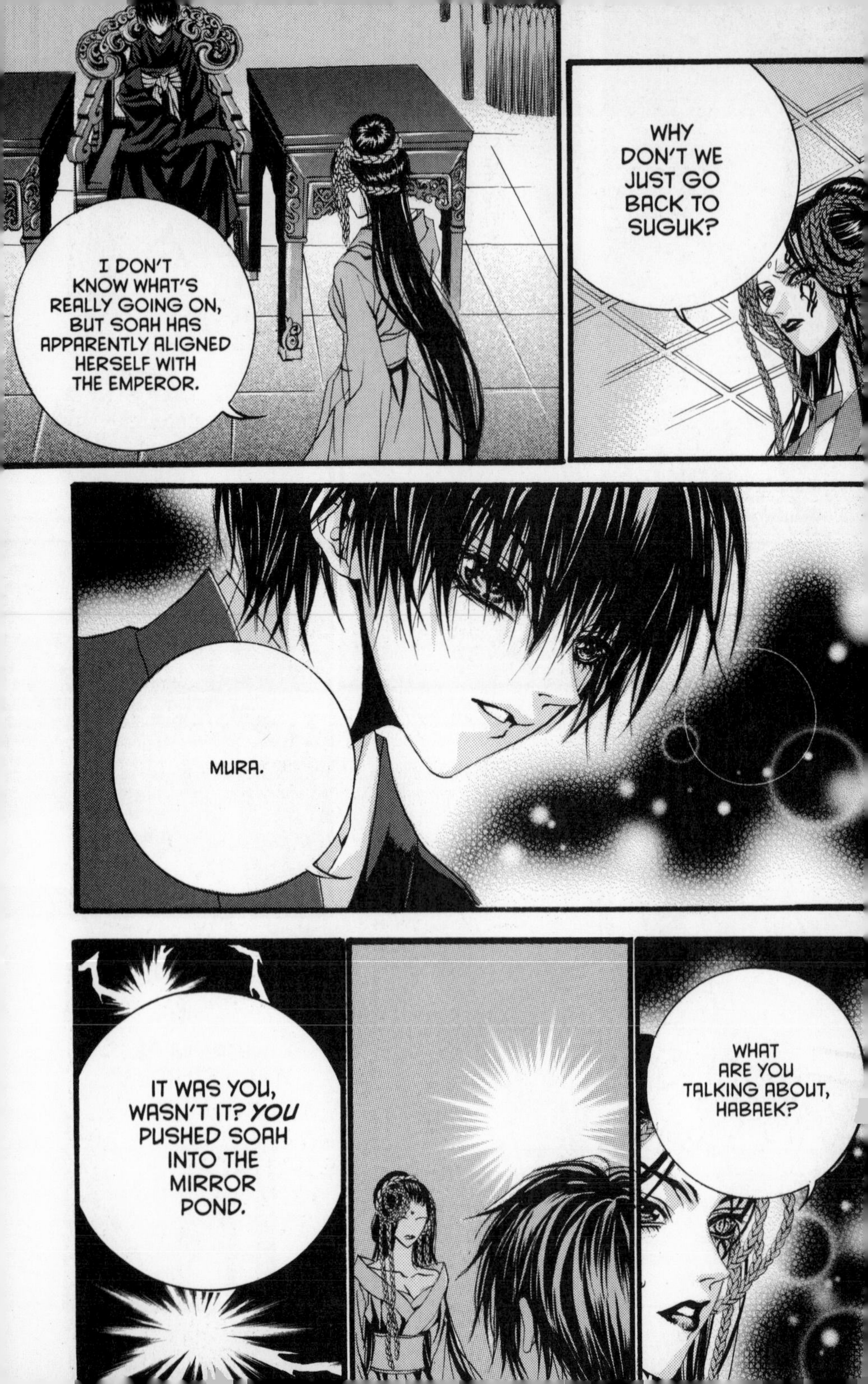
I DON'T KNOW WHAT'S REALLY GOING ON, BUT SOAH HAS APPARENTLY ALIGNED HERSELF WITH THE EMPEROR.
WHY DON'T WE JUST GO BACK TO SUGUK?
MURA.
IT WAS YOU, WASN'T IT? *YOU* PUSHED SOAH INTO THE MIRROR POND.
WHAT ARE YOU TALKING ABOUT, HABAEK?

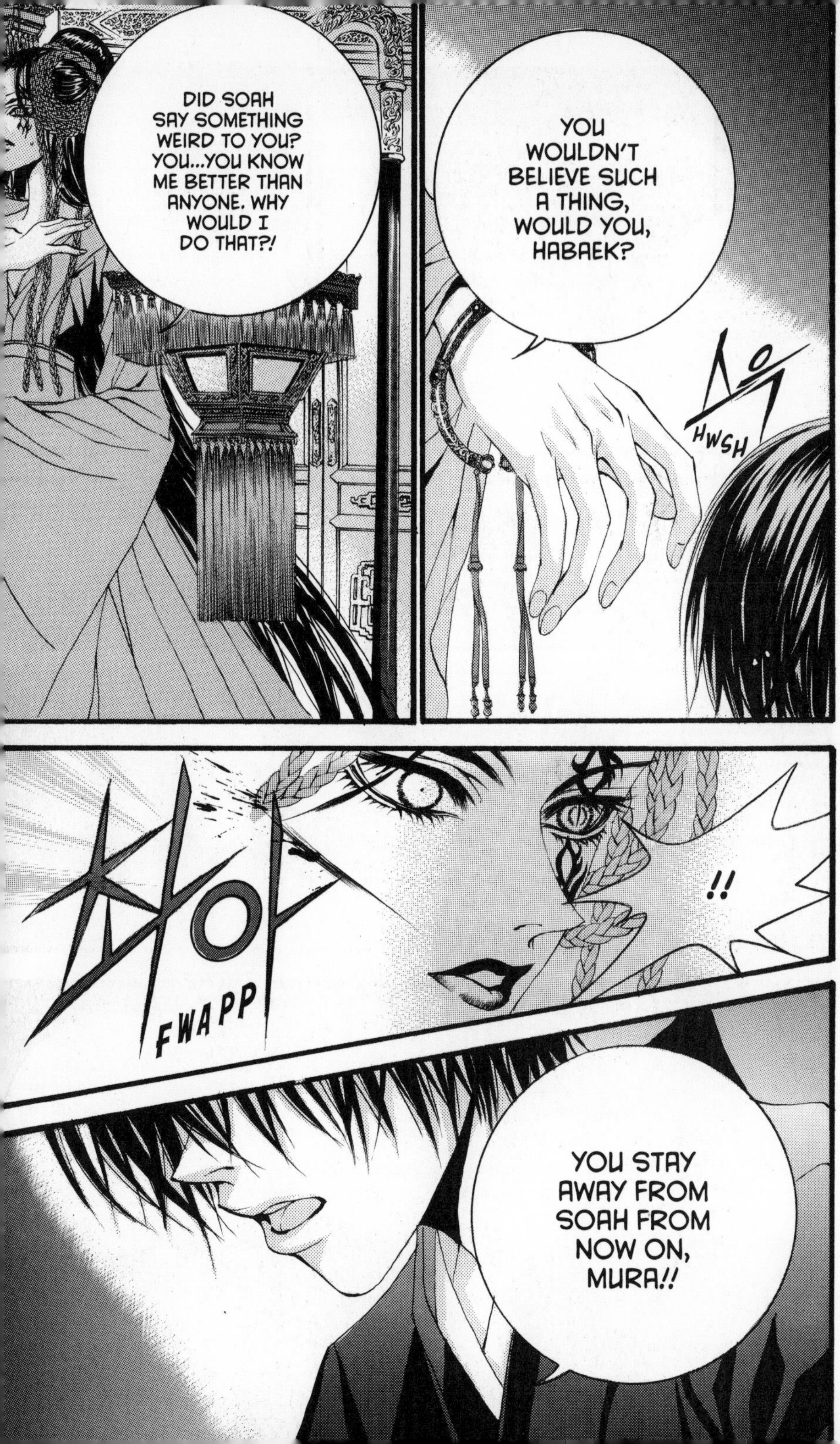
DID SOAH SAY SOMETHING WEIRD TO YOU? YOU...YOU KNOW ME BETTER THAN ANYONE. WHY WOULD I DO THAT?!
YOU WOULDN'T BELIEVE SUCH A THING, WOULD YOU, HABAEK?
HWSH
FWAPP
!!
YOU STAY AWAY FROM SOAH FROM NOW ON, MURA!!

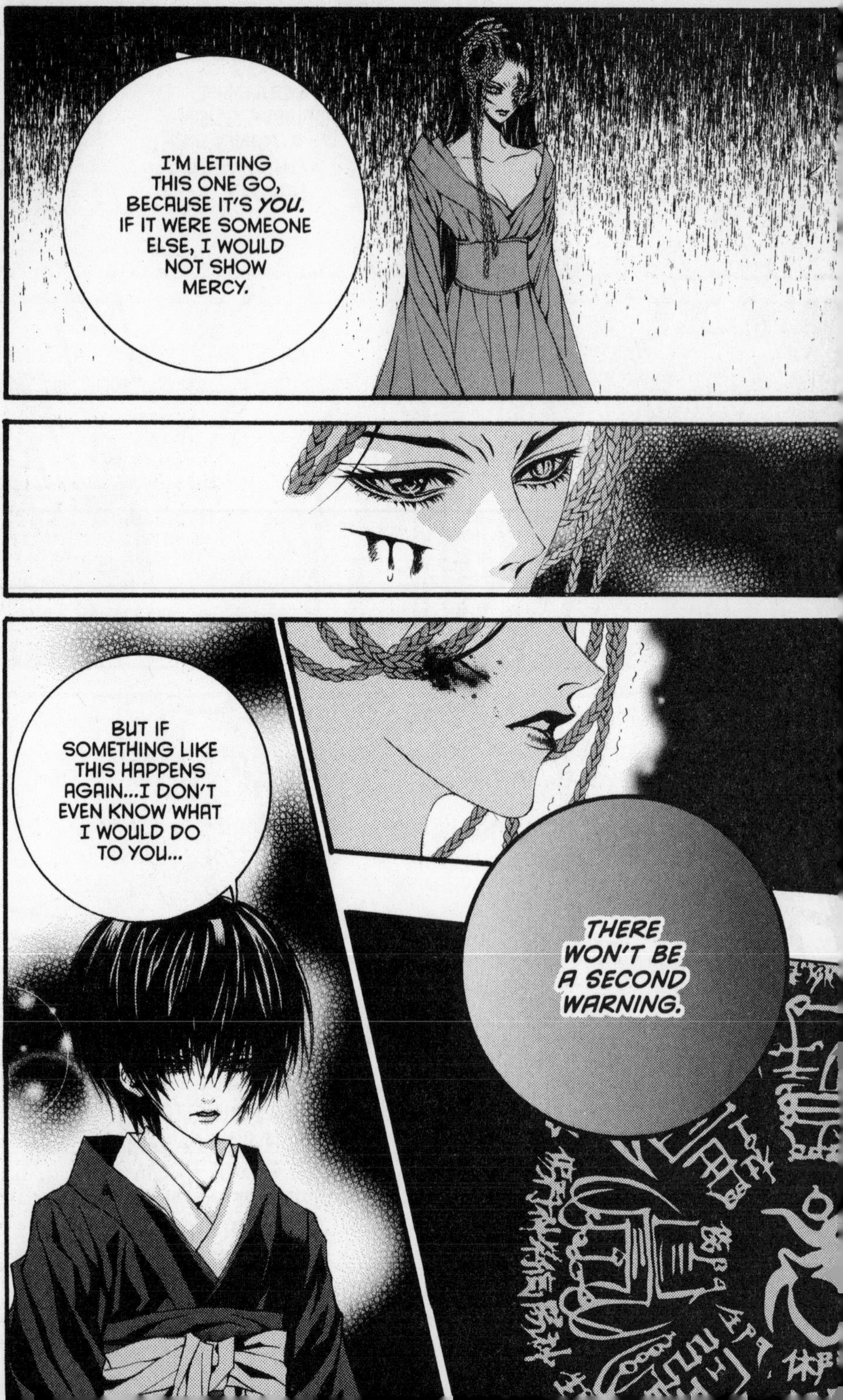
I'M LETTING THIS ONE GO, BECAUSE IT'S *YOU.* IF IT WERE SOMEONE ELSE, I WOULD NOT SHOW MERCY.
BUT IF SOMETHING LIKE THIS HAPPENS AGAIN...I DON'T EVEN KNOW WHAT I WOULD DO TO YOU...
THERE WON'T BE A SECOND WARNING.

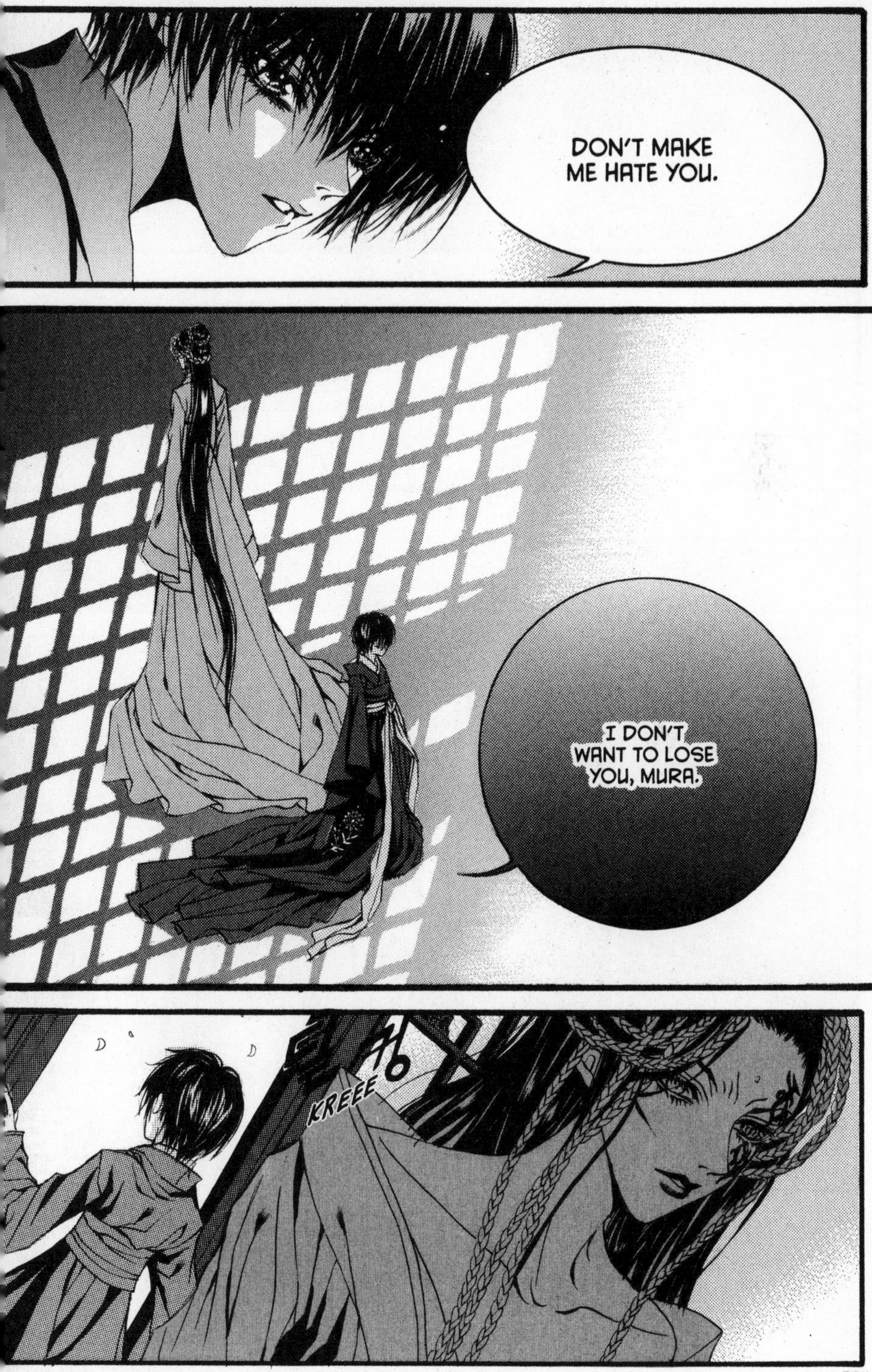
DON'T MAKE ME HATE YOU.
I DON'T WANT TO LOSE YOU, MURA.
KREEE

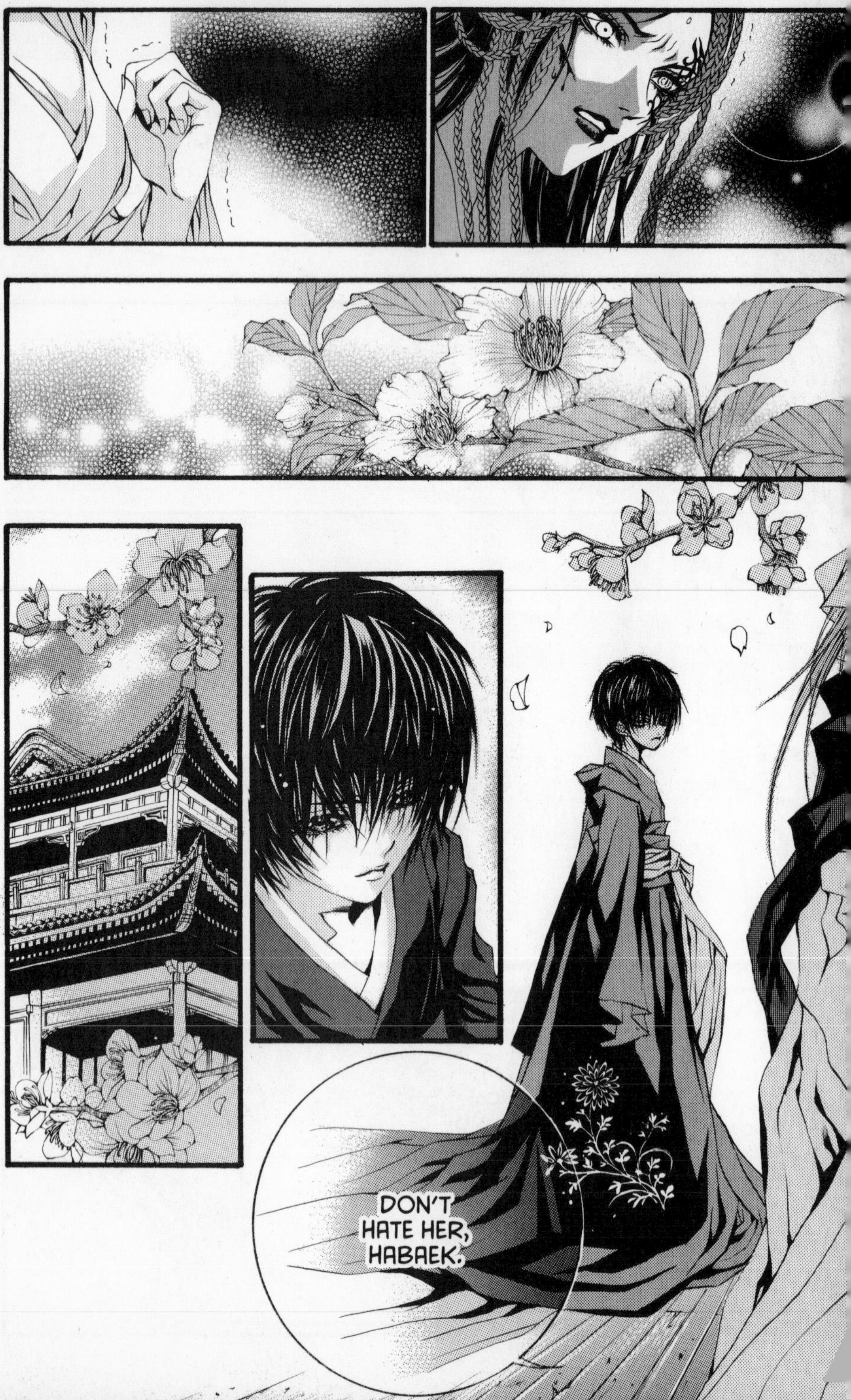
DON'T HATE HER, HABAEK.

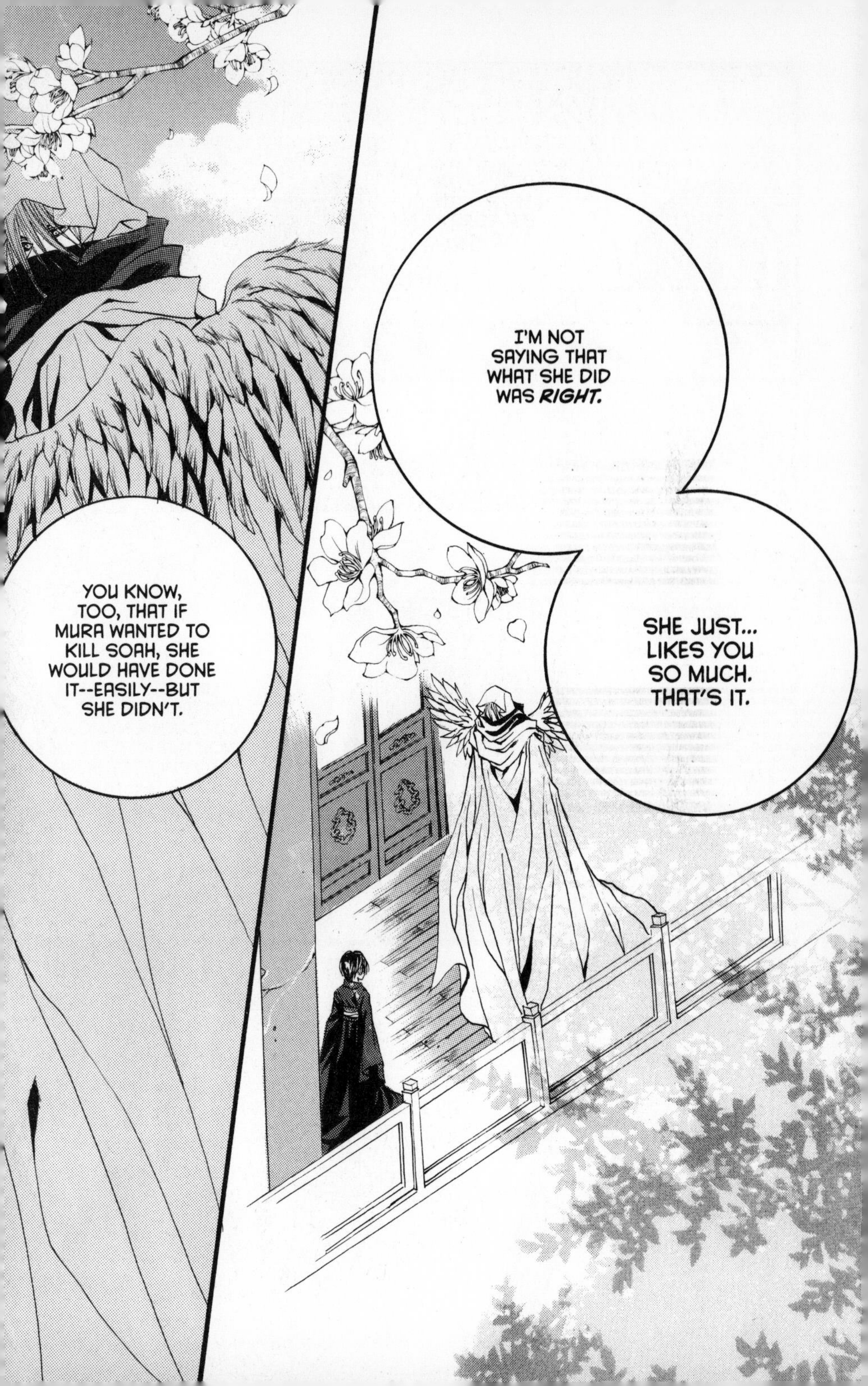
I'M NOT SAYING THAT WHAT SHE DID WAS *RIGHT.*
SHE JUST... LIKES YOU SO MUCH. THAT'S IT.
YOU KNOW, TOO, THAT IF MURA WANTED TO KILL SOAH, SHE WOULD HAVE DONE IT--EASILY--BUT SHE DIDN'T.

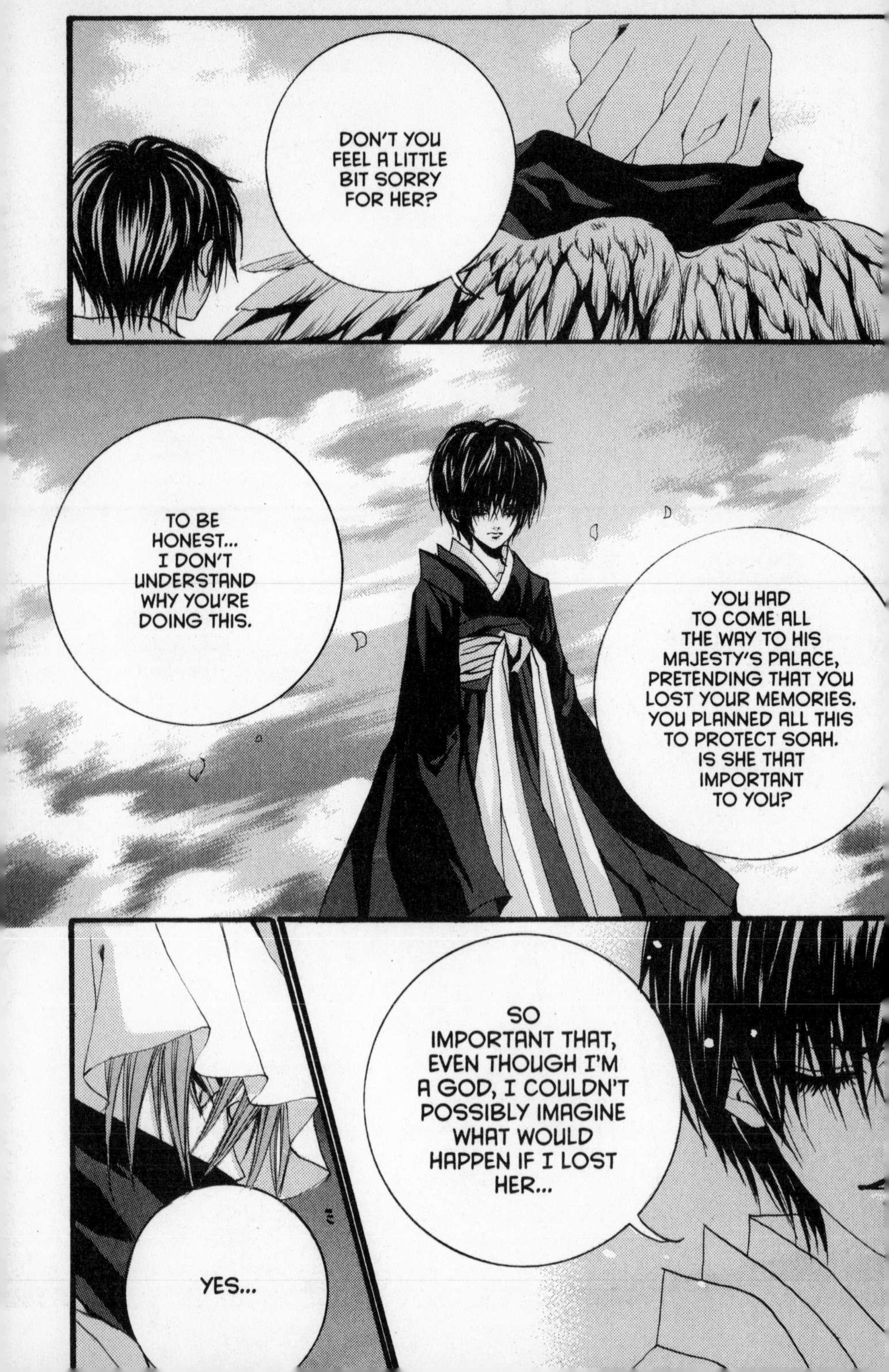
DON'T YOU FEEL A LITTLE BIT SORRY FOR HER?
YOU HAD TO COME ALL THE WAY TO HIS MAJESTY'S PALACE, PRETENDING THAT YOU LOST YOUR MEMORIES. YOU PLANNED ALL THIS TO PROTECT SOAH. IS SHE THAT IMPORTANT TO YOU?
TO BE HONEST... I DON'T UNDERSTAND WHY YOU'RE DOING THIS.
SO IMPORTANT THAT, EVEN THOUGH I'M A GOD, I COULDN'T POSSIBLY IMAGINE WHAT WOULD HAPPEN IF I LOST HER...
YES...

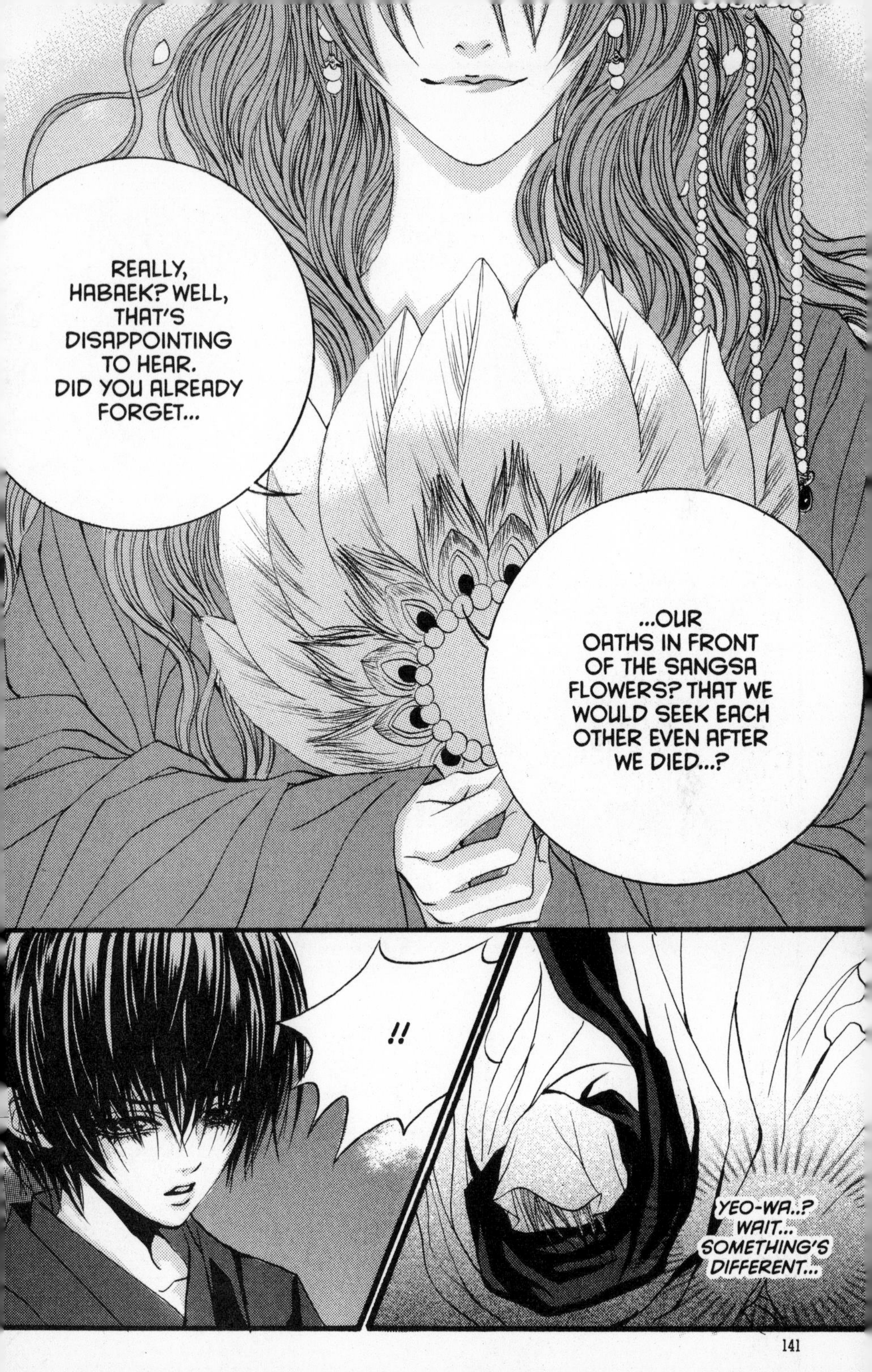
REALLY, HABAEK? WELL, THAT'S DISAPPOINTING TO HEAR. DID YOU ALREADY FORGET...
...OUR OATHS IN FRONT OF THE SANGSA FLOWERS? THAT WE WOULD SEEK EACH OTHER EVEN AFTER WE DIED...?
!!
YEO-WA..? WAIT... SOMETHING'S DIFFERENT...

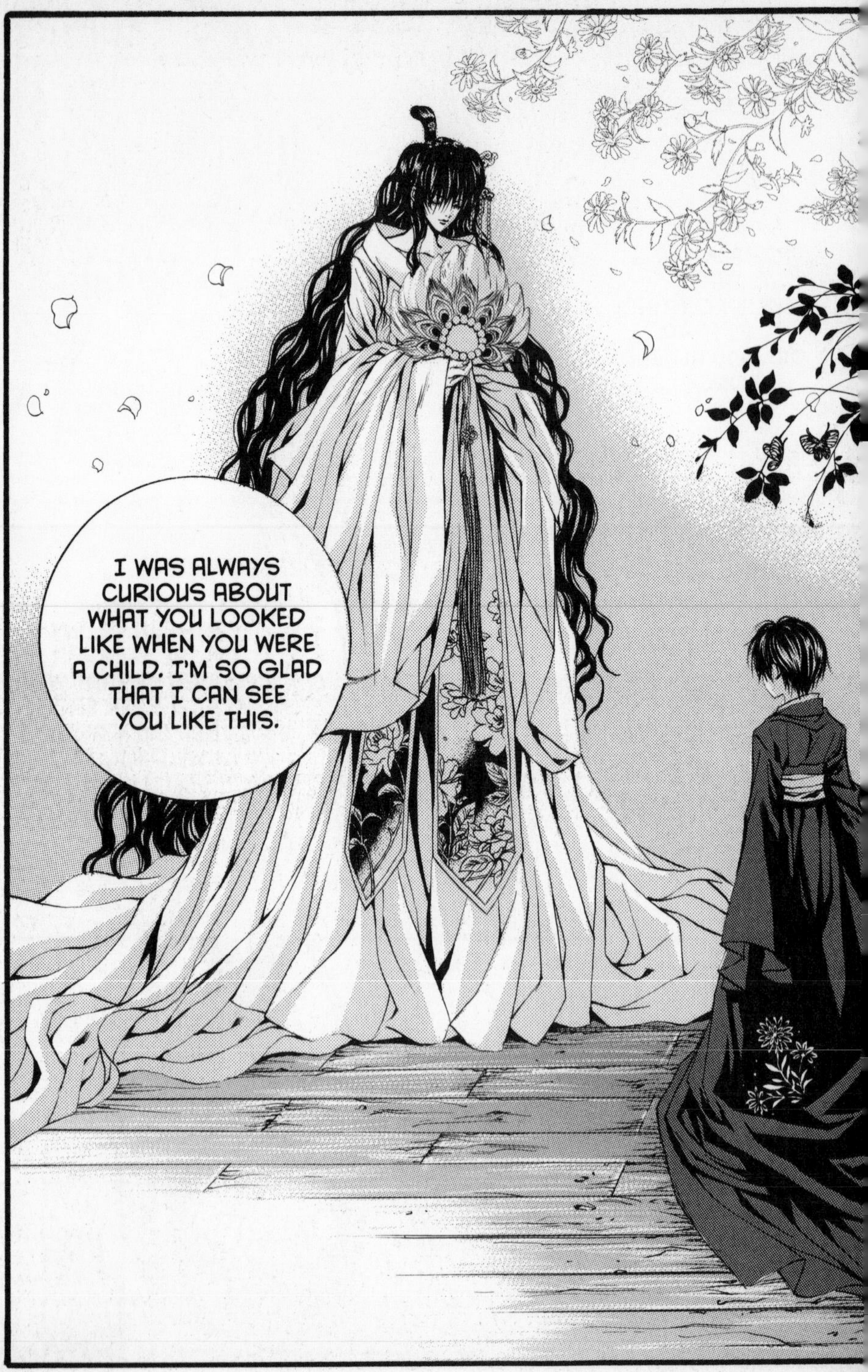
I WAS ALWAYS CURIOUS ABOUT WHAT YOU LOOKED LIKE WHEN YOU WERE A CHILD. I'M SO GLAD THAT I CAN SEE YOU LIKE THIS.

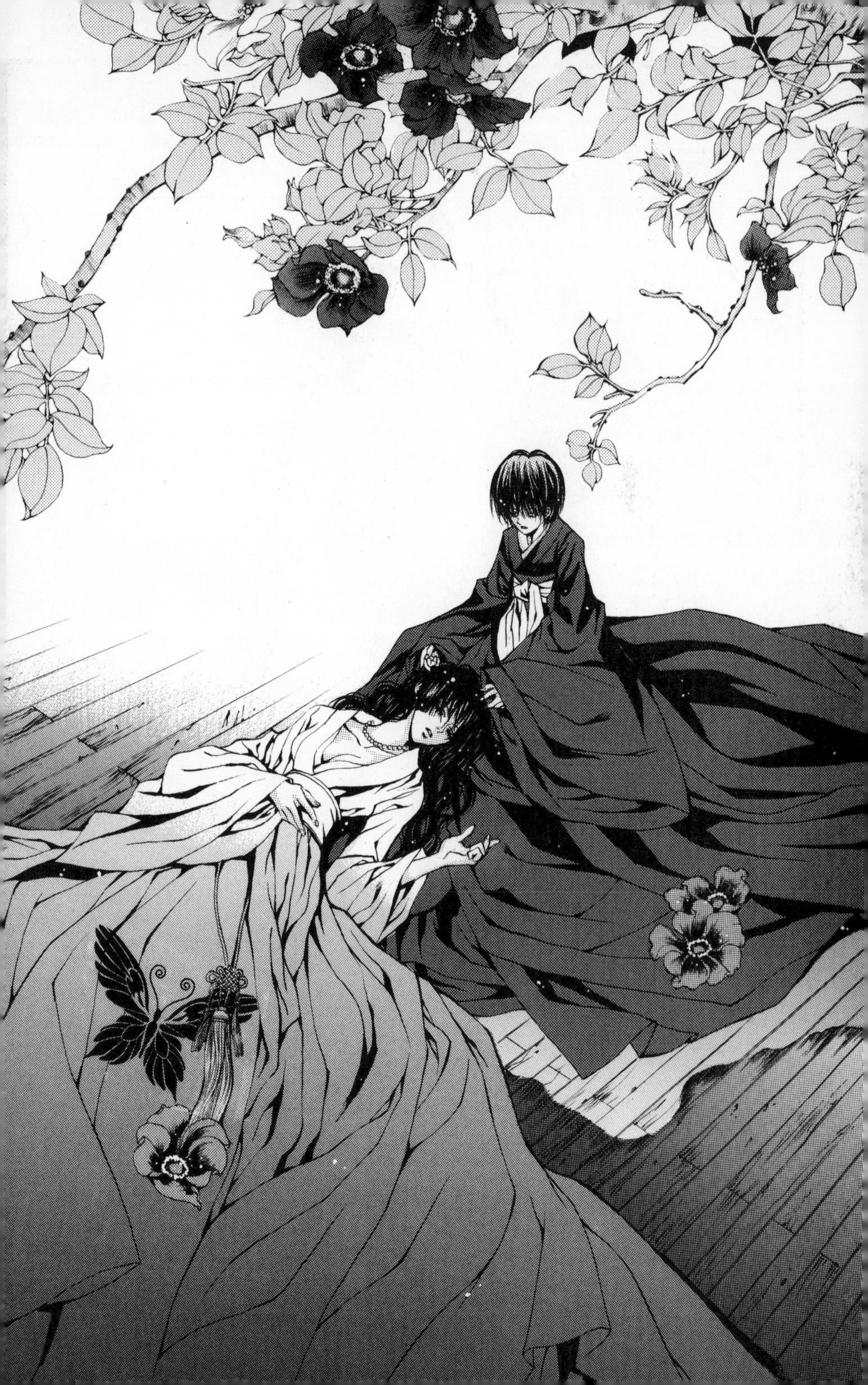

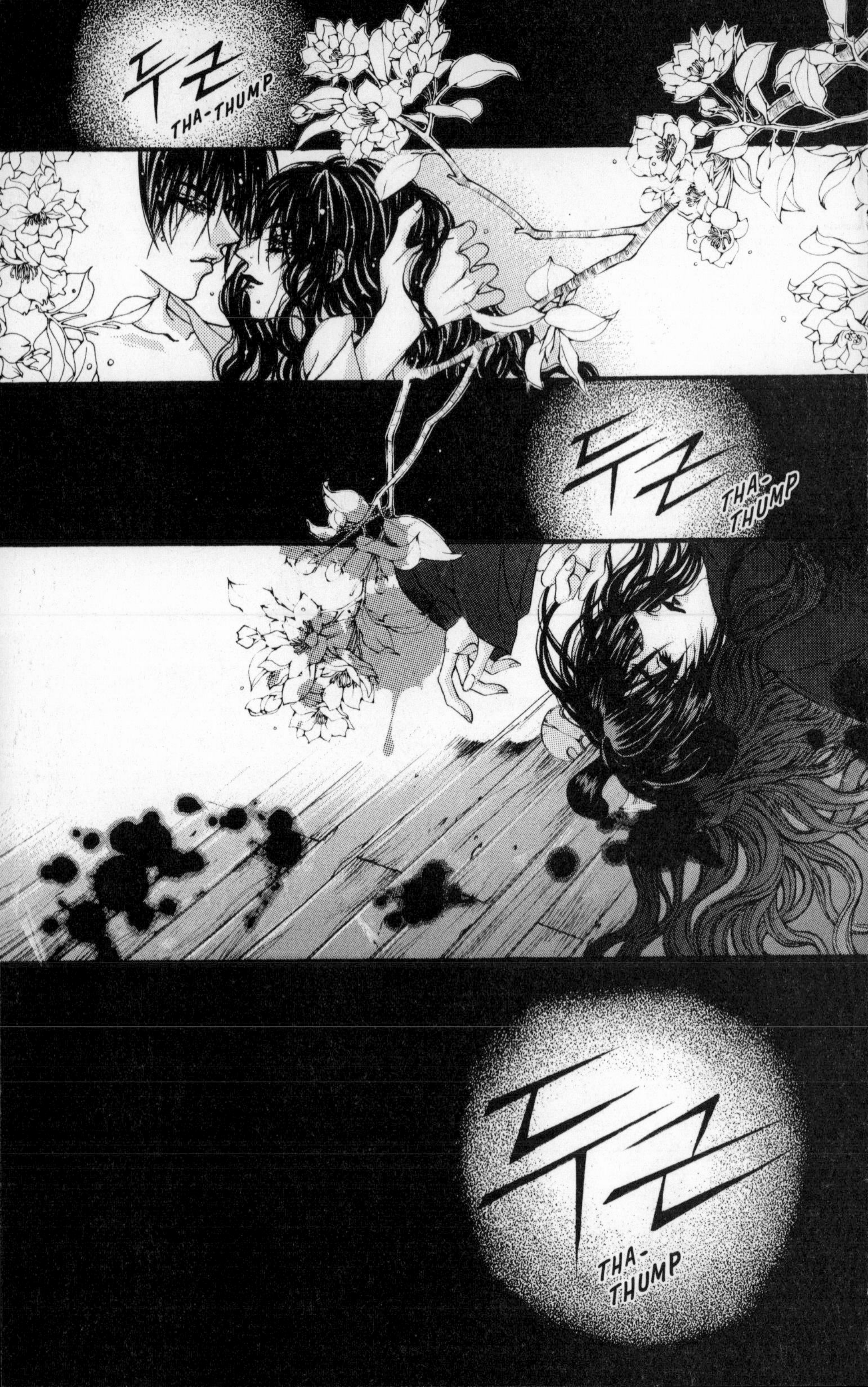
두근
THA-THUMP
두근
THA-THUMP
두근
THA-THUMP

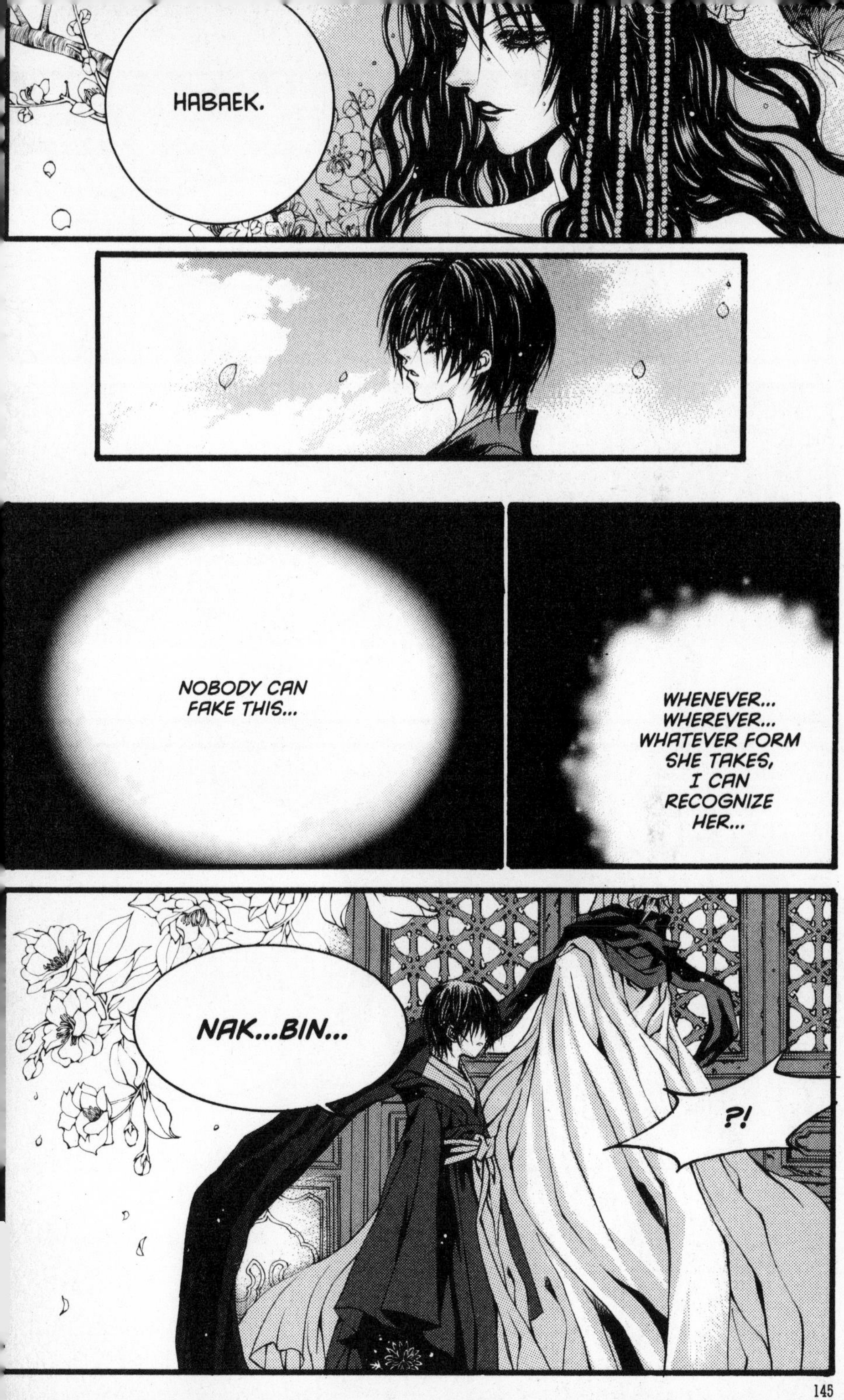
HABAEK.
NOBODY CAN FAKE THIS...
WHENEVER... WHEREVER... WHATEVER FORM SHE TAKES, I CAN RECOGNIZE HER...
NAK...BIN...
?!

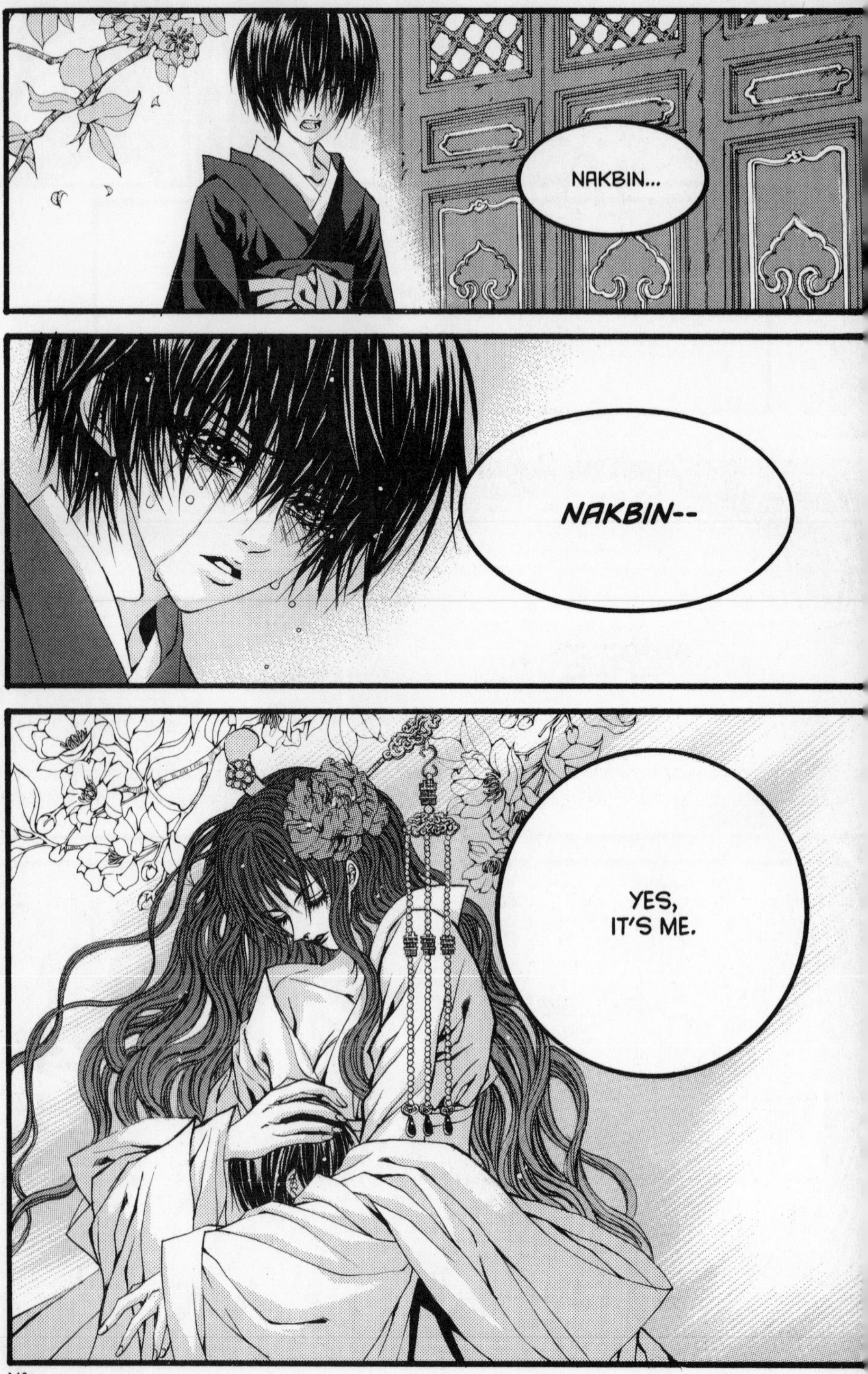
NAKBIN...
NAKBIN--
YES, IT'S ME.

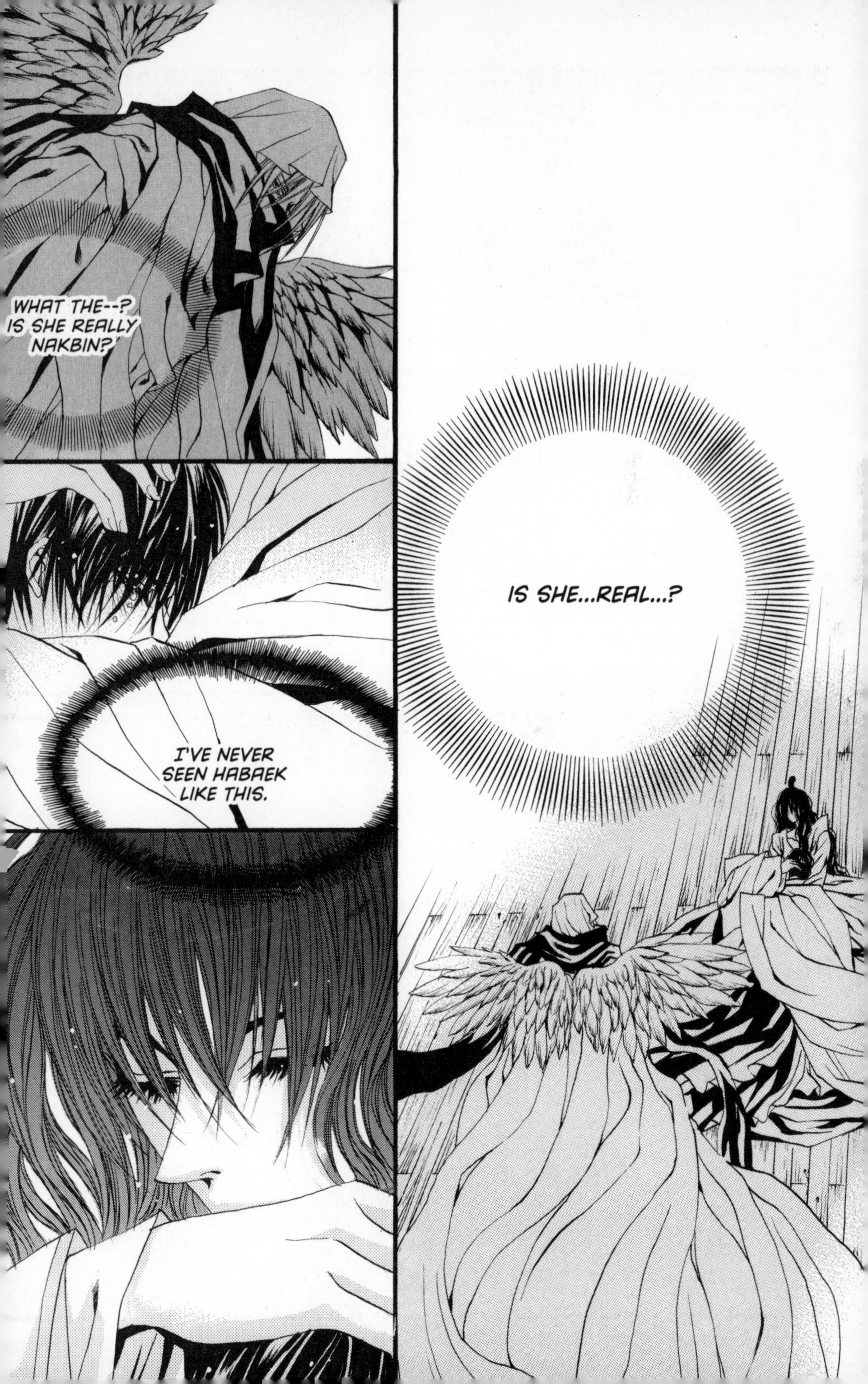
IS SHE...REAL...?
WHAT THE--? IS SHE REALLY NAKBIN?
I'VE NEVER SEEN HABAEK LIKE THIS.

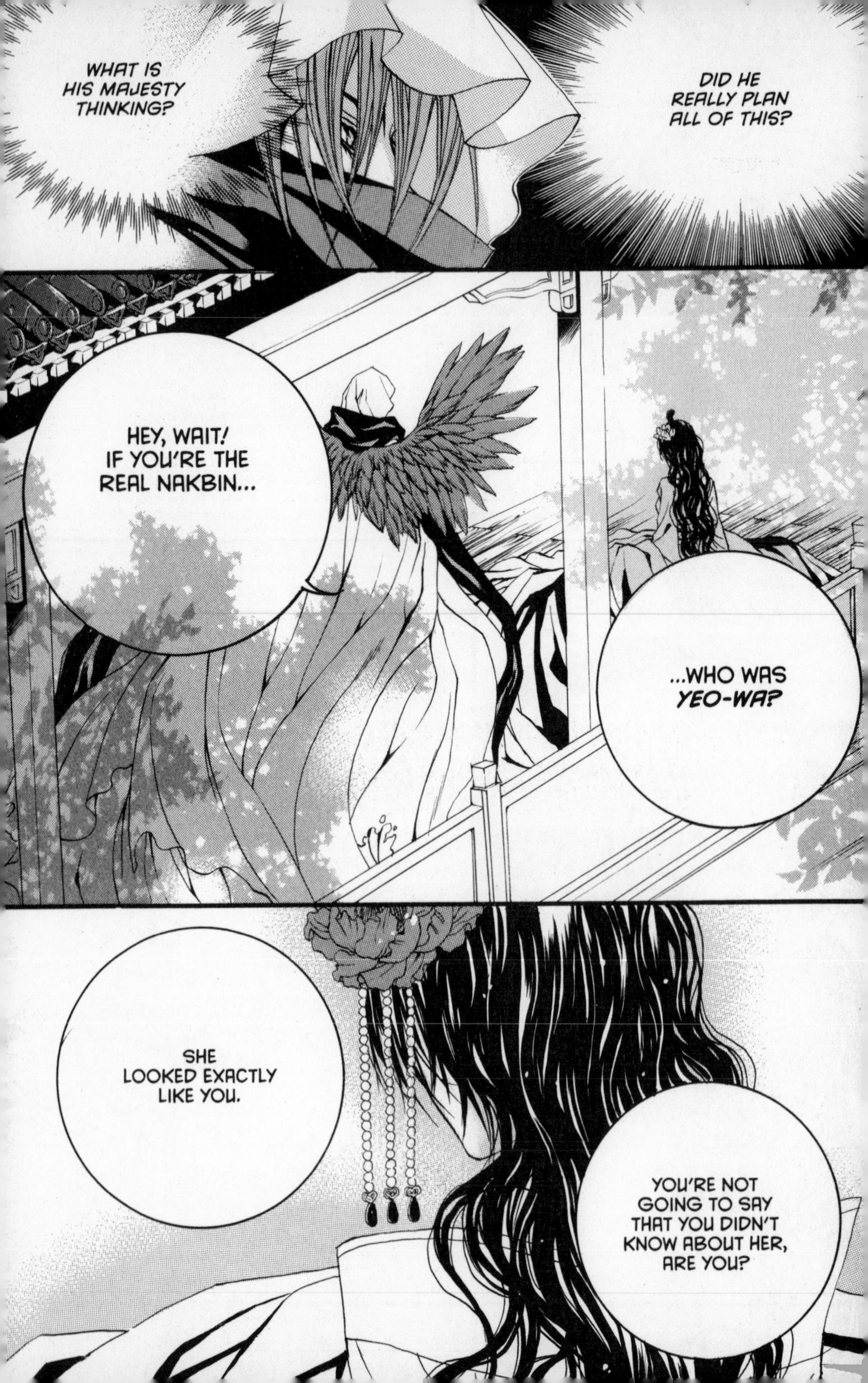
DID HE REALLY PLAN ALL OF THIS?
WHAT IS HIS MAJESTY THINKING?
...WHO WAS *YEO-WA?*
HEY, WAIT! IF YOU'RE THE REAL NAKBIN...
SHE LOOKED EXACTLY LIKE YOU.
YOU'RE NOT GOING TO SAY THAT YOU DIDN'T KNOW ABOUT HER, ARE YOU?

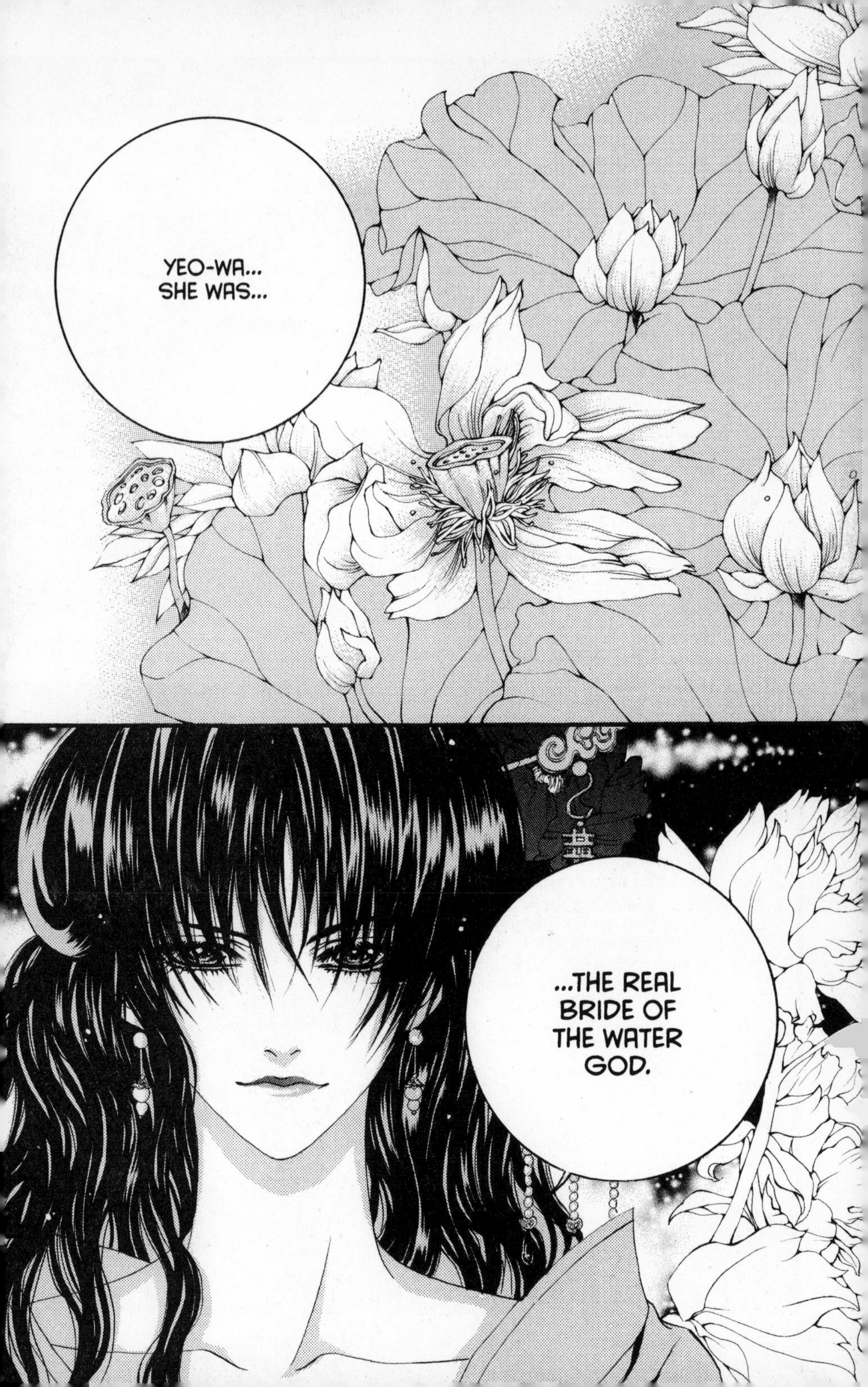
YEO-WA...
SHE WAS...
...THE REAL
BRIDE OF
THE WATER
GOD.

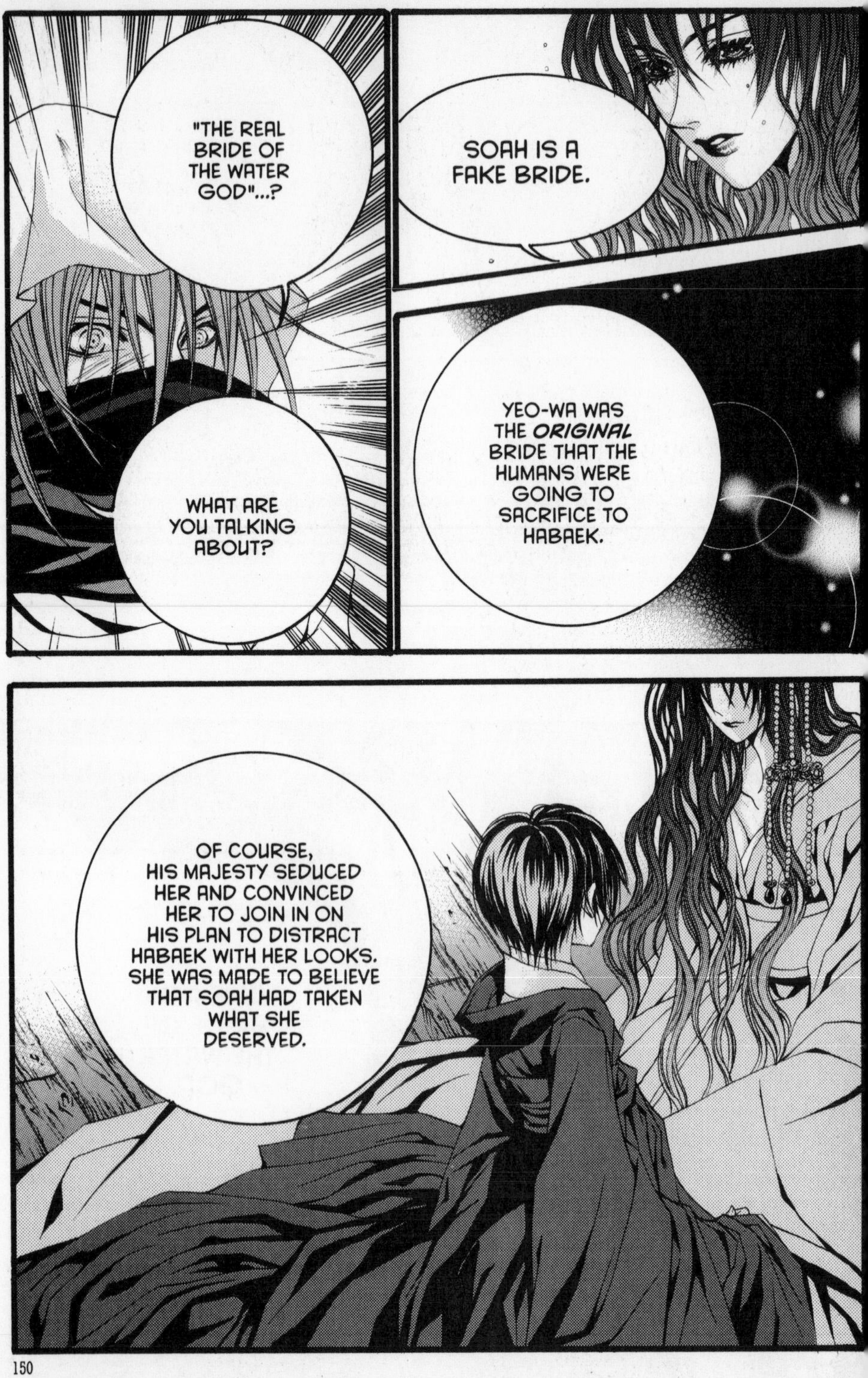
"THE REAL BRIDE OF THE WATER GOD"...?
WHAT ARE YOU TALKING ABOUT?
SOAH IS A FAKE BRIDE.
YEO-WA WAS THE *ORIGINAL* BRIDE THAT THE HUMANS WERE GOING TO SACRIFICE TO HABAEK.
OF COURSE, HIS MAJESTY SEDUCED HER AND CONVINCED HER TO JOIN IN ON HIS PLAN TO DISTRACT HABAEK WITH HER LOOKS. SHE WAS MADE TO BELIEVE THAT SOAH HAD TAKEN WHAT SHE DESERVED.

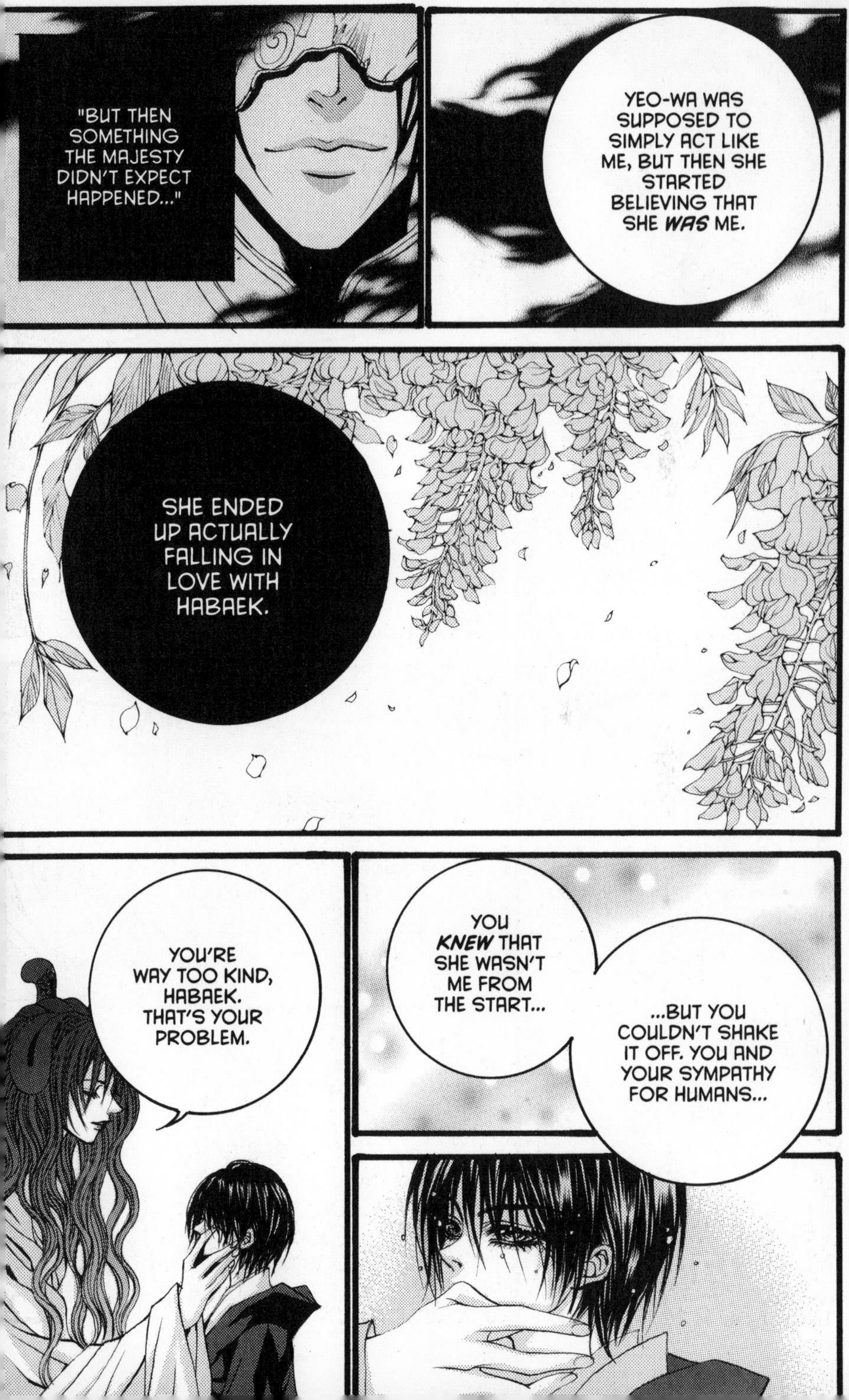
"BUT THEN SOMETHING THE MAJESTY DIDN'T EXPECT HAPPENED..."
YEO-WA WAS SUPPOSED TO SIMPLY ACT LIKE ME, BUT THEN SHE STARTED BELIEVING THAT SHE *WAS* ME.
SHE ENDED UP ACTUALLY FALLING IN LOVE WITH HABAEK.
YOU *KNEW* THAT SHE WASN'T ME FROM THE START...
...BUT YOU COULDN'T SHAKE IT OFF. YOU AND YOUR SYMPATHY FOR HUMANS...
YOU'RE WAY TOO KIND, HABAEK. THAT'S YOUR PROBLEM.

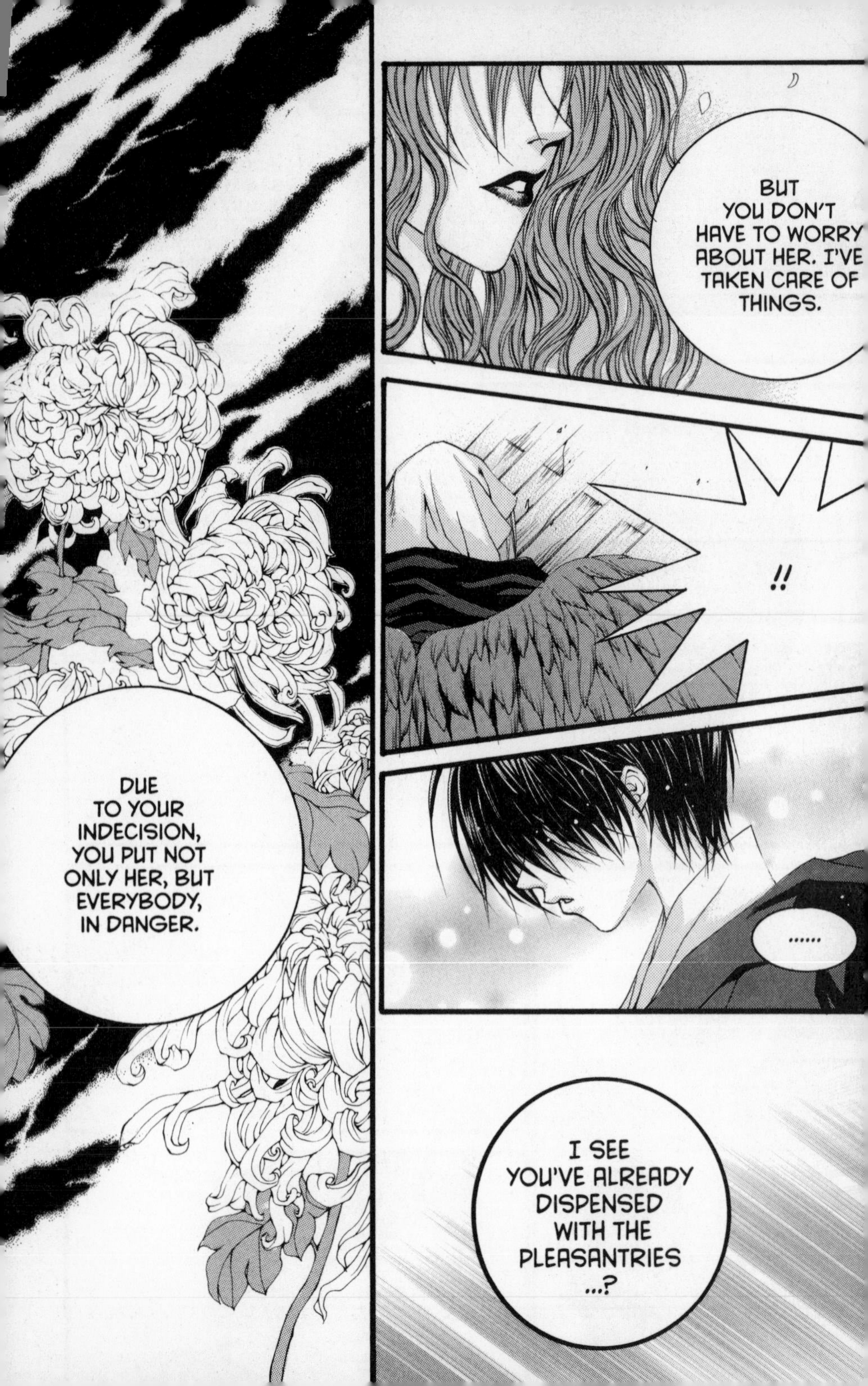
DUE TO YOUR INDECISION, YOU PUT NOT ONLY HER, BUT EVERYBODY, IN DANGER.
BUT YOU DON'T HAVE TO WORRY ABOUT HER. I'VE TAKEN CARE OF THINGS.
!!
......
I SEE YOU'VE ALREADY DISPENSED WITH THE PLEASANTRIES ...?

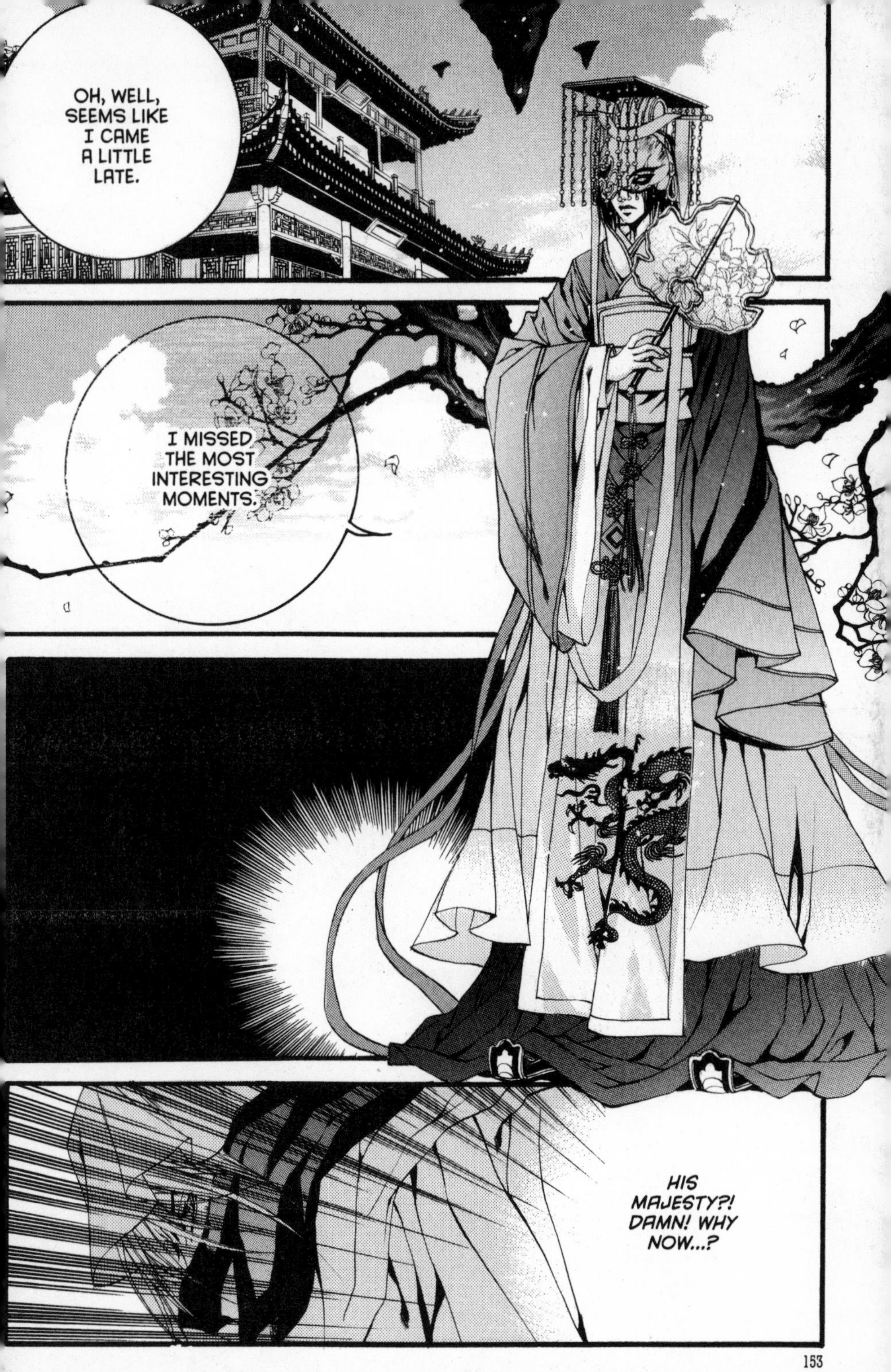
OH, WELL, SEEMS LIKE I CAME A LITTLE LATE.
I MISSED THE MOST INTERESTING MOMENTS.
HIS MAJESTY?! DAMN! WHY NOW...?

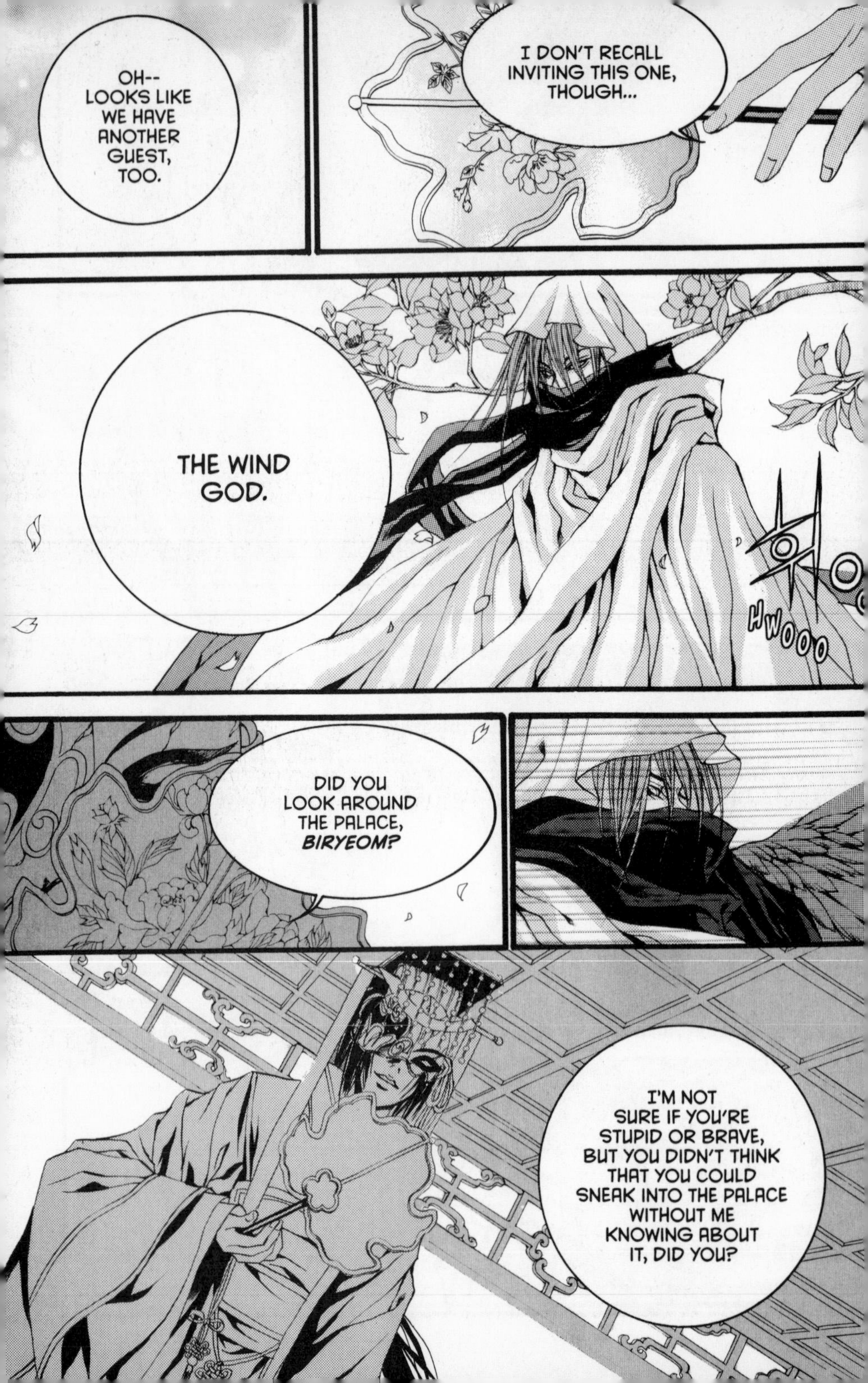
OH-- LOOKS LIKE WE HAVE ANOTHER GUEST, TOO.
I DON'T RECALL INVITING THIS ONE, THOUGH...
THE WIND GOD.
HWOOO
DID YOU LOOK AROUND THE PALACE, *BIRYEOM?*
I'M NOT SURE IF YOU'RE STUPID OR BRAVE, BUT YOU DIDN'T THINK THAT YOU COULD SNEAK INTO THE PALACE WITHOUT ME KNOWING ABOUT IT, DID YOU?

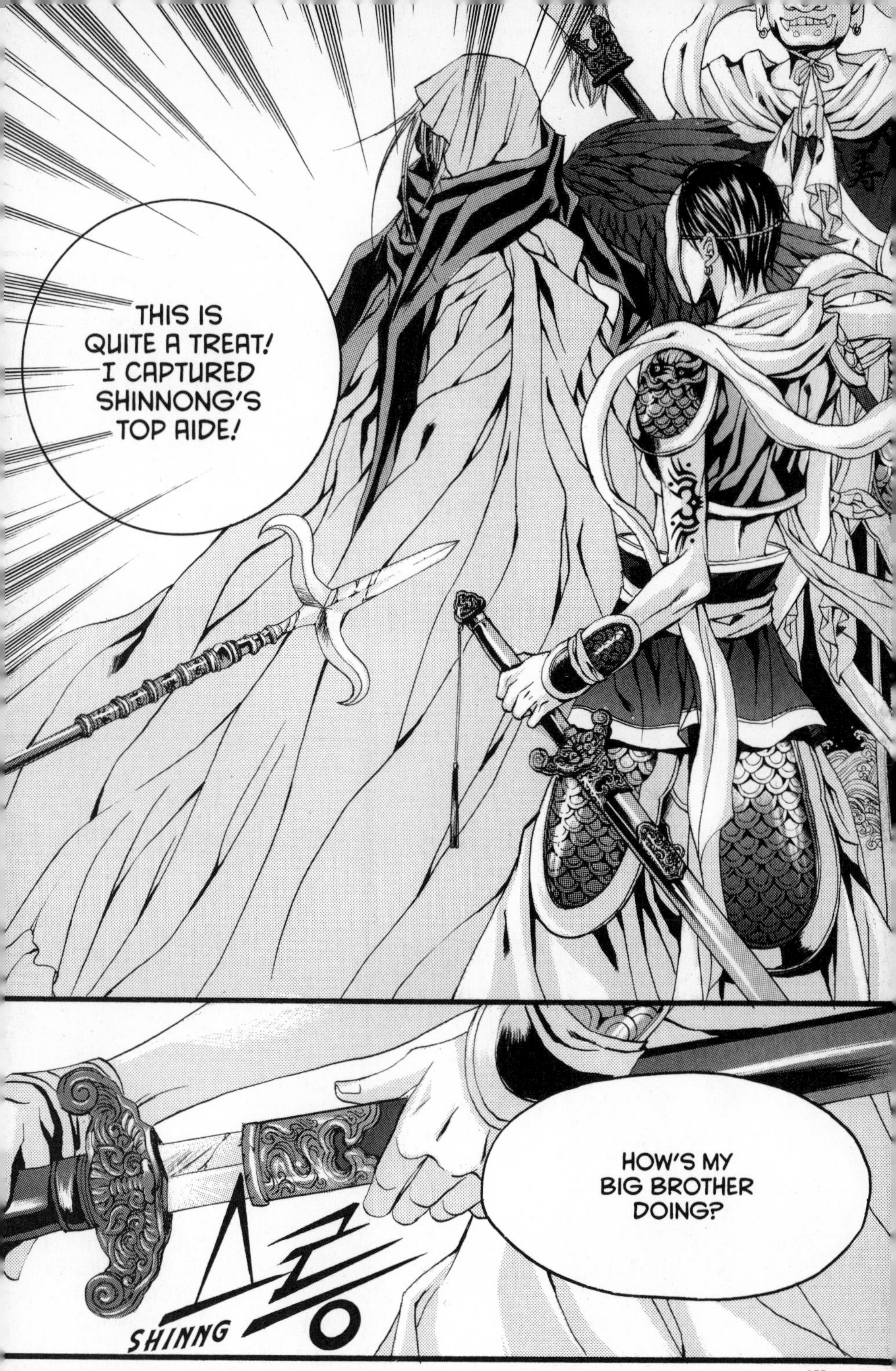
THIS IS QUITE A TREAT! I CAPTURED SHINNONG'S TOP AIDE!
HOW'S MY BIG BROTHER DOING?
SHINNG

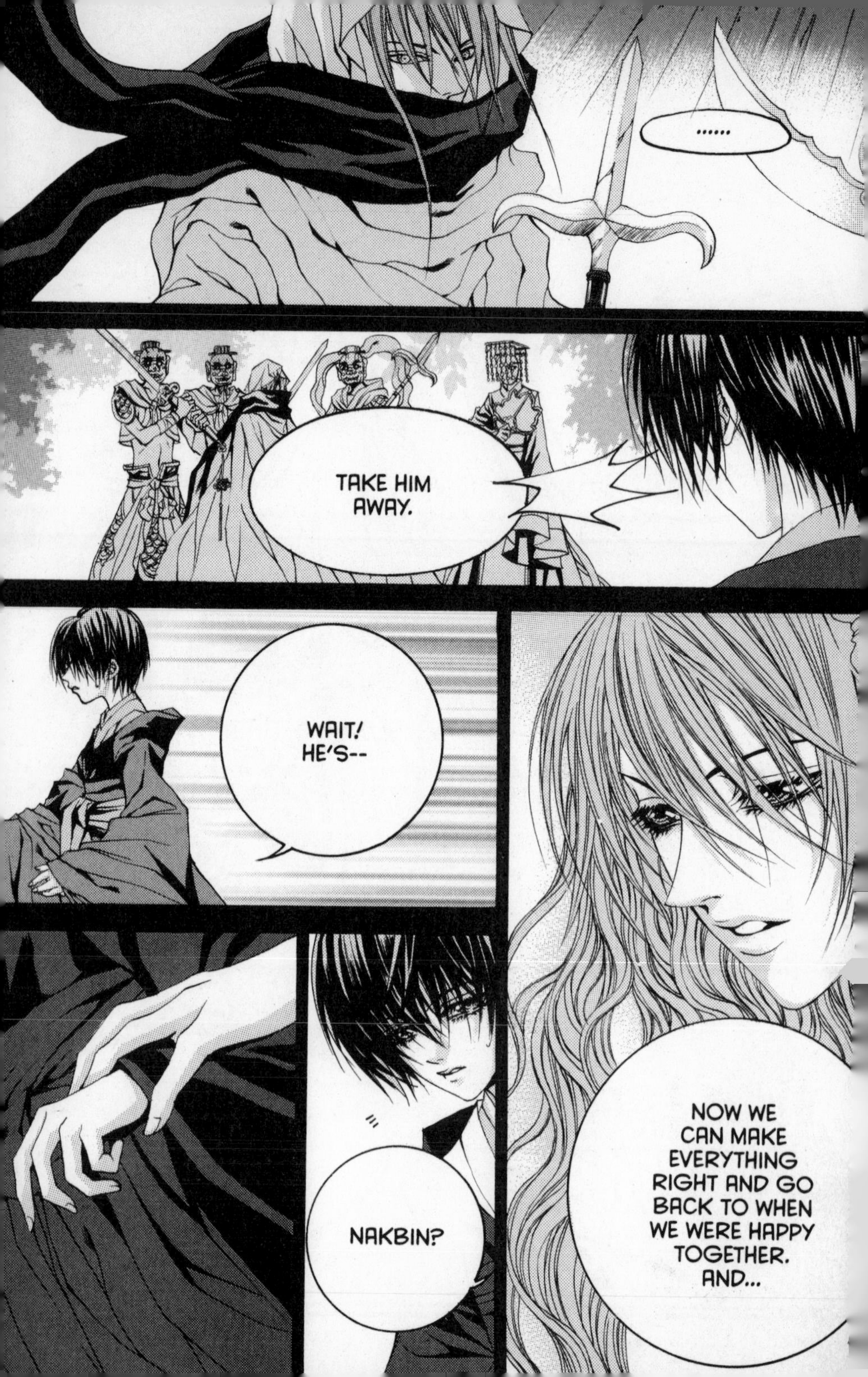
......
TAKE HIM AWAY.
WAIT! HE'S--
NOW WE CAN MAKE EVERYTHING RIGHT AND GO BACK TO WHEN WE WERE HAPPY TOGETHER. AND...
NAKBIN?

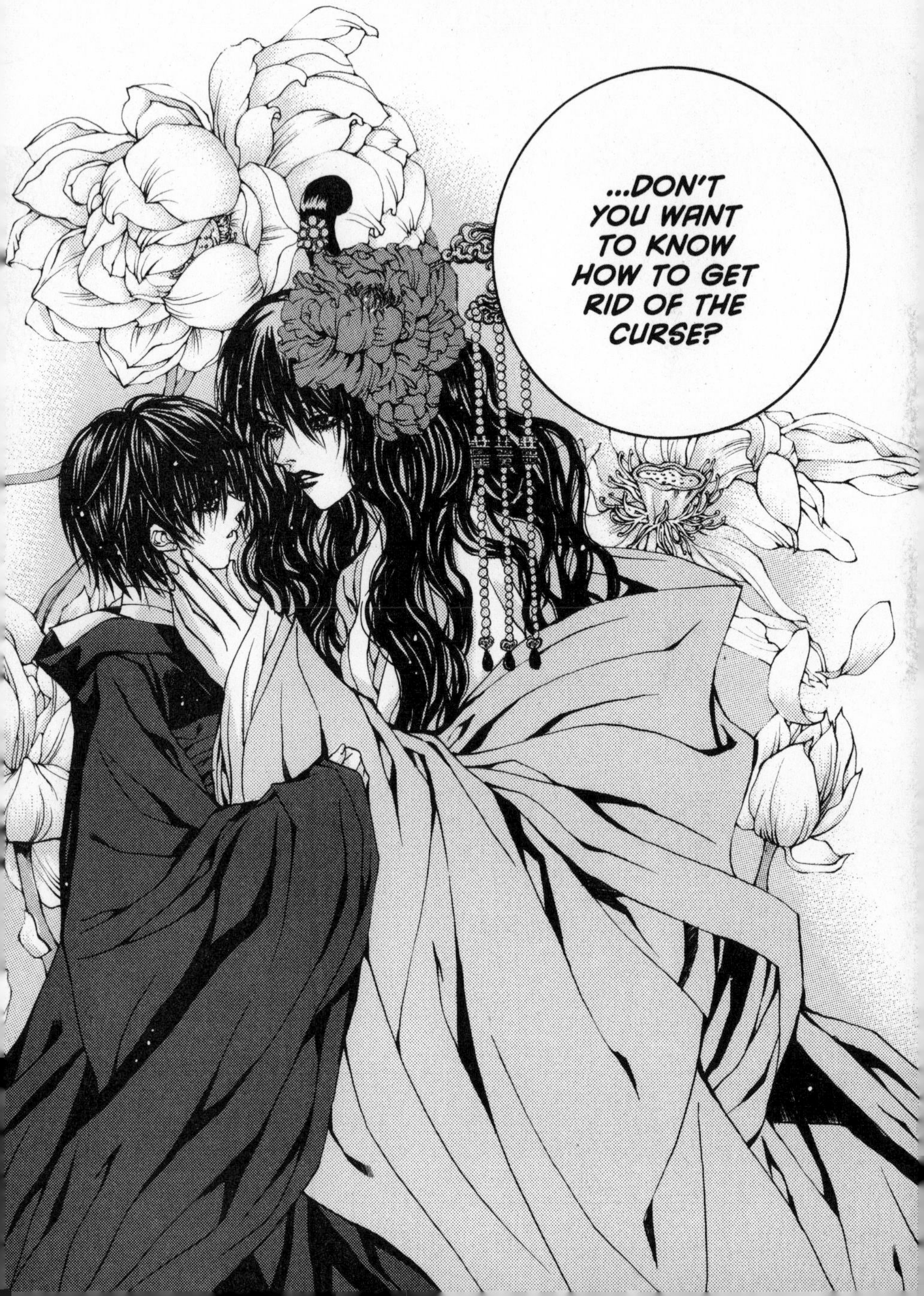
...DON'T YOU WANT TO KNOW HOW TO GET RID OF THE CURSE?

BRIDE of the WATER GOD

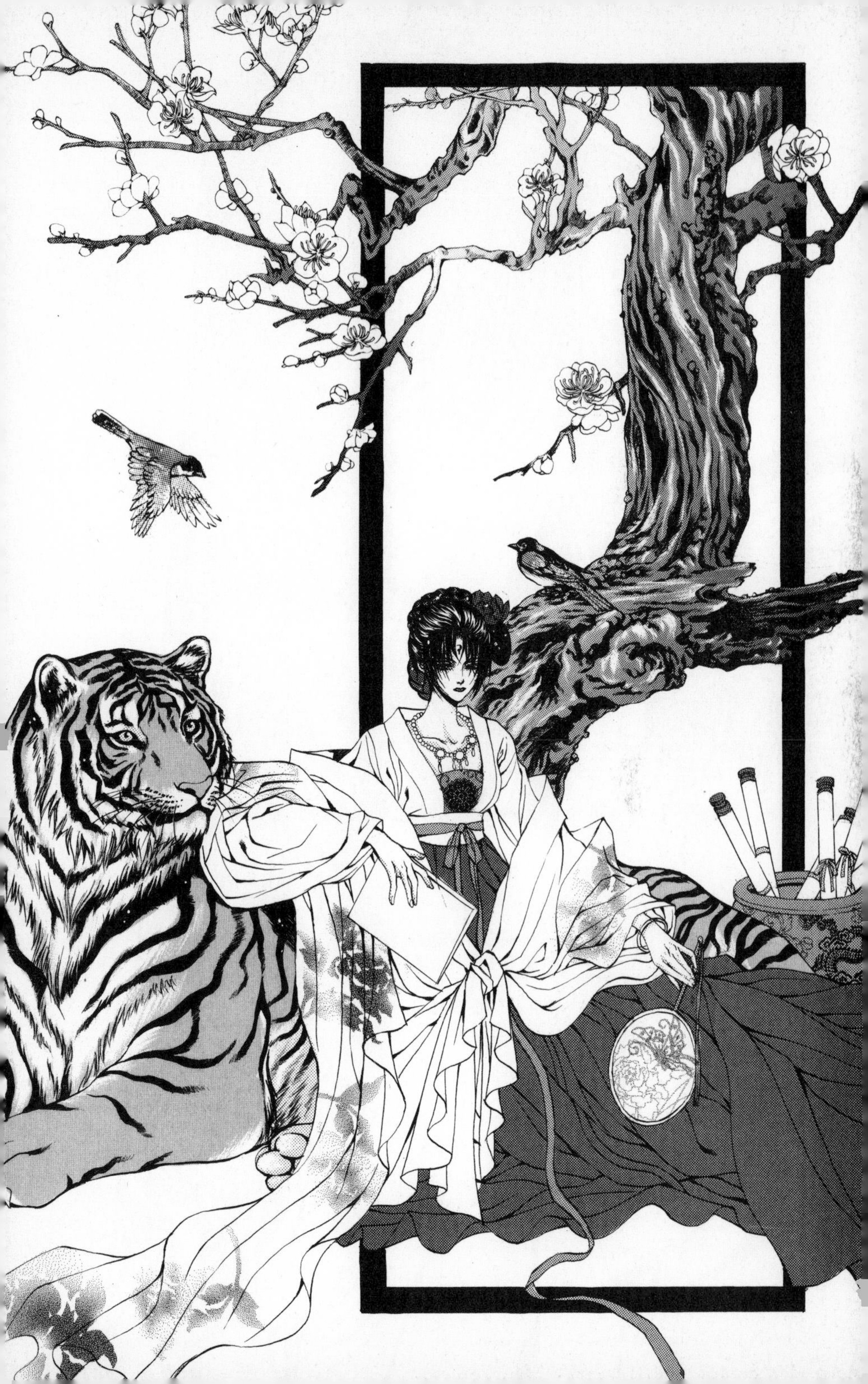

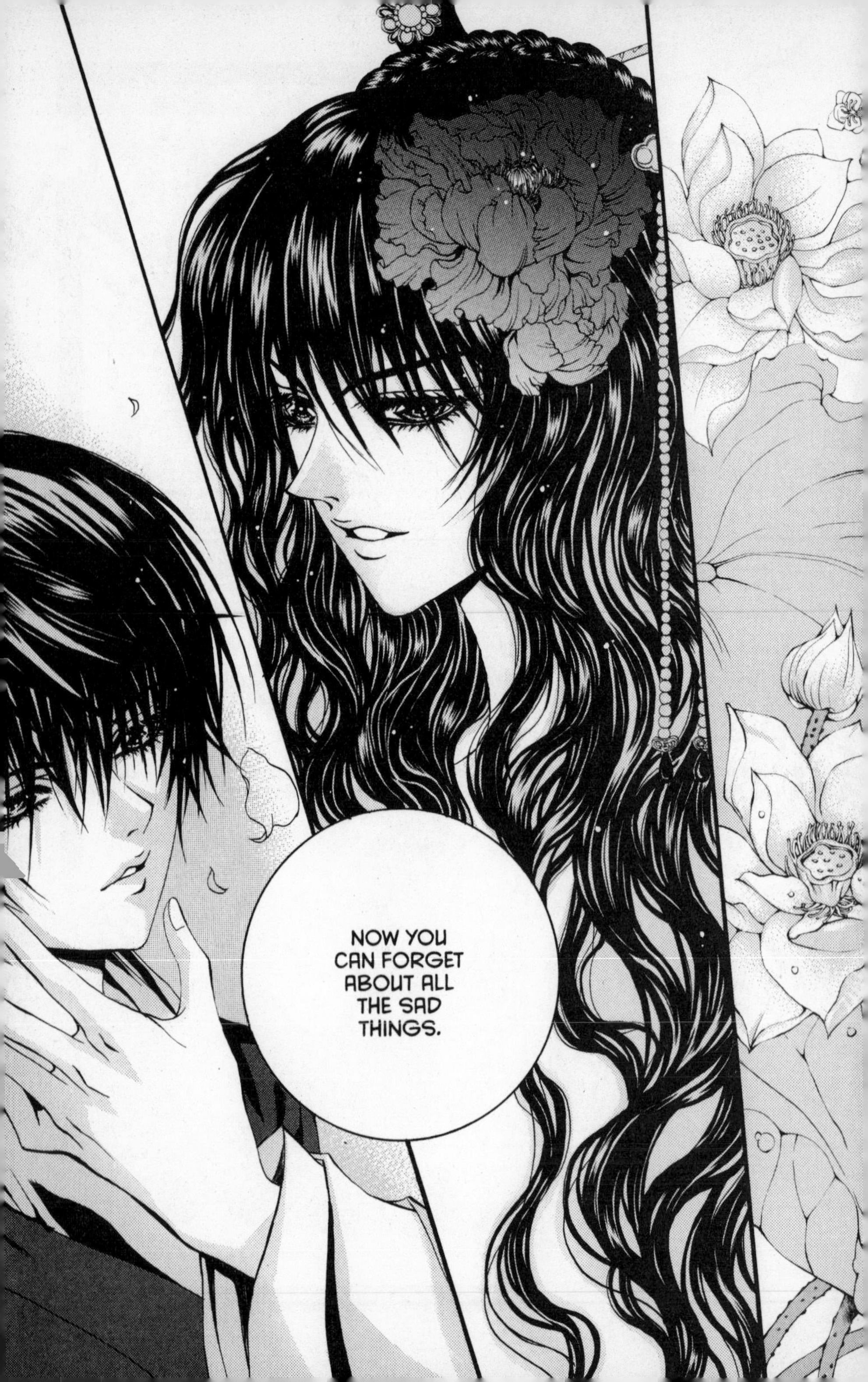
NOW YOU CAN FORGET ABOUT ALL THE SAD THINGS.

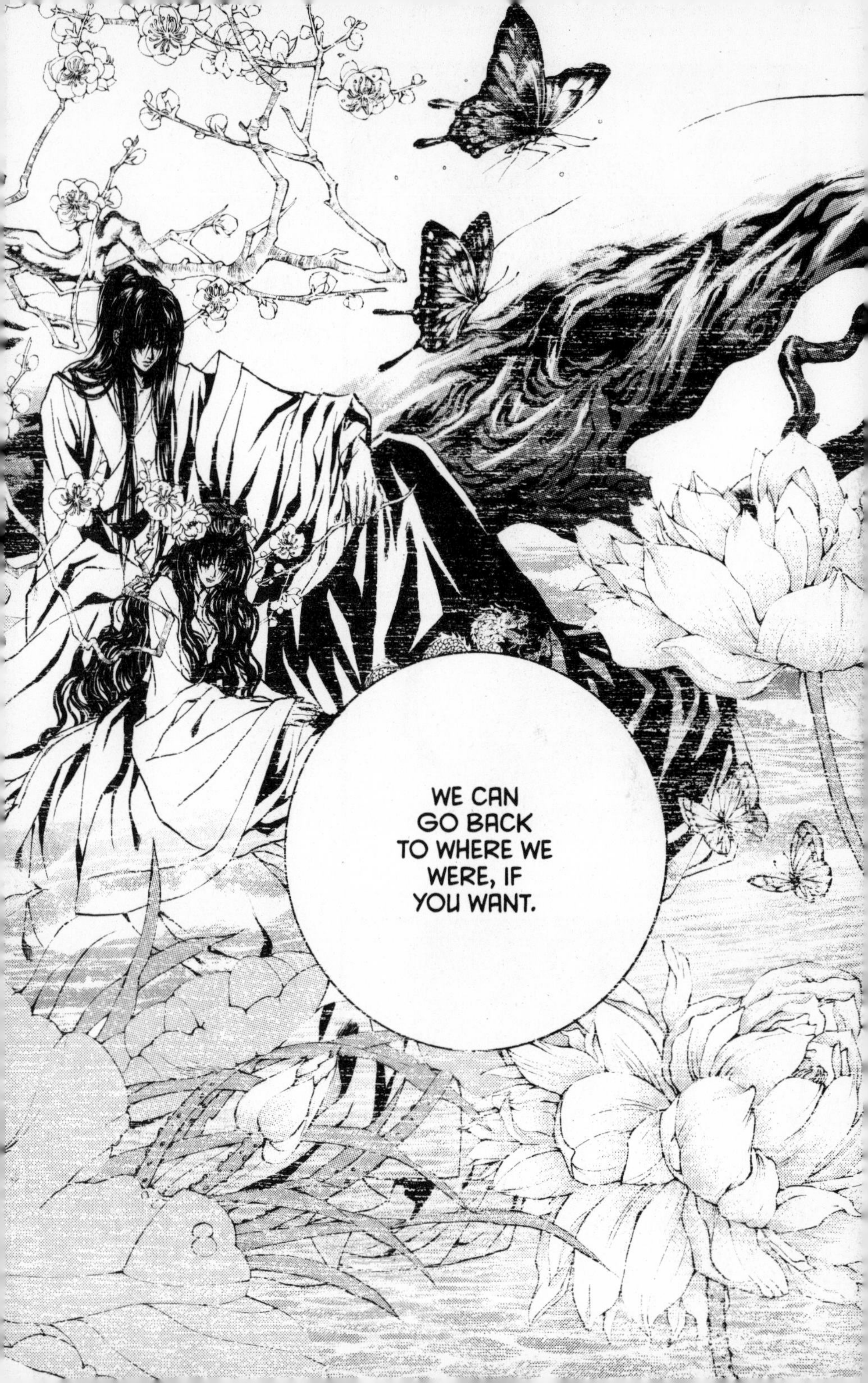
WE CAN GO BACK TO WHERE WE WERE, IF YOU WANT.

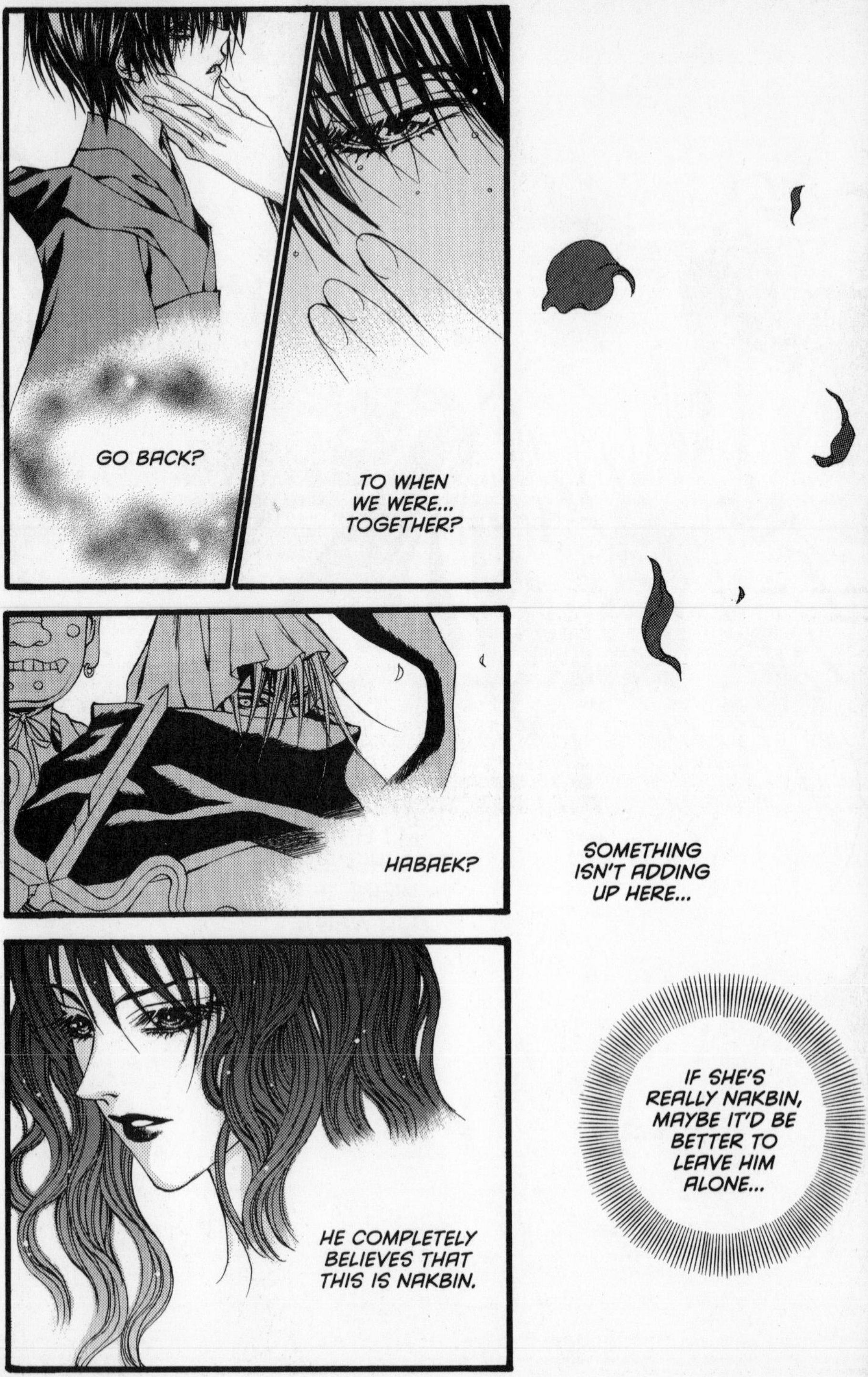
GO BACK?
TO WHEN WE WERE... TOGETHER?
HABAEK?
SOMETHING ISN'T ADDING UP HERE...
HE COMPLETELY BELIEVES THAT THIS IS NAKBIN.
IF SHE'S REALLY NAKBIN, MAYBE IT'D BE BETTER TO LEAVE HIM ALONE...

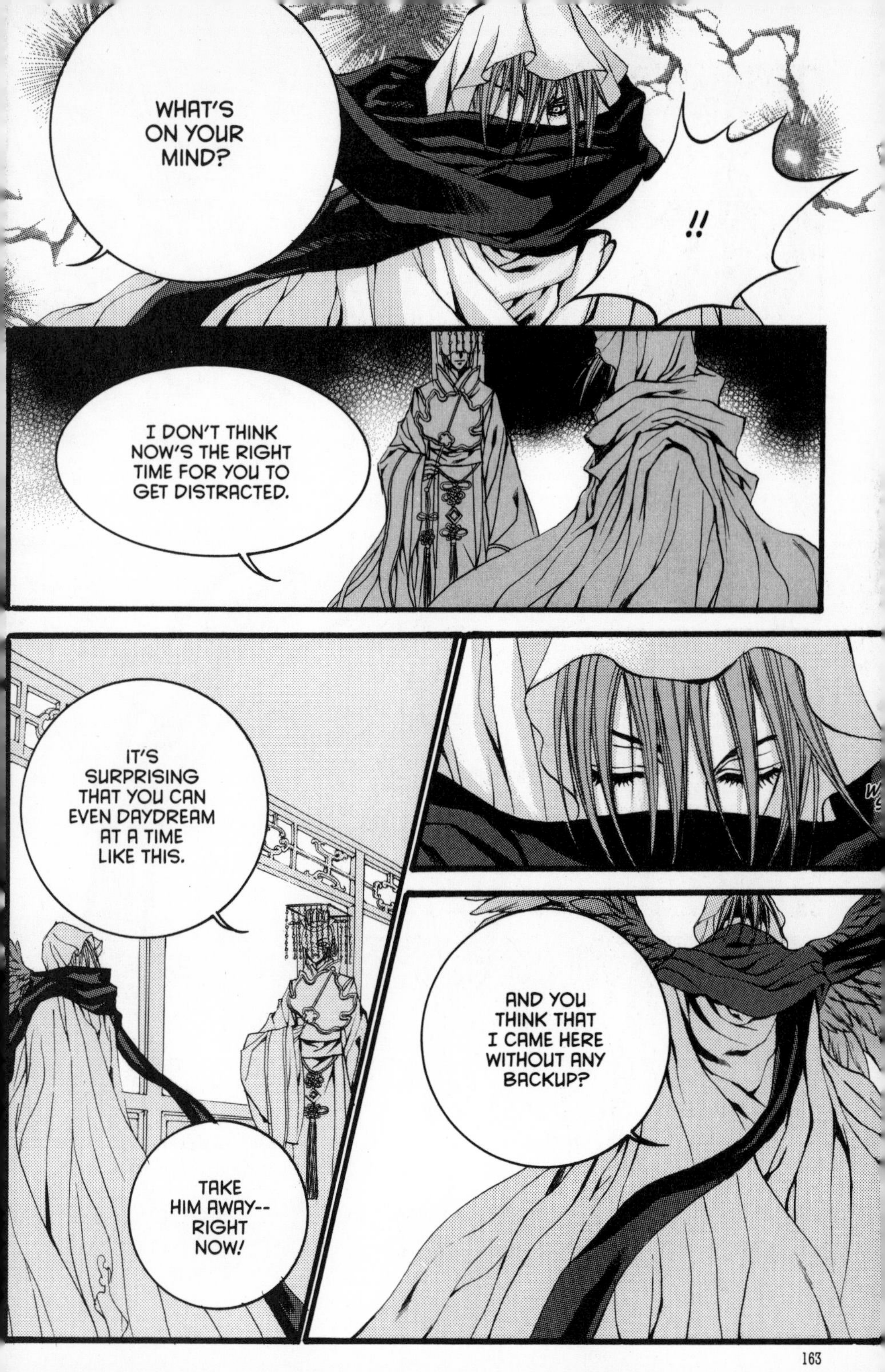
WHAT'S ON YOUR MIND?
!!
I DON'T THINK NOW'S THE RIGHT TIME FOR YOU TO GET DISTRACTED.
IT'S SURPRISING THAT YOU CAN EVEN DAYDREAM AT A TIME LIKE THIS.
TAKE HIM AWAY-- RIGHT NOW!
AND YOU THINK THAT I CAME HERE WITHOUT ANY BACKUP?

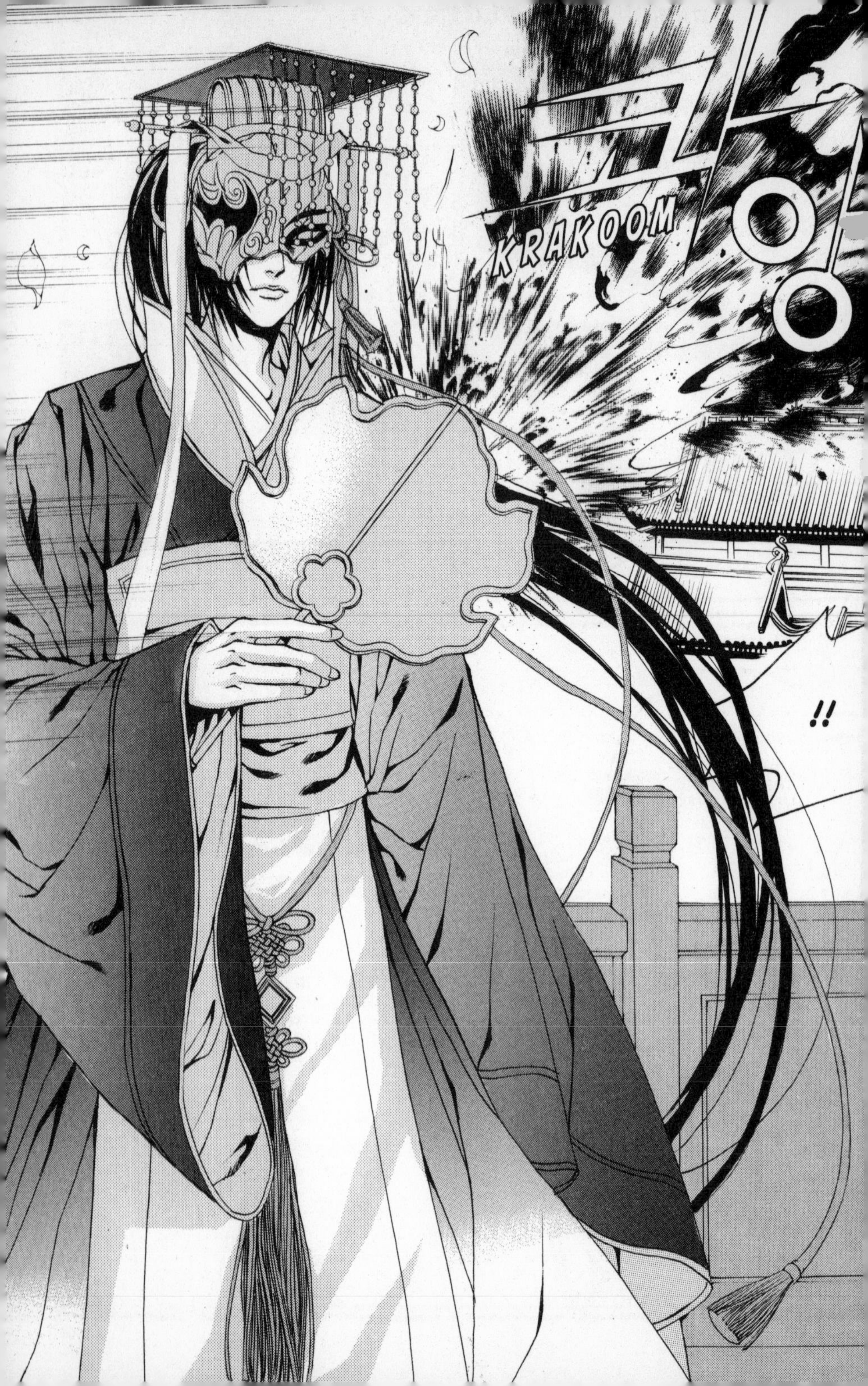
KRAKOOM
!!

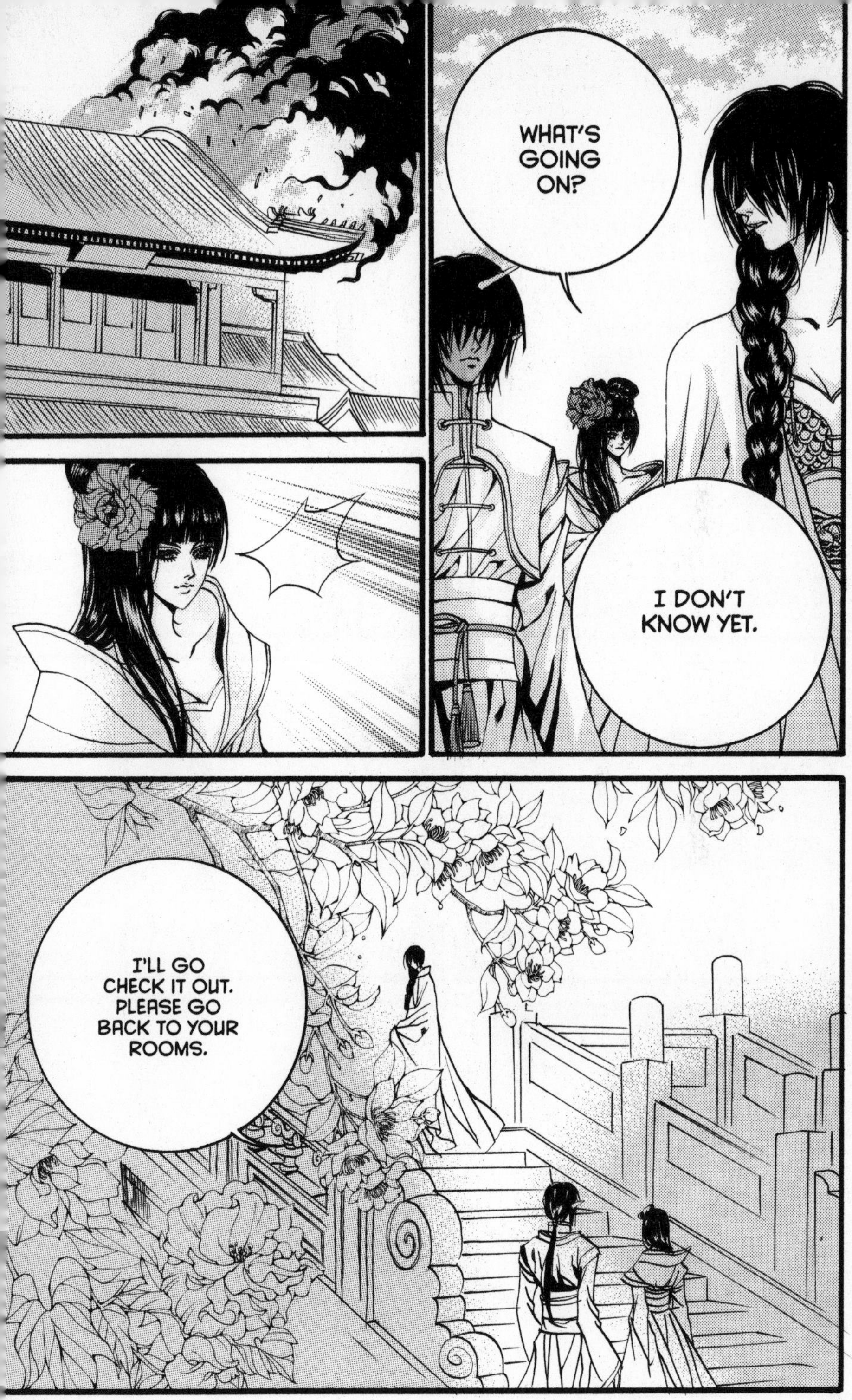
WHAT'S GOING ON?
I DON'T KNOW YET.
I'LL GO CHECK IT OUT. PLEASE GO BACK TO YOUR ROOMS.

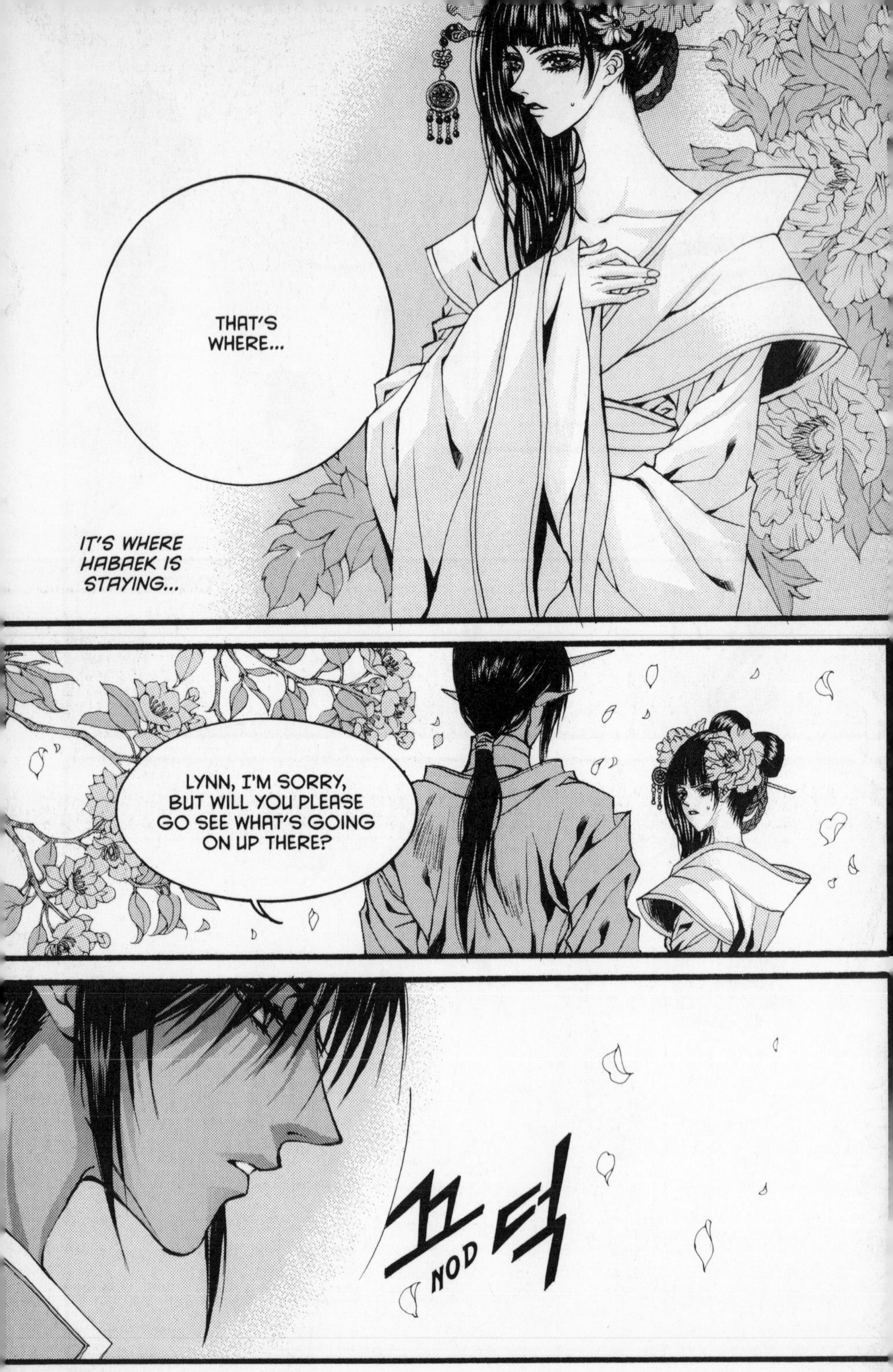
THAT'S WHERE...
IT'S WHERE HABAEK IS STAYING...
LYNN, I'M SORRY, BUT WILL YOU PLEASE GO SEE WHAT'S GOING ON UP THERE?
끄덕
NOD

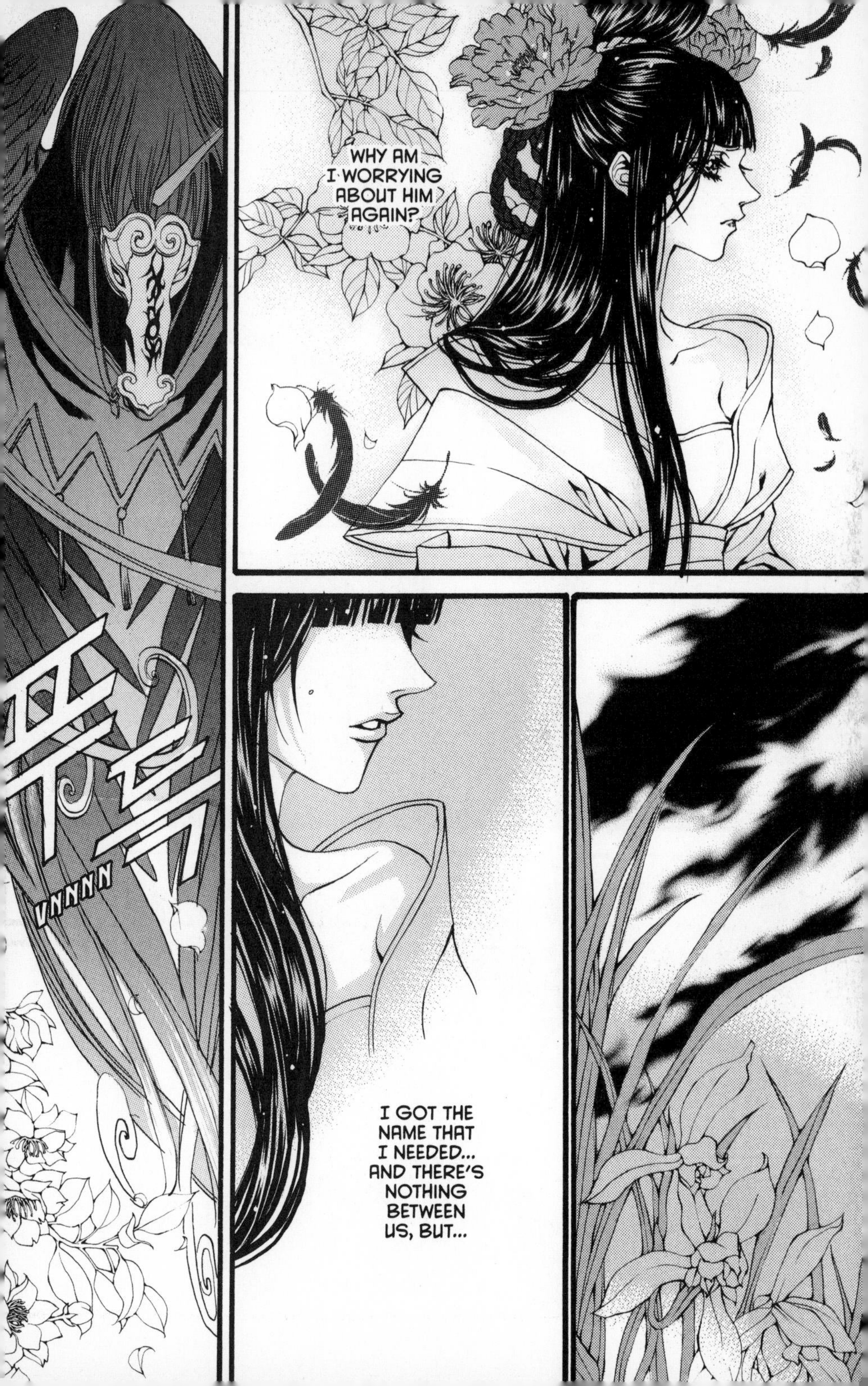
WHY AM I WORRYING ABOUT HIM AGAIN?
VNNNNN
I GOT THE NAME THAT I NEEDED... AND THERE'S NOTHING BETWEEN US, BUT...

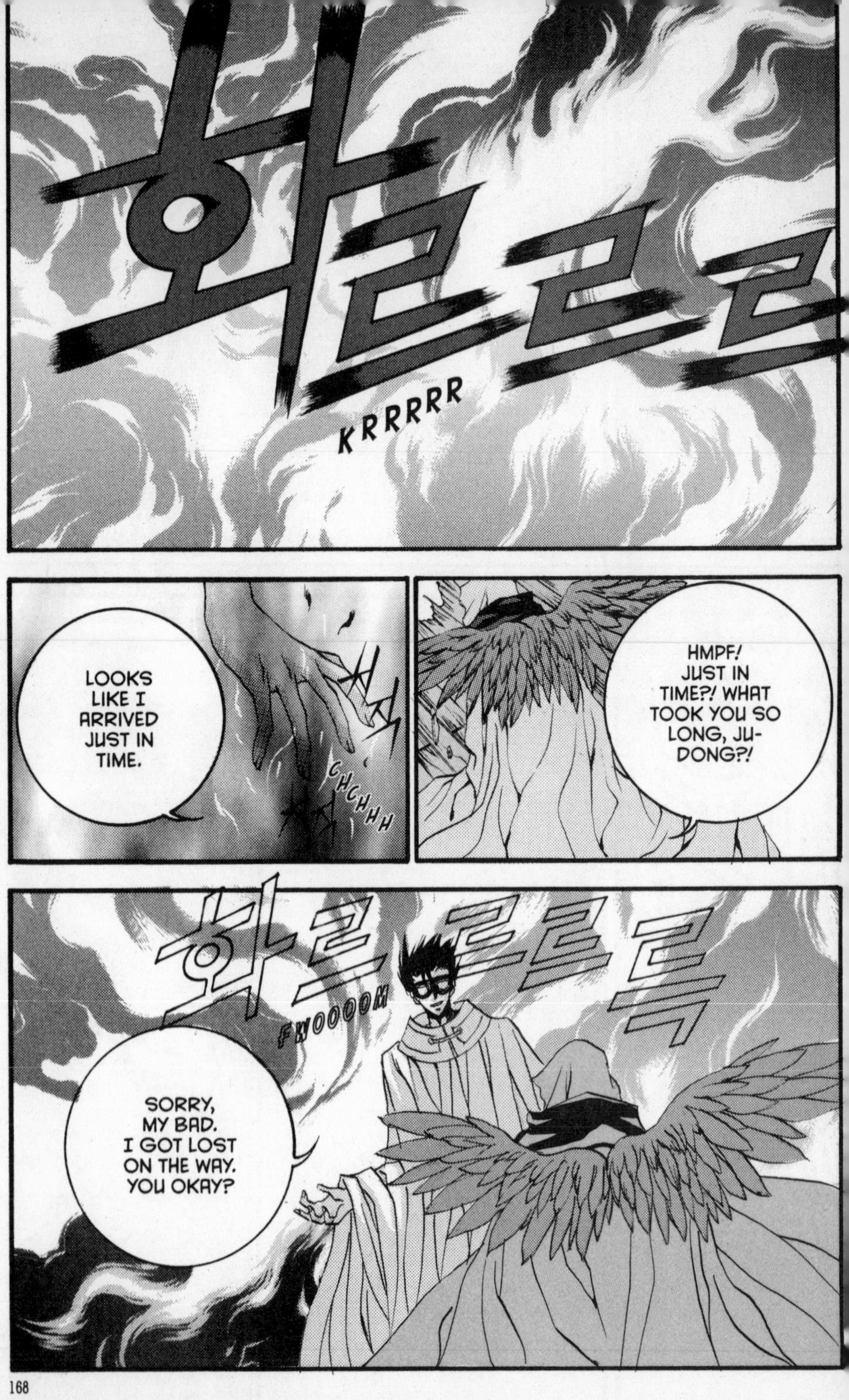
화르르
KRRRRR
LOOKS LIKE I ARRIVED JUST IN TIME.
CHCHHH
HMPF! JUST IN TIME?! WHAT TOOK YOU SO LONG, JU-DONG?!
FWOOOOM
SORRY, MY BAD. I GOT LOST ON THE WAY. YOU OKAY?

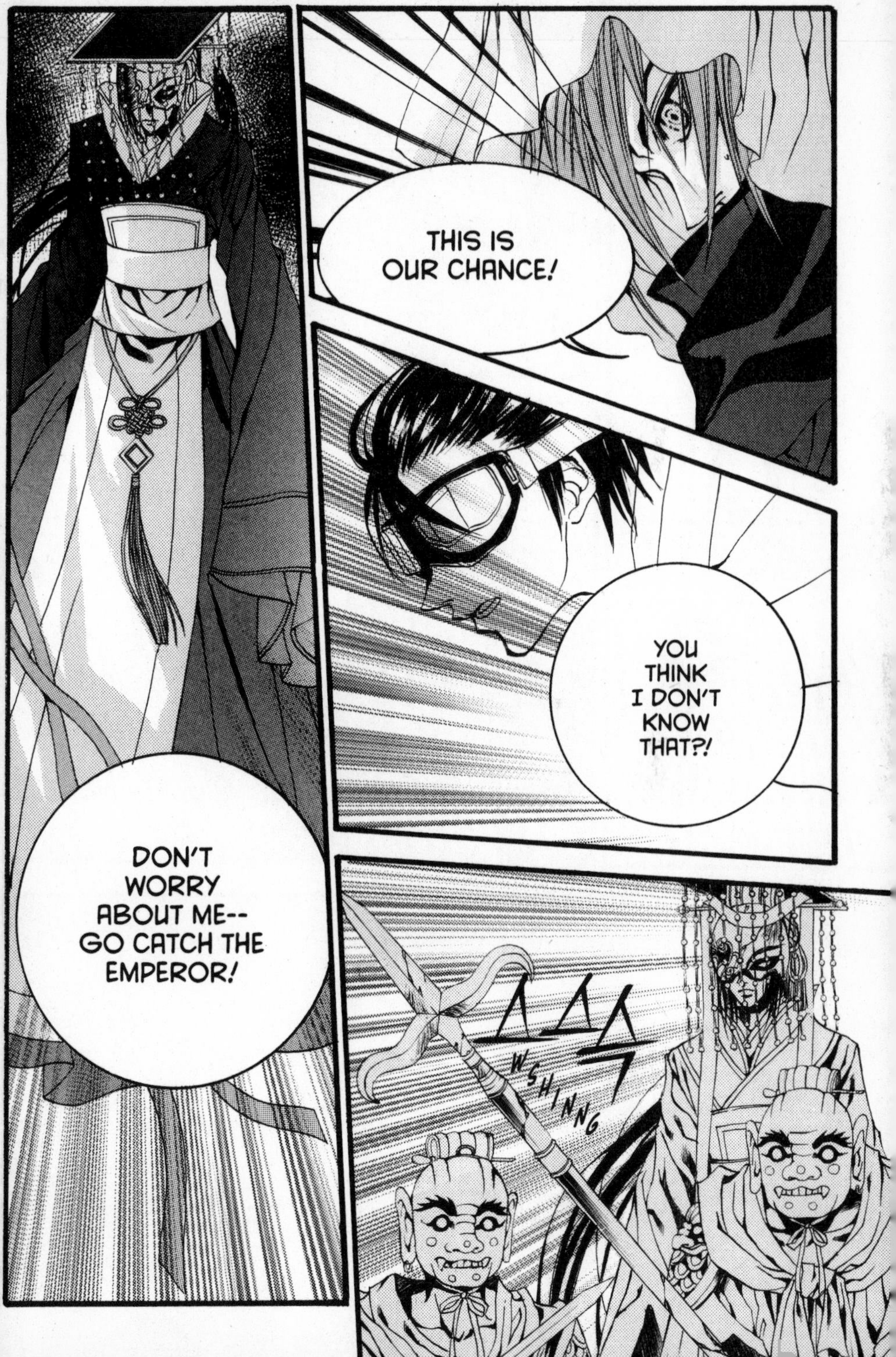
THIS IS OUR CHANCE!
YOU THINK I DON'T KNOW THAT?!
DON'T WORRY ABOUT ME-- GO CATCH THE EMPEROR!
WSHINNG

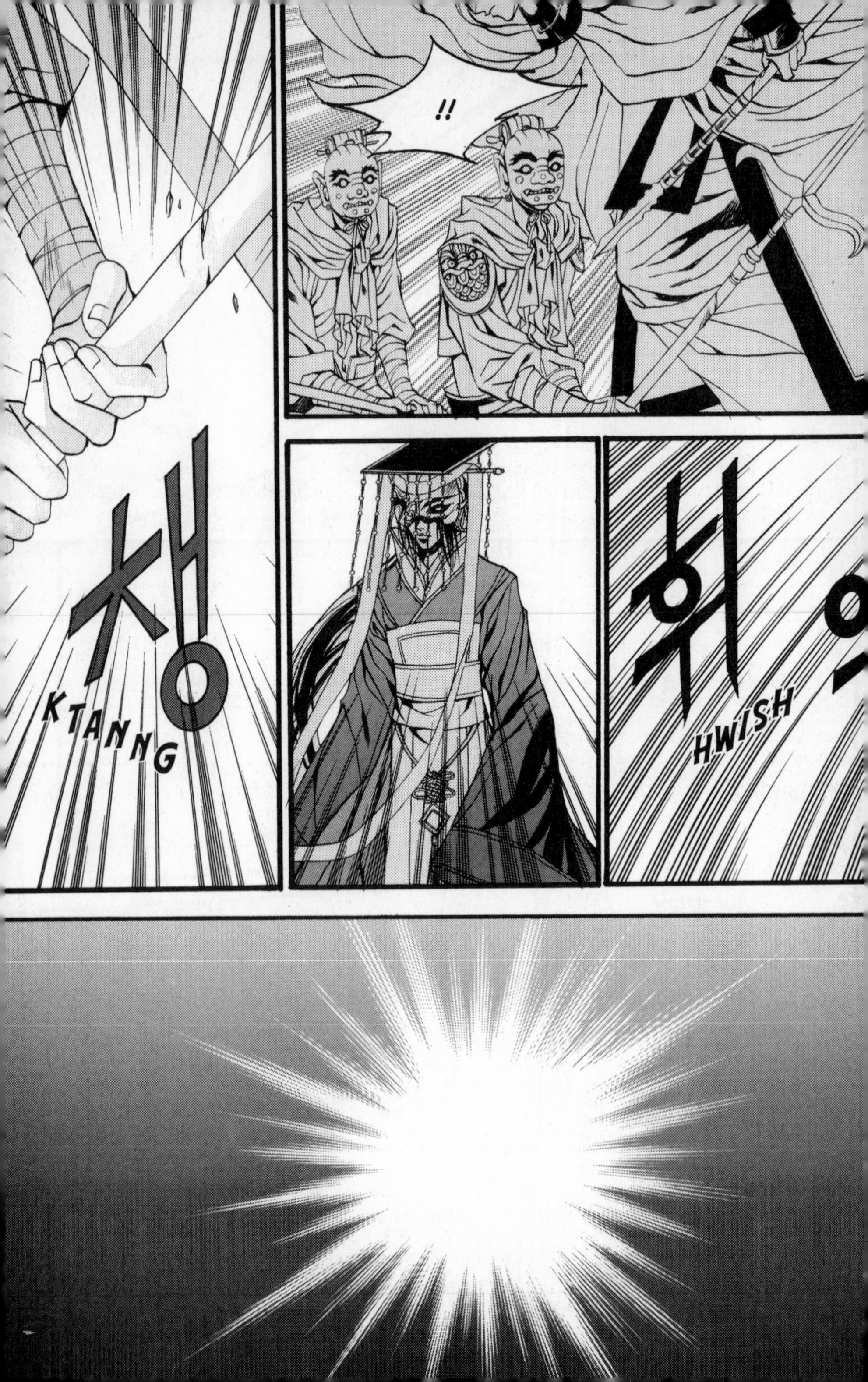
!!
챙
KTANNG
HWISH

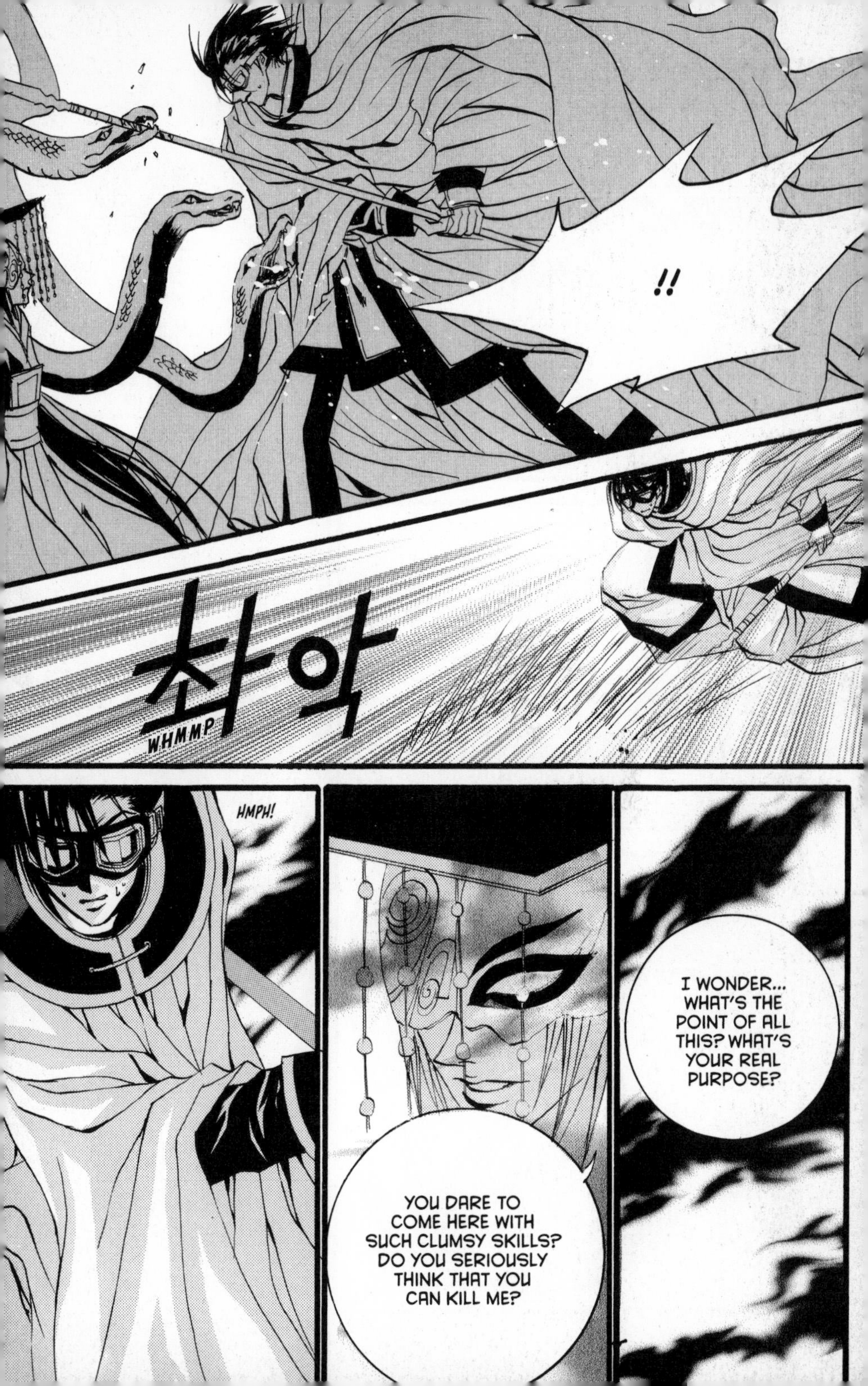
!!
촤악
WHMMP
HMPH!
YOU DARE TO COME HERE WITH SUCH CLUMSY SKILLS? DO YOU SERIOUSLY THINK THAT YOU CAN KILL ME?
I WONDER... WHAT'S THE POINT OF ALL THIS? WHAT'S YOUR REAL PURPOSE?

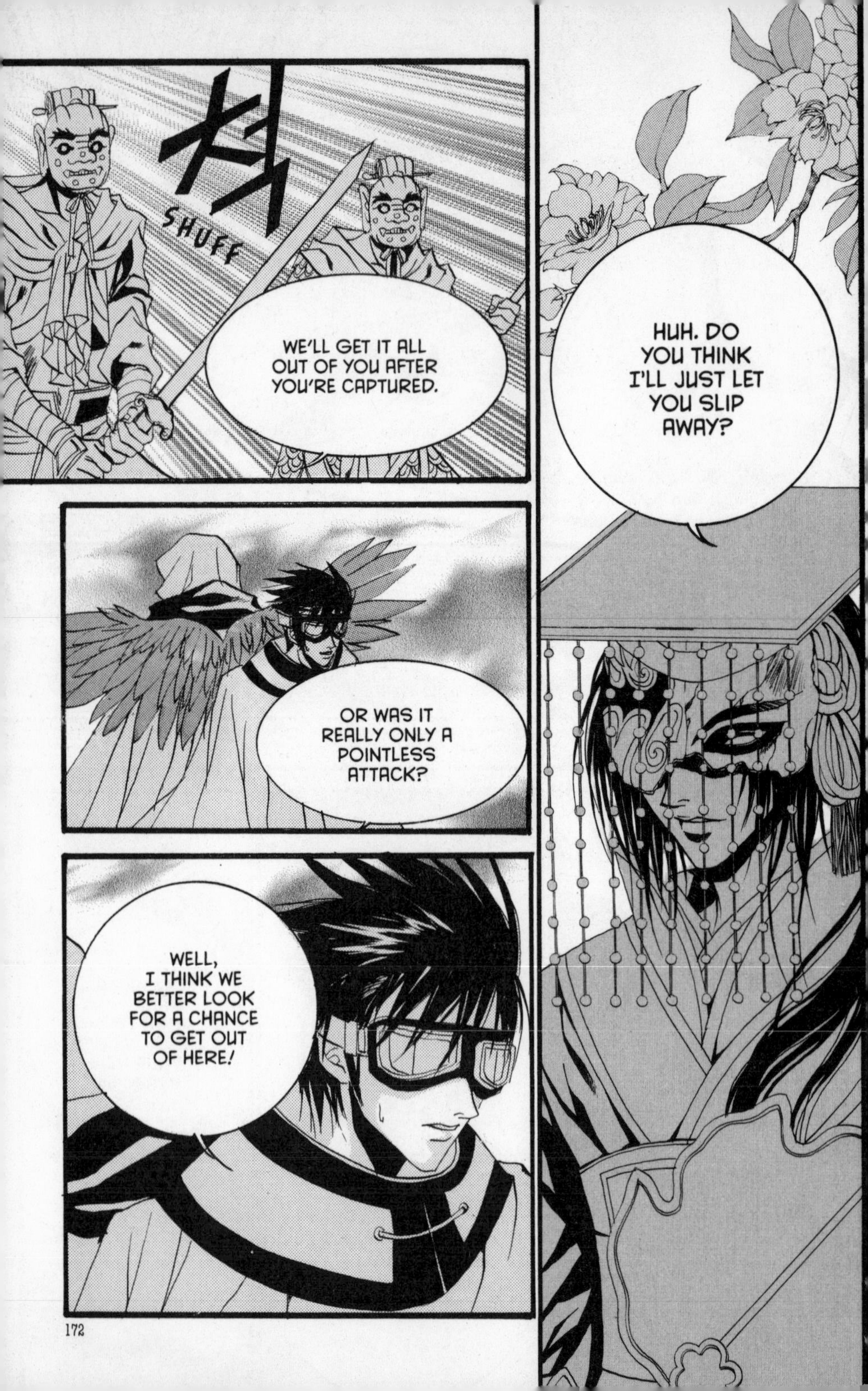
SHUFF
WE'LL GET IT ALL OUT OF YOU AFTER YOU'RE CAPTURED.
OR WAS IT REALLY ONLY A POINTLESS ATTACK?
WELL, I THINK WE BETTER LOOK FOR A CHANCE TO GET OUT OF HERE!
HUH. DO YOU THINK I'LL JUST LET YOU SLIP AWAY?

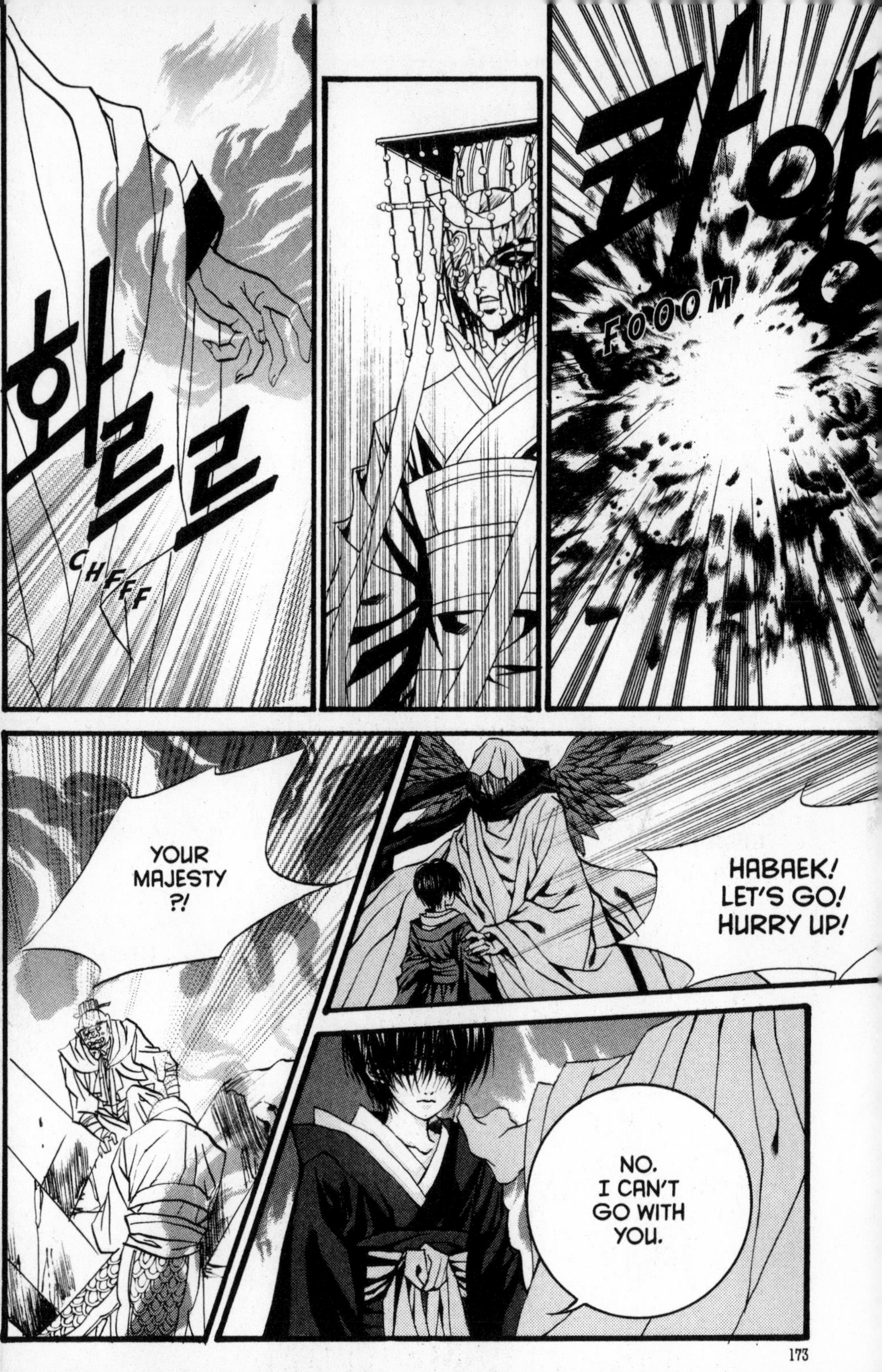
화르르
CHFFF
콰앙
FOOOM
YOUR MAJESTY ?!
HABAEK! LET'S GO! HURRY UP!
NO. I CAN'T GO WITH YOU.

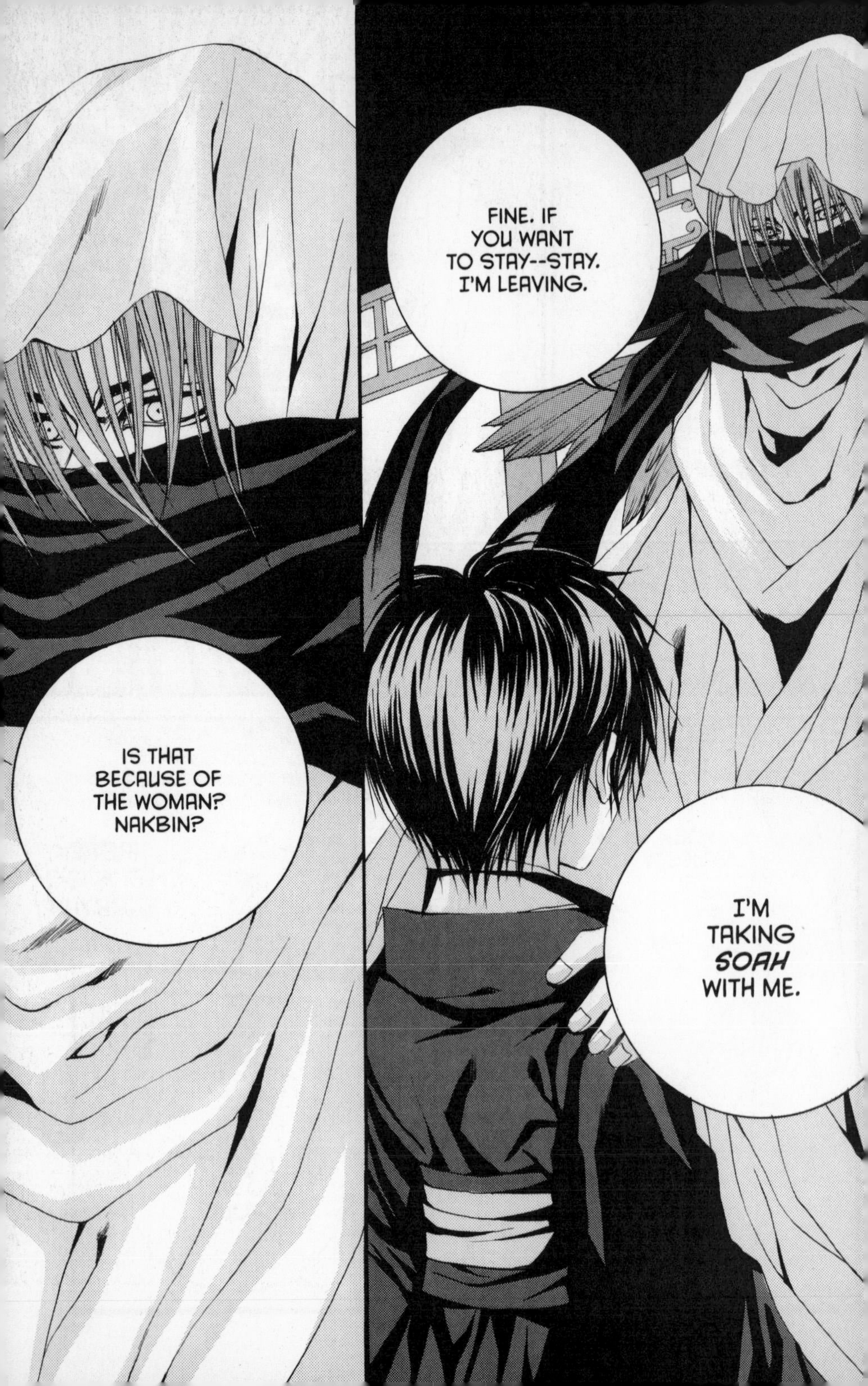
FINE. IF YOU WANT TO STAY--STAY. I'M LEAVING.
IS THAT BECAUSE OF THE WOMAN? NAKBIN?
I'M TAKING *SOAH* WITH ME.

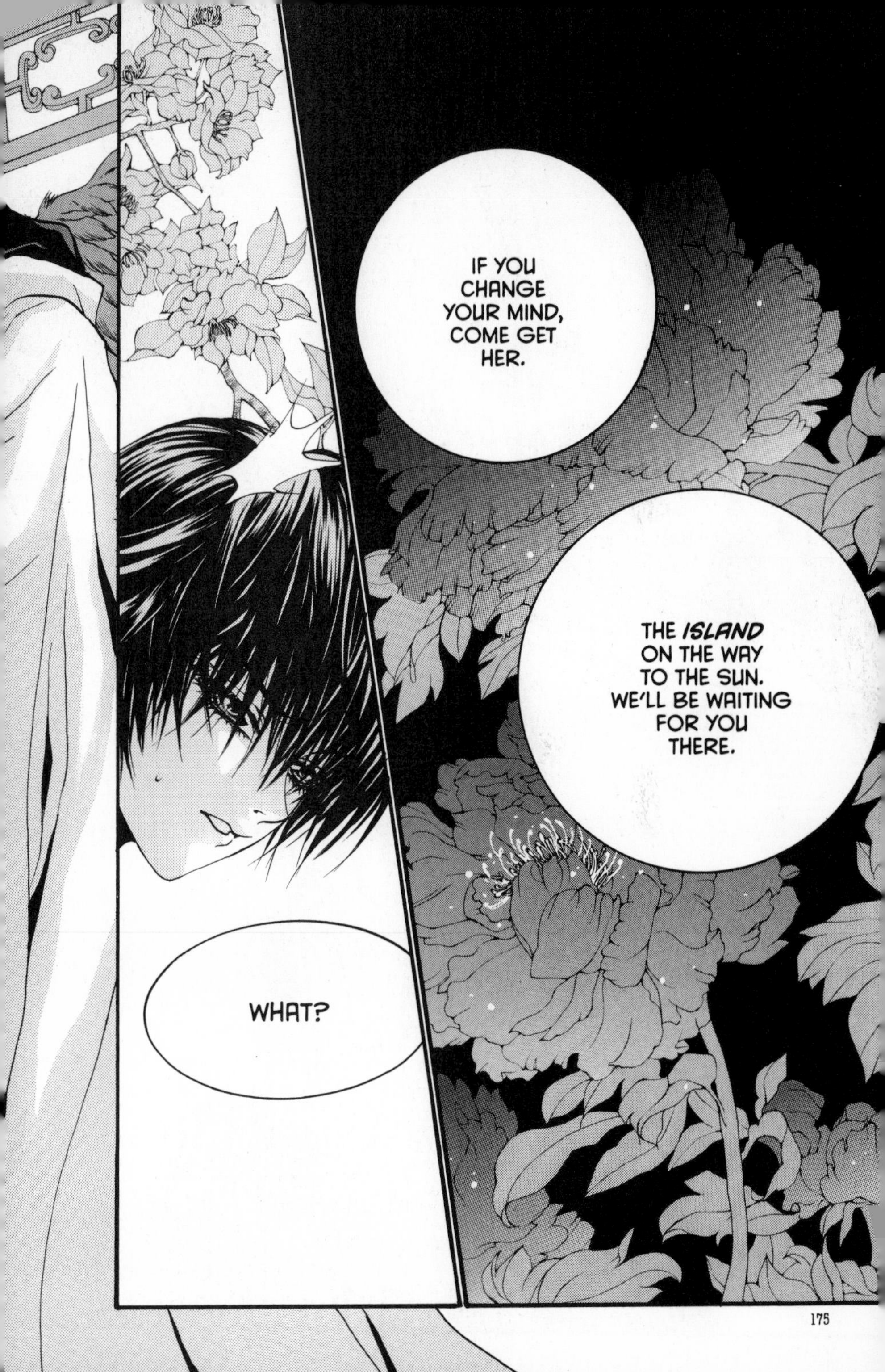
IF YOU CHANGE YOUR MIND, COME GET HER.
THE *ISLAND* ON THE WAY TO THE SUN. WE'LL BE WAITING FOR YOU THERE.
WHAT?

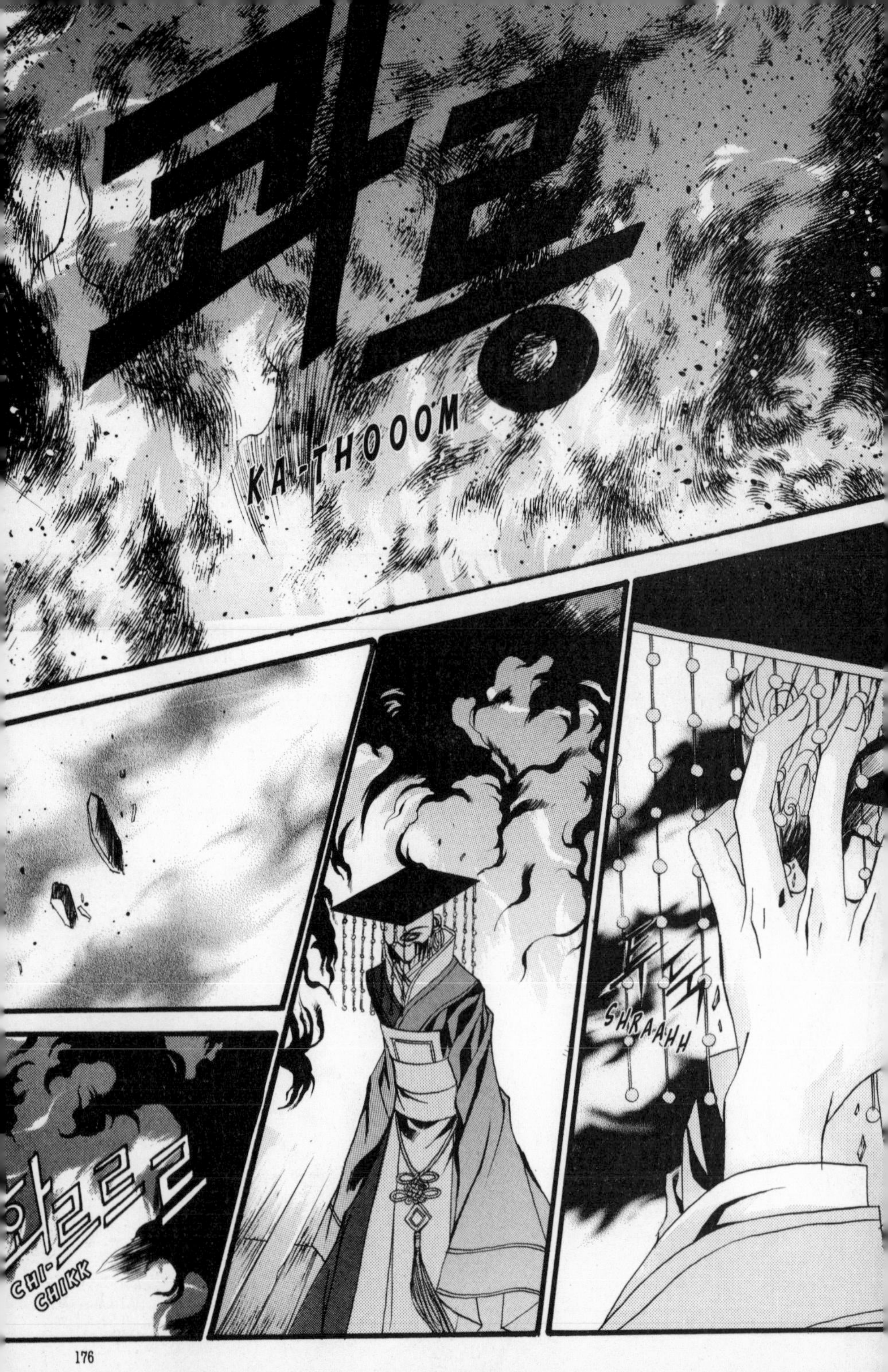
KA-THOOOM
CHI-CHIKK
SHRAAHH

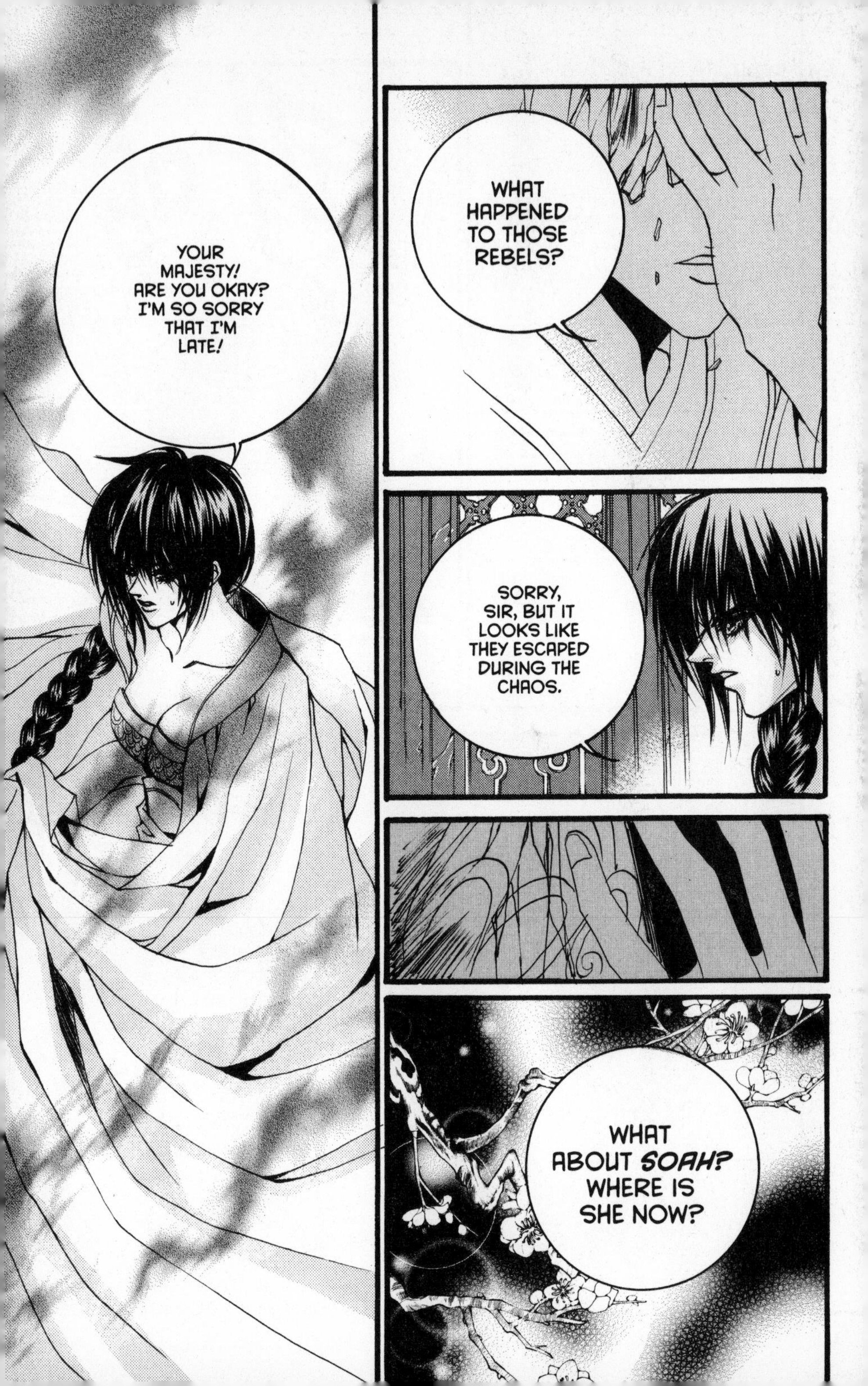
YOUR MAJESTY! ARE YOU OKAY? I'M SO SORRY THAT I'M LATE!
WHAT HAPPENED TO THOSE REBELS?
SORRY, SIR, BUT IT LOOKS LIKE THEY ESCAPED DURING THE CHAOS.
WHAT ABOUT *SOAH?* WHERE IS SHE NOW?

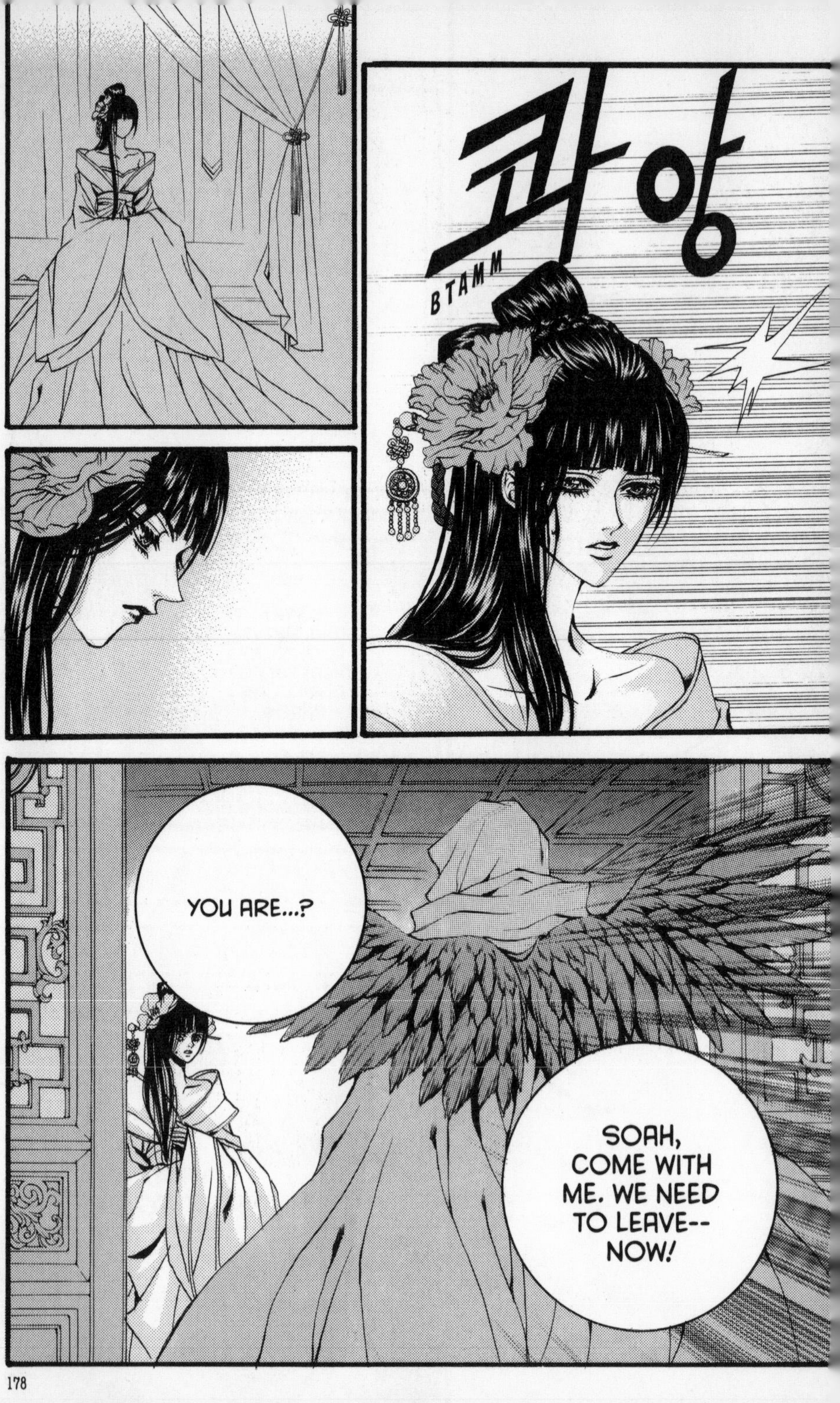
콰앙
BTAMM
YOU ARE...?
SOAH, COME WITH ME. WE NEED TO LEAVE-- NOW!

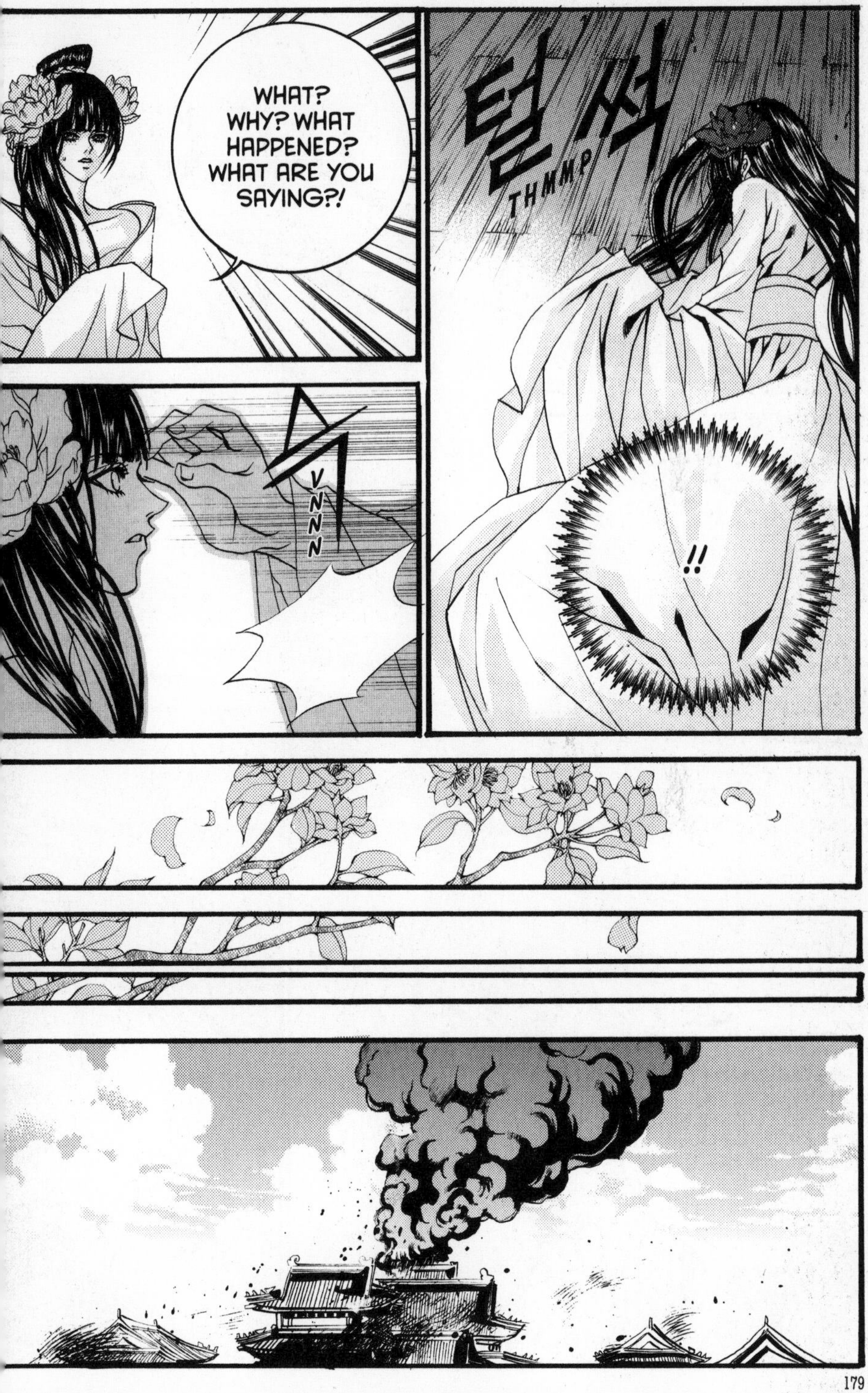
WHAT? WHY? WHAT HAPPENED? WHAT ARE YOU SAYING?!
털썩
THMMP
VNNN
!!

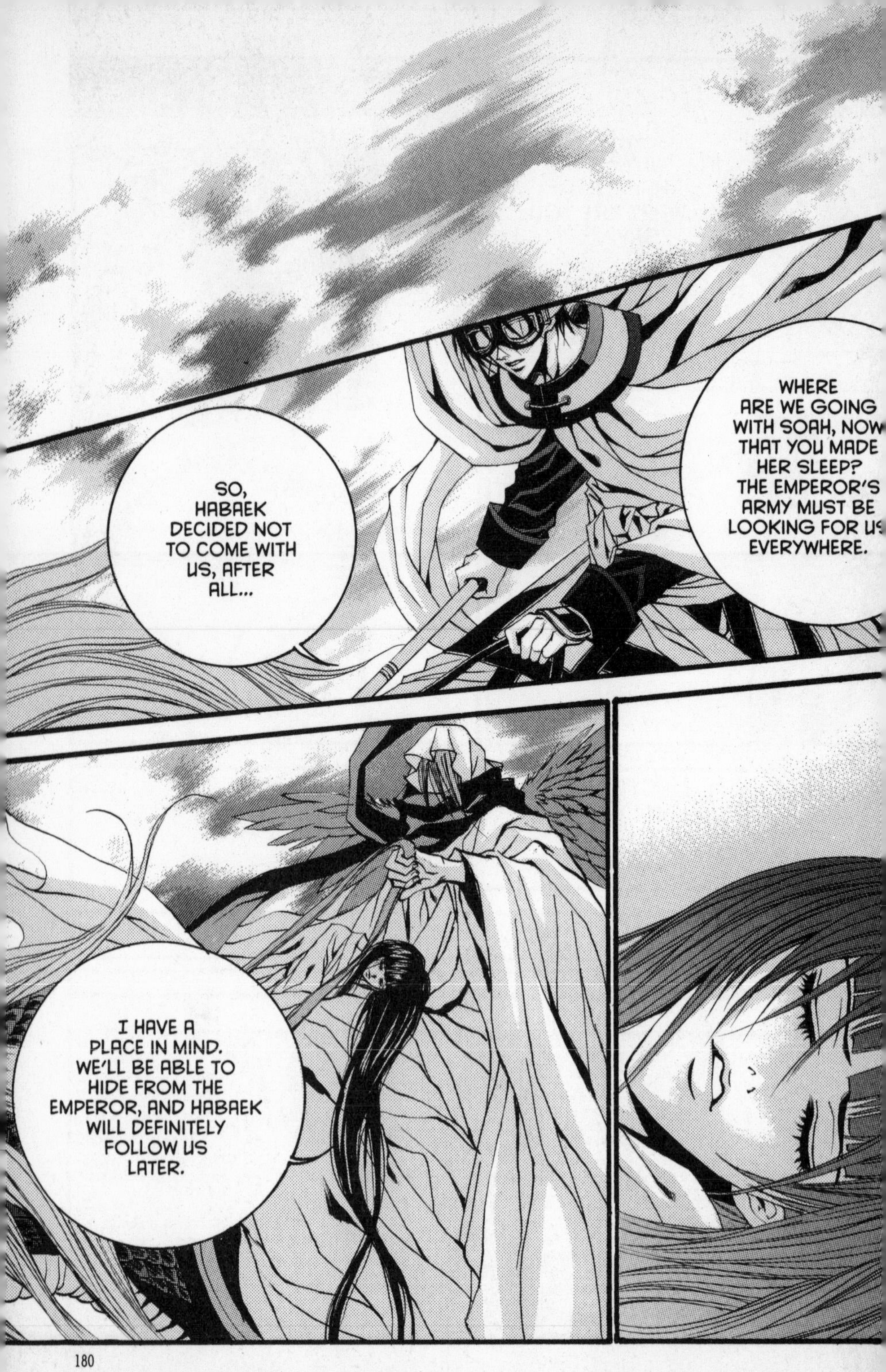
WHERE ARE WE GOING WITH SOAH, NOW THAT YOU MADE HER SLEEP? THE EMPEROR'S ARMY MUST BE LOOKING FOR US EVERYWHERE.
SO, HABAEK DECIDED NOT TO COME WITH US, AFTER ALL...
I HAVE A PLACE IN MIND. WE'LL BE ABLE TO HIDE FROM THE EMPEROR, AND HABAEK WILL DEFINITELY FOLLOW US LATER.

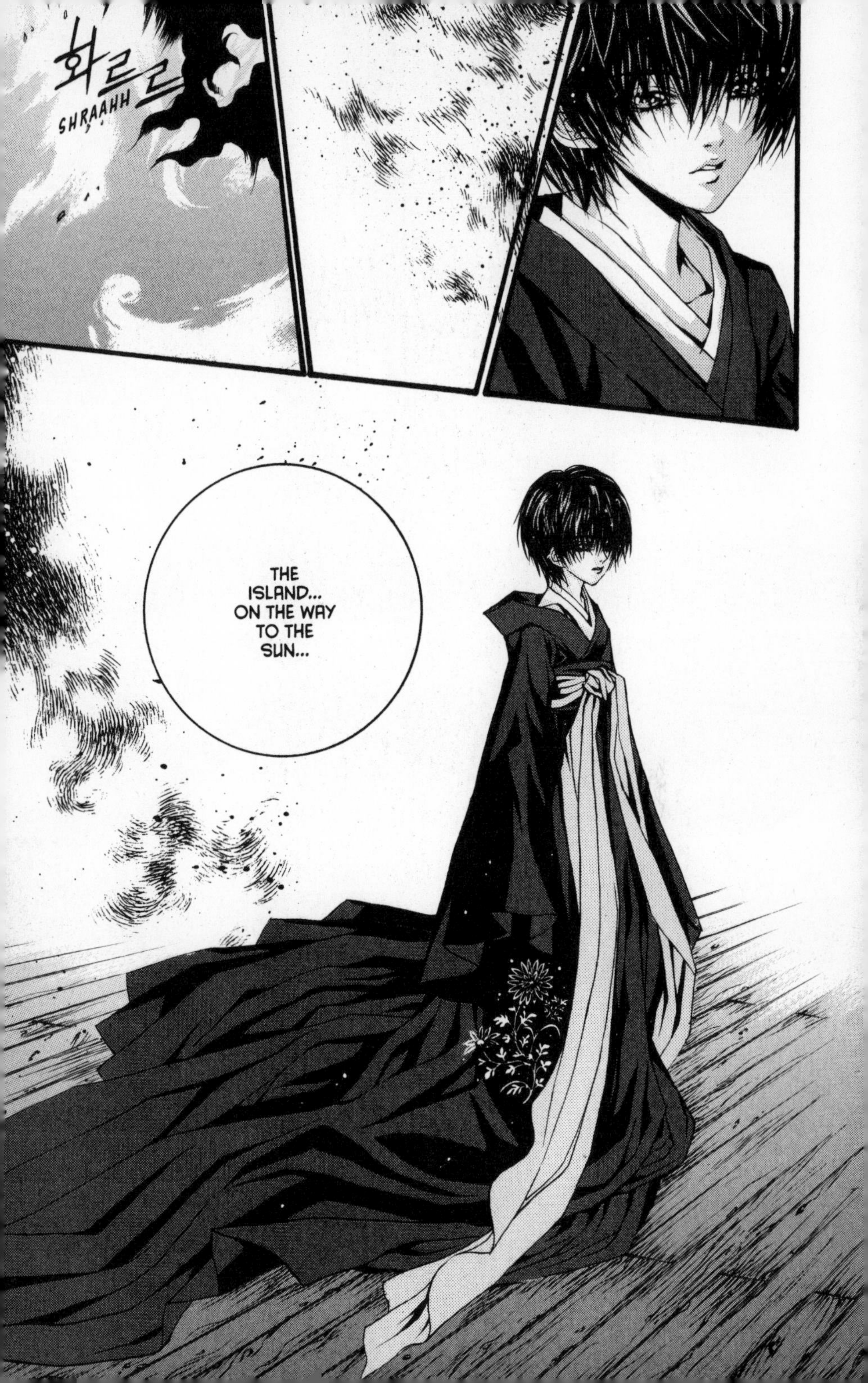

화르르
SHRAAHH
THE ISLAND... ON THE WAY TO THE SUN...

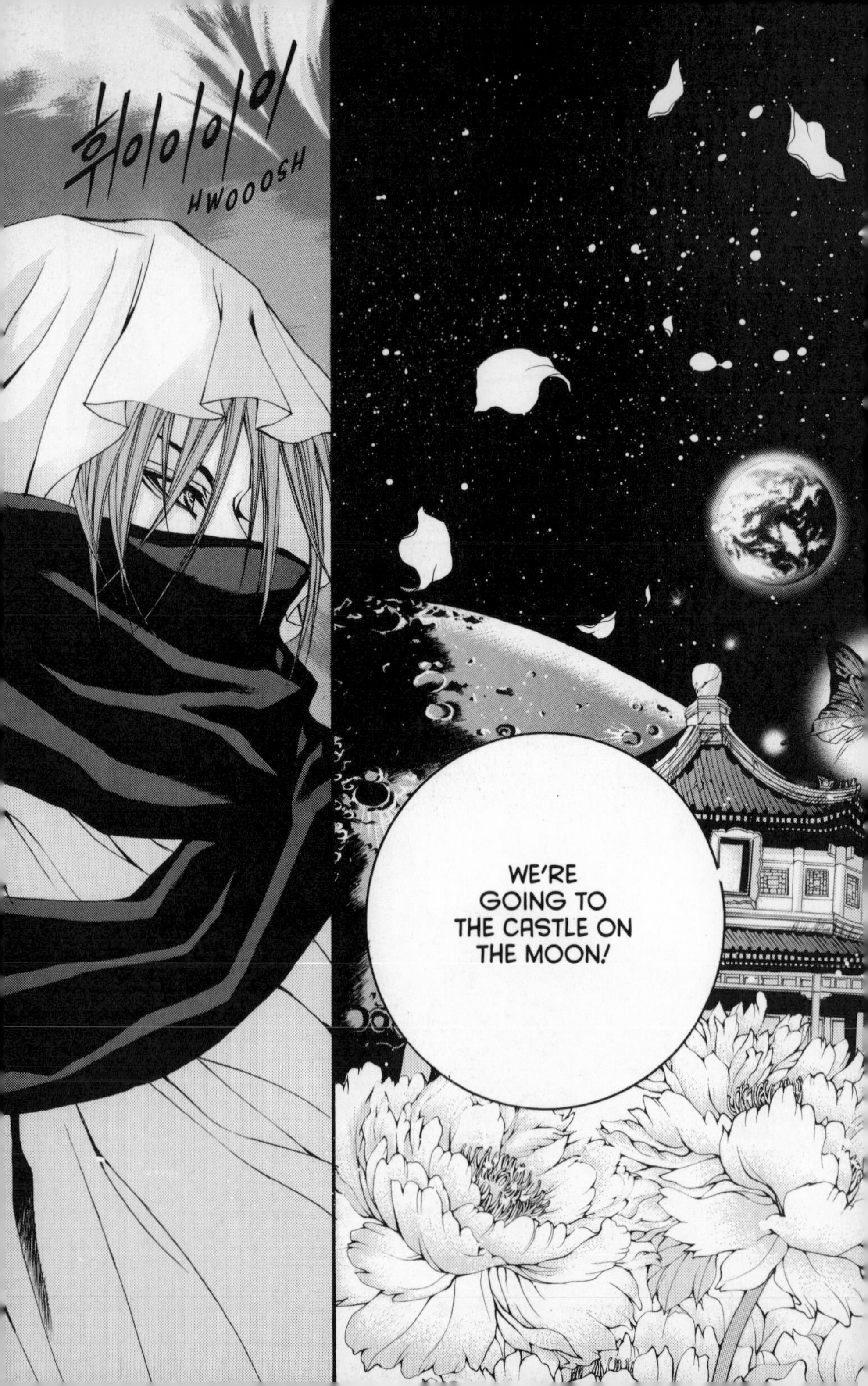

휘이이이이
HWOOOSH
WE'RE GOING TO THE CASTLE ON THE MOON!

BRIDE of the WATER GOD

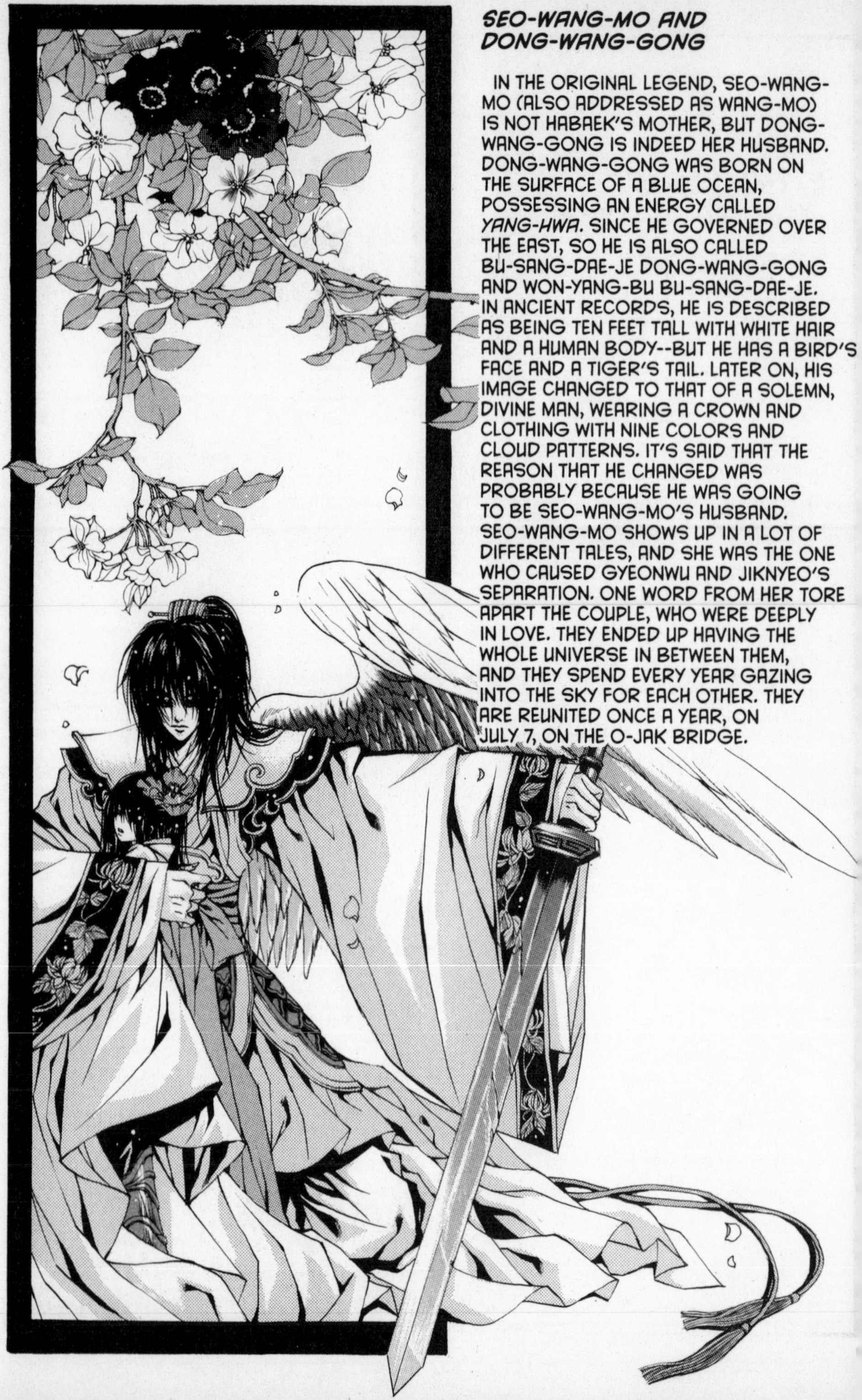

SEO-WANG-MO AND DONG-WANG-GONG

IN THE ORIGINAL LEGEND, SEO-WANG-MO (ALSO ADDRESSED AS WANG-MO) IS NOT HABAEK'S MOTHER, BUT DONG-WANG-GONG IS INDEED HER HUSBAND. DONG-WANG-GONG WAS BORN ON THE SURFACE OF A BLUE OCEAN, POSSESSING AN ENERGY CALLED *YANG-HWA*. SINCE HE GOVERNED OVER THE EAST, SO HE IS ALSO CALLED BU-SANG-DAE-JE DONG-WANG-GONG AND WON-YANG-BU BU-SANG-DAE-JE. IN ANCIENT RECORDS, HE IS DESCRIBED AS BEING TEN FEET TALL WITH WHITE HAIR AND A HUMAN BODY--BUT HE HAS A BIRD'S FACE AND A TIGER'S TAIL. LATER ON, HIS IMAGE CHANGED TO THAT OF A SOLEMN, DIVINE MAN, WEARING A CROWN AND CLOTHING WITH NINE COLORS AND CLOUD PATTERNS. IT'S SAID THAT THE REASON THAT HE CHANGED WAS PROBABLY BECAUSE HE WAS GOING TO BE SEO-WANG-MO'S HUSBAND. SEO-WANG-MO SHOWS UP IN A LOT OF DIFFERENT TALES, AND SHE WAS THE ONE WHO CAUSED GYEONWU AND JIKNYEO'S SEPARATION. ONE WORD FROM HER TORE APART THE COUPLE, WHO WERE DEEPLY IN LOVE. THEY ENDED UP HAVING THE WHOLE UNIVERSE IN BETWEEN THEM, AND THEY SPEND EVERY YEAR GAZING INTO THE SKY FOR EACH OTHER. THEY ARE REUNITED ONCE A YEAR, ON JULY 7, ON THE O-JAK BRIDGE.

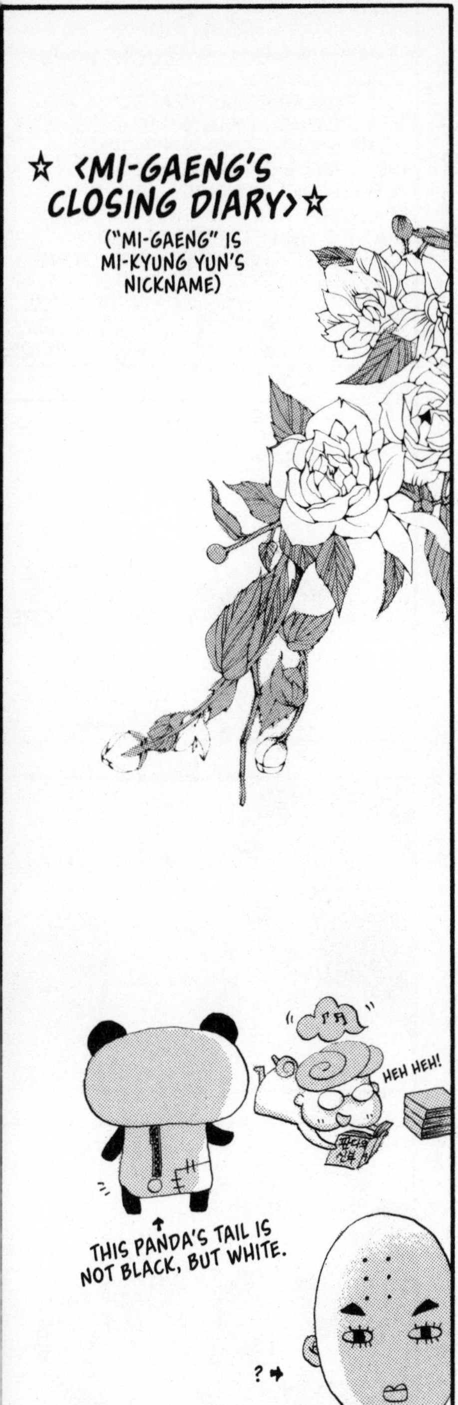
☆ <MI-GAENG'S CLOSING DIARY> ☆
("MI-GAENG" IS MI-KYUNG YUN'S NICKNAME)
HEH HEH!
THIS PANDA'S TAIL IS NOT BLACK, BUT WHITE.
?

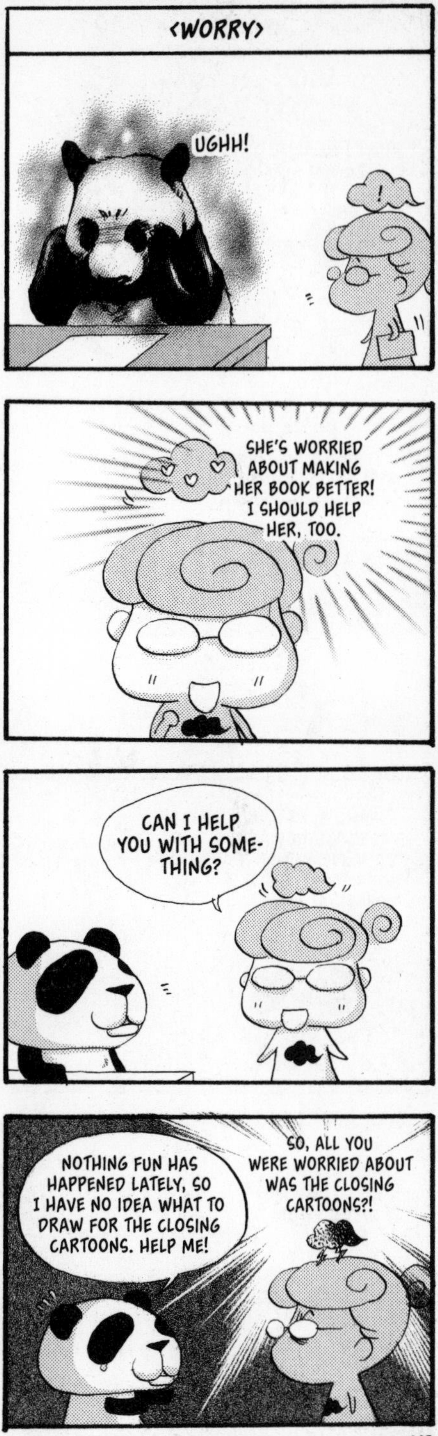
<WORRY>
UGHH!
SHE'S WORRIED ABOUT MAKING HER BOOK BETTER! I SHOULD HELP HER, TOO.
CAN I HELP YOU WITH SOME-THING?
NOTHING FUN HAS HAPPENED LATELY, SO I HAVE NO IDEA WHAT TO DRAW FOR THE CLOSING CARTOONS. HELP ME!
SO, ALL YOU WERE WORRIED ABOUT WAS THE CLOSING CARTOONS?!

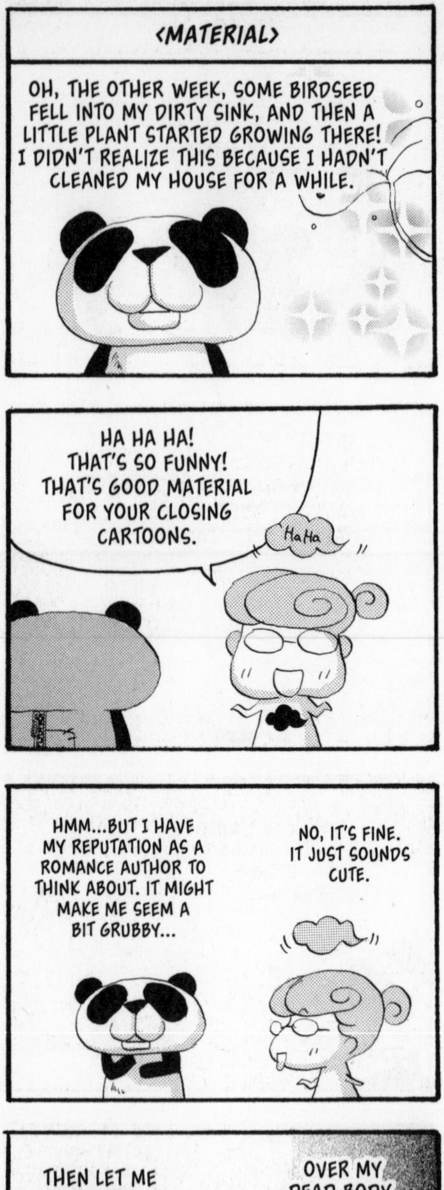
<MATERIAL>
OH, THE OTHER WEEK, SOME BIRDSEED FELL INTO MY DIRTY SINK, AND THEN A LITTLE PLANT STARTED GROWING THERE! I DIDN'T REALIZE THIS BECAUSE I HADN'T CLEANED MY HOUSE FOR A WHILE.
HA HA HA! THAT'S SO FUNNY! THAT'S GOOD MATERIAL FOR YOUR CLOSING CARTOONS.
HaHa
HMM...BUT I HAVE MY REPUTATION AS A ROMANCE AUTHOR TO THINK ABOUT. IT MIGHT MAKE ME SEEM A BIT GRUBBY...
NO, IT'S FINE. IT JUST SOUNDS CUTE.
THEN LET ME WRITE IT AS IF IT WERE *YOUR* STORY!
OVER MY DEAD BODY. (SUPER FIRM VOICE)

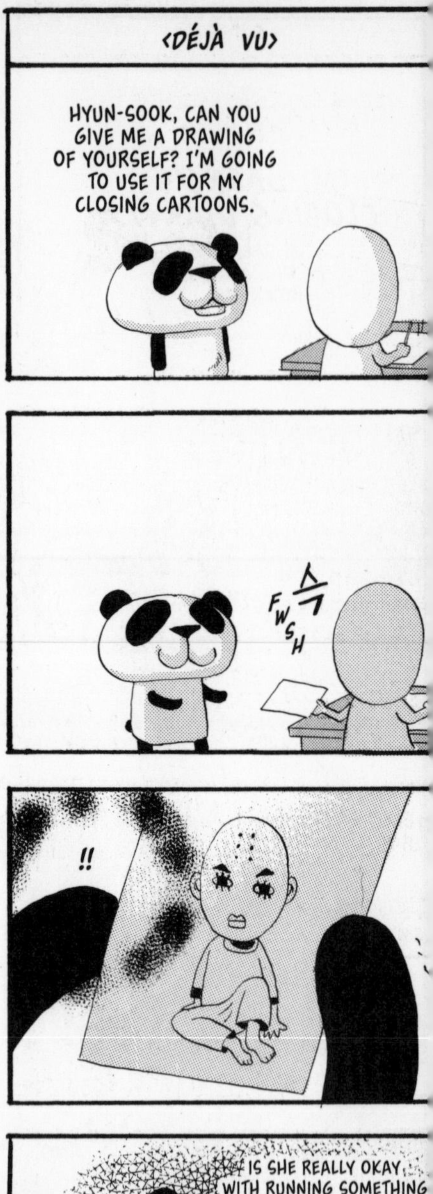
<DÉJÀ VU>
HYUN-SOOK, CAN YOU GIVE ME A DRAWING OF YOURSELF? I'M GOING TO USE IT FOR MY CLOSING CARTOONS.
FWSH
!!
IS SHE REALLY OKAY WITH RUNNING SOMETHING LIKE THIS ? OH, WAIT, THIS FEELS FAMILIAR! IT FEELS LIKE SOMETHING LIKE THIS HAS HAPPENED BEFORE!

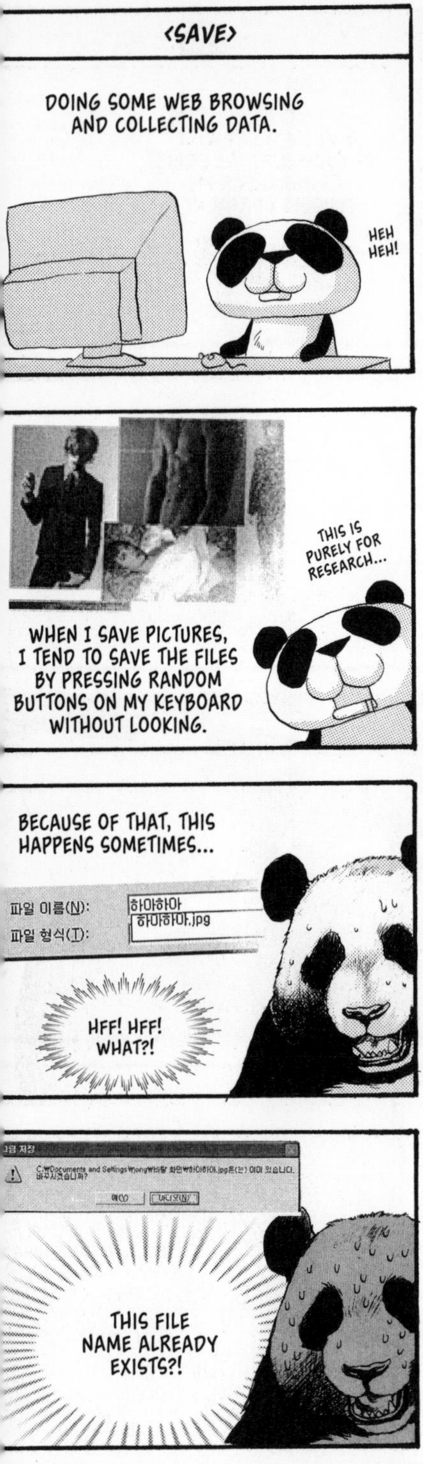
<SAVE>
DOING SOME WEB BROWSING AND COLLECTING DATA.
HEH HEH!
THIS IS PURELY FOR RESEARCH...
WHEN I SAVE PICTURES, I TEND TO SAVE THE FILES BY PRESSING RANDOM BUTTONS ON MY KEYBOARD WITHOUT LOOKING.
BECAUSE OF THAT, THIS HAPPENS SOMETIMES...
파일 이름(N): 하마하마
파일 형식(T): 하마하마.jpg
HFF! HFF! WHAT?!
THIS FILE NAME ALREADY EXISTS?!

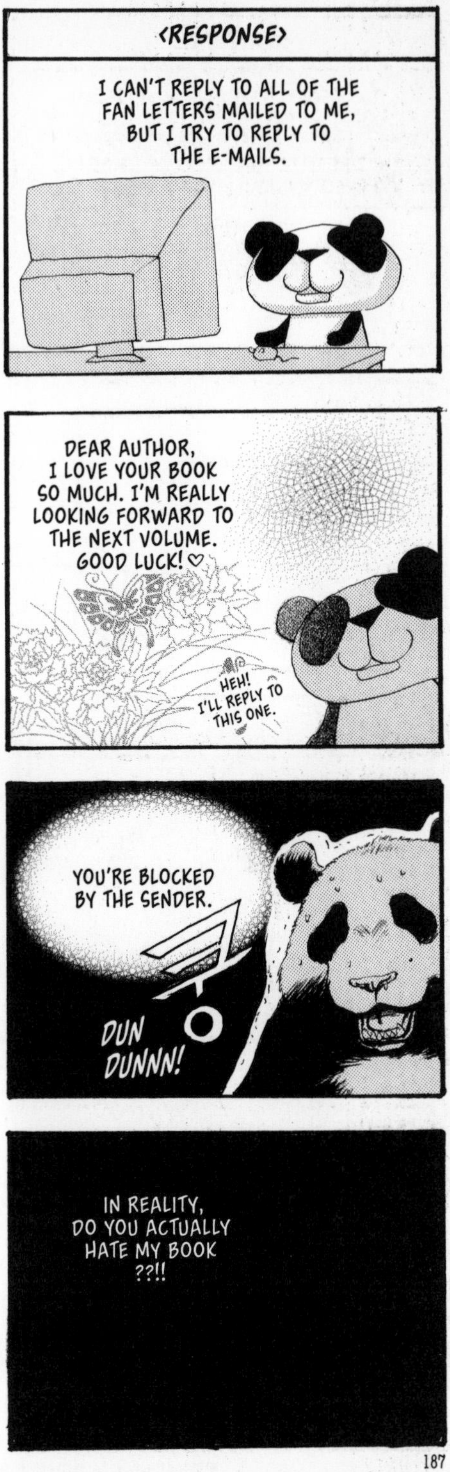
<RESPONSE>
I CAN'T REPLY TO ALL OF THE FAN LETTERS MAILED TO ME, BUT I TRY TO REPLY TO THE E-MAILS.
DEAR AUTHOR, I LOVE YOUR BOOK SO MUCH. I'M REALLY LOOKING FORWARD TO THE NEXT VOLUME. GOOD LUCK! ♡
HEH! I'LL REPLY TO THIS ONE.
YOU'RE BLOCKED BY THE SENDER.
DUN DUNNN!
IN REALITY, DO YOU ACTUALLY HATE MY BOOK ??!!

I ORDERED SOME PAPER MAGNETS FROM A WEB STORE. I PUT *BRIDE OF THE WATER GOD* ILLUSTRATIONS AND LOGOS ON THEM, SO I CAN USE THEM FOR FAN-EVENT PRIZES.

OH, THEY'RE SO CHEAP. I'LL ORDER SOME!

IN A FEW DAYS...

딩동~
DING DONG

WHO IS IT?

BRIDE OF THE WATER GOD-NIM?!

SOMEWHAT DISAPPOINTED FACE →

--?!

NO WAY...?!

ARE YOU REALLY... *BRIDE OF THE WATER GOD*-NIM?

YES... *BRIDE OF THE WATER GOD*.

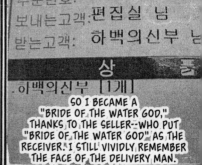

주문번호:
보내는고객: 편집실 님
받는고객: 하백의신부 님

상
하백의신부 [1개]

SO I BECAME A "BRIDE OF THE WATER GOD," THANKS TO THE SELLER--WHO PUT "BRIDE OF THE WATER GOD" AS THE RECEIVER. I STILL VIVIDLY REMEMBER THE FACE OF THE DELIVERY MAN.

188　　THE KOREAN DELIVERY SLIP SAYS, "SENDER: EDITORIAL TEAM-NIM, RECEIVER: BRIDE OF THE WATER GOD-NIM, PRODUCT: BRIDE OF THE WATER GOD (ONE BOX)."

My editor calls Dong-Wang-Gong the "Feeble Father." Sorry I couldn't draw you better, Dong-Wang-Gong! T.T (← crying face) Come to think of it, Mui's indecisive personality has to have been inherited from his father. In *Bride of the Water God*, the female characters do seem stronger than the men. ^^; (← sweating face)

—Mi-Kyung Yun

CREATOR PROFILE

Born on October 14, 1980. Majored in Animation at Mokwon University.

Received the silver medal for Seoul Media Group's "Shin-in-gong-mo-jeon" ("New Artist Debut Competition") for *Na-eu Ji-gu Bang-moon-gi* (*The Journey of My Earth Visit*) in 2003.

Received a "Shin-in-sang" ("Best New Artist") award from the Dokja-manhwa-daesang organization for *Railroad* in 2004.

Currently publishing *Bride of the Water God* serially in the Korean comics magazine *Wink*.

BRIDE of the WATER GOD

When Soah's impoverished, desperate village decides to sacrifice her to the Water God Habaek to end a long drought, they believe that drowning one beautiful girl will save their entire community and bring much-needed rain. Not only is Soah surprised to be *rescued* by the Water God instead of killed; she never imagined she'd be a welcomed guest in Habaek's magical kingdom, where an exciting new life awaits her! Most surprising, however, is the Water God himself, and how very different he is from the monster Soah imagined . . .

Created by Mi-Kyung Yun, who received the "Best New Artist" award in 2004 from the esteemed *Dokja-manhwa-daesang* organization, *Bride of the Water God* was the top-selling *shoujo* manhwa in Korea in 2006!

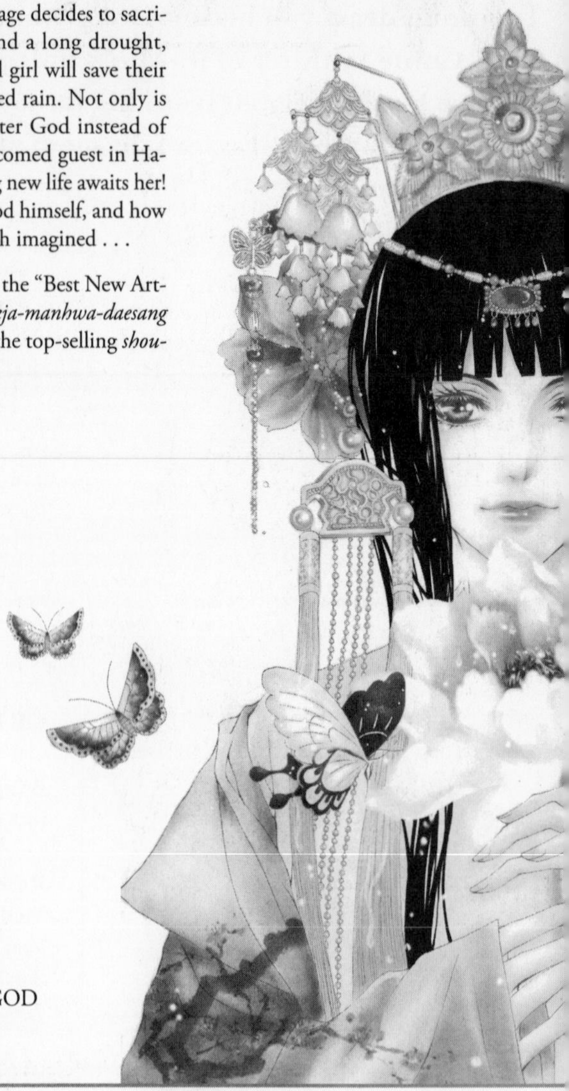

Volume 1
ISBN 978-1-59307-849-2

Volume 2
ISBN 978-1-59307-883-6

Volume 3
ISBN 978-1-59582-305-2

Volume 4
ISBN 978-1-59582-378-6

Volume 5
ISBN 978-1-59582-445-5

Volume 6
ISBN 978-1-59582-605-3

Volume 7
ISBN 978-1-59582-668-8

Volume 8
ISBN 978-1-59582-687-9

Volume 9
ISBN 978-1-59582-688-6

$9.99 each

Previews for BRIDE OF THE WATER GOD and other DARK HORSE MANHWA titles can be found at darkhorse.com!

PARK JOONG-KI'S

S·H·A·M·A·N
WARRIOR

A lavishly illustrated fantasy series with violent, breakneck action sequences and imaginative, memorable characters! Outlawed by the kingdom they once served, the Shaman Warriors of Kugai are a dying breed of disturbingly powerful, mystical fighting machines. As a young Shaman Warrior, Yaki's inherited powers have yet to awaken, but the heartless leaders of Kugai are determined to kill her and put an end to her legendary bloodline. When Batu—her hotheaded guardian—sneaks through dangerous territories to hunt the Death Lord who assassinated Yaki's father, the girl embarks on her own treacherous path of self-discovery.

Volume 1 ISBN 978-1-59307-638-2

Volume 2 ISBN 978-1-59307-749-5

Volume 3 ISBN 978-1-59307-769-3

Volume 4 ISBN 978-1-59307-819-5

Volume 5 ISBN 978-1-59307-859-1

Volume 6 ISBN 978-1-59307-895-9

Volume 7 ISBN 978-1-59582-332-8

Volume 8 ISBN 978-1-59582-381-6

Volume 9 ISBN 978-1-59582-453-0

$12.99 each

Previews for *SHAMAN WARRIOR* and other DARK HORSE MANHWA titles can be found at darkhorse.com!

AVAILABLE AT YOUR LOCAL COMICS SHOP OR BOOKSTORE. To find a comics shop in your area, call 1-888-266-4226. For more information or to order direct: On the web: darkhorse.com. E-mail: mailorder@darkhorse.com. Phone: 1-800-862-0052 Mon.–Fri. 9 AM to 5 PM Pacific Time.

DARK HORSE MANHWA

【 translucent 】
translucent

Can you see right through her?

By Kazuhiro Okamoto

Shizuka is an introverted girl dealing with schoolwork, boys, and a medical condition that has begun to turn her invisible! She finds support with Mamoru, a boy who is falling for Shizuka despite her condition, and with Keiko, a woman who suffers from the same illness and has finally turned *completely* invisible! *Translucent's* exploration of what people see, what people think they see, and what people wish to see in themselves and others, makes for an emotionally sensitive manga peppered with moments of surprising humor, heartbreak, and drama.

VOLUME 1
ISBN 978-1-59307-647-4

VOLUME 2
ISBN 978-1-59307-677-1

VOLUME 3
ISBN 978-1-59307-679-5

$9.99 Each!

Previews for *TRANSLUCENT* and other
DARK HORSE MANGA titles can be found
at darkhorse.com!

AVAILABLE AT YOUR LOCAL COMICS SHOP OR BOOKSTORE
To find a comics shop in your area, call 1-888-266-4226. For more information or
to order direct: • On the web: darkhorse.com • E-mail: mailorder@darkhorse.com
• Phone: 1-800-862-0052 Mon.–Fri. 9 AM to 5 PM Pacific Time.

DARK HORSE MANGA

Kosuke Fujishima's

Oh My Goddess!

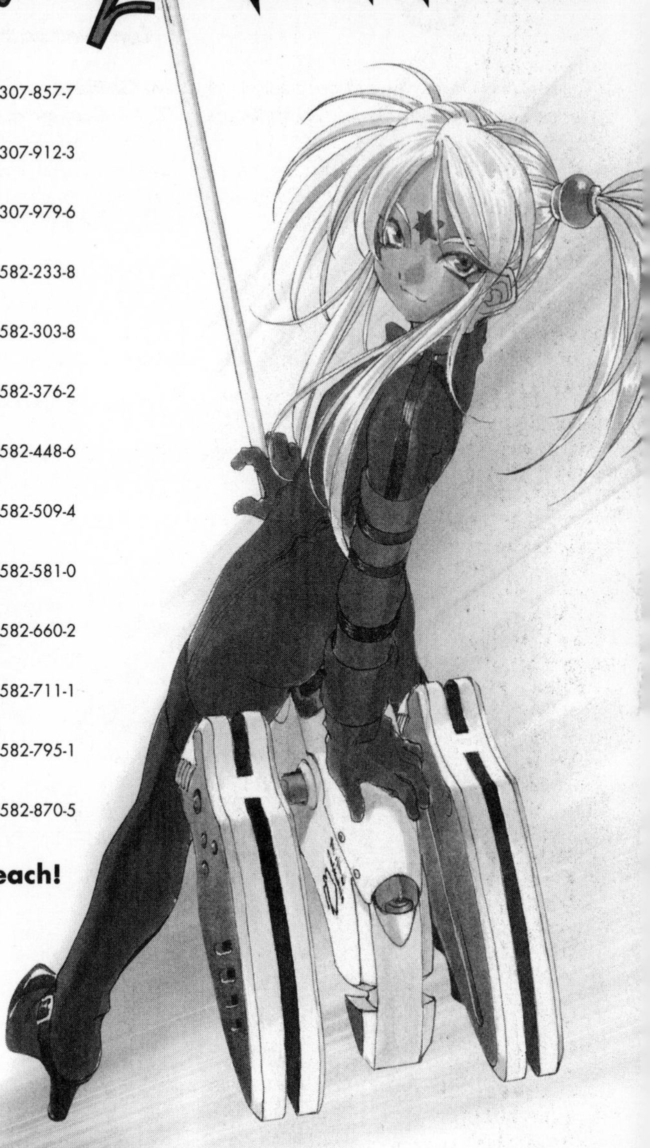

Volume 1
ISBN 978-1-59307-387-9

Volume 2
ISBN 978-1-59307-457-9

Volume 3
ISBN 978-1-59307-539-2

Volume 4
ISBN 978-1-59307-623-8

Volume 5
ISBN 978-1-59307-708-2

Volume 6
ISBN 978-1-59307-772-3

Volume 7
ISBN 978-1-59307-850-8

Volume 8
ISBN 978-1-59307-889-8

Volume 22
ISBN 978-1-59307-400-5

Volume 23
ISBN 978-1-59307-463-0

Volume 24
ISBN 978-1-59307-545-3

Volume 25
ISBN 978-1-59307-644-3

Volume 26
ISBN 978-1-59307-715-0

Volume 27
ISBN 978-1-59307-788-4

Volume 28
ISBN 978-1-59307-857-7

Volume 29
ISBN 978-1-59307-912-3

Volume 30
ISBN 978-1-59307-979-6

Volume 31
ISBN 978-1-59582-233-8

Volume 32
ISBN 978-1-59582-303-8

Volume 33
ISBN 978-1-59582-376-2

Volume 34
ISBN 978-1-59582-448-6

Volume 35
ISBN 978-1-59582-509-4

Volume 36
ISBN 978-1-59582-581-0

Volume 37
ISBN 978-1-59582-660-2

Volume 38
ISBN 978-1-59582-711-1

Volume 39
ISBN 978-1-59582-795-1

Volume 40
ISBN 978-1-59582-870-5

$10.99 each!

Winner of the 2009 Kodansha Award! Discover the romance classic that's America's longest-running manga series!

AVAILABLE AT YOUR LOCAL COMICS SHOP OR BOOKSTORE
To find a comics shop in your area, call 1-888-266-4226
For more information or to order direct: • On the web: darkhorse.com
• E-mail: mailorder@darkhorse.com • Phone: 1-800-862-0052 Mon.–Fri. 9 AM to 5 PM Pacific Time.

publisher
Mike Richardson

editor
Philip Simon

editorial assistant
John Schork

digital production
Jason Hvam

collection designers
David Nestelle & Tina Alessi

Special thanks to Davey Estrada, Michael Gombos, Heejeong Haas, and Cara Niece.

English-language version produced by DARK HORSE COMICS.

BRIDE OF THE WATER GOD Volume 9

Dark Horse Manhwa, a division of Dark Horse Comics, Inc.
10956 SE Main Street, Milwaukie, OR 97222
DarkHorse.com

To find a comics shop in your area, call the
Comic Shop Locator Service toll-free at 1-888-266-4226

First edition: October 2011
ISBN 978-1-59582-688-6

1 3 5 7 9 10 8 6 4 2
Printed by Lake Book, Inc., Melrose Park, IL, U.S.A.